RETURNING

A L S O B Y
NICHOLAS LEMANN

———

Transaction Man:
The Rise of the Deal and the Decline
of the American Dream

Redemption:
The Last Battle of the Civil War

The Big Test:
The Secret History of the
American Meritocracy

The Promised Land:
The Great Black Migration and
How It Changed America

LEMANN

RETURNING

A

SEARCH FOR HOME

ACROSS

THREE CENTURIES

NICHOLAS LEMANN

Liveright Publishing Corporation

A Division of W. W. Norton & Company
Independent Publishers Since 1923

Frontispiece: The family grave where Bernard and Harriet Lemann, and many other family members, are buried, Metairie cemetery, New Orleans. LINDA RENO

Copyright © 2026 by Nicholas Lemann

All rights reserved
Printed in the United States of America
First Edition

For information about permission to reproduce selections from this book, write to Permissions, Liveright Publishing Corporation, a division of W. W. Norton & Company, Inc., 500 Fifth Avenue, New York, NY 10110

For information about special discounts for bulk purchases, please contact W. W. Norton Special Sales at specialsales@wwnorton.com or 800-233-4830

Manufacturing by Lakeside Book Company
Book design by Barbara Bachman
Production manager: Gwen Cullen

ISBN 978-1-63149-841-1

Liveright Publishing Corporation, 500 Fifth Avenue, New York, NY 10110
www.wwnorton.com

W. W. Norton & Company Ltd., 15 Carlisle Street, London W1D 3BS

Authorized EU representative: EAS, Mustamäe tee 50, 10621 Tallinn, Estonia

1 0 9 8 7 6 5 4 3 2 1

For Judith

Contents

JACOB LEMANN ┈┼┈ **MARIE ESTELLE BERTHELOT**

(1809–1887) *(1821–1878)*

BERNARD LEMANN ┈┼┈ **HARRIETT FRIEDHEIM**

(1841–1899) *(1850–1897)*

MYER LEMANN ┈┼┈ **CARRIE ABRAHAM**

(1858–1930) *(1869–1927)*

MONTEFIORE MORDECAI LEMANN ┈┼┈ **NETTIE ELISE HYMAN**

(1884–1959) *(1893–1946)*

ALICE LEMANN ┈┼┈ **LEO FELLMAN**

(1889–1989) *(1878–1934)*

THOMAS BERTHELOT LEMANN ┈┼┈ **BARBARA MANN LONDON**

(1926–2023) *(1926–1999)*

STEPHEN BERTHELOT LEMANN

(1930–1995)

NICHOLAS BERTHELOT LEMANN

(1954–)

NANCY ELISE LEMANN

(1956–)

CORALIE LEMANN ········ LAZARD KAHN

(1862–1954) *(1850–1928)*

MARY ANNA ········ JULIAN BECK
FELLMAN FEIBELMAN

(1913–2009) *(1897–1980)*

The

LEMANN

FAMILY

TREE

Part One

LEAVING

ON PREVIOUS PAGE

Palo Alto plantation, just outside Donaldsonville, painted
by Marie Adrien Persac in the 1850s.

THE SUMMER I WAS NINETEEN YEARS OLD, I HAD TWO JOBS IN New Orleans. One was working as a reporter for what we used to call an underground newspaper, the *Vieux Carre Courier*, whose office was in a spare, dusty loft at the back end of the French Quarter. The other was assisting someone who had gotten a grant to write a history of a briefly flourishing New Orleans literary magazine of the 1920s called *The Double Dealer*, also located in the French Quarter, which had been early to publish William Faulkner, Ernest Hemingway, Allen Tate, and Robert Penn Warren. It was 1973. Some people who'd been fifty-years-ago versions of me, young people working at *The Double Dealer* or at least in its orbit, were still alive. My job was to find them and interview them. I spent the summer ping-ponging between the present (the *Courier*) and the past (*The Double Dealer*), between journalism and history, between political crusading and literary sleuthing.

It was inevitable that I would end up in the study of Ben C. Toledano that summer. Ben C. (never Ben) was news in the present, a Republican back when they were rare in New Orleans, who frequently ran unsuccessfully for office. He was also New Orleans's leading collector of Southern literature: the study, cool, kept in semidarkness to protect the books, was lined from floor to ceiling with signed first editions of the work of every Southern novelist who was even moderately well-known. Ben C. was someone whose political life was based on accusing the establishment of being corrupt—by his lights, if not many other people's, too liberal—so he was a font of advice about what shady arrangements I ought to look into. He also knew everybody in town who might have something to say about *The Double Dealer*.

On one of my visits, Ben C.—disinhibited, dough faced, with a stiff, pomaded stand of iron gray hair, dressed as usual in a white shirt so stiffly starched that it could have stood up on its own without him in it—walked me around the four walls of the study, plucking books out here and there, telling me where he'd found each one and how he'd gotten it signed. He accompanied his narrative of acquisition with gossipy anecdotes and brief reviews. He arrived at the culmination of the tour: what he considered the greatest of all Southern novels, Warren's *All the King's Men* (to the ever-familiar Ben C., the author was Red Warren). I hadn't read it, even though it was set in an unnamed state that was obviously Louisiana, where Warren had taught at the state university through most of the 1930s and had watched at first hand the rise and fall of our dictatorial populist governor, Huey Long. Ben C.'s endorsement sent me straight to the Basement Book Shop, housed in an ancient, askew yellow shotgun house, whose grouchy and opinionated owner, Tess Crager, had known the *Double Dealer* crowd back in the 1920s, to buy a copy. Mrs. Crager often forbade her customers, at least the ones like me whom she knew, to buy books they asked about, because she thought they were junk, but in this case she gave her consent.

Some books change your life because they lead you to experience the world in a new way. Others lend a kind of grandeur to the life you're already living, the life that you may sometimes think of as mundane or futile or insignificant, much as you don't want it to be. That was *All the King's Men* for me. Written in a lush, consciously poetic prose that you don't encounter so often anymore in American literary fiction, it elevates politics to the level of myth: hubris, doomed love, domination, tragedy, betrayal, murder, suicide, revelation. The pertinence to my own situation was obvious. Jack Burden, the narrator, was the lonely, searching, discontented scion of a prominent Southern family, more strongly drawn to observation than to action. So was I. He was torn between loyalty to the place he came from and an impulse to overturn its social order. So was I. He did historical research and journalism—both grounded in a need to investigate things you aren't supposed to know. So did I. In particular, he wound up spending a great deal of time looking in old family records. And so did I—though that came much later. In *All the King's Men*, all this was vastly consequential. Therefore I could take it as a demonstration that my own preoccupations were more than merely passing adolescent enthusiasms.

In the South, the supreme event between the time *All the King's Men* was published in 1946 and the time I read it was the public peak of the civil rights movement—something the novel in no way anticipates. Another book that was a touchstone for me in those days was *The Burden of Southern History*, by C. Vann Woodward. (It's dedicated to Robert Penn Warren.) Woodward wrote history for Southern liberals, in which the Jim Crow regime represented a terrible wrong turn, not the essence of the region. The South could have, should have, moved beyond its feudal economic system, but appeals to race solidarity had distracted the attention of its plain people, to their eventual sorrow—especially if they were Black, but even if they were white. It was this version of Southern history that Martin Luther King Jr., who'd obviously read Woodward, offered up in his magnificent speech on the steps of the Alabama State Capitol at the end of the Selma to Montgomery march in 1965.

Besides Jack Burden, another literary figure I identified with was Faulkner's Quentin Compson, who, at the end of *Absalom, Absalom!*, as a student at Harvard (as I too was that summer), having recounted the long and terrible Southern history of his own family, is left shouting helplessly, *"I dont hate it! I dont hate it!"* Woodward offered a way not to hate the South, if its being your home made that painful. You could see its past as a series of tragic mistakes—and, in the present, you could hope that the South, as the only region of the country fully acquainted with defeat and failure, could lead America out of its self-deluding preoccupation with triumphant success, into a more realistic form of consciousness. I was ready to enlist as a soldier in that mission.

Another thing I remember about my visits to Ben C. was that he was preoccupied with my being Jewish. Every time I came to visit he brought it up. He loved being transgressive, and in that time and place you weren't supposed to talk about such things. Jews in New Orleans were a tiny group, whose status felt eternally provisional, dependent on our being unobtrusive. Having it brought up made me uncomfortable—most people were discreet enough not to. Anyway, a Southerner was what I was. But Ben C. would obsessively offer up lists of who in New Orleans was Jewish, who didn't want people to know they were Jewish, who was too Jewish, who might or might not be Jewish. In that last category he put himself. Toledano is a standard name for Sephardic Jews, referring to Toledo, the Jewish center of medieval Spain. The C. in Ben C. was for Casanas, his mother's name before she married—also possibly Sephardic. In the way that there was always gossip in the world I grew up in about who might have "a touch of the tarbrush," meaning that they were Black and passing, Ben C.'s mother was known, as he liked to tell me, as the Jewish Queen of Carnival—in the present, an impossibility— because she had been a member of the city's one-day reigning couple on Mardi Gras in 1929, and . . . people wondered. He could talk to me about these things because he knew that my own family had a similar liminal status in New Orleans.

On the Jewish calendar, it was 5733, not 1973. History is longer and slower to unfold when enumerated in that way. My great-great-grandfather, Jacob Lemann, born and raised in the village of Essenheim, Germany, arrived in New Orleans as a young man, alone, in 1836. In Jewish-American time, that was long ago, making us an old family. In unhyphenated Jewish time, Jacob came here in 5596. The time between then and now feels to me like merely a moment in Jewish history. Jacob was born in 1809, at a time when his village in Germany was under the dominion of France. Just a few years earlier the French emperor, Napoleon Bonaparte, had made Jews citizens. It was astonishing that Jews could be understood, even by themselves, as anything but an entirely separate tribe, enclosed, self-governing, barred from living in most places or working in most occupations; mysterious, fetishized, feared, and despised by outsiders; only hazily aware themselves of what the non-Jewish world was like. Napoleon soon backpedaled: for Jews to become full members of society, they had to become normal by non-Jews' lights, for example by giving up their traditional occupation of moneylending and by adopting conventional first and last names. And soon after that, he fell from power and the part of Germany he no longer controlled began reinstituting the traditional restrictions.

Jacob was part of a small but coherent Jewish migration from the Upper Rhine River Valley—southwest Germany and Alsace—to Louisiana. What drew these people to this destination was that it was an unusually prosperous place, where the traditional Jewish skills could find a ready market and there were no official rules telling Jews what they could and couldn't do. Perhaps they felt that something that had long eluded Jews could be achieved there. But the reason Louisiana was so prosperous was that it was one of the world's principal locations for producing sugar, on cane plantations that were home to a particularly harsh form of slavery—the escape from which is central to our own mythology. Jacob, illiterate in English, quickly and steadily made his way upward in this setting. He married a teenage girl, Marie Berthelot, a Cajun, also illiterate in English. Twenty years into their American life, they began relocating to New York City. Marie converted to Judaism. Their firstborn child, Bernard, my great-grandfather, was by his late twenties an enthusiastic consumer of high culture—literature, opera, theater— and an observant Jew.

When the Civil War began, the family chose to leave the country temporarily and return to Germany. When the war ended, they returned to Louisiana rather than New York. They used the postwar chaos of the Deep South as an opportunity to acquire a string of plantations in sugar country. Bernard, the young aesthete, became a merchant and a midlevel agricultural baron. He and his wife, Harriet Friedheim, were leading members of the Jewish community, and parents of ten children, eight of whom survived to adulthood, four of whom they sent to Harvard to be educated. One of these was my grandfather, Montefiore Mordecai Lemann, who grew up to become a prominent lawyer in New Orleans, and, along with his wife, Nettie Elise Hyman, a full participant in the social and political life of an American German-Jewish elite that had its heyday in the first half of the twentieth century and has since evanesced, thanks to assimilation, intermarriage, and conversion.

My parents, Thomas and Barbara London Lemann, the fourth American generation of the family, aspired to become fully mainstream—still Jewish but in ways that entailed no particularity in how we conceived of ourselves and how we lived, finally freed of the restrictions that, despite their not officially ever existing in America, had somehow never stopped reappearing. It was unmissable that I came from a plantation-owning family and that I was being raised in a race-pervaded culture, in which one couldn't get through even a few hours of an ordinary day without being reminded that white supremacy was the prevailing order. That explains why, at the time of my encounters with Ben C. Toledano, I thought of myself as a Southerner, and also why I had fastened on the civil rights movement, something that people in homes like ours were aware of as an approaching force that proposed to change our way of life, as a means of remaining loyally Southern without having to retain whites' traditional sense of what that entailed.

Being Jewish was far more mysterious to me. I knew almost nothing about the Jewish aspect, as opposed to the Southern aspect, of my family's history. It was more the way other people, like Ben C., thought of us, than the way we thought of ourselves. Why couldn't it be a lightly held and inconsequential ethnic identity, something a little quaint or exotic, adding a touch of spice, but nowhere near life-determining in the way that racial identity was in our world? I knew that some time when I was a small child, a member of our family had taken on a research project that ended in his depositing a large collection of material—records, letters, diaries—in the manuscript collection at Tulane University, just a few blocks from our house.

Much as I was coming to discover that I loved investigating, looking at these family papers was one investigation I made a point of not undertaking. Present-day political machinations and misdeeds, and the literary history of New Orleans, were far more compelling. Maybe I was afraid of what the family papers would reveal: a past I wouldn't be proud of. It wasn't until decades later, and a lifetime of investigating everything but this, that I decided it was time to look. Now I'm going to tell you what I discovered, not just about the people I come from, but also about myself. What my original exemplar of investigation, Jack Burden, said at the end of *All the King's Men* also applies to me, I think: "It is the story of a man who lived in the world and to him the world looked one way for a long time and then it looked another and very different way. The change did not happen all at once."

PALO ALTO

In *All the King's Men*, Jack Burden periodically visits his family's elegant rural homestead, in a place called Burden's Landing. For me the equivalent is Palo Alto plantation, a short distance outside the town of Donaldsonville, Louisiana, where my family has lived for 180 years. (To make the comparison to Burden's Landing more exact, there's a nearby hamlet called Lemannville.) There is a dreamy picture, rendered in soft light blues and greens, of Palo Alto, made some time shortly after it was built, before my family owned it. The artist, Marie Adrien Persac, a French-born architect and draftsman, traveled through sugarcane plantation country in the years before the Civil War, making flattering images of houses on commission from their owners.

In the picture, a small white-sailed schooner sails lazily along calm, broad, pacific Bayou Lafourche. Gentlemen in stovepipe hats and ladies in elegant dresses stand on the opposite bank, looking across the bayou at the plantation. Palo Alto itself is a complex of several buildings enclosed by a picket fence. A horse and buggy passes by on the road. In *All the King's Men*, Burden's Landing, a coastal town, plays as an instantiation of the kind of economic class system that gave rise to populists like Huey Long. It's impossible to see Palo Alto in that way: it's deeply, inextricably embedded in slavery. Persac's drawing comes across as a typical antebellum Southern planter's version of plantation life as a pastoral idyll. There are only white people in the picture, but the evidence of how the place operated is there: next to the columned main house are a sugarhouse, a shed, an overseer's house, a double row of slave cabins. Palo Alto means "tall tree" in Spanish: that's pastoral too. But the name is actually a tribute to a military triumph, the battle at Palo Alto in 1846, the first major encounter of the Mexican-American War, just before construction of the plantation began. The name indicates a practical project, a dream of conquest, behind the elegant scrim represented by the pretty moniker.

I still visit Palo Alto every so often. My cousin Peter lives there with his partner, DeeDee DiBenedetto, who's descended from Sicilian laborers who were imported by Louisiana planters after emancipation to work on the sugar plantations. (One of the old country lanes that runs through Palo Alto's cane fields is called Dago Road, after the planters' favored epithet for Italian immigrants.) DeeDee is an ex-Marine, an ex-police officer, a private investigator, a local historian, and an expert on paranormal phenomena—she insists that the ghost of one of the nineteenth-century Lemanns patrols the grounds at Palo Alto.

When I was growing up, we would make regular trips to Palo Alto so that we could understand where we came from. In those days Peter's parents, Bubs (my father's first cousin) and Camille, he in a seersucker or linen suit, she in a light sundress with her hair pinned up in a bun, presided over the plantation. They kept pet peacocks that wandered around behind the house. They'd show us how to milk cows and to harvest eggs from the henhouse and give us sticks of fresh sugarcane to suck on for a treat. The house was pervaded by the past. The windows, of wavy old glass, had people's names scratched into them, supposedly with diamonds from engagement rings. The rooms, full of old, heavy wood furniture, were still, hot, with tall ceilings and plaster walls. In the attic there were boxes filled with old pictures of stiff-looking people taken a very long time ago, and handwritten ledger books that recorded ancient transactions in an elaborate script. There was a small dungeon underneath the house, a reminder of slave times. Sometimes Bubs would pull my father aside to have a private conversation about something children weren't supposed to know about.

Today Palo Alto is a plantation, a bed-and-breakfast, a rentable wedding venue, a shooting range, a hunting lodge, and a right-of-way for underground oil and gas pipelines. Most of the nearby plantations stand empty; keeping the place going requires a good deal of effort. Sometimes Civil War buffs with metal detectors come by and ask Peter and DeeDee for permission to hunt for spent bullets, out in front of the house where the saplings in Persac's picture are now broad old oak trees, hung with Spanish moss, which keep the grounds in a deep shade. A lightly used county road runs along the bank of the bayou, some distance in front of the house. On the broad front porch, where Peter likes to sit in a rocking chair smoking a pipe, it's quiet. You don't feel very closely connected to the world as it is now.

Donaldsonville, if it ever actually conformed to the Persac rendering, doesn't any longer. Bayou Lafourche is a muddy ditch. The center of town, where my cousin Bubba sells tractors at Lemann's Farm Supply, is struggling. Donaldsonville is mostly Black and heavily poor. It feels hollowed out. All through the surrounding countryside, you see abandoned wooden shacks yielding to voracious deep green vines. The original Donaldsonville was built for a purpose—supplying the fledgling United States with sugar via slave labor—that has long since lost its economic and moral underpinnings, so the present Donaldsonville is left to contend with the fate of places that for a time had a business rationale powerful enough to have lent them the illusion of being also the seat of a small civilization. The dominant enterprise in town, pervasively evident from its gassy smell, is a complex of factories that make up the world's largest production facility for nitrogen fertilizer, which it would be challenging for even a modern-day Persac to render appealingly. A panel of experts appointed by the United Nations Human Rights Council in Geneva recently visited the area, declared it to be an example of environmental racism, and called on the federal government to stop allowing chemical plants to be built there.

Race is impossible to miss in Donaldsonville, unless you want to make a determined effort not to notice it, but nothing there is noticeably Jewish, except for a small cemetery indicating a former, now ghostly presence. Peter and DeeDee are Catholic. But, as in my long-ago visits to Ben C. Toledano, around the edges of our officially Southern family story, Jewish items keep manifesting themselves in unexpected ways. They don't fit, but they don't go away—or they seem to go away and then reappear in ways you couldn't anticipate. Some years ago I got a call from a friend of mine: there was a story in that day's *New York Times* about a demonstration in Jerusalem staged by West Bank settlers, protesting a liberal Israeli government's efforts to create a Palestinian state. The story quoted someone named Hanan Lemann, who compared himself with the settlers on the American frontier who had wrested the land away from the Indians. They hadn't had to give the land back, why should the Israelis?

My friend wanted to know whether he was any relation. I checked and found out that he was. Another of my father's first cousins, Bernard Lemann, born in Donaldsonville, became a professor at Tulane. He devoted himself professionally to architectural preservation—cataloging plantation and plantation-like old houses in New Orleans and the countryside around it. He was the one who had assembled our family papers and donated them to Tulane. Politically, he was the most obviously left-wing member of the family, a conscientious objector during the Second World War and a converted and practicing Quaker. Hanan, whom I had known growing up as John, was Bernard's oldest son. Now he was an Orthodox

Israeli; today he has twenty-five grandchildren and seven great-grandchildren. I went to see him a few years after the *New York Times* story. By that time he had moved from the West Bank to an apartment in Jerusalem. There was a copy of Persac's drawing of Palo Alto hanging in the front hall. The original used to hang in the front hall of Palo Alto until it was auctioned off, as the possessions in old family homesteads often are—too valuable to keep. The buyer was anonymous, so nobody knows where it is now.

THE GEIGER COUNTER

When I was growing up, New Orleans's days as a minor literary center seemed to lie far in the past. The people I interviewed about *The Double Dealer* were elderly; I was getting to them just in time, and they hadn't been replaced. There was one major exception, though—Walker Percy, another scion of a plantation family (cotton, in the Mississippi Delta), who had become a medical doctor, converted to Catholicism, and, after a serious illness, turned to writing fiction. A lean, shy man with white hair and deep-blue eyes, he lived semireclusively in a small town some distance from New Orleans. He was a mentor to my sister and my stepmother, both novelists. I knew him slightly.

Percy's first and best-known novel, *The Moviegoer*, shares with *All the King's Men* a lonely, alienated hero who has distanced himself from the prominent family he comes from, and who finds it much easier to engage in Southern life as an observer than as a participant. His name is Binx Bolling. The action of the novel takes place over a few days at the height of Mardi Gras season, New Orleans's central ritual. I identified intensely with Binx, as I did with Jack Burden, but there was one passage that jumped out at me, because it showed me a bright outer boundary to the territory of my identification. "Whenever I approach a Jew, the Geiger counter in my head starts rattling away like a machine gun," Binx tells us, "and as I go past with the utmost circumspection and with every sense alert—

the Geiger counter subsides." That was me. Even if I thought I was like Binx, he didn't think so. In real life, Percy thought of himself as a philosemite, but that entailed seeing Jews as belonging to a special category, different from other people. He regularly urged the Jewish writers he knew in New Orleans to tell their story. He believed there was something about us, some profound realm of knowledge and experience, about which we could clue in the rest of the world, to its great benefit.

What Percy didn't realize was that aspiring writers like my sister and me, Jewish though we were, were not equipped to write the book he wanted to read. We could not answer his questions, and our ignorance was not accidental, it was the product of a fiercely enforced family policy. My own curiosity was initially about the South, not about Jewishness. Although by adolescence I was accustomed to thinking of myself as a rebel, in this regard I was operating in harmony with the way my family and the other Jewish families we knew in New Orleans preferred to identify themselves.

Most of what one knows growing up one knows through general absorption of the prevailing atmosphere. Those scenes in movies where a single incident in the past explains everything that follows are properly understood as an effective form of dramatic license. But in this case, for me as a particular kind of Jew, there actually was a scene, which I remember vividly.

In the 1960s, when they were in their thirties and I was in elementary school, my parents built a large and elaborately planned house in a carriage-trade neighborhood in New Orleans. I think of it as their Palo Alto, a midcentury-modern version of a plantation house, transposed from the countryside to a city. It stood on a corner, concealed from public view behind high, opaque wooden fences. An opening admitted visitors to a driveway that gave onto a large graveled plaza with an old moss-draped live oak tree standing magnificently in the center. The façade of the house was red brick with floor-to-ceiling plate-glass windows. Like Palo Alto it had a gabled roof sloping down toward the entrance, and columns running across the front façade. It was built for entertaining; to a visitor it offered a sense of an entrance, a procession. In addition to the grand live oak at the entrance, there was another one in the back-yard, displayed through another wall of plate-glass windows. My father decided to give the house a name—Quercus, after the Latin name for live oaks, *Quercus virginiana.*

Quercus was designed so that the bedroom where my parents slept was on the first floor. My sister and I had our bedrooms on the second floor. Father, who was small and elaborately courtly—crew-cut, bespectacled, studious, not athletic—spent his life cycling through a series of intense, highly particular, time-limited obsessions. He devoted most of his time during evenings at home to sitting at a built-in desk in the corner of the library, surrounded by file folders and small, precise objects he had collected, pursuing his many interests. So when, one evening in the late 1960s, not long after we had moved in, Father climbed the stairs and knocked on my door, it was clear that something unusual was going to happen.

Father wanted to have a serious talk. Usually he presented himself with a carefully calibrated mix of seriousness and playfulness—as when he would write outraged (or were they mock-outraged?) letters to publications, as he often did, about their grammatical errors. Very occasionally, though, the playfulness disappeared. The hint of a smile left his face. This usually happened when an essential aspect of the social order we inhabited—officially graceful and carefree, but resting on a rock-solid set of unstated rules about who occupied what place and where the boundaries of acceptable behavior were— had to be affirmed.

He asked me whether I had gotten an invitation in the mail to attend a junior-division Mardi Gras ball called Squires. Yes, I had. It had arrived printed on heavy cream-colored stationery, with my name and address beautifully hand-calligraphed on the enve-lope. Inside was a stiff card with a lot of fancy language about the king and his court commanding my presence. Father looked at me. I think he took it amiss that I wouldn't have told him about the invitation, with pride and even excitement, rather than keeping it to myself. "Well," he said, "do you plan to go?" I said no. I don't want to give myself too much credit here for having a fully developed social conscience; it was more that for a thirteen-year-old boy, the prospect of getting dressed up and spending an evening in a cavernous auditorium unpersuasively done up as a royal tableau, presided over by eighth graders wearing costumes of silk and satin that supposedly had temporarily transformed them into sceptered and plumed kings, queens, dukes, and duchesses, sounded somewhere between dull and terrifying.

What Father had in mind, it was clear, was that our encounter in my room would be one of those moments when a young man is inducted into a previously concealed zone of the adult world. You are the first Jew ever to be invited to the Squires ball, he said, gravely, each word landing with a portentous thump. It was important that I accept, because it would be a step in the direction of progress. As an aspect of the invitation, I could designate two or three guests who would be permitted to sit in the balcony of the auditorium and watch the ball, but not to dance on the floor. It is essential, Father went on, that when you do this, you not place any other Jews on your list of guests. People think we are clannish. If I invited Jewish guests, it would reinforce the impression, and that might bring the breakthrough that was within our reach—us, meaning the Lemanns, and if that went well, others like us—to a halt.

From earliest childhood, everybody in New Orleans knows about Mardi Gras. Though it's officially a Christian holiday, Jews are no exception. During the weeks before the beginning of Lent, the streets are constantly shut down for parades. Tractors pulling the floats—tall, flimsy, brightly colored constructions—rumble along; they bear balconies full of hard-drinking members of the organization sponsoring the parade, costumed in masks and hoods and gaudy costumes, who fling handfuls of cheap beads, coins, and trinkets to ecstatic, begging crowds with outstretched arms. That is the outer, visible Mardi Gras, but there is also an inner, more private Mardi Gras, in which some of the same organizations, called krewes, put on balls. Every year, every krewe has a king, a middle-aged man wearing a crown and a pasted-on beard, attended by a coterie of younger dukes and pages, and a queen, a nineteen- or twenty-year-old girl who is also a debutante that year, attended by a court made up of other debutantes. The breathless accounts of these balls in the newspapers would describe the king and queen making a stately procession through the auditorium, waving scepters at their grateful subjects.

Symbolically, such scenes were in keeping with the rest of the lives of people like us. Most of us lived in big, old wooden houses, waited on by a coterie of servants. The men presided over calm downtown business offices—often of family businesses. No function in our world was more important than the selection of every year's Mardi Gras royalty. It was the obsessed-over, gossiped-about token of high prestige, the way professional rather than social tokens are in the world I live in now. (What made Binx Bolling's alienation vivid and palpable, at least to New Orleans readers, was that he refused to participate.) Children, as they became teenagers, began what would be years of training to take their part of the Mardi Gras system. But not if they were Jewish. We were insiders who were also outsiders. We led comfortable lives that had very strict limitations.

Father told me the story of how this had come to be. In our family, we did not operate by the precept that if something was important, it would be a good idea to talk about it. Better not to, unless it was unavoidable, and that made candid occasions like this especially portentous. I remember him taking off his glasses, which made him look unprotected, vulnerable, uncharacteristically confidential. The first Rex, the king of the most public Mardi Gras parade and ball, a man who rolled through the city's most prominent avenues on a papier-mâché throne perched on top of a float, wearing a shiny golden outfit, a crown, silk stockings, and golden boots, magnanimously waving his scepter while tens of thousands of people in the streets cheered, had been a Jew named Lewis Salomon. That was in 1872, which wasn't so very long after people like us had arrived in Louisiana as backpack peddlers—and yet we were completely accepted.

But Salomon was also the last Jewish Rex. Why? Because, Father said, not long after Salomon's one-day reign over New Orleans, *they* had started arriving en masse. *They* were the other Jews. They came from Russia, or some other godforsaken place in Eastern Europe that no Jews like us had ever visited. They had traveled to America in large numbers, jammed into the holds of ships. On arrival, they lived in squalid slums in big cities. They looked different, with odd black costumes and head coverings. They spoke Yiddish. They kept kosher. They prayed frequently and incomprehensively. Even those who had managed to climb out of poverty often operated their businesses in sharp, ungentlemanly ways. At the same time that they were making money through unsavory practices, they were also left-wing. The majority, normal mainstream Americans, found them repellent.

I wasn't sure Father had ever encountered such Jews in person. Certainly I had not. But they were lodged firmly in our consciousness, partly because we knew they were lodged in the consciousness of people whose approval we sought. The central problem for us—dignified, prosperous, and well-established Jewish people who had come here from Germany rather than Russia—was that, incredibly, the rest of the world didn't appreciate the enormous difference between us and *them*. Instead, we were all simply Jews. So *they* had ruined the almost complete advancement of us.

But now here we were in the present, and Father had become hopeful. Many decades had passed since the days when impossible-to-miss boats filled with Russian Jews—their large, raggedy families crowded against the railings on the deck, looking desperately wanting and weary—were sailing into American ports. We were living in a modern world. Religion and ethnicity were surely going to fade in importance. In New Orleans, where our large extended family had lived for generations, people knew us well enough to see that, while we made no attempt to hide who we were (that would have been impossible anyway, because in our intensely provincial milieu, everybody knew everything about everybody else), we bore no trace of the negative traits that people, frankly including us, associated with Jews. We spoke softly, in faint Southern accents. We lived quietly in decorous, stolid houses. We associated ourselves with good causes, and they didn't necessarily have to be Jewish causes. We had earned a measure of respect.

I can see that somebody might encounter a story like this today and wonder why we took something like my invitation to the Squires ball so seriously. All sorts of things about the enclosed and enveloping environment of my childhood are difficult to explain, except by saying that we knew intimately the deep-rooted mores of the milieu we inhabited and only hazily those of the wider world. My conversation with Father would have taken place just after the 1967 war in Israel, something that was a riveting event for most American Jews. We never spoke about it. One could also ask why, as white Southerners living deep inside a racial caste system, surrounded by Black people in subordinate positions, the racial revolution going on all around us didn't command our full attention. It didn't. But the details of life inside the Mardi Gras krewes were central, riveting. For our family, it was hard to be completely indifferent to our exclusion from them. When you have nearly everything, what you don't have exerts an illogically large claim on your attention. Mardi Gras membership was what we didn't have. Father believed it to be attainable, if only we would comport ourselves properly.

Father's visit to my room ended with a quick negotiation and a deal, accomplished, as conflicts in our family always were, without raised voices, reddened faces, or tears. His concession to my self-righteous objection was that I didn't have to go to the Squires ball. My concession to his deep concern that this delicate step forward not play out disastrously and ruin everything was that I would send in the card indicating that I had accepted the invitation. Father must have thought I would come around eventually—this way my options would remain open. He returned to his desk downstairs and to his hobbies. Not wanting to hurt him, and lacking any information that might contradict his account of our precarious but promising place in the world as Jews, I directed my curiosity elsewhere. I would have been unable to explain what set off the Geiger counter of other people in New Orleans because it was our family's mission not to set it off at all.

ORIGINS

If we had been completely rational (but who is?), it would have been obvious that being Jewish must represent something more than just an impediment, manifesting other people's prejudices. We had a tribal history, a religious history, and a specific family history. We just didn't know what it was. Father was a fierce seeker of information of a certain kind, and so was I, of another kind, but it was part of our family pact about Jewishness that this was information we would not seek. In *All the King's Men*, Willie Stark, the political boss, adeptly uses his dominating power to direct Jack Burden's investigating energies to the task of digging up dirt on Stark's enemies, including the patrician residents of Burden's Landing. But they seem to be exemplary, Jack says. No, says Stark: "There's always something." What the something was about my own patrician family, I didn't know—there was a lot to want not to know, if you were a plantation-descended Jewish Southerner aspiring to leave the meaning of those two of your historical tributaries behind. But of course it was there, once I had decided, much later, to look for it.

The research library at Harvard Business School has a vast collection, made up of more than twenty-five hundred large white cloth-bound volumes that are as solid and heavy as building materials, of reports compiled by a firm initially called the Mercantile Agency, then R. G. Dun, then Dun & Bradstreet, which, beginning in the 1840s, sent agents all over the United States to inspect businesses and give an opinion of their creditworthiness. Clerks in New York entered the agents' field reports into ledger books, in neat handwriting so tiny that the library staff lends you a magnifying glass so you can read it. There are reports on Vanderbilts and Rockefellers, and also, mainly, on innumerable small businesses scattered through the remote reaches of rural America. A whole volume is devoted to Ascension Parish, Louisiana, the home of my family, and there on the first page is a series of entries devoted to Jacob Lemann, my immigrant great-great-grandfather.

The first entry is from January 1848: "Jew, one of the best of his kind. In business 10 or 12 years. Deals fairly, pays promptly, has real estate and Negroes ['has' must mean 'enslaves'], appears permanent and is considered a fair exception of what Jews generally are." An agent who visited three years later wrote: "Came here in '36 without ten cents, is an active, energetic money making fellow, looks sharp to #1, owns two houses and a store house. Real estate here worth $8000, in another parish worth $4000 and some in Cincinnati; he says he is worth $30,000. Considered good for ordinary purchases."

Here is a report from another, less friendly agent, filed a few months later: "Can't give him much of a character as he is a Jew. Believe he is not over honest in his dealings. Commenced as a butcher and was accused of killing old mules and selling them for meat. Traded in horses, then speculated a little in Western produce, married a Christian, and now keeps a plantation store. Makes a good deal by shaving notes. Is liberal to his family, but only gives to the poor when he knows the whole Parish will hear of it. Don't think his credit stands high in Commercial Circles. He has some $5000 in real estate and perhaps some $25,000 in all (notes and mortgage). Is pretty shrewd in business, but owed his success greatly to good luck; never was known to lose in a transaction."

Over the next few years the reports begin to take on a rising note of respect, showing perhaps that if you make some money and hold on to it, the circumstances of your arrival begin to fade out of memory. In December 1851 Jacob is a "keen shrewd business man."

In August 1852 he is a "man of good character." In May 1853 "his name here would be very good." In January 1854 Jacob tells the visiting agent that he has bought a house in New York City. In June 1856 the agent reports that Jacob, twenty years after he arrived in Louisiana without ten cents, has sold his store in Donaldsonville to a man named Bienvenue Mollere, and has begun making summer trips to Newport, Rhode Island.

I'm aware of only two photographs of Jacob Lemann, albumin prints made when he was an old man, whose stiffness was surely dictated by the limits of the equipment in those days, but that still leave the impression that people back then actually *were* stiff—human versions of ancient statuary. Anyway, Jacob, during the last decade of his life, was in fact ancient. He stared directly, even fiercely, at the camera through light clear steady eyes. He had a craggy face and a white beard. In one photograph he is wearing a formal, tightly buttoned black frock coat; the other shows just his face. Jacob left behind many progeny but not a lot of material that would give a sense of what was in his heart and mind. He never learned to write in the Roman alphabet, except for a stylized figure that stands for his signature; his documentary record is made up of numbers in ledger books, and scribblings in Hebrew characters. The only way available to understand him is through his actions, the choices he made.

Jacob was born the same year as Abraham Lincoln, 1809. Essenheim, his village, is an old, quiet town that sits up on a ridge, surrounded by vineyards that must have been there for centuries. Growing up, I had known that at the age of twenty-seven, alone, he somehow traveled 450 miles to the Atlantic port of Le Havre, France, at the mouth of the Seine, bustling from trade to and from the New World, and booked passage on a ship bound for New Orleans. But about his life in Germany I knew nothing until I started investigating, and neither did anybody else in my family. It was a blank, and not an object of great curiosity either. A few years ago, with Judith, my wife, I went to Essenheim and hired a guide, a local historian

Jacob Lemann in his midseventies, made by a photographer in Cincinnati.

named Stefan Mossel, to help me learn what I could about my family before Jacob came to America.

Today an Ashkenazi Jew is someone whose origins are European outside of the Iberian Peninsula, but back in the Middle Ages the Ashkenazim—named after a minor biblical character—were Jews who lived in a tightly limited section of western Germany around the ancient towns of Worms, Speyer, and Mainz, which are arrayed in a line along the Rhine River. Jews turned up there as early as the year 300, having, at least according to legend, made their way from the Holy Land to Italy and then marched northward alongside the Roman legions. Essenheim is a short distance outside of Mainz. I have it in my head that I came from people, whom I picture as small, dark, strange, hunched under the weight of their backpacks, who arrived there by foot on some unimaginably long-ago date and then devised a way to get by and to pray and study and propagate. I'm not sure I'm so very different from them.

There's an eight-hundred-page book published in 1927, the year after my parents were born, called *A History of the Jewish People*. It's just the kind of one-volume summary of a vast theme that adorned the shelves of many middle-class American Jews who deeply respected scholarly knowledge but hadn't had the means to achieve it themselves. *A History of the Jewish People* is a good example of what's known as the *Leidens-und-Gelehrtengeschichte* school of Jewish history—

suffering and learning. Under the heading of learning, Gershom ben Judah, a great Jewish scholar, established a school in Mainz in the late tenth century. Rashi, the most revered of all the Jewish medieval sages, was trained in Worms and Mainz. Under the heading of suffering, the corner of Germany where Jacob Lemann was born was the site of an endless procession of bloody persecutions of Jews.

In 1012 all Jews were expelled from Mainz; Gershom's own son converted to Christianity so he could stay. The first mass killing of Jews in Europe took place in Mainz in 1096; more than a thousand Jews were murdered in a savage frenzy by Crusaders. In all, in this section of Germany, Crusaders murdered ten thousand Jews; perhaps because this kept them so busy, they never got to Jerusalem, their supposed destination. Even now some congregations remember these events in a special prayer on Yom Kippur. What was it about our tiny subcategory of humanity that generated this bloodlust? It was supposed to be that we were religious infidels and that we had money we had unfairly extracted from other people, but that doesn't account for the great variety of circumstances in which so many people felt that the answer to their suffering was to inflict far greater suffering on Jews. There were further massacres in my family's home ground in 1146, in 1221, in 1235. We were burned at the stake. We took our own lives, and sometimes our own children's, to avoid being slaughtered. We were intermittently required to wear yellow hats when we went out in public, or to sew yellow badges on our clothing. In the fourteenth century, the Black Death, another in the series of disasters that were attributed to us, set off a wave of Jew killing. In Strasbourg, the stately queen city of this section of the Rhine, with a large cathedral and old narrow streets lined with substantial half-timbered houses, eighteen hundred Jews were rounded up on the Sabbath, brought to a cemetery, and burned alive. In 1650 the Jews, now blamed for the horrors of the Thirty Years' War as we had been for the Black Death, were forced to remove themselves from wherever they lived within the city walls of Mainz and find new homes somewhere else.

Were Jacob Lemann's forebears, my forebears, living in the Rhine River Valley then? If they were, how did they avoid being killed? Did they put out of their minds what seems now like a looming, ever-present possibility that the mob might come for them one day, or did they imagine, as we sometimes do now, that such things could never happen again? One legend of the origin of the Eastern European Jews, the people from whom, much later in America, we were so eager to differentiate ourselves, is that after the Crusades they fled from Germany to Poland and Russia, hoping that by resettling they would be out of danger. If the people I came from decided to stay in Germany, did that signal a confidence that they could operate safely, quietly, in a hostile environment? Did they calculate that the benefits of staying would outweigh the risks? Or were they simply accustomed to the lives they were living, as people usually are—unless they can't be any longer?

Stefan Mossel took us to the town hall in a village called Nieder-Olm, just outside of Essenheim. We walked down a flight of steps to a basement. There, in a barren, linoleum-floored, fluorescent-lit room with a small metal Christmas tree sitting incongruously in the corner, he opened the arklike doors of a gray metal cabinet, pulled out a stack of ancient ledger books containing handwritten records of births, marriages, and deaths, and spread them out on a small table.

Napoleon's army conquered this part of Germany in 1796. Because the French Revolution had given all people living in France the status of citizens, Jews became French citizens. This means the local civil officials began including Jews in record books—which is why much of what I learned about my family's German origins was recorded in French. The first relative of mine whose name appears in the official records was a man whose name was listed as Feist Lamech. The next in my line, born in 1766, was listed as Beretz Lamech. Jacob Lemann was his son. In 1808 Napoleon required Jews to adopt last names, which they'd never had before: Beretz Lamech meant, simply, Beretz the son of Lamech. Beretz took the last name Lehmann; his siblings took the last name Mayer. Then, in 1812, when Jacob was three years old, Beretz died, at the age of forty-six. The house in Essenheim where the family lived is no longer standing. Stefan Mossel sent me an old picture, showing what he thinks was the Lehmanns' house, a comfortably worn, thick-walled, tile-roofed building just off the main street. Evidently there weren't enough Jews in Essenheim for them to have been restricted, or to have restricted themselves, to one street. Other houses in town where Jews lived—Mayers and Urnsteins—are still standing on the main street. They are solidly built two-story structures, indicating a measure of prosperity.

All up and down the Rhine Valley, whether they were officially subjects of France or of a German principality, Jews had always lived as a separate tribe—really a separate nation, an Israel in the form of an archipelago of small communities. They were legally barred from most occupations and from owning land. They followed the traditional dietary laws. They were educated by rabbis in Jewish schools, which made them among the few ordinary Germans with any education at all. They wrote in Hebrew characters, even when they were writing in German. They dressed in ways that would have distinguished them visually from non-Jews. They were self-governing, by communal authority, though ultimately answerable to the local prince.

This was the life that Jews had lived, generation after generation, in this corner of Europe. Before they came under French rule, German Jews had no formal rights as we understand them (and neither did most other people). Jews were usually not permitted to live in cities, only in villages, and there they usually lived in *Judenstrassen*, Jewish streets. The great Gothic cathedral of Strasbourg, once the tallest building in the world, had two carved figures on either side of one of its portals, Ecclesia (erect, proud, bearing a cross and a chalice), symbolizing Christianity, and Synagoga (blindfolded, head bowed, forlornly carrying a broken spear and a book), symbolizing Judaism. That the superiority of the mighty Catholic Church over a tiny non-Christian tribe was worth advertising so prominently is a sign of the peculiarly large space we occupied in the mind of the majority. Beginning in 1388, all Jews in Strasbourg were required to leave at sunset and the city gates were locked behind them.

Almost all Jews in the Rhine Valley, at least those who weren't destitute, engaged in some combination of peddling, trading livestock and dry goods, shopkeeping, and moneylending, which for centuries had been the only paying endeavors that were open to them. As *A History of the Jewish People* puts it, "Jew and merchant were synonymous terms." My own forebears are listed in the record books as, depending on whether Essenheim was under French or German control, *Handelsman*, *marchant*, or *marchant des bestiaux*. To judge by the way they lived, my family were probably *Schutzjuden*, Jews who lived under an annually granted letter of protection from the local prince, in return for which they had to pay special taxes that were higher than everyone else's. Jews did not have the freedom to live where they wanted without this kind of special permission. Often their freedom to marry was also restricted, because of the authorities' felt need for protection from a too-large local population of Jews—even though Jews did not have the means to protect themselves. And after the fall of Napoleon, in 1814, and the end of French control of our part of Germany, the long-familiar restrictions and outbreaks of anti-Jewish violence began again. It wasn't until the unification of Germany as a modern nation, in 1871, that German Jews were fully emancipated. By that time Jacob Lemann was long gone.

As a wealthy old man living in faraway rural Louisiana, Jacob used to get importuning letters from people in Mainz. A niece, one of the Mayers, wanted a dowry so she could get married; a needy woman reminded Jacob that she had helped his widowed mother raise him and felt this merited repayment. But there isn't any evidence to indicate what his life was like before he left for America— how he and his undoubtedly overburdened mother lived, how he was educated, what work he did, how wrenching the decision to

emigrate all by himself was. It's tempting to turn people in the past
into mere actors, semiconscious, lacking the self-awareness that we
have, moving forward toward their inevitable destinations without
a lot of thought, as if pulled along by a towline. But that can't possibly be right. How could it not be emotionally overwhelming for a
young man to move halfway around the world alone with no definite prospects, not knowing as we do how his adventure would turn
out? Among my family's papers, I found a memoir of a departure
from Alsace, in 1864, left by a relative of ours by marriage named
Felix Kahn, one of seven children of a poor family who left for the
New World one by one. Felix had only just turned fifteen when he
immigrated to Brazil. Here is how he remembered his departure:

> Finally the 18th of May arrived—I shall never forget this day.
> The most profound circumstances are engraved in my heart
> with characters of bronze. Well I remember this scene. My
> God! How I cannot forget it. All those who have left their
> well beloved parents, for a country far away, not knowing
> when they can return, will understand that which I felt, and
> that it will be impossible to write of it. When I said goodbye
> to my mother, she took me to her heart and covered me with
> kisses—and me, my God! I am not yet free of the pain. The
> coachman was in a hurry. I released myself from my moth-
> er's embraces. I ran like a fool and took myself away from
> the paternal home where I was born and had grown up. The
> goodbyes of my grandmother were heart-rending, for she felt
> she would never see me again.

Jacob left behind nothing that shows him to have been capable of
expressing himself so floridly. The record we have of his departure
from Germany is a passport that he kept for the rest of his life and
that his descendants preserved after he was gone. He was part of
a distinct movement: thousands of Germans, including German
Jews, made their way from the Rhine Valley to Le Havre in the

1830s, bound for America, with New Orleans a common desti-nation. Great multiple-masted wooden sailing ships would come from New Orleans to Le Havre bearing cotton from the South's slave plantations. Wagons would meet them and then take the cot-ton back to Strasbourg, the commercial center of Alsace's grow-ing textile industry. The wagons would return to Le Havre bearing people—emigrants like Jacob. There, hard by a port filled with ships and a shoreline jammed with four- and five-story buildings thrown up to accommodate the boom times, the emigrants would stay in cheap boardinghouses. By day they would reconnoiter on the quays, looking for a ship's captain or an agent with whom they could strike a deal for passage to America. Jacob's passport shows him turning up in Darmstadt, not far from Essenheim, on July 23, 1836, then in Strasbourg on August 2, in Paris on August 13, in Le Havre on October 7, and finally in New Orleans on November 26, seven weeks later. The officials who stamped his passport listed his occu-pation variously as merchant or butcher.

GO FORTH

It took some effort to get to see these documents connecting me more than two hundred years back in Father's family history. It would have been close to impossible for my mother's family. She had grown up in, for someone in her generation, a much more conven-tional American Jewish household than Father's, in the small blue-collar city of Perth Amboy, New Jersey. Her father was the town's first pediatrician. Until Mother went off to college, the family lived in a modest house divided horizontally into two apartments. They lived downstairs and a collection of relatives, who had to be partly supported by my grandfather because of the effects of the Depres-sion, lived upstairs. A Conservative synagogue stood two or three blocks away. Mother's sister once told me that if I wanted to under-stand what their childhood was like, all I had to do was read the first chapter of Philip Roth's *American Pastoral.* Fair enough: the

The main commercial street of Perth Amboy, New Jersey,
when Mother was a young woman there.

time period was the same, Roth's Newark was only twenty miles away, and Mother's Perth Amboy was an immediate environment that was at once entirely Jewish and enthusiastically, self-consciously all-American, full of optimism, the furthest thing from the doomed and dreamy South.

But there was something that wasn't so cheerful. Somewhere a generation or two back in Mother's family, and probably the other proudly middle-class families of Perth Amboy too, were the Lower East Side slums. These were never to be discussed. People had been desperate, hungry, disordered. Was it completely impossible that they could fall back into the abyss? Maybe not. When I was a boy, Mother would sometimes drive me past a soup kitchen called the Ozanam Inn that was on the way between Quercus and Father's office downtown. She would point to the long line of defeated-looking men standing outside. "See those men?" she'd say. "Every one of them made just one mistake, and that's where they wound up." Years before Mother was born, her father's father, a poverty-bred *no-goodnik*, had won an illegal lottery, made a small windfall, and abandoned his family; my grandfather had managed to acquire a medical license at an early age after an unspecified, but evidently not large, amount of higher education, and then he went to work supporting the family. He grew a moustache to make himself look older. Mother told me that once when she was a girl, a strange man had approached her on Perth Amboy's main shopping street and said he was her missing grandfather. She ran home and told her parents, who sternly admonished her never to speak to him again, if he should turn up, which he didn't. He died alone in a rooming house in Newark.

Mother's parents would instantly and firmly shut down my occasional inquiries into their family history. They wanted to focus on the bright future, not the mysterious but undoubtedly unpleasant past. Father's firm uninterest in his own Jewish history came not so much from wanting to erase it as to remake it, so that we would have been descended from European aristocrats—or at least from an eternally upper-class Jewish family, on a level with the Sassoons or the Ephrussis. At one point he hired someone to design a heraldic shield for us. What he and Mother, with their different backgrounds, had in common was an impulse to create a clean slate in the present, devoid of poverty, devoid of discrimination, devoid of religion, devoid of what Jews call Yiddishkeit. Jewishness felt as if it had a strange power to ruin everything, unaccompanied by much countervailing benefit.

Mother and Father were married in 1951 in the living room of her parents' house. By that time, her parents, doing better, had moved a short distance away from the apartment where Mother had grown up, into a house right on Raritan Bay, with a broad porch and no relatives as their housemates. Before the ceremony, Father spotted a basket of *kippot*, skullcaps worn on religious occasions, that had been put out for the men to wear, and hid them away. Mother and her family, thrilled about her propitious mar-

riage to someone from a much less modest background, got the
message. I don't remember anything Jewish ever being mentioned
during my long childhood visits to Perth Amboy. After Mother
died, I was surprised to find out that in high school she had been a
Hebrew school teacher at the synagogue, Congregation Beth Mordecai. Today Perth Amboy is a mainly Latino city, with very few
Jews left; like Philip Roth's Newark, it was a one-generation Jewish paradise for people climbing the American ladder, a step up
from where they had come from, a step below what they were preparing their children for. Congregation Beth Mordecai has been
reconsecrated as a church.

In New Orleans, we belonged to Temple Sinai, a grand, sand-
colored, neo-Moorish building on St. Charles Avenue, founded
in the late nineteenth century by German Jews, including my relatives. My great-grandparents, my grandparents, and my parents,
along with quite a few other Lemanns, lived within a short walk of
the temple, as if we were unusually prosperous shtetl dwellers, in a
neighborhood of spacious old houses and live oak trees whose thick
roots had extended over long years to the point that they had broken
through the sidewalks. The rabbi, Julian Feibelman, was married
to one of my innumerable cousins. When I was a child Father took
us to the temple just once a year, on Thanksgiving; Mother didn't
come. He'd tell us that this was a holiday for all Americans, not just
for Jews, who were to his way of thinking not a separate people, just
a group of religious congregants like any other.

Mother and Father sent us to the temple's Sunday school, where
he had gone as a child, but not with a lot of enthusiasm. A few years
ago, at the American Jewish Archives in Cincinnati, I came across
a series of letters Father had written to Julian Feibelman during the
time I was growing up. One was from 1966, complaining that I had
brought home a magazine for Jewish children that Father found
objectionable. "It has, to my mind, an undue orientation toward
the State of Israel and matters taking place there," Father wrote.
For many years after that, Father waged a lonely campaign against

Israel's ever being mentioned at Temple Sinai, or the Israeli flag's being displayed there alongside the American flag. "Temple Sinai is a house of worship, not a foreign policy organization!" he'd say indignantly. Israel was maximally threatening to his preferred version of being Jewish. It was unavoidably different, impossible to miss, combative, surrounded by enemies, and indicative of a sense of Jewish particularity. Father loved to travel, including in the ancient world, but Israel was one place he never went.

Julian answered Father's letter, in a patient but unmistakably exasperated tone, observing that you can't please everyone. And he had a complaint of his own, about an assignment on Hanukkah that my sister had submitted, which "caused us much more of a problem than, I daresay, any magazine or textbook would induce." It's easy for me to guess what Nancy must have said in the paper. I had absorbed Father's habit of being closely attuned to, so as to avoid, anything that might bring people's disapproval; Nancy was more candid, exuberant, unrestrained. She probably had said forthrightly in her paper that we did not celebrate Hanukkah in our house. Instead, Christmas was an occasion of great and elaborate joy for us. In our attic were boxes full of beautiful Christmas ornaments, taken out every year after we had brought home our tree, and there were also wreaths on our front door, an annual ceremonial reading by Father of "A Visit from St. Nicholas," caroling, a lavish Christmas dinner—the whole schmear, as we wouldn't have put it. Julian's letter went on to chastise Father: if a child of the temple was getting one message at Sunday school (pro-Hanukkah, no doubt) and the opposite message at home, it put the school in an impossible situation.

A few months later, Father wrote another complaining letter to Julian. I had gotten a very low grade, 53 out of 100, on a Sunday school test about the early history of Reform Judaism back in Germany. (Until I saw Father's letter, I had no memory of this. I don't think I cared much about how I did in Sunday school, or felt that hearing about the opening of a splendid Reform temple in Hamburg in 1844 had anything to do with me.) Father included the test with his letter, along with my latest school report card, which was much better. My performance on the test, to his mind, represented a failure on Temple Sinai's part rather than on my part. The temple had failed to capture my interest. Father told Julian that, in the face of relentless complaints from both his children about being bored in Sunday school, he was inclined to stop insisting that we go. Of course it's the rare child who doesn't protest being subjected to religious education—mine certainly did—so Father's reaction showed how important his children's Jewishness was to him: not very.

Around this time, unaware of this correspondence, I asked Father's permission to quit Sunday school. He said I should go see Cousin Julian and tell him why I wanted to quit. If I could obtain his blessing, it would be okay. Julian was a small, immensely dignified man with a round, deeply creased face. He was seventy years old, thirty years into his reign at Temple Sinai, proud of the measure of prominence he had achieved as one of the South's leading rabbis. I picture him in dark, floor-length, embroidered velvet robes, though he couldn't have been dressed that way when we met in his office. I put my case before him: Every year we had two classes, Jewish history and Hebrew, and each one was the same every year, the first featuring the stories of the biblical patriarchs and the second devoted to teaching us the characters in the Hebrew alphabet. It was boring. Julian looked at me impassively, revealing nothing. Knowing what I know now, I think he must have been relieved. He was one nod of his wise head away from getting Father off his back. What I remember is his assenting, with a minimalist oracular opacity. I was free.

This happened when I was about the age I would have become a bar mitzvah, had I grown up in a more typical Jewish environment. At Temple Sinai we had confirmations instead, the way Episcopalians, a denomination we greatly admired, did. Father had been confirmed at Temple Sinai when he was sixteen, but I was not. In fact I can't remember our doing anything explicitly Jewish for years. Somehow, though, if our aim was to attain a blessedly Jewishness-free consciousness, it didn't work. Our membership in this mysterious and heavily freighted category of people was still ever-present, hovering around us in the air, troubling, undefined, unresolved.

What was I missing? To be more specific, what if I had been bar-mitzvahed? It's something I wonder about now, but at the time, even if I was vaguely aware that bar mitzvahs existed somewhere far away from us, I had no idea what actually happened at one. Now I know. A bar mitzvah spends several years learning about the traditional Jewish Sabbath morning service, in which the bar mitzvah ceremony is embedded. He becomes familiar with the order of the service and with the prayers, and learns how to say at least some of them in Hebrew. At the climax of the ceremony, the boy is called to the Torah—meaning, he is summoned to a platform where a group of elders of the congregation are gathered, called by his Hebrew rather than his secular name, and put in front of a mysterious, sanctified long parchment scroll, dense with hand-inscribed Hebrew characters arrayed in columns, and—at least in the case of a well-prepared bar mitzvah—asked to read aloud.

Many Jews, at least American Jews today, are used to thinking of themselves as having a comfortable, casually worn ethnic identity, but you can see that here, unavoidably, the bar mitzvah is being removed from the mainstream and relocated as a Jew. He uses a different name and speaks a different language—a particularly challenging one if he's reading from the Torah scroll, because, in addition to the alphabet's being different, there are no vowels and the reading must be done in a distinctive singsong trope. The Torah itself is not reading matter, it's magic. It's handled with ritual and reverence, honored with prayers before and after it's read. Letting it fall would be a disaster. It is divided into fifty-two weekly portions. Every Saturday morning Jews read one of them out loud and then listen to a comment delivered by a rabbi, a member of the congregation, a learned visitor, or, in this case, a bar mitzvah. People who are observant have read every weekly portion dozens of times; the idea is that, unlike any other book, this one, a peculiar stitched-together collection of stories and recitations of rules, cannot ever yield the entirety of the wisdom it contains. There's always something new— not just new, so vital that life really ought not be lived without it— that each year's reading of each week's portion offers.

As a journalist and a professor, I operate in a culture that imagines itself to be capable and rational. Whatever is going on in the moment, we analyze it. If it's a problem, we believe we can solve it. We don't assume that there are limitations to smart humans' capabilities, to their power of understanding. Entering the world of Torah study requires thinking of yourself differently. Whatever is in that week's portion—fire, flood, liberation; peculiarly detailed instructions about animal sacrifice; poetry; excruciatingly long genealogical lists; unacceptable practices like slavery, concubinage, polygamy, and war crimes—is, at least in the moment, more important, more pertinent, than whatever is going on in the world. It has a special power if you submit to it. Why? Did God write the Torah? Did He reveal it to Moses atop Mount Sinai? Even if one wants to dodge those questions, as I do, participating in Jewish services requires acting as if the answers to them might be yes.

The Torah leads into a vast ocean of commentary, much of it written many centuries ago in a highly elliptical style by rabbis living in medieval villages. The premise is that the Torah, on one hand, contains all possible wisdom and is usefully applicable to all situations in the present, but, on the other hand, is full of unclarities, contradictions, and elisions. None of this can be simply a mistake— God doesn't make mistakes—so it requires study and explication. To make this even more complicated, the commentators usually don't come to a conclusion, they merely disagree eruditely. (The Talmud, the vast compendium of ancient and medieval Jewish law and commentary, begins with a long, unsettled dispute over the proper time to say the evening prayer.) All Jews should participate in this ongoing disputation—even a bar mitzvah. So preparing for a bar mitzvah also requires an encounter with the commentary on at least one's weekly portion. The premise is that even a thirteen-year-old boy can—must!—add something of his own to a never-ending two-millennium-long conversation. That's what it means to be an adult member of the community. And so it also means, at least if you conduct a portion of your life outside the confines of the *kahal*, the community, coming at the world in an unfamiliar way, having to negotiate constantly between two quite different forms of identity and consciousness.

Because Jacob Lemann's departure from Germany is on my mind, I would like to imagine that, if I had a bar mitzvah, my Torah portion would be Lech Lecha, which takes up chapters 12 through 17 of the Book of Genesis. And because it's likely that Jacob studied Lech Lecha himself, studying it might serve as a way to engage in informed speculation about his state of mind as he was leaving; my text was plausibly his text too. Lech Lecha is not one of those boring Torah portions that bar mitzvahs dread being assigned. It begins with a bang. God appears to Abram, a seventy-five-year-old man living with his barren wife, Sarai, in a village in what is now Turkey, and offers a stirring possibility—no, given the source, a certainty: "Go forth from your native land and from your father's house to the land that I will show you. I will make of you a great nation." The main storyline of the Torah begins here.

Dispatched on their unlikely journey by God, this elderly couple make their way to Egypt, where Abram essentially offers up Sarai to Pharaoh as a mistress and is rewarded with great riches. God puts an end to that episode. Long years of wanderings and wars follow. Sarai instructs Abram to consort with her servant, Hagar, so that he can have a child, and he does—call him Ishmael. Then, when Abram is ninety-nine years old and Sarai is ninety, God reappears and creates His covenant with our people: Abram will have himself and all the males in his household circumcised, God will at last give Sarai a child, the couple will be renamed Abraham and Sarah, and their numerous descendants will eventually be given the land of Canaan as an everlasting holding. Can we just immerse ourselves in the indelible, undeniable power of this story? Here we have longing, sin, an epic journey, adventure, miracles, and some awfully complicated relationships.

But this is a bar mitzvah, so, sorry, we will have to engage with Lech Lecha in the Jewish manner, which is not so straightforward. A very long time ago, we were driven out of the land God promised us in Lech Lecha. We no longer had the magnificent Temple in Jerusalem, and we still don't. Scattered all over the world, we have focused intensely on studying the Torah. It's what binds us into a people. Perhaps because of its supreme importance and therefore its familiarity, we pass right through its main narrative. Instead we look for small mysteries, unanswered questions, and lacunae, and then try to explain them. We look for meanings beyond the obvious meanings. For example, Rashi began his interpretation of Lech Lecha at the very beginning, with the first two words. Why did God say "go forth," instead of just "go"? It couldn't be just happenstance or idle wordplay. There must be a reason.

Rashi finds a great deal more than is obviously there in that one extra word: "GET THEE OUT (literally, go for thyself)—for your own benefit, for your own good: there I will make of you a great nation whilst here you will not merit the privilege of having children." None of this is in the text. Rashi feels free to make Abram's first encounter with God into more of a transaction and less of a simple command: stay, and remain childless, or go, and become rich and fruitful. Perhaps God knew already, as we don't at that point, what a highly imperfect person Abram (like all the biblical patriarchs) was—a man capable of telling Pharaoh that Sarai was his sister, and of assenting to the banishment of Hagar when Sarai became enraged with her for becoming pregnant. Did God know that Abram was not sufficiently noble to make his terrifying journey without a material deal-sweetener?

All this speaks to the idea that in reading Lech Lecha, and for that matter every other Torah portion, we assume, at least for the purpose of a bar mitzvah, that this ancient document, containing nothing we would accept today as factual or scientific evidence, can still guide us. The Torah—physically unwieldy, unreadable without special training, often dull or indecipherable, full of material that offends modern sensibilities—rationally ought not to have bounded so many millions of people's lives for so many years, but it did. Even now, when I see it taken out of the ark and unrolled to the proper passage, I can't help feeling that there is an underlying order in the world, a stanchion against whatever is the disaster of the moment. It's hard to explain in the language I'm accustomed to using to explain things, but the Torah's power, for those who choose to submit to it, is undeniable. It endures. Nothing else endures.

If Jacob Lemann, childless like Abram and also wifeless, had looked to Lech Lecha for guidance when he departed Germany for Louisiana, what would he have derived from it? Abram's journey, God told him through their various conversations, would bring him riches, and descendants as numerous as the stars in the sky, and a land populated by people we'd now call Jews. Jacob was moving from his small, constricted, but covenanted environment to a country that would be far less friendly to a Jewish life, at least in the short run, but far more friendly to Jews. The Comte de Clermont-Tonnerre, a French aristocrat and politician, gave a "Speech on Religious Minorities and Questionable Professions" in 1789, just a few months after the Revolution (and twenty years before Jacob was born), in which he declared, "We must refuse everything to the Jews as a nation and accord everything to the Jews as individuals." If this was the choice Jacob was making, his journey was different from Abram's: away from the covenant, not toward it. He would be fully emancipated, he would have a chance to prosper far beyond what would have been possible in Germany, but he would not be able to keep kosher, or even to pray, since that requires a company of ten Jewish adults. He would surely have to violate the Sabbath.

Jacob would be arriving in a strange land built on slavery, even as he himself instantly became a white man with all the rights he hadn't had back home—indeed, rights very few Jews had anywhere in the world—in a new nation that liked to compare itself with a biblical promised land. Was Louisiana Canaan, or was it Egypt? Was he leaving in order to return, or simply leaving? He had a lot to figure out—and also, like Abram, money to make and offspring to produce (according to a genealogy-adept cousin of mine, there are 643 people produced as a result of his marriage to Marie Berthelot alive today). But, for all the mysteries and complications of Lech Lecha, its pertinence seems clear on one point: a Jewish exile, a wanderer, is better understood as a seeker than as an escaper: someone who aspires to live a life under God's law but in different circumstances, not to live a life unbounded by the covenant. Jacob could have made himself into an exemplar of Clermont-Tonnerre's maxim, happily trading Jewish life for individual rights. Or he could free himself of the restrictions imposed by non-Jews and then try to find his way back to the incomparable rewards of Jewish life. That's a choice his descendants have had to make too—including me.

SUGAR COUNTRY

If it seems odd that Jacob should have chosen Louisiana, rather than some part of America closer to Europe, as his destination, it shouldn't. During the decades before the Civil War, a distinct emigrant wave of Jews who lived along the upper reaches of the Rhine River left home and came to Louisiana. Most of them were not desperately poor, and their lives were not in immediate danger. Most of them came as single young men. Pretty much all of them had the same original occupation: some combination of peddling, shopkeeping, moneylending, and trading in livestock.

The Upper Rhine River Valley is a very pretty place. The river is narrow, constrained by steep banks containing gorgeous, pacific, green vineyards and ancient towns. Jewish immigrants like Jacob were coming to the banks of a very different river. The Mississippi in those days was wide, muddy, and flood prone. You wouldn't have called it beautiful. Its banks were flat and weedy. The towns along its course were rough and raw. Epidemics and disastrous storms swept through regularly. Louisiana wasn't an obviously better place to be than Germany. But some combination of the constraints of their lives back home and the opportunities in America was enough to induce these young men to find their way to Le Havre and then to spend weeks sailing across the Atlantic Ocean.

When they arrived in Louisiana, they kept doing what they had been doing back home, and their culture was tight enough that they were able to maintain a network of business connections, across what would now seem to have been unimaginable distances and barriers to communication, with other German and French Jews, in other parts of the United States and in Western Europe. Louisiana was an attractive destination because many people there spoke French and some spoke German, because life in an agricultural region was familiar to this group of immigrants, because there was an economic role for the Jews to fill, and, most of all, because it was a booming area, where, if you were white and had a head for business, you could arrive with very little and quickly make money.

The reason Louisiana provided such abundant opportunity to someone like Jacob was that it had an economy and a political order that rested on slavery: the dominion, in the place where he settled, of a small number of white people over a far larger number of Black people whom they legally owned. I think of Jacob's generation of Jewish immigrant peddlers (*colporteurs*, as they were called in Louisiana), trudging along rough country roads with their wagons or backpacks in the pestilential heat, alongside the leveeless Mississippi, as people God had decided to test, as He had tested the founders of our tribe. What they wanted most of all, surely, was to establish themselves and prosper. They were not particularly intellectual or artistic or scholarly. There is no sign that, before they boarded their ships, the prospect of moving to a slave society troubled them. They had no evident impulse to present themselves with a series of profound moral challenges, both about being Jews and about being human—but that is what life brought them.

In 1791, the most significant Black rebellion in the history of the New World, soon led by Toussaint-Louverture, began in Saint Domingue, the French colony that is now Haiti. Up to that point, Saint Domingue and other Caribbean islands supplied most of the Western world's sugar from large plantations whose owners were white and whose workers were Black Africans and their descendants. That uprisings were rare didn't mean they weren't deeply lodged in whites' consciousness, including even as late as during my lifetime. It's easy for me to imagine how heavily the Haitian Revolution, whose origins could be told as a story of large numbers of escaped slaves, in hidden encampments in the woods, practicing voodoo before campfires as a prelude to doing to whites what whites had done to them, would have landed with sugarcane planters. The "devastation of the French sugar islands by servile insurrection," as a white Southern historian put it long ago, made it look as if more Toussaints would emerge on other islands.

In 1794, during the most radical stage of the Revolution, France abolished slavery in all its colonies. (Napoleon reinstated it some years later.) Abolitionist sentiment was growing in Britain too. Where could white planters grow sugarcane, harvested with enslaved labor? Louisiana had been thought to be too far north, insufficiently tropical if less burdened by pangs of conscience about slavery. But in 1795, Etienne de Bore, a French-descended owner of an indigo plantation, demonstrated, thanks to the labor of eighty slaves, that sugarcane could be commercially grown and processed there. Quercus stands on land that is a stone's throw from the site of de Bore's plantation.

In 1803 Louisiana became part of the United States, which was far more friendly to slavery than France, its former owner. A few years later, Congress banned the transatlantic slave trade, which elevated the importance of the large slave market in New Orleans, whose commerce in humans included enslaved people marched down from the Upper South in coffles by traders to be sold to plantation owners in the Lower South. At the market, enslaved Black people would be paraded before buyers who would poke and prod them, inspecting them for signs of their potential for hard physical labor, childbearing, and rebelliousness—this last criterion checked by inspecting their backs for marks of the lash.

Beginning in the earliest years of the United States, Congress placed a series of heavy tariffs on imported sugar, in order to encourage domestic production—which really meant subsidizing slaveholding plantations in Louisiana. From the beginning of the nineteenth century until the Civil War, sugar cultivation in one small section of southern Louisiana was a bonanza for the planters. Louisiana sugar country, which had more than 1500 planters and nearly 140,000 enslaved Black people by 1850, accounted for 95 percent of sugar production in the South and 25 percent in the world. Donaldsonville, where Jacob settled, was the principal town in sugar country. It was this circumstance that drew him there.

The largest of the Louisiana sugar planters were among the richest people in the United States. Some of them, even if they had started with nothing, learned to get themselves up as aristocrats. They built grand plantation houses placed so as to be on display to people passing by in boats on the river, bred racehorses, entertained opulently with wines, china, and silver imported from Europe. (Most movies you've seen that are set on Southern plantations—*12 Years a Slave, Interview with the Vampire, Django Unchained, Hush . . . Hush, Sweet Charlotte*—were filmed on Louisiana sugarcane plantations, not far from Palo Alto, that had been built in the decades before the Civil War; in the most recent film version of *All the King's Men*, a sugarcane plantation represents a house in Burden's Landing.) An awestruck Southern historian writing in the 1950s captured the planters' preferred way of presenting themselves: "In approaching by steamboat a typical sugar plantation, one first saw 'the house,' the master's dwelling. It was an institution of the Southern scene glorified in literature and lore. . . . Within high-ceilinged rooms and shaded verandas flowed the domestic and social life of the plantation community. Like the manor house of an earlier day, it was and yet remains the highest symbol of the grandeur of the ante-bellum sugar civilization." It was an automatic assumption in the milieu of my childhood that the people who lived in these plantation houses really were aristocrats, people of ease and refinement, deserving automatic admiration and even deference. The plantations were seen as monuments of civilization, worth preserving and honoring, even past the middle of the twentieth century.

Such was the façade. Behind it lay, primarily, slavery. The planters always insisted that the only way to operate their plantations was with enslaved, African-descended labor. They justified themselves with not just economic necessity but also supposedly inviolable historical and biological laws and even biblical sanction that permitted their systematic dehumanization of fellow humans. Many planters had no trouble keeping their own children, the result of the sexual aspect of their total dominion over the people they owned, in slavery, or selling them away from the people who cared about them. They usually claimed that most slaves appreciated the system and led far better lives than white laborers in the North. But events gave the lie to that. In 1811 the largest slave uprising in American history took place just a few miles down the Mississippi from Donaldsonville, in an area called the German Coast. A group of two hundred Black people gathered on a sugar plantation and began marching toward New Orleans, killing two white planters and burning down five plantation houses as they went. Within a few days, a larger and better armed white force had put the rebellion down. The Blacks' main leader, Charles Deslondes, was hunted down by dogs in a swamp. The white militia that caught him first cut off his hands and then burned him alive.

In all, ninety-five Black people were either killed on the spot or executed later after a trial. Their heads were cut off and put on pikes for the world to see. Afterward the planters did everything they could to make sure that future uprisings by sugar country's heavy Black majority would be impossible. They forbade or tightly restricted slaves' movements between plantations, even to see their spouses and children. They formed patrols to travel through the swamps looking for escapees. They limited Black people's access to anything that might be empowering, like marriage, literacy, and religion. Occasionally the planters experimented with importing European immigrant labor, but repeated experiments failed and that redoubled their determination to defend slavery at all costs.

Sugar plantations were factories as well as farms. On Southern cotton plantations, the cotton left in the form of ginned bales, lightly processed. On sugar plantations, the cane left as hogsheads of refined sugar and barrels of molasses. That meant a plantation had to have a sugarhouse, running around the clock at the year-end harvest season and staffed by skilled craftsmen, to turn cane into sugar, quickly, before it spoiled. The demand for labor—to drain swamps for cultivation, to plant and cut cane, to cut down trees so the wood could be burned in sugar refineries, and to operate the sugarhouse—was relentless. Solomon Northrup, the author of *Twelve Years a Slave*, was rented out by his cotton-planting owner to a Louisiana sugar plantation that was desperate for workers, and there, he reported, he was paid a small quantity of cash in return for working on Sundays, because the sugarhouse had to operate seven days a week.

A recent historian who is not a Southerner described life on the plantation without a hint of grace or ease: "Louisiana's sugar order left a brutal imprint on those who worked the line and whose days were atomized, routinized, and divided by the ticking clock. . . . Late antebellum sugar plantations hummed with the energy of the machine age and reverberated with the groans of exhausted slaves; field work and mill labor continued day in and day out with oppressive regularity and mind-numbing monotony. As ruthless and intrusive capitalists, the sugar masters modernized their immense agricultural enterprises and exploited the clock, the plantation layout, shift work, and the division of labor coldly and rationally to maximize slave labor." Some plantation owners would press older female slaves into service as wet nurses, so as to put young mothers back to work earlier and to avoid the natural contraceptive effects of nursing, in the hope of hastening the next pregnancy. Nonetheless, the work was so relentless and harsh that the natural population increase of slaves on sugar plantations was below what it was on cotton plantations. One way to account for the incompatibility of accounts of life on sugarcane plantations would be to say that the planters were either evil or morally impaired. Another would be to say that the planters chose to see what they wanted to see. The owner of a plantation that was substantial enough to afford him aristocratic pretensions often thought of himself as the benign protector of a grateful flock of simple Black peasants, not so different from feudal lords in Europe, many of whom deluded themselves in the same way. (Back in the Germany that Jacob Lemann left, when a large piece of agricultural land was sold, the peasants on the land, though not technically enslaved, were conveyed to the new owner.)

The person who carried out the daily brutality of slavery was usually the plantation overseer, who functioned as a shield from unpleasantness for the owner. William Minor, a leading Louisiana sugar planter, wrote out a lengthy list of instructions for his overseers, which began this way: "He must treat all the Negroes with kindness and humanity both in sickness and in health." If an overseer didn't do that, surely he would understand that Minor, and people like him, preferred not to know about it. And the overseer had his own overseer, an enslaved Black man called a driver, who was charged with keeping his own people in line in return for a measure of special treatment. An eyewitness to life on the Louisiana sugarcane plantations during the heyday of slavery was the Connecticut-born Frederick Law Olmsted, later to become America's leading landscape designer, but then a young journalist. Olmsted, a clear-eyed young adventurer with flowing hair and a moustache, spent several years in the 1850s traveling through the South and filing dispatches to the just-founded *New York Times*, under the byline "Yeoman." He described the social ordering of a labor gang on a Louisiana plantation this way:

> First came, led by an old driver carrying a whip, forty of largest and strongest women I ever saw together. They were all in a simple uniform dress of a bluish check stuff, the skirts reaching little below the knee; their legs and feet were bare; they carried themselves loftily, each having a hoe over the shoulder, and walked with a free, powerful swing, like *chasseurs* on the march. Behind them came the cavalry, thirty strong, mostly men, but a few of them women, two of whom rode astride on the plow mules. A lean and vigilant white overseer, on a brisk pony, brought up the rear.

Like many visitors, Olmsted found sugar country to be a kind of supercharged version of what the antebellum South was generally, with more extreme conditions, more dramatic disparities between the condition of the fortunate few and the unfortunate many, and more heated justifications of the system from the people who controlled it. He spent a good deal of time with planters, receiving their celebrated gracious hospitality and listening to their apologia. Olmsted personally came down here: "I must confess that there seems to me room for grave doubts if the capital, labor, and especially the human life, which have been and which continue to be spent in converting the swamps of Louisiana into sugar plantations, and in defending them against the annual assaults of the river, and the fever and the cholera, could not have been better employed somewhere else." That would be my own preferred interpretation, too, but I have to contend with knowing that if, as Olmsted preferred, the Louisiana sugarcane plantations had never been created, Jacob Lemann might not have been motivated to come to America, and I wouldn't be here. In Germany, my generation of Jews was never born.

Sugar country was perpetually desperate for credit, because running a plantation required constant infusions of money and the crop was sold only once a year. Financially, slavery may have been even more important to planters as a source of credit than as a source of forced labor. Enslaved people were not only bought, sold, and traded, they were financial assets, used as collateral for the loans the planters always needed. The major planters in sugar country borrowed from factors in New Orleans—financiers who would lend them money and help them take their crops to market. Planters who were too small to get the factors' attention dealt with people like Jacob Lemann, Jews who moved through the countryside selling them goods, making small-scale loans, buying loans and reselling them, and trading: what they knew how to do because it was what their forebears had been doing for centuries back in France and Germany. Because slaves in sugar country sometimes made a little cash, Jewish peddlers sold goods and extended credit to them too. In a country with no stores, the Jews established stores. The timing of Jacob's arrival in Louisiana was especially propitious because it closely preceded a banking crisis, whose result was that for fifteen years sugar country had a severe shortage of traditional lenders, which opened the way for nontraditional lenders like him.

These Louisiana Jews were people whose central animating myth was of their liberation from slavery, and whose organizing principle of daily life had been Jewish observance. And here they were seeking opportunity in an environment that required accepting slavery (of other people) as a given and living secular lives. If you take the trouble to look, the past, one's own past, often doesn't behave as one would like it to. How does one grapple with that? It's possible that my descendants will learn about things I did that will trouble them, and may not have troubled me. I hope they will not dismiss me. I don't want to dismiss my own ancestors, now that for me, because I investigated and learned things, they are no longer just names to be honored, opaque, stripped of the messiness of being human. Even so, truly understanding them is a difficult project. It's hard to know from this distance what they thought and how they felt; all that's possible is to find out what they did.

THERE'S ALWAYS SOMETHING

The first time Jacob Lemann's name turns up in an official record after his arrival in New Orleans in 1836 is in the 1840 federal census. There he is the head of a household in Donaldsonville, with his last name spelled Lemann rather than Lehmann. Also in the household are four "free colored persons" and three white males. These must have been employees of the earliest version of the family store, run out of a home, as the Jews' stores back in Essenheim were. And there is also a white woman, under the age of twenty, listed as a member of the household. That would have to be Jacob's wife, my great-great-grandmother, who was born as Marie Estelle Berthelot in Thibodaux, Louisiana, some distance away on Bayou Lafourche, and baptized in a Catholic church there. Father, during his heraldry phase, entertained the hope that the Berthelots might have been descended from French nobility, but it seems more likely that they were French-Canadian fur trappers who had moved to Louisiana from somewhere in Missouri or Illinois. Family legend has it that Marie was working as an au pair in Donaldsonville when she met Jacob, and that her family was unhappy about the marriage. She would have been sixteen or seventeen years old. They were together until she died in the 1870s. In 1841 Jacob and Marie's first child, my great-grandfather, Bernard Lemann, was born. (A second child, named Isaac, was born a year later. He died at the age of one.)

Not long after that, Jacob's and Marie's names begin appearing regularly in the elegantly handwritten (often in French) official records of property transactions kept in the Ascension Parish courthouse. Dozens of these, executed in a flowery and often impenetrable legal jargon, march across the pages of the parish clerk's thick record books. In most cases both Jacob and Marie have signed the document, Jacob with the stylized signature that was the only thing he ever learned to write that wasn't in the Hebrew alphabet, Marie with an X, because, as one recording clerk put it, "Mrs. Lemann, having declared not to know how to write or sign, made her ordinary mark in the presence of the same witnesses, after due lecture of this act." The transactions begin in the early 1840s at amounts in the hundreds of dollars. They gradually escalate to sums in the tens of thousands by the late 1850s. Jacob was in two overlapping businesses: operating his store on the Donaldsonville town square, and buying and selling assets of all kinds—primarily land.

When Willie Stark sends Jack Burden off to investigate Judge Montague Irwin, of Burden's Landing, looking for misdeeds, Jack can't believe he'll find anything. But Willie is right: there's always something. What about for Jacob Lemann? Again, there's always something—something a great deal more weighty than the minor professional lapse Jack turned up about Judge Irwin. The old Ascension Parish records reveal that among the assets Jacob bought and sold during the years of his rise were enslaved people. I found fourteen of these transactions of human beings in all, involving eighteen people. In the first record, from 1844, Jacob sold "Louisa a mulatto woman aged about twenty years and Lewis alias Steam Boat a negro man aged about forty years," for $832. Just a few days later, for $2020, he bought Arianne, "trente trois ans," and her four small children, Edouard, Maria, Alfred, and Virginie. In 1848 he sold Ned Henry, "aged about twenty-seven years acquired by the vendor as a runaway at a sheriff sale," along with the same Arianne, with only three of her children, for $5000. In 1851 he bought Emma, age eighteen, for $200. In 1852 he bought and then immediately sold Alfred, a fourteen-year-old boy, for $800. A few months later he bought Judy Cole, age thirty-one, and her two children, Peyton and Henry, for $1210. Later that year he sold Emma, whom he had bought the previous year, for $628. In 1857 he sold King, age thirty-five, whom he had bought at a local auction, for $1300. I don't know anything else about these people or their descendants. Some of those descendants must still be living in Donaldsonville, as some of Jacob's descendants are.

Jacob was not operating plantations, so he evidently wasn't looking for laborers he could compel to work in the cane fields. He was a middleman, as Jews so often have been. The 1850 census shows him owning no slaves. Usually he had bought the Black people whom he was selling at a public auction after somebody had defaulted on taxes, or from a widow whose husband had recently died, and their bodies were conveyed along with a piece of land. Jacob was looking for underpriced assets that he believed he could sell later at a profit. During this time the antislavery movement was well underway, though certainly not in Louisiana sugar country, but if its arguments ever made an impression on Jacob, there's no evidence of it. His own records consist entirely of cryptic columns of figures, sometimes accompanied by a private shorthand made up of German words rendered in the Hebrew alphabet (perhaps he didn't want any information about his business to be accessible to prying eyes). Black people were valuable not just as workers but also as property that could be bought, sold, or mortgaged, and Jacob obviously didn't feel constrained from doing those things if the opportunity arose as he looked for investment. And in the larger sense, he was getting rich in an economy that was thriving because it was entirely based on slavery.

Ever since I sat in the Ascension Parish clerk's office looking at these records, I can't get them out of my mind. As late as the 1930s, when one of the New Deal agencies paid for a project to translate the old records out of French into English and to type them up so they would be easier to read, the project was limited to land transactions—no livestock or Black people. That's a sign of the ambient level of moral awareness in Louisiana, back when it was casting nearly 90 percent of its votes for Franklin Roosevelt. And shouldn't Jacob, as a Jew, have seen the wrong in slavery? Evidently he did not. The Torah is full of references to slavery, treating it as something far below, say, idol worship on the scale of immorality. At best one can say that the Torah tries to create rules for slaveholders, including Jewish ones, while exulting in the collective emancipation of the Jews as a people. Could Jacob have been obeying some inner compass that would be utterly foreign and offensive to us today? All

I can do with these questions, given the opacity to me of Jacob's inner life, is to say that there is a direct causal connection between his involvement with slavery, which I would consider evil even if he did not, and the life I'm able to live today. It's my job, not his, to do what I can to make amends, if that is even possible. I cannot remove slavery from our family's history—my history.

The Lemann store had established itself within ten years of Jacob's arrival in the United States as the leading retailer in Donaldsonville. In 1846, the year he became a naturalized citizen of the United States, he took out an advertisement in a local newspaper, obviously written for him by somebody else, announcing that he had a wide array of goods acquired from "friends in Cincinnati and New York," including carriages, carts, harnesses, "negro clothes," whiskey, wine, tobacco, lard, salt, and sugar. He operated a saddler's shop, "where various planters can have work of any kind made to satisfaction on the shortest notice." He was willing to part with any item he carried for cash, credit, or barter.

In one of the old parish records, created in 1848, Jacob confers power of attorney over the store and his investment properties to a man named Joseph Cire for six months, because he is planning an extended visit to New York. It's obvious from the store advertisement I just quoted that Jacob was operating within a network that went far beyond Louisiana. That was how he got the goods he sold in the store, and probably also the money he was using to buy land and enslaved people. The network was made up mainly of other German-Jewish immigrants. Just as, in Louisiana, Jacob extended credit to his customers and to the people he traded with, outside of Louisiana other German Jews extended credit to him. They trusted one another. They spoke the same language.

What becomes clear as you follow his trail forward in time through the records is that Jacob had more in mind in New York than merely making business connections. He was beginning to move his family there. The evidence I have would indicate that he was seeking not a hometown that wasn't based on slavery, and not a richer cultural life, but a way to be more actively Jewish than Donaldsonville could provide. In 1852, in New York, Marie came before a court of three rabbis and informed them that she was married to a Jew, had given birth to a Jewish son who had been circumcised, and had herself just recently been immersed in a bath of ritual purification. She was officially converted to Judaism and renamed Miriam.

The presiding official at this ceremony was German-born Max Lilienthal, the most prominent German-Jewish rabbi in the United States, the first American rabbi who held a degree from a university. Lilienthal stood as a living emblem of the hope that German-born Jews could find a miraculous life in America, one previously unknown in the whole great sweep of Jewish history, which would combine all the freedoms accorded to non-Jews in enlightened societies with the full benefits of Jewish observance. In 1846, not long after he arrived in the United States, Lilienthal told his people back home that he was writing them from "New York, from the God-blessed country of freedom, the beautiful ground of civic equality! The old Europe with its restrictions lies behind me like a bad dream." Following Marie's conversion, she and Jacob had a second wedding ceremony, at Congregation Ansche Chesed, then housed in an elegant newly constructed building on the Lower East Side, which still stands.

In 1854 Jacob and Miriam bought a small house in Newport, Rhode Island, not yet a resort with grand seaside mansions. This wasn't a location they had chosen by accident or merely because of its climate advantage over New Orleans. The house was just a short distance from the Touro Synagogue, whose home, an austere, imposing painted brick structure built in 1763, is the oldest Jewish house of worship still standing in the United States. Judah Touro, the only son of the synagogue's founding religious figure, had moved to New Orleans in the early nineteenth century and had become its most rich and prominent Jewish citizen. In 1790 George Washington visited the Touro Synagogue; in preparation he wrote a

The *ketubah* (marriage contract) for the religious
remarriage of Jacob and Miriam (formerly Marie)
Lemann in New York City, 1852.

letter to the congregation promising, astonishingly, that the United
States would always be a nation without official religious prejudices,
and that every one of "the children of the stock of Abraham" shall
"sit in safety under his own vine and fig tree and there shall be none
to make him afraid." Like Max Lilienthal, the Touro Synagogue
partook of a powerful dream of what kind of Jewish life might be

possible in America—though at that point it wasn't possible in Donaldsonville.

In 1856, Jacob sold his store, with all its contents, to his chief clerk, Bienvenue Mollere, for just under $15,000, and signed a legal document promising never to engage in shopkeeping in Donaldsonville again. The next year he sold the land under the store to Mollere for $10,000. The year after that, 1858, Jacob and Miriam bought a house in New York City, on Twenty-Third Street, which was then filling up with substantial brownstones. Bernard's much younger brother Myer—perhaps named for the family's Mayer relatives back in Essenheim, as Bernard was probably named after Jacob's father, Beretz—was born in New York not long after that.

When Judith and I went to Essenheim, our guide, Stefan Mossel, told us he had a couple of surprises for us, beyond the official records of births, marriages, and deaths that were stored in the basement of the town hall of Nieder-Olm. He took us to the Essenheim town hall. There, in the kitchen, sitting on a metal dolly, was a massive stone, eight inches thick, with a carved inscription in Hebrew. Stefan told us that it was one of two cornerstones that had flanked the front door of Essenheim's synagogue, built in 1857, one inscribed in Hebrew, the other, now lost, in German. The Hebrew inscription said that the synagogue had been a gift from Jacob Lemann.

So, nearly twenty years after he had left, Jacob returned to Essenheim as a Jewish philanthropist. We walked around the corner and saw the empty, weedy lot where the small, solid synagogue had once stood. It had operated from 1857 until 1935, when the Nazis forced all the Jews in Essenheim to move to Mainz, a few miles away, which had a much larger Jewish community. On Kristallnacht, November 9, 1938, both of the synagogues in Mainz were burned, and afterward a heavy tax was levied on the Jews to pay for the damage. In 1942 and 1943 all the Jews who remained in Mainz, 1336 people, were deported to concentration camps. In Essenheim, the synagogue was turned into a storehouse. There is a brief old film clip showing it during that period. The missing German-language

Stolpersteines, brass plaques memorializing victims of the Holocaust,
set in the pavement in front of the former home of the Mayer family,
our relatives, in Jacob Lemann's home village of Essenheim, Germany.

cornerstone commemorating Jacob Lemann's gift is clearly visible.
Inside the holy spaces, ducks wander around among piles of junk. In
the 1970s, the deteriorating building was finally demolished. On the
main street of Essenheim, in front of one of the old half-timbered
houses, there are small square brass plaques set in the pavement—
Stolpersteines, which one sees all over Germany in front of murdered
Jews' homes—memorializing three of my Mayer relatives who were
shipped off to the camps.

From the Essenheim town hall, Stefan took us to a village
called Jugenheim, which is the site of the cemetery where, from
the sixteenth through the nineteenth centuries, all the Jews in the
area were buried. A friend of Stefan who lives there walked with
us out to the edge of the village and then down a rough dirt road
that ran between cow pastures. There, a few hundred yards outside of town, was the Jewish cemetery, which isn't marked on any
map and would have been impossible for us to find on our own.
On Kristallnacht, Jugenheim's small synagogue had been burned
down and the Jewish homes and businesses vandalized; soon

after, the Hitler Youth desecrated the cemetery. It was easy for me to picture the scene—frenzied teenage boys given free license to have fun destroying the small monuments that were what was left of ordinary Jews' lives. Why be confined solely to going after live Jews?

After the war the boys were identified and made to return to the cemetery and repair the damage they had inflicted, but evidently, if that was a rehabilitation program, it didn't last long. Today the cemetery is a peaceful landscape of mostly toppled headstones resting under tall shade trees, surrounded by a low metal fence. Jacob, during the same period when he made the gift to build the synagogue in Essenheim, also commissioned a rather grand new headstone, considerably taller than me, for the grave of his father, who had died when he was three years old. Miraculously, it still stands untouched in the Jewish cemetery. One side is inscribed in Hebrew,

The Jewish cemetery outside the village of Jugenheim, Germany, was never fully restored after its desecration by Nazi youth during Kristallnacht in 1938. Jacob Lemann's parents are buried there.

the other in German. The German side says it is the grave of Peraz Lehmann, put up by Sohn Lehmann—who would be Jacob, the son.

Stefan had one last surprise to tell us about. In 1859, not long after the opening of the new synagogue Jacob had commissioned, his half brother, Joseph Lehmann, one of the children of Jacob's father's first marriage, was murdered in his home in Essenheim, evidently by a knife-bearing attacker who broke in and stabbed him to death. Stefan showed us the official police report describing the murder scene: "His dead body lay outstretched on the floor of the living room with his arms bent above his body, was dressed with jerkin, trousers, vest, shirt and slippers, the kerchief lay loose round the neck, on the side of his head lay the lost kippah." From this you get a picture of a prosperous, and still religiously observant, businessman. The crime was never solved.

Later, Stefan sent us a slightly different account of the murder that he had found and translated from German into English, written by a man named Adam Probst, a Christian farmer who lived on the same street as Joseph Lehmann, a few houses away. Probst wrote: "About nine o'clock in the evening Joseph Lehmann was murdered in his own home. A strong hit shattered his skull, whereupon his death took place instantly. A golden clock, he still wore that day, was taken from him, his desk was opened and probably a lot of money stolen, because the desk was completely depleted." From Probst's point of view, Joseph had it coming. His account went on: "Lehmann was a big usurer and he probably was not completely without money. A suspicion actually rests on his own family, because he was an unjust father, an evil man. His children had to live in poverty although he possessed a fortune from which they all could have lived decently. However, proof cannot be delivered against them. By the way, the murdered had many more enemies than friends, and if the nefarious act remains covered, that will teach the future."

It's hard to read this and feel that the Essenheim to which Jacob returned was a place where Christians and Jews lived in prosperous harmony—but perhaps I say that because I know what happened three-quarters of a century later. Jacob had left Essenheim young, alone, much poorer, and willing to venture outside the confines of a Jewish life, including marrying a non-Jewish woman. Now he had come back as a successful middle-aged man, prosperous enough to erect these monuments, and observant enough to put his money and energy into specifically Jewish remembrance. Marie had become Miriam, their marriage had been religiously consecrated, they evidently belonged to two congregations, one in Newport and one in New York, and he was able and willing to invest in the future Jewish life of Essenheim—which, not so many years afterward, forced its long-established Jewish residents to leave, and then joined them into an undifferentiated mass of millions of other Jews and murdered them with industrial efficiency. No Jews live in Essenheim now.

SCHOOL DAYS

I'd say it counts as evidence that Jacob and Miriam's move to New York was for religious reasons that they sent Bernard, their eldest child, up north first, ahead of the rest of the family, in 1855, when he was fourteen years old. It counts as evidence because they had placed him in a religious boarding school for Jewish boys, presided over by Samuel Myer Isaacs, a Dutch-born rabbi who was as prominent as Max Lilienthal, but much more religiously strict—what we'd now call Orthodox. Isaacs saw it as his mission to be a fierce protector of Jewish religious life, against whatever erosion of it Jews' ambition to join the American mainstream might entail. (This tension was hardly limited to one moment in the mid-nineteenth century, of course. It's embedded in my daily life today.)

Isaacs had two sons who became prominent: Myer, a judge, and Abram, a rabbi. They, along with Bernard and other boys, were students at the school, which was in the Isaacs family's townhouse. Bernard was moving from a sizable town in the Deep South—Donaldsonville's population back then was about double what it is now—but one where only a handful of Jews lived, to the biggest city in the United States. New York had just become the country's first city with more than half a million residents. Its tallest structures were still church steeples, but it had a number of five- and six-story buildings, and its Jewish population, rapidly growing because of immigration from Western Europe, was already above ten thousand, large enough to support a substantial Jewish community life.

A few years ago, a friend of mine gave me a copy of a book Abram Isaacs had published in 1928, when he was an old man, called *School Days in Hometown*. It's a novel, aimed at an audience of Jewish teenagers, about the early days of his father's school, with the students' names and some of the details changed. One day a rumor spreads among the students that "a little colored boy" will soon enroll in the school. Will that induce everyone to leave? Before the question can be settled, the boy arrives, and he's white—"small of size with piercing dark eyes, a little snub nose, a face somewhat tanned by the sun, of very rapid speech, and clasping a banjo, with his long wiry fingers, close to his side." His name is Edward Lazarus, and he's from a town in Louisiana, near New Orleans, "in the heart of a vast plantation."

The reason there was any demand for a Jewish boarding school was that Jacob was far from the only immigrant Jewish peddler who had come to, and prospered in, a part of America where it was not yet possible to form a full-fledged Jewish community. In the novel, Edward's father had written the head of the school, saying that he cannot obtain a Jewish education for his son at home, so, "Now that he is nearly eleven I wish him to be reared in his ancestral faith and at the same time be prepared for college." And, indeed, embodying his father's dream of a double life that was not possible in Donaldsonville, Bernard was a student and boarder at Samuel Isaacs's school, and also a student at the secular Collegiate School (which still exists as New York's most elite all-boys' private school), then a one-man operation run by an undoubtedly non-Jewish man named George Payn Quackenbos.

Under Isaacs, Bernard learned Hebrew, kept kosher, and observed the Sabbath and the other Jewish holidays; under Quackenbos (as a fragile, ancient student notebook of Bernard's reveals) he wrote, in a gorgeous cursive, compositions with titles like "The Fall of Sebastopol" (the crucial defeat of Russia in 1855, during the Crimean War, big news at the time), "Oriental Countries," and "The Mohammedan Religion." Isaacs founded a fortnightly newspaper called *The Jewish Messenger,* initially staffed by his students, which was published until 1902. At the top of the masthead of the first issue, dated January 1857, is "B. Lemann & Co., Proprietors"—that must be an inside joke—and fifteen-year-old Bernard, Myer Isaacs, and another boy are listed as the co-editors. The first issue has two articles that Bernard—the son of two functionally illiterate people, but now evidently fluent in at least three languages—had translated into English from French publications.

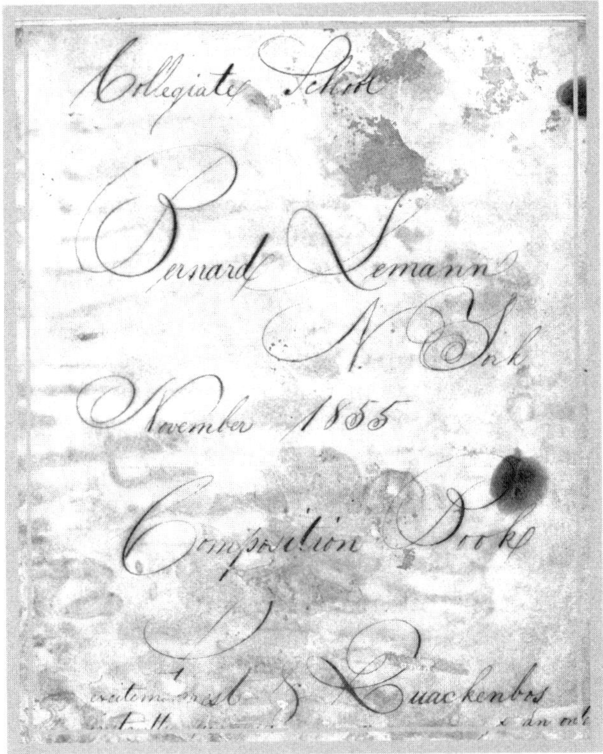

Thirteen-year-old Bernard Lemann's composition
book at Collegiate School in New York City, 1855.

In *School Days in Hometown*, Abram Isaacs subjects Edward Lazarus to a terrible, unidentified disease. He is confined to the school infirmary, where he lies in bed, wanly clutching his banjo but unable to play. He wanes. He waxes. At one point Edward seems to have recovered enough to accompany his parents on their annual trip to Europe—but then, no, after Isaacs has wrung every possible drop of pathos out of the story, Edward succumbs, and "his treasured banjo resting on the bed could no longer respond to his loving touch." The schoolhouse rings with sobs and shrieks. His parents "learn of their little son who had passed so quickly from life to death and from death to life everlasting."

In real life, Bernard took flight—in particular, intellectually. The vocabulary we use now to describe the progress of immigrant families through the generations doesn't seem apt for him. Was he becoming assimilated? It doesn't seem so, since he was able to be engaged, enthusiastically, not dutifully, in Jewish activities to a far greater extent than his parents in Louisiana. And he was also imbibing non-Jewish high culture in great eager gulps, something that also wasn't available to his parents, since they weren't educated. I know this because spread between two archives, one in New Orleans and one in Cincinnati, are a dozen pocket-sized notebooks, with lined paper and leather covers, that Bernard kept through his eventful late teens and early twenties. They are sturdier and more legible than one would have any right to expect, but still daunting to touch and hold. For how many American Jews in the mid-nineteenth century can one have access to daily activities and thoughts? It feels as if the little books might evanesce at any moment, called back into the emptiness of most of the past.

The notebooks run from 1858 through 1868, and then there is an undated one called "Miscellania: Thoughts Culled from My Reading; Essence of Books; Notes; Quotations; Striking Passages; &c, &c, &c." It begins with an inscription: "'Read for the glory of our Creator and the relief of men's estate'—Bacon." At the beginning of this period, hardly twenty years after his father had arrived in

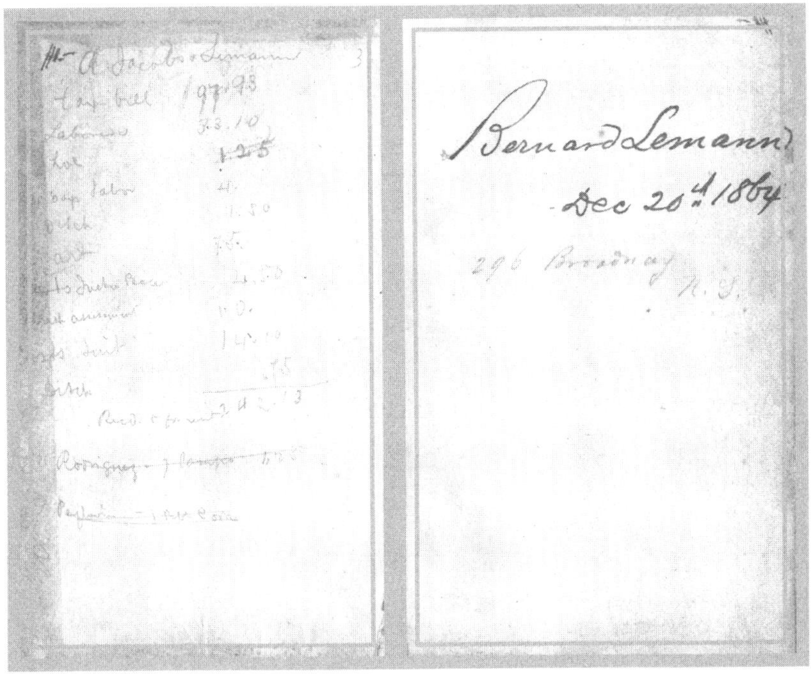

One of the diaries Bernard Lemann kept
during his travels in Europe, 1864.

Louisiana alone and with nothing, Bernard was living the life of
a well-off young Jewish patrician in New York. Once his parents
had bought their house in New York, his mother moved there and
Bernard lived with her rather than at Isaacs's boarding school. Most
Saturdays he'd go to synagogue and then to the Isaacses for a Sabbath lunch. He took music lessons and went for rides on one of a
pair of horses his father had bought. He performed minor business
chores for his father, particularly writing letters in English, which
Jacob never mastered. He danced quadrilles at balls, went to the
opera when that was the grandest entertainment spectacle available
(Mozart's *Don Giovanni* and Verdi's brand-new *La Traviata*) and
the theater (including the first run of *Our American Cousin*, the play
Abraham Lincoln was watching when he was assassinated a few
years later). He spent summers at his family's house in Newport,
where he made careful lists of the flowers he wanted to plant.

Bernard's social circle seems to have been entirely Jewish, and he was proud to participate in Jewish causes, to fast on Yom Kippur, and to observe the other Jewish holidays. After a little Jewish boy in Bologna named Edgardo Mortara was abducted in 1858 from his family by the Catholic Church, because his nurse claimed that she had secretly baptized him as an infant, Bernard attended a Jewish protest meeting held at a concert hall on Broadway, to demand the boy's return to his family. The Mortara story, which transfixed Jews everywhere, and, for a while, much of the rest of the world, began when the Italian police turned up at a Jewish family's home in Bologna and forcibly removed their six-year-old son, because, by his nurse's testimony, he was now a Christian. He was never returned to his family; his mother died a pitiful death and his father was permitted to see him only a few times. Edgardo wound up as a Catholic priest, living into the 1940s. The story seems to us today to combine implausibility with a maximal, hard-hitting emotional logic in the same way as the operas Bernard loved. How deeply foreign and threatening Jews must have seemed, if the separation of a child from his parents because he'd had a brief moment's notional connection to Christianity seemed warranted, even required! And this at a time when Bernard was beginning to acquaint himself with the Christian world, from a position firmly within the Jewish world. Was an American like him really fully protected from the ancient provisionality of Jewish status and Jewish rights whose survival into the mid-nineteenth century the story demonstrated?

Bernard was a copious reader. Before he had left his teens, he had plowed through at least some of the work of Dickens, Sterne, Trollope, and Austen; Shakespeare, Longfellow, Macaulay, and Tennyson; Goethe, Tocqueville, Byron, and Molière. He read the fledgling American magazines *Harper's* and *The Atlantic*, and also the *Edinburgh Review*—all publications where he would have encountered abolitionist sentiments that were rarely openly expressed back in Louisiana, if anyone even harbored them. He wrote out in his notebook a lengthy summary of the history of the Roman Empire, drawn from the *Encyclopedia Britannica*. He was especially moved by George Eliot's first novel, *Adam Bede*, whose hero is a carpenter who stands in moral contrast to the callow son of a landowner—moved because, as he wrote in his notebook, "it treats the low people and lowly life, but the author's genius has rendered the subject most attractive."

Bernard somehow found his way to an immensely controversial theological work of the day, *The Pentateuch and the Book of Joshua*, by John William Colenso, an Anglican bishop who had been sent to South Africa and had become a champion of the Zulu people and an antislavery crusader. Colenso's work exposed Bernard to views that were deeply threatening in two different environments he knew at first hand: the South, because of Colenso's opposition to racism, and the orbit of Rabbi Samuel Isaacs, because Colenso also believed that the Torah itself was not the unadulterated word of God as revealed to Moses at Mount Sinai. It was typical of Bernard to record the obviously discordant and contradictory views he encountered in his reading with an almost unnatural calm, never giving his own opinion. It was as if he saw dispassion as the price of admission to the new worlds he had the still fresh and unusual opportunity, for a Jew, of exploring. Bernard gamely set down Colenso's religious arguments in his journal, saying that he found them to be "very strong," without going one step further and saying that he agreed. And the encounter with Colenso didn't dampen his inclination to be observant.

During this period, the late 1850s, Jacob was often back in Louisiana. Now that he no longer owned his store, he made his living as a midlevel financier in credit-hungry, bank-deprived sugar country, lending money to cash-poor cane planters who operated below a scale where they could have attracted the attention of the prominent sugar factors in New Orleans. Marie Adrien Persac, the draftsman who had sentimentally rendered Palo Alto and other plantations for their owners, also produced, in 1855, for a commercial establishment in New Orleans, an elaborate and beautiful map showing

every plantation on the Mississippi River between Natchez, Mississippi, and New Orleans.

There you can see names that appear in the Ascension Parish clerk's
curlicued French-language records of Jacob's loans, or in the sections
of Bernard's notebooks where he set down business information for
his father: Valery Landry, Oscar Ayraud, Fernando Rodriguez, The-
ophile Bouchereau, their landholdings forming a rough collar surrounding the town of Donaldsonville. Jacob would lend them a few
thousand dollars, at 8 percent interest, and they would put up their
landholdings, and sometimes also their slaves, as collateral. By this
time Jacob's name appears in the records as a resident of New York
or of Newport; by every indication, he thought of himself as having
relocated permanently to the North. Perhaps he intended to develop
business interests there, or perhaps he thought of himself as a long-
term, long-distance financier in sugar country. Some of the most
prominent German-Jewish fami-

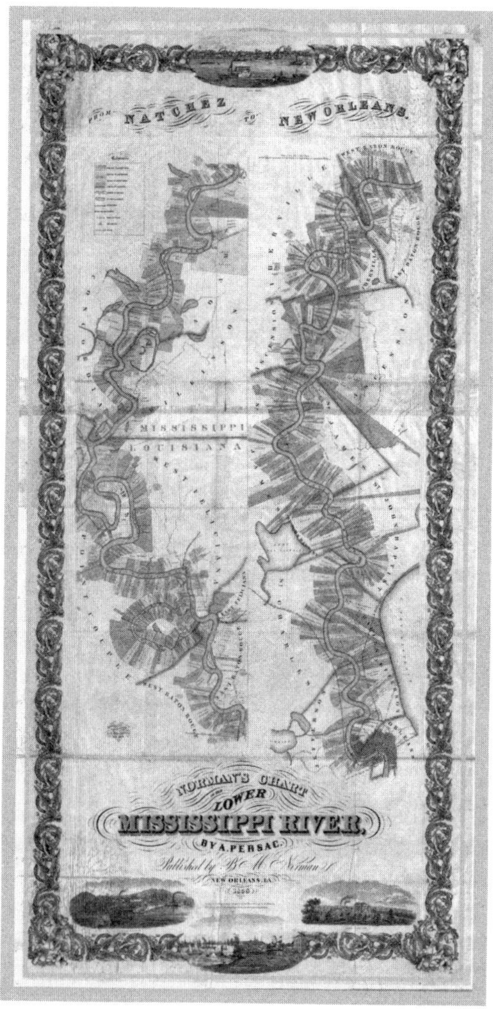

A map of the plantations along the Mississippi
River in 1858, made by Marie Adrien Persac.

lies in the United States, like the Lehmans and the Seligmans, had initially settled in the South and then moved north and helped create a tight business and social culture there for our little subtribe. Why not the Lemanns too?

"LES FEDS ONT DETRUIT DONALDSONVILLE"

And then came the Civil War.

When I was growing up, I had no idea that our family had ever lived in New York. If Father knew, perhaps he chose not to tell me, because by the time I was a child we were so thoroughly Southern that it would not have comported with the way we saw ourselves. It was a given in our milieu, automatically assumed rather than argued, that the Confederacy had been a noble cause. We sang "Dixie" and Confederate anthems in stout, proud voices at school and at summer camp. At Tulane, a few blocks away from Quercus, the fraternities, well into the 1970s, staged an annual Old South week where the boys would ride through the streets on horseback in gray uniforms and the girls would dress up in ruffled white gowns with hoop skirts. Anything with a plantation association—a recipe, an architectural style—was automatically enhanced.

As children we accepted these as verities, as children do. I would like to be able to tell you that something about them struck me as morally wrong, but what I remember instead is wondering why we didn't speak proudly about our family members who had served in the Confederate army, as other families we knew did. Standing at the edge of the New Orleans business district was a statue of Robert E. Lee mounted on a tall, pale fluted column. (The city government removed it in 2017.) When we were small, Father would sometimes haul out a heavy reel-to-reel tape recorder and capture our precociousness for posterity. My sister remembers my solemnly reciting a poem I had written about General Lee for a class in elementary school for one of these sessions—in her rendition of my voice (I had trouble with my *r*'s), it went, "Genewal Lee, so noble, so bwave . . ."

These don't seem to have been Jacob Lemann's attitudes in the 1860s. Hardly more than a month after Confederate troops had captured Fort Sumter from the United States, Bernard Lemann was in Newport, boarding a steamer bound for Liverpool. Jacob, Miriam, and little Myer came to the dock to see him off. Bernard had just turned twenty, prime age for a soldier. Jacob was not, it appears, in the mood to subject his firstborn son to an American *akedah*, on behalf of either side. (Northern families with money could pay for substitutes for their sons. Southern families could not, and almost nobody of military age didn't serve. About half of Confederate soldiers became casualties.) The family business was in Donaldsonville, but the Lemanns' residence, their main social circle, and their religious life were all in New York. There is no evidence that the Confederate cause stirred their hearts, and a declaration of loyalty to the Confederacy would have destroyed their prospects in New York. Anyway, as soon became clear, Donaldsonville was a dangerous place to be.

But an open alliance with the Union would be perilous, too, at least for business, since Jacob couldn't afford to lose everything he had in Louisiana to expropriation by what was now the government of a hostile power. Just after the end of the summer of 1861, a time when a Confederate victory seemed possible—the Union army had been forced into a humiliating retreat to Washington, D.C., after losing the Battle of Bull Run—Jacob borrowed a very substantial sum, $24,000, from one of his German-Jewish friends in New York, whom he also empowered to rent or sell his two houses. Then he, Miriam, and Myer sailed for Europe. They obviously wanted to avoid having to declare allegiance to either side—even though their move to New York now looks like a signal of allegiance—lest they bet wrong and lose everything. Bernard met them in Paris in October. In November Jacob had Bernard draft a letter to a business associate in New Orleans, saying, "I beg to make known that I am in Europe to all my friends & acquaintances who may be ignorant of the fact. And I further beg of you to take all of the steps necessary for the protection of my property & the welfare of my interests. It would, perhaps, be requisite that you inform the proper authorities that I am residing in Europe, for I understand that the property of residents in the Northern States is to be confiscated, & it might be thought that I still reside in New York." Relocating to Europe was his insurance against confiscation.

During Bernard's months alone in Europe, he lived the life of a young gentleman on a *Wanderjahr.* "What a delightful country this is to live in & enjoy life," he wrote in his diary soon after arriving in Paris. Jacob had made a connection in New York to August Belmont, the German-Jewish representative of the Rothschild family in America, so Bernard crossed the Atlantic bearing a note from Belmont that entitled him to make withdrawals from the Rothschild bank in Paris. He lived well. He looked at pretty girls promenading in the public gardens, he drank Bordeaux wines, he rented horses and rode in the Bois de Boulogne. He saw a hippopotamus in the Jardin des Plantes. He got a glimpse of the King of Sweden and of the Comtesse de Castiglione when they visited Paris. He consumed culture copiously: opera, theater, literature. He visited Marseille, Toulouse, Lyon, Geneva, Stuttgart, Hamburg. If Bernard felt tormented that the country of his birth had come apart and that many young men his age were dying in battle (we now know the number: 600,000, considerably more than died in all other American wars put together), he didn't show it in his diaries. Maybe he had an ability, which I can see as having been passed down through the generations, to train himself not to see what there would be no immediate benefit in seeing.

Before leaving for Europe, Bernard wrote down the dates of all the Jewish holidays (not just the ones even non-Jews have heard of; also, Shemini Atzeret, Hoshana Rabbah, Shavuot) on the opening page of his journal; he always celebrated them enthusiastically, usually in a synagogue. He functioned, via transatlantic mail, as a secretary for his father, translating instructions Jacob had rendered in Hebrew characters into business letters written in English and mailed to people in Louisiana and New York. He read *The Times* of London, where he encountered among other things, dispatches from the South from its Civil War correspondent, William Howard Russell. (He noted that Russell had spent a night—June 10, 1861—in Donaldsonville; there, Russell saw the local "society, which consisted of several gentlemen and various Jews playing games unknown to Hoyle, in oaken barrooms flanked by billiard tables.") Bernard closely followed the news of the Civil War—recording, in a neutral tone, the victories of both sides.

Let's not skip too quickly over the unusualness of the life Bernard was living. Not only was he an expatriated solo twenty-year-old, an officially nonaligned party in the most destructive war in American history; he was also a Jew traveling freely through country after country in Western Europe, partaking of whatever cultural riches, Jewish and non-Jewish, were on offer wherever he happened to be. It was arrestingly new and highly unusual for a Jew in Europe to be able to do that. Full Jewish emancipation in Germany wouldn't be complete for another decade. Bernard's freedom of movement would have been less unusual in the United States, but in Europe, the idea that a Jew could go anywhere and do anything, dressed, I would guess, in secular garb, had pretty much never materialized, through all the centuries of Jewish history. One could say, well, Bernard was an American—and he *was* a U.S. citizen, but at that moment it was much clearer that the Lemanns were Jews than that they were Americans, since both the outcome of the war and the family's future plans were unclear. His father, not so many years earlier, couldn't possibly have traveled from country to country by himself, checking into hotels and attending performances wherever he pleased—let alone his grandparents, great-grandparents, and all the other Ashkenazim from whom he was descended.

Europe was debating whether this ancient, peculiar, despised, useful tribe should be admitted to modern society. Jews, too, were debating whether they should want to pay whatever price there might be for leaving the comforts and wonders of life in their own community. Regularly, though not as regularly as he read literature, Bernard read essays in prominent publications debating what was known as the Jewish question. As with the events in the Civil War, he carefully made note of what he had encountered, without taking sides. He read the philosemitic novel *The Jew of Denmark*, by Meir Aron Goldschmidt, and the antisemitic novel *Jud Süss*, by Wilhelm Hauff: the first showing a Jewish hero's devastating encounters with an irredeemably hostile non-Jewish world, the second recounting the rise and, finally, the violent public murder of a Jewish financial advisor to a German duke.

I spent some time following Bernard's tracks as a reader. I wondered how he could have summoned the dispassion to read descriptions of the category he belonged to as if it stood utterly apart from the rest of humanity, without showing any reaction. Perhaps in the 1860s that would have felt more expected than it does now. He read a long essay in *Chambers's Papers for the People* called "Jewish Life in Central Europe," which laid out in obsessive anthropological detail the practices of traditional Jews, in a tone that was meant to be admiring—the essay began by saying, "It is admitted on all hands that the Jews are one of the most remarkable people on earth"—but left a deep impression of its subjects' alienness. Circumcision, phylacteries, dietary laws, peculiar naming customs, Talmud reading, legends and superstitions, the strange gyrations accompanying prayer, the Sabbath as a too-brief temporary release from the overwhelming filth and misery of ghetto poverty; and then, as soon as the old restrictions were lifted, the nearly instant transition to a sophisticated, intellectualized, politically liberal culture, a love of elegant clothing and jewelry, and the establishment of control of banking and the press—all this bore some relation to Bernard's family's life and history, but couldn't have felt right on the money, so to speak.

Then there was an article in the *Westminster Review*, one of England's leading intellectual publications, that recited the long, disastrous history of Jews in Western Europe—pogroms, forced conversions, expulsions, requirements to stop trading and lending money as the price of admission to the citizenship—but ended on a sympathetic and optimistic note. The Jews' negative traits may have been overstated (for example, "their love of money, though a frequent, is not by any means a universal characteristic") and their positive ones (braininess, a love of law and of justice, devotion to charity) underappreciated. The time may have come for them finally to become full members of society.

In the Jewish world in Europe, the *Hasklalah*, the Jewish Enlightenment, was underway, at least in some of the cities Bernard was visiting, much more so than it had been when Jacob left his village in 1836. At least some Jews were leaving their *Judenstrassen* and being permitted to educate themselves secularly and to enter previously forbidden businesses and professions. In 1844 a grand, soaring, twin-towered Reform temple opened in Hamburg, meant to stand for the hope that for prosperous Jews there was a new way to be Jewish that would not be so tribal, peculiar, and restricting; and, ten years later, in counterreaction, an equally grand Orthodox synagogue in Frankfurt opened to demonstrate that Jews who had left the ghettos could remain loyal to their traditions. (Both of these ceased to function in 1938, after Kristallnacht.) Bernard was taking all this in without indicating, at least in his diaries, what kind of Jewish life he wanted to live. This was a moment when things seemed possible for Jews that had never been possible before, and when, also, there were constant reminders, of which he was well aware, that the hopes of that moment might wind up being pure fantasy. For now, he was able to experience the joys of the larger world and the joys of Jewishness at the same time, as doubtless none of his forebears ever had. Whatever warnings he encountered, he couldn't possibly have foreseen how temporary this intoxicating moment would turn out to be: in only seventy-five years, everything that he saw aborning would be gone, not just re-restricted, wiped out.

During his solo wandering period, Bernard's health was poor.

He suffered terribly from maladies that don't fit comfortably into our vocabulary of disease: boils, headaches, "glands," "colic." He spent weeks at a spa in the French Pyrenees, where the chief doctor prescribed a series of baths, draughts, and poultices that appear to have had little effect, and it didn't occur to Bernard that he might have been in some kind of emotional distress, as a lonely young man elegantly escaping a war that was tearing apart everything he knew. Nonetheless, when he got word that his family would soon join him in Paris, "I actually danced with joy at the news." After they arrived, his regular diary entries about his maladies diminished considerably.

The Lemanns first rented rooms in Paris, which was being transformed under the vision of Georges-Eugène Haussmann into a grand modern city of boulevards, squares, monuments, and palatial railway stations, and then relocated to Biebrich, *"un charmant petit village sur the Rhin"* in Germany (that year Bernard, who liked to learn languages, kept one diary in French and another in English) that wasn't far from the village where Jacob had grown up. There, in 1862, Jacob and Miriam's fourth and last child, Coralie, was born (she died the year I was born). Bernard's relentless program of intellectual self-improvement continued—he began taking weekly German lessons—along with his business assistance to his father, his regular visits to synagogues, and his close attention to the news from America. The family developed a circle of friends in Germany, other Jews from the area who were also entering the promising world of possibilities that were becoming available; it wasn't a lonely exile. Nevertheless, on March 30, 1863, Bernard wrote in his diary, "It appears very probable that we shall return to America in a month or two." Jacob left first, then Miriam and the younger children, and finally, in October, almost two and a half years after he had left, Bernard arrived in New York. By that time New York's prosperous German Jews had built an all-encompassing world for themselves, which, judging by Bernard's round of activities, was not much inconvenienced by the war. He spent a few weeks there, socializing with Jacobses, Schiffers, Stettheimers, Levys, Cohens,

Goldsmiths, and Hesses. He flirted at parties and danced with girls he found attractive. In December he left for Louisiana. He arrived in New Orleans on December 13 and boarded a steamboat for Donaldsonville. He arrived at two o'clock the next morning. "Sleep at hotel in a room containing eight beds, all occupied," he wrote in his diary after his first night back.

Returning to Donaldsonville at that moment was a gamble. It meant going from an almost surreally safe environment to an obviously dangerous one. In April 1862, Admiral David Farragut of the Union navy had led a flotilla of vessels past two forts that stood at either side of the mouth of the Mississippi River, sailed a hundred miles upstream, and captured New Orleans, which after that was under military occupation. Farragut's victory helped turn the tide of the war because it severely reduced the Confederacy's access to the continent's main internal transportation artery. The territory that was firmly in the hands of the United States extended only so far up the river. Port Hudson, another hundred miles upstream from New Orleans, was still under Confederate control. Donaldsonville, by then a substantial small town with proud brick buildings along its short main street, was halfway between the two. It was valuable contested territory. Informal militias, called partisan rangers by the Confederates and guerrillas by the Union, roamed through sugar country making raids on the Union army.

One company stationed itself on the bank of the river in Donaldsonville and fired at Union vessels as they passed by. Farragut sent emissaries to Donaldsonville with the message that if the firing continued, he would send a flotilla up the river and bombard the town and its surroundings until everything there, and at the nearby plantations, was destroyed. The partisans wouldn't listen. On August 9, 1862, Farragut's forces arrived and began firing on Donaldsonville from the river, and troops under his command went ashore and burned down buildings in town and plantation houses in the countryside. *Les Feds, sous les orders de Farragut, ont detruit*

Donaldsonville," Bernard, who was in Germany reading about these events, noted with typical calm in his diary.

When Jacob, and then Bernard, arrived there, the town stood in ruins. Why return to a place in that desperate condition? They had decided not to be Southern last-standers, as their two-stage departure, first for New York and then for Europe, makes clear. The war was closer to its beginning than its end; most white people in sugar country were not convinced that the Union would win. The whole area was still an active battle zone. I can't make myself understand their return as anything but a business decision, which means that it also demonstrates that these people I came from put business ahead of their personal safety. Jacob had decided that it was necessary for him to be physically present to protect his interests. He wanted to establish relations with the federal forces. He was ready to gamble that they were going to prevail, and he was prepared to deal with them as commercial counterparties, not as an occupying enemy force.

During the summer of 1863, the Confederates began moving through sugar country again, with the hope of getting far enough south to be able to recapture New Orleans. In late June a large force attacked a fort the Union had constructed in Donaldsonville, at the confluence of the Mississippi River and Bayou Lafourche. That did not succeed, but the Confederates kept staging skirmishes in the countryside. On July 13, Union forces marched out from Donaldsonville along the banks of Bayou Lafourche until they reached the grounds of Palo Alto plantation. There they met a Confederate force that had been waiting for them. Their encounter was an especially bloody one: as one Southern historian put it, it was "a sorry, humiliating affair for the Union forces," a rout that left 459 Union casualties compared with only 33 for the Confederates. What Union troops were left retreated to Donaldsonville. The metal-detector-bearing Civil War buffs who occasionally turn up at Palo Alto today are still looking for the remains of this battle.

Just a few days earlier, on July 4, 1863, General Ulysses Grant's long, brutal, and effective siege of Vicksburg, Mississippi, had ended with a Confederate surrender; and on July 9, so had General Nathaniel Banks's siege of Port Hudson, downstream from Vicksburg. These victories finally gave the Union unimpeded dominion over the river. Also on the fourth, the Union won the Battle of Gettysburg, ending the Confederate army's thrust into Union territory. The war continued, but from then on, it's clear in retrospect, the Confederacy was doomed. The Union army soon sent fresh troops to reestablish its control of Donaldsonville and the surrounding countryside. That was the situation when Bernard arrived at the end of the year.

THE NEW ORDER

If you have ever encountered the assertion that the purpose of the Civil War, from the Union point of view, was to abolish slavery and to establish racial justice, you'll need to extract it from your mind in order to understand the situation in Donaldsonville when Bernard arrived. Lincoln hadn't run for president in 1860 on an abolitionist platform, only on opposition to the extension of slavery into Western territories. Most Union soldiers were not, to their minds, putting their lives on the line for abolition or for the cause of full citizenship for Black people. During the war, when the U.S. army took possession of Confederate territory, as it did in Louisiana sugar country, Black people enslaved on plantations flocked to the military encampments (including the one in Donaldsonville), hoping to be freed from bondage. General Benjamin Butler, soon to become the military commander in New Orleans, had deemed these people "contrabands" and refused to return them to the plantation owners. He put some of them to work and turned the rest away to fend for themselves. Butler refused to pay the contrabands, as if they were still slaves, and when he took command in New Orleans he quickly moved to restart the plantation economy—with Black people working under compulsion. "I assure you it is quite impossible to free them here and now without a San Domingo," he wrote a Cabinet member in Washington, thinking of Toussaint-Louverture's revolution. "There is no doubt that an insurrection is prevented only by our bayonets."

In Lincoln's 1862 annual message to Congress, issued on December 1 of that year, he proposed that all the slave states be required to abolish slavery by 1900, in return for financial compensation from the national government. Bernard took note of this in his journal, during the time when he was trying to teach himself to write in French: *"Les nouvelles de N.Y. parlent du Message de Lincoln qui declare que les negres qui devienments libres pendant la guerre surtout ont toujours libres."* Only a month later, Lincoln issued the far more immediate and consequential Emancipation Proclamation—but, as Bernard also wrote in his journal, the parts of Louisiana under federal control were exempted. Benjamin Butler's Union-operated forced-labor regime for Black people in sugar country remained in place. Knowing that should temper any impulse to think of the Emancipation Proclamation as a complete victory. Another item in the category of complicating the picture we have of Union sentiment is that in New York, the anti-abolition Democratic Party had swept to victory in all contested offices in the 1862 elections; and, not long after that, in the summer of 1863, as Bernard wrote, "in N.Y. there have been riots, occasioned by the enforcement of the Conscription. Several buildings have been burned, fifty negroes killed." These were the New York draft riots, urban rampages still unmatched in American history: Irish immigrants who'd received draft notices from the troop-starved Union army attacked first the army's recruiting offices and then Black people, anywhere they could find them. President Lincoln had to send troops directly from the battlefield at Gettysburg to New York to put the riots down.

In Louisiana, as the Union got sugar country firmly into its grasp, white planters despaired. They regarded the situation as, in the words of one Southern historian, "the destruction of a graceful civilization." The Louisiana sugar crop of 1861, brought in when the plantations were still under Confederate control, was the largest ever recorded: more than 450,000 hogsheads, worth more than $25 million. Because so many enslaved Black people realized, after the Union's conquest of New Orleans, that their owners had lost the ability to treat them as chattel property with impunity, the crop fell precipitously in 1862, to 87,000 hogsheads, worth $8 million. In 1864 it was only 10,000 hogsheads. The Southern historian I just quoted continued his lamentation: "For the sugar planters, the gay, light days of faraway war were ended. No longer did they relax on their verandas, drinking mint juleps and discoursing on the ineffectiveness of the naval blockade and the impending collapse of the Northern economy. . . . Desolation brooded over the plantation country." The son of one of sugar country's most prominent planters, temporarily self-exiled to Texas, wrote: "The days (emphatically days of darkness & gloom) succeed each other bringing nothing but despondency with regard to the future—Our beautiful Parish is laid waste & is likely to become a desert. . . . There can be no crop made in the country and of course starvation will be the dreadful consequence." These long-ago sentiments feel very familiar to me, because I was still hearing versions of them when I was growing up: the plantation South as paradise lost, reduced to a smoking, unrecoverable ruin.

White planters lived deep inside a mental world they had created to help them justify the racial order they had created in sugar country. They had convinced themselves that the Black people they had bought and compelled to work appreciated their generosity and grace. The historian I've just been quoting described the most intense period of plantation labor—by his account, eighteen hours a day—this way: "Rigorous as was the toil of the harvest, the blacks apparently enjoyed that season more than any other. Masters boosted their morale with generous portions of food, whiskey, tobacco, and coffee, giving the entire process an atmosphere of frolic." On the other hand, the planters also believed that, in Black-majority sugar country, they were always at risk of a rebellious element among the enslaved coming to the fore, as it had not so long before during the German Coast uprising—hence the patrols that were a regular part of plantation life. Therefore, the same historian wrote, "plantation folk lived in fear of servile insurrection during much of the war." This sharp Black binary in the white mind, into good (contented, deferential) and bad (vengeful, terrifying), was something I encountered even when I was a child, a century later. Sex was an especially charged category. In a society that was built to handle mixed-race births only if they were to Black mothers, the uprisings whose possibility was ever present would surely have included Black men having their way with white women, which, as one planter put it, would amount to "an act . . . unparalleled in the history of the world."

In the concrete realm of plantation balance sheets, emancipation was a disaster for the planters not only because it entailed the loss of their enslaved labor force, but also, perhaps even more, because slaves were financial assets—sellable, tradeable, and, most important in credit-hungry, bank-deprived sugar country, usable as collateral for loans. "The impoverishment of the South's propertied class is a unique event in American economic history," another Southern historian wrote; he thought the only comparable situation ever, anywhere, was the Russian Revolution. And one could add to this picture of utter bleakness in the planters' minds a large element of political uncertainty. Would the United States now abolish slavery in the areas it controlled? Whom would it compensate after the war, the slaveholders or their former slaves? All this was unclear, and would remain unclear for quite some time. (One reason the 1864 crop was so small is that many Black Louisianans hoped they would gain access to land—so why go back to work as field hands?)

In 1863, Benjamin Butler was replaced as commander in New Orleans by Nathaniel Banks—like Butler a former Massachusetts politician, but a much more physically commanding figure, handsome, with a bristly moustache, than the overweight, rheumy-eyed Butler. In 1864, Banks took a step toward actually abolishing slavery in sugar country by establishing a system of payment for Black people who worked on plantations: initially, two dollars a month for male field hands, one dollar a month for female, for no more than twenty-six days a month of work. Anyone who wanted to operate a plantation under these rules first had to swear an oath of loyalty to the United States government. This ruled out many of the plantation owners; the Confederacy hadn't surrendered yet.

In this situation, Jacob Lemann detected opportunity. Why? Why wouldn't he have resumed his life in New York, or have remained in Germany? For Jacob and other Jews in particular, there was an additional concern. In December 1862, General Grant had issued an order banning all Jews from the territory that was under his control in next-door Mississippi, because he felt Jewish cotton traders were using the Union army's presence as an opportunity to look for quick profits. (Father's mother's family were cotton traders in Mississippi at the time, so I may well be related to some of these people.) This was the only official, stated government ban on Jews in American history. It drew immediate strong condemnation, and within days President Lincoln reversed the order. But surely one could not have been entirely confident that such sentiments would not reappear; the impulse to blame the Jews has very often presented itself, in many different places at many different times, when people are suffering. And for Jews, there's always a lurking wariness that, no matter how well things seem to be going, everything can always be abruptly snatched away, as has happened so many times in the past.

Over the years I've known a number of self-made businessmen. There's a fierce protectiveness that they feel about their laboriously built-up enterprises, an unwillingness to walk away—could that have been Jacob's motivation? Or did he see some kind of bright future for sugar country—as a site of possibilities, not the smoldering wreckage of a vanished society—that eluded the vision of other white people? (*His* civilization hadn't vanished.) Or perhaps he felt that the chaos of the situation made his in-person presence in Donaldsonville necessary, and made his previous life as someone who could live in New York while operating business interests in Louisiana impossible. In any event, what he had at that point was the loans he'd made to midlevel planters, and all of them had failed. Just as he'd started in the mid-1830s as a backpack peddler, he started over in the mid-1860s as a defaulted-on lender. He couldn't have thought it was possible that his creditors would pay him back.

What he could get that had value was their land, not their money. One could say: business is business, what's the difference? But for a Jew, acquiring agricultural land was a momentous step to take. In Europe, down through the centuries, we had almost always been forbidden to own land. Traditionally we had made our living from what we could carry on our backs and in our heads. We moved around. We walked down country roads with full backpacks and laden carts, buying, selling, lending, trading. The Lemanns had moved around quite a lot during the previous ten years, maintaining the tradition at a higher level of luxury. When your business is owning land, you can't do that. You're attached to one place. The Lemanns were Americans, having sworn the required oath of loyalty; they were also Jews—perhaps still, at that moment, principally; but now they would also be Southerners. Jacob's return to Louisiana may have been an exigent economic decision, but for the rest of us, the as yet unborn, its effects went beyond immediate practicality. It meant that we would be Southerners too.

Bernard, after a couple of months in Donaldsonville trying to helping his father collect on his delinquent loans, spent most of 1864 and 1865 back in the North. The Civil War was still raging, through dozens of brutal battles that produced hundreds of thousands of casualties, but in New York Bernard returned to the life of a culturally and intellectually inclined young Jewish socialite. His diaries record many parties lasting long past midnight, where he'd dance with Esther Cohen, Bertha Jacobs, Bertha Hess, Lizzie Joseph, and many other girls. He went to the theater and the opera, sometimes to see productions in French and German. He bought a pair of yellow kid gloves. He had his portrait painted. He rode a horse his father owned through the open expanses of brand-new Central Park. He fasted on Yom Kippur. He read Thoreau, Poe, Thackeray, Sir Walter Scott, John Stuart Mill, and the firsthand accounts of British explorers.

A way of being Jewish in America was presenting itself to Bernard, entailing—it looks from this distance,

Bernard Lemann in his early twenties, in New York, just before he moved back to Louisiana, circa 1865.

at least—the promise of comfortable participation in both the growing, thriving Jewish community and the larger life of the nation. Bernard paid close attention to politics and current affairs. He read *The Cotton Kingdom*, by Central Park's principal designer, Olmsted—declining in his journal, typically, to comment even privately on its fierce condemnations of slavery. He attended a speech by George McClellan, the vain former Union commander who'd been fired by Lincoln and then ran against him as the Democratic nominee in the 1864 presidential election on a platform of nonendorsement of abolition. He took his little brother to see a grand parade through the city, culminating in a mass meeting in Union Square, to celebrate a string of Union victories. In addition to keeping up with the debates about American politics, Bernard also kept up with the debates about the future of the Jews in Europe. He read works by Heinrich Heine, one of the first German Jews to write for a wider audience, and Gotthold Lessing, one of the first Germans to write sympathetically about Jews. He and Myer Isaacs, his old schoolmate, organized a Purim Association—Bernard was its inaugural president—that held a grand masquerade ball, where the guests were costumed as characters from fairy tales and Shakespeare, dined on a kosher repast, and danced to music by the Seventh Regiment Band, from which he didn't get home until 3:30 a.m. He rented out the family's substantial townhouse on Twenty-Third Street and moved to its smaller wooden home in Newport, and then he took care of the details of the sale of both houses.

The Civil War ended with Robert E. Lee's surrender in April 1865, followed a few days later by the assassination of Abraham Lincoln in a Washington theater, which Bernard reported in his diary, showing more emotion than he usually did: "The death of Prest. Abraham Lincoln took place this morning. He was brutally murdered last night in Washington at Ford's Theater by a pistol shot from the hand of John Wilkes Booth, the tragedian. The city goes into spontaneous mourning. An attempt was made also to assassinate Sec. Seward." A few days later Bernard, like many other shocked and grieving New Yorkers, was out in the street to see six matching black horses pull a canopied caisson bearing Lincoln's coffin through Union Square and on to City Hall for a two-day public viewing. He joined what he described as an "immense crowd" lined up to see the embalmed corpse in an open casket. This was one of the last times when Bernard would have seemed like a New Yorker, or, more broadly, like a mainstream Jewish American. He was headed for another country (no longer literally, but in fact): the South. As the war that had launched his years of well-heeled wandering came to an end, so did his long absences from Louisiana—forever, except for brief trips. By the end of November 1865, he had returned to

Donaldsonville, obviously intending to stay. On the last page of his diary for that year is pasted an ornate printed business card:

BERNARD LEMANN,

Dealer in

DRY GOODS, CLOTHING, NOTIONS, BOOTS

SHOES, HATS, HARDWARE, CROCKERY

GROCERIES, FURNITURE, CARTS, PAINTS

OILS, SADDLERY, BUGGIES, IRON, STEEL,

NAILS, PAPER, LIQUORS

&C. &C. &C.

Donaldsonville, La.

PLANTERS

It seems that Jacob's and Bernard's attempts to collect on the loans Jacob had made to plantations around Donaldsonville were unsuccessful. There's evidence: in early 1865 Myer Isaacs, Bernard's school friend in New York, wrote a letter to General Banks, the commander of the U.S. Army of the Gulf in New Orleans, on behalf of Jacob Lemann. The letter appears to have followed a brief in-person meeting with Banks that Isaacs had somehow been able to obtain. At this moment, Grant was months into a siege of Petersburg, Virginia, not far from the Confederate capital of Richmond, and Lee's army was reduced, isolated, and starving. A Union victory was plainly imminent. Jacob, Isaacs explains, is a loyal citizen of the United States who owns five mortgages on sugar plantations, together worth more than $100,000. Three of the five mortgage holders have died in the war. A fourth has disappeared and is rumored to have fled to Mexico. Only one is still in Louisiana, and, in common with the others, he isn't making interest payments. Hence Isaacs's request: Would

Banks order a forced sale of the five plantations to Jacob? In return, Banks promises, Jacob will operate the five plantations himself and make them fruitful again.

It's obvious that Banks did not instantly agree to Jacob's request and issue an order, because it took some time to resolve the failed loans. But Jacob was relentless, and eventually successful, in pursuit of his goal. Through a combination of means, including purchases at bargain prices, lawsuits, conventional foreclosures, and forced sheriffs' sales, within five years after the end of the Civil War he had acquired all the plantations that owed him money, plus several more. He acquired Peytavin plantation, just downriver from Donaldsonville, in 1865, Palo Alto and Bouchereau in 1867, and then Dugas, Souvenir, Diaz, Rodriguez, Crescent, Perseverance, Pedesclaux, Raccourci, and Viala. Together these holdings formed a contiguous semicircle of land surrounding Donaldsonville; you could not enter the town without passing through Lemann lands. Our family had become Jewish lords of the manor. Not so long ago, in upstate New York, I met a Southern expatriate who, after we were introduced, complained bitterly about his family's beloved plantation having been lost to the Lemanns after the war. And it's hard to imagine that as his family handed down the story, our being Jews—moneylenders, ruthless—would have been omitted.

Bernard had to devise a way of life for himself, as a bachelor in his twenties, in this rough, rural, ruined place. The performances he had attended in New York and in Europe were out of reach. He could still read. He was able to hold on to his love of dances and parties, but now his social circle was no longer exclusively Jewish. Social occasions were less frequent, but, because people had to travel a considerable distance on rough roads to get to them, they lasted even further into the night, at a higher level of gaiety, than parties in New York did. In May 1866 he attended the wedding of one of the Ayrauds (who were Catholic, like almost everyone in Ascension Parish), the same family who had owned Palo Alto before the Lemanns acquired it. But in June he noted that he was *not invited!*

to the wedding of one of the Landrys (also Catholic), who had owned Souvenir and Peytavin. Was being Jewish the reason?

The Lemanns did not instantly remake themselves from merchants and moneylenders, their traditional occupation, into landed gentry. Instead, they reopened their store in the center of town and created a small-scale business empire that integrated it with their agricultural interests. When Jacob had sold his store to Bienvenue Mollere a decade earlier, in connection with his move to New York, Mollere was supposed to pay in installments. With the coming of the war, he, like Jacob's planter-creditors, stopped paying. Jacob sued him and repossessed the store and the land where it stood. Now, with the reopening of the store, Jacob was a sugarcane planter, a factory owner (because his sugarhouses converted cane into processed sugar and molasses), a retailer, a lender (because the store extended credit to its customers), and, to some extent, a practitioner of his old vocation of buying and selling all sorts of assets. He had wound up using what Jews had always been permitted to do, small-scale moneylending (in this case, to plantations), to attain the status of a kind of back-country tycoon. It's hard to imagine that this wasn't resented, but Ascension Parish as the war was ending was a place where not many people would have been equipped either to stand in Jacob's way or to compete with him.

Most other whites saw Donaldsonville's surrounding plantations as irreparable, because, they believed, their successful operation had to rest on the enslavement of a Black labor force. Jacob disagreed. Two German-Jewish families in New York, the Schiffers and the Jacobses, were his principal financiers and occasional business partners. (Another name I found in the family business records was Ben Toledano, probably the grandfather of the man who introduced me to *All the King's Men*; this would indicate that the Toledanos were indeed Jewish, since that's mainly whom Jacob traded with.) In 1867, Bernard, acting as Jacob's scribe, wrote to the Schiffers: "Business is better here than it was before. All the negroes work and have money, which they spend in the stores at Donaldsonville."

Sugarcane plantations, because of their factory aspect, mainly paid Black workers cash wages; Jacob had put himself in a position in which the Lemann field and factory hands, forced to live as quasi-serfs after emancipation, had little choice but to spend their wages, or buy goods on credit, in the Lemann store in Donaldsonville or one of its small branches out in the countryside.

Recent historians have jettisoned the old view of Southern planters as landed aristocrats; now they're likely to be portrayed as having been the most efficient and hard-hearted capitalists the world has ever known, practically the inventors of the global financial system. (As one historian put it, referring to the textile mills in the north of England, "Without Mississippi there is no Manchester.") I would guess that Jacob more likely thought of the prewar planters as non-Jewish quasi-incompetents who had been too passive or sentimental in looking after their interests during the war, and too firmly committed to slavery as the only possible basis for prosperity in the sugarcane business—which created an opening for him. In 1872 his future son-in-law, the Alsatian-born Lazard Kahn, who was twenty-one years old, trying to start a business in Selma, Alabama, and already fluent in English, wrote to a Jewish friend in Cincinnati, "The men who still continue to plant may be divided into two classes: first, those who have abided by the results of the late war, who have energetically gone to work and have now, since the war closed, acquired a snug fortune; second, are those who after the war having become deprived of their slaves have never looked the future straight in the face and insist on declaring it an impossibility to work or manage 'free labor.'"

Some years ago, an amateur historian, a lawyer in Washington named Elliott Ashkenazi, wrote a book called *The Business of Jews in Louisiana, 1840–1875*, which has a chapter devoted to Jacob. Ashkenazi made his way through the large collection of family papers at Tulane University and wound up with a highly favorable, not to say cheerleading, view of Jacob and Bernard. They were competent and, compared at least with the more florid prewar planters, prudent

in business and frugal in their personal lives. The reports on the
Lemanns by the business inspectors from R. G. Dun, when they
passed through Donaldsonville in the years after the war, were far
more uniformly glowing than they had been back in the 1840s and
'50s. It hadn't taken the Lemanns very long to go from being sleazy
Jews to upstanding business leaders, whose tribal identity was barely
worth mentioning; success brought respectability.

One of the Dun inspectors, visiting in 1870, said this about Jacob:
"Doing a good business, in trade several years, age about 50 [actu-
ally, he was about 60]. Character habits and capacity good. Owns
real estate worth $50 to 100m, and is certainly worth $50m clear. He
is shrewd [is that code?] and intelligent business man. Commenced
life about 20 years ago as a pedlar and has accumulated enough of
wealth to purchase several plantations. Prospects fair." Bernard, a
couple of years earlier, as he was just starting out in retailing under
his own name, got an even better review: "Bernard Lemann age
about 30 [actually, he was 26], single, stock worth about $15 or 20m.
Temperate honest and reliable. He is also a son of Jacob Lemann, a
very wealthy planter of the parish. Bernard has succeeded very well,
is very attentive to business." A year later: "Good character, temperate, thrifty. Makes money, pays promptly, general confidence is on
him in this community. Received goods on consignment and sells
some on commission. Future very promising." One could read this
and think, optimistically: this young man, and no doubt his descendants, are now completely accepted.

I've been through the family's business records myself, in the
library at Tulane, and I can see what the inspectors were talking
about: there are endless ledger books, letter books, conveyance
records, loan agreements, and orders to suppliers, transforming
agricultural toil and commercial self-supply into neat, irrevocably
logical rows of figures, meticulously recorded in impeccably inked
handwriting. Every field hand's wages and purchases at the store are
noted to the penny, and so are the sales of every barrel of sugar and
hogshead of molasses. Wagons, implements, and seed are paid for.

Problems—bad weather, broken equipment—are noted, solutions planned. In a few photographs that have survived, you encounter half a dozen formally dressed, moustachioed clerks sitting at desks in a room in back of the store, creating these records. They stare implacably at the camera, practically nailed in place, communicating a sense that they occupy a definite and fixed place in a fully designed social order.

Bernard's life was changing during these postwar years, more devoted to business, less to parties, performances, and reading. His wandering, culture-devouring youth was drawing to a close. For a time he still traveled to New York occasionally and temporarily took up life in his old social circle, but that didn't last very long. In the spring of 1870, at a Purim ball in New Orleans, where immigrant German-Jewish families who had prospered in the plantation economy presented their daughters as debutantes, following days of nervous and expectant dress fittings and hairdressings, he met the "stately and beautiful" (as Bernard's sister Coralie put it, many years later) nineteen-year-old Harriet Friedheim, born in a small town in the Rhine River Valley not far from the Lemanns' German home, and raised in New Orleans from the age of three.

Harriet was one of ten children. What I know about her is that her parents died when she was young and she was then looked after by a large network of cousins, that two of her brothers served in the Confederate army, that she played the piano, and that, when she went back to Germany and visited her relatives many years later, she found that most of them were quite religious. Within just a few weeks of their first meeting, Bernard and Harriet were married in the large, stolid living room of a family friend, by New Orleans's leading rabbi, Isaac Leucht, who was also born in the same part of Germany. A photograph of them from their early years together shows Harriet wearing a heavy, floor-length, shiny, ruffled black dress, with a mass of dark hair someone had carefully arranged in a pile above her head, and a level, steady, serious look. She's standing, with a protective hand on the shoulder of Bernard, who's sitting.

The newlywed Bernard and Harriet Lemann, circa 1870.

He looks just a shade more insouciant, with a thin moustache, wavy pomaded hair, and a bow tie, his legs crossed.

Before Bernard and Harriet had been married twenty years, they had produced ten children, eight of whom lived to adulthood. Just twelve years after her last child was born, Harriet died, at the age of forty-six. It seems that the two of them didn't spend a lot of time apart, so very little correspondence between them has survived. An exception is a very long and excited letter Bernard wrote in November 1870, six months into their married life. He was at Palo Alto and Harriet was in New Orleans, already pregnant with their first child. On the morning after Election Day, Bernard reported, a group of men had been seen on the opposite bank of the Mississippi from Donaldsonville—a weedy, muddy, forbidding, uninhabitable, ungoverned stretch of land—preparing to board a boat, cross the river, take the ballot boxes from the Ascension Parish courthouse, and bring them back across the river to be counted. These men were Republicans, meaning that they were the party of the Union, and, more recently, of Donaldsonville's newly enfranchised Black majority. They were afraid that the Democrats, unrepentant former Confederates who not so long ago had been conducting raids on Union troops in Donaldsonville, would steal the election.

This wasn't a misplaced fear. During the decade following the end of the Civil War, Louisiana was in a state of unremitting bloody political chaos. Just as the Civil War wasn't so clearly about abolishing slavery, the Reconstruction period, after the war, can be understood as a kind of low-grade second Civil War, fought over the question of what kind of lives the former Confederacy's millions of no longer formally enslaved Black people would live. Violence was constant, though sporadic, and it may have been all the more horrific because it didn't involve armies meeting on a field of battle, but, instead, what we'd now call terrorism, ruleless and unexpected, aimed mainly at denying Black people the right to vote. The success of my family's postwar business ambitions depended on how well they could navigate through this environment. That and also, perhaps, what call their conscience placed on them.

Just after the war, Louisiana, like other Southern states, passed laws meant to reinstitute a racial order that was as close to slavery as possible. The passage of new federal constitutional amendments (the Fourteenth in 1868, the Fifteenth in 1870) conferring citizenship and voting rights on Black Louisianans, enforced by the still occupying U.S. army, was meant to override the South's intentions. But whites launched an organized armed resistance that lasted through the end of Reconstruction in 1877. Campaigns, elections, and inaugurations were especially prone to attacks by white paramilitary organizations with names like the Knights of the White Camellia and the White League (as well as the one whose name we still remember, the Ku Klux Klan), which were made up of die-hard Confederate veterans and were informally affiliated with the Democratic Party. When these groups' attention shifted from their primary object, Black people, other people who were identifiably different could be subjected to their malign activities: Italians, Jews. In 1866, an attempt to hold a state constitutional convention in New Orleans produced a violent killing spree by ex-Confederates and their allies, who furiously shot, stabbed, and clubbed to death a group of politically organized Black people. As in most incidents of Reconstruction violence, the whites worked themselves up into an uncontrollable frenzy, as if something pent up within them had been released; they kept attacking even the bodies of people who were already dead. The incident left forty-six Black people dead and sixty more wounded.

During and after the 1868 elections, in incidents of political violence all over the state, nearly eight hundred Black people were killed. Things got worse in the 1870s. After the 1872 elections, two men, one from each party, each with an armed force under his command, both claimed to be the duly elected governor of Louisiana. A few months later, on Easter 1873, the bloodiest incident during the entirety of Reconstruction in the South took place in the town of Colfax, Louisiana, on the Red River, when dozens of Black men were murdered during another political conflict. Whites set a Black-occupied courthouse on fire, murdered anyone who tried to escape, and then went rampaging through the countryside looking for more Black people to kill. In September 1874, a force of five thousand white militiamen staged a victorious battle in the heart of the New Orleans business district against federal troops and held the government offices for three days, until fresh army troops dislodged them.

In rural places like Donaldsonville, the violent outbreaks followed a script. Plantation country was Black-majority and essentially all Black voters were Republicans, so Republicans would almost certainly win elections that were fair. The Democrats developed techniques to prevent this. Sometimes they would stage armed confrontations at Republican political rallies or at polling places, aiming to prevent Black people from voting; sometimes, afterward, if the Republicans claimed victory, the Democrats would seize power by force, claiming fraud; sometimes in these cases they would hear that a Republican militia was coming to unseat them, and would ride off into the countryside to stage a battle. For most whites, there was essentially no psychological distinction between one of these election confrontations and the eternally feared advent of a "Negro mob" bent on pillage, theft, and the despoilation of white women that was assumed to be every Black man's most cherished aim.

Since he had returned to Donaldsonville, Bernard made note in his diary whenever there was a local murder, which was occasionally. The Lemanns, being white, wouldn't seem to have to fear for their lives in this environment, but they might have to fear for their ability to do business. That they were immune to other white planters' end-of-civilization fantasies didn't mean they were guaranteed safe passage through a postwar period that felt more like a guerrilla war than peacetime. In 1867, Jacob, communicating via Bernard, wrote to one of the men in New York who were financing his postwar reestablishment in business in Donaldsonville, "In reference to the political trouble which you mention as being a hindrance to the prosperity of this section of the country, I assure you I have no fear that they will injure the sugar plantations." But in November 1870, the violence came to Donaldsonville, in more than episodic form—and this was one of those cases where its most prominent victim was not Black. He was a Jew.

The Democrats were in Donaldsonville, on the west bank of the Mississippi, in control of the courthouse. The Republicans, who wanted to get their hands on the ballot box, were on the east bank. As their boat was crossing the river, Democrats positioned on the west bank opened fire. One Republican was wounded and the boat turned back. Bernard, who was at the family store, just a short distance from the river, heard the gunfire and hurried to Palo Alto to look after his mother, who was there alone. While he was there, a visitor arrived, and, as he wrote Harriet, "we heard that a force of militia several hundred in number were halted on the road a little way below our house, while opposite the house and a little above were men from town, all armed with muskets, to prevent the other from getting to town." The election dispute had attracted more participants and had spread beyond the banks of the river. The militia Bernard had heard about was mainly Black. Its aim was to get to the courthouse and take possession of the ballot box, since the party crossing the river by boat had been repulsed. The men from town with muskets were white.

Soon Bernard heard gunfire again, which sounded like it came from quite near Palo Alto. He took his mother to the factory building on the plantation where sugar was refined, figuring that would be a safer hiding place than the house itself. Bernard's letter to Harriet went on: "After a while a negro came running along the levee and reported that they were coming in great numbers from St. James"—the neighboring parish—"and would set fire to the town." To picture this, it's necessary to understand that in our part of Louisiana, the countryside doesn't mean reassuring pastureland. It means swamps, jungles, uncharted streams, wild animals: a territory where, especially in the white imagination, anything is possible. Bernard hurried back to the store to retrieve his business records. There he heard that the Republican boat had once again crossed the river to get the ballot boxes, and that Donaldsonville's leading Democrat, a Confederate veteran named William C. Lawes, and its leading Republican, a Jewish merchant named Marx Schoenberg, each of whom claimed to be Donaldsonville's rightful mayor, had decided to go meet the militia together and plead for peace.

"In the town I am told no one slept all night," Bernard wrote. Morning brought the news that both Lawes and Schoenberg were dead, killed on land owned by one of the Lemanns' business partners from New York, the Jacobs family. Believing that the militia was going to march into town and destroy everything, Bernard's first impulse was to protect Donaldsonville's Jews. He helped arrange for horse-drawn carts to take what Jewish women and children he could round up—including Marx Schoenberg's three small children, whom somebody had dropped off at Palo Alto—away to safety, as if this were an outbreak of anti-Jewish violence back in Germany. By nightfall, as invariably happened at the denouement of these rumored destruction-bent Negro uprisings in the rural South during Reconstruction, the militia had inexplicably dispersed and calm had returned to Donaldsonville. "I tell you we have had exciting time, but I thank God it is all over," Bernard wrote. He was aware that Harriet, a city girl, might not have been enthusiastic about the prospect of spending her adult life in the environment he had just described. "I am glad you were not here. You must not feel uneasy at all for everything is perfectly quiet, as usual." Bernard promised to send her fresh pecans and cane syrup, and brought his letter to an end: "With my love, dearest darling, and hundreds of kisses. Your fond & devoted Bernard."

In accordance with religious law, Marx Schoenberg was buried the day after he had died, in Donaldsonville's Jewish cemetery. His tombstone carries this legend: "In memory of Marx Schoenberg, Born in Germany, 1833, Murdered November 9, 1870. May he rest in peace." What happened? Schoenberg was like one of those central characters in a murder mystery whom many people want dead. A report on him from an R. G. Dun inspector, not long after Schoenberg had arrived in Donaldsonville, said: "Makes it a point never to pay a just debt unless sued. Is fond of lawsuits, gives no care to his business and loses ground. Anyone giving him credit is sure to need a lawsuit." Another report, a few months later: "Not doing much. Bad pay and often sued, is very fond of litigation. About 35 suits have been brought against him since 66. Paid the amount sometimes before and sometimes after judgments. Has family. No business capacity. Credit very bad." But these deficiencies would pale compared to the offensiveness, to local whites, of a white man's having been a highly visible radical Republican, which is to say allied with Donaldsonville's Black voting majority. In the language of the white South, Schoenberg had been a scalawag. During the 1868 election season, recently appointed as postmaster of Donaldsonville, he received death threats and had to hide out in New Orleans for a while. When he returned and became mayor, the Democratic city council reduced his salary to one dollar a year.

As always with incidents of racial political violence in the Reconstruction South, there were two versions of how Schoenberg had died. They appeared in newspapers affiliated with the two political parties. In the Democratic version, he had been killed by the Negro mob—just deserts for his having believed that Black people would treat a white man as an ally. In the Republican version, he had been killed by William Lawes, the Democratic pretender to the mayoral throne. Another theory, which came later from a U.S. government investigator, was that the militia, intending to shoot Lawes, had also shot Schoenberg by accident. What's indisputable is that Schoenberg's body was found with six bullet holes, but Lawes's was found shot and then hacked to pieces with the short, razor-sharp, machetelike knives that plantation workers used to cut down stalks of sugarcane.

Most whites in Donaldsonville could hardly believe what they were seeing during Reconstruction. An Army officer named Joshua Addeman, in a memoir he published in 1880, told a story about being posted to Donaldsonville as commander of a regiment of Colored Troops, just after the war. One of his duties was to act as a judge in disputes, and in one case he ruled in favor of a recently enslaved woman against a white man. "I presume this was the first occasion in the experience of many of the spectators, in which the sworn testimony of a negro was received as against that of a white person," he wrote. Such a thing was unheard of, before and after Reconstruction: white people were always right, Black people were always wrong. The whites who were present, Addeman wrote, "scowled upon the proceedings with the intensest malignity," but for the Blacks, "it was evident that the year of jubilee had come at last." People were more religious when Addeman was writing than they are now, so his readers would have known he was referring to God's commandment, recorded in the Book of Leviticus, that every fifty years masters must free their slaves.

Another item on white Southerners' standard list of the horrors of Reconstruction was the short-lived Freedmen's Bureau (1865–1872), a small new federal agency charged with overseeing the transition out of slavery, through education, health care, housing, and possibly land ownership for the formerly enslaved, which was operating in Donaldsonville. Most white planters refused to pay the tax levied to support the bureau's activities. As the bureau's local administrator noted bitterly in a report he sent to one of his superiors,

"No palpable reason for thus withholding their aid is assigned, other than that the Freedmen has no business to have the least degree of Education." The formerly enslaved, to the minds of their former masters, should not have economic options except for being field hands and house servants, or any political knowledge that would acquaint them with concepts like rights or would make them aware of how different conditions were in other parts of the country. Better to ensure that they'd be incurably stuck where they were.

What was Bernard politically? As someone who had left Donaldsonville to avoid serving in the Confederate army and who had returned and sworn an oath of allegiance after the Union had established control of the town, he obviously was not a Democratic bitter-ender. He faithfully paid the Freedmen's Bureau tax, noting every occasion in his journal. A few years after Schoenberg's murder, in 1873, he was one of the organizers of a biracial but white-majority "Merchants' Ticket" that ran in the local elections on a platform of Donaldsonville's honoring the bonds it had issued in 1866 to finance its postwar rebuilding. That would indicate that he was a moderate Republican of sorts. But within a few years, Reconstruction had ended, and within a few more years, there was no Republican Party to speak of in Louisiana, thanks to the success of the Democratic terrorists. The year of jubilee that Addeman wrote about had not come; instead, it soon became inconceivable—for another century—that a Black woman could successfully testify in court against her white employer. The Lemanns didn't work to create this reactionary regime, but after it had arrived, they took operating within it as a given. They attended to business. In 1881, Myer Lemann, Bernard's much younger brother and business partner, became the second Jewish mayor of Donaldsonville, after Marx Schoenberg. He evidently served without ruffling anyone's feathers. In the early twentieth century, Bernard's son Walter was also mayor. There's a bronze plaque memorializing his service mounted at the foot of the levee in Donaldsonville.

OLD FAMILIES

After the Civil War, the United States was put to the test, morally, by the activities of the white terrorists in the South, who were prepared to ignore the outcome of the war when it came to the basic rights of the formerly enslaved. How committed would the country be, and for how long, to the project of guaranteeing full citizenship to the great majority of Black America who were still living in the South? The nation was poised at the edge of industrial boom times, a period of big cities, big business, American power. Reconstruction was the North's idea, not the South's, but as it wore on, the North's patience began to wane. There was a limit to the white North's racial sympathy, which was never especially powerful in the first place. Getting to the other side of Reconstruction promised prosperity, old troubles forgotten. So the troops were withdrawn from the former Confederacy and the South was permitted to create its formal, legal exception to the Constitution, the Jim Crow system. In the Lemanns' home territory, Louisiana sugar country, this obviously reordered life for Black people: the end of formal slavery actually elevated the importance of race, which now had to become the basis of a large, all-pervasive system of laws and practices establishing the color line. We Jews watched all this with special attention. We had long and deeply felt experience with categorical exclusion. Could this social tidal wave miss us entirely? Should we consider ourselves involved, or resistant, or avoidant?

Just as the German Jews of rural Louisiana had a kind of precarious privileged status—economically established but not fully accepted, useful to others but necessarily on guard against their intermittent rage—so too did a limited, distinct group of Black people known as Creoles, or free persons of color. In 1872, a member of this group named Josephine DeCuir, who like the Lemanns had expatriated herself to Europe during the war and returned as it was ending to look after her business affairs, bought a first-class ticket on a steamboat from New Orleans to the place upriver where she owned a plantation. The steamboat's captain told her that now, in the postemancipation world, she was a Negro and couldn't ride in the first-class section. She sued. The case wound up in the U.S. Supreme Court, which ruled against her: the steamboat had the right to impose any conditions on passengers it wanted, including racially discriminatory ones. The DeCuir case was one of a string of Louisiana cases that came to the Supreme Court in the years after the Civil War—the *Slaughterhouse Cases* (1873), *U.S. v. Cruikshank* (1876), and finally *Plessy v. Ferguson* (1896)—all of which weakened the power of the federal government to override local authority and so laid a legal foundation in support of the end of Reconstruction and the advent of the Jim Crow system. The reason DeCuir was on the steamboat was that she was trying to recover some of the value of a large plantation she and her husband—Creole slaveholders—had owned. All the problems that white plantation owners had, plus being on the receiving end of racial discrimination now that Creoles were no longer legally distinct and privileged, spelled the end of her former life.

I spent some time not long ago with Winston DeCuir, Josephine's great-grandson, who is the first Black graduate of Louisiana State University law school, and his wife, Barbara. They had also invited Donald and Ronald Bajoie, brothers and partners in a contracting business, old friends of theirs, also Creoles. We spent a few hours talking in their house, a comfortable ranch-style place in Baton Rouge, filled with cultural touchpoints that were familiar to me as a Louisianan: well-worn pots and pans in the kitchen, a recreation-room bar, a gun rack, a hunting dog dozing in a cage, a pickup truck in the driveway and a flat-bottomed fishing boat in the garage, walls decorated with family photographs, crucifixes, American flags, and LSU football paraphernalia. People like them are an entrée into Louisiana's Black history because their families have been there so long and have passed stories down through the generations. It's easier to move backward through them than to move forward from the people whose names—usually only first names—are recorded in old records of slave sales, denied the dignity of being fully identified. The four of them took me on a breakneck ride through Louisiana's racial history, going back to 1699, when the first DeCuir arrived in the Deep South, as they had lived it and as it had been passed down to them through their large extended families.

The way one got to be Creole is through interracial unions that produced children. When I was growing up, just before the passage of the civil rights laws, interracial marriage was a crime—miscegenation—but in the early days when Louisiana was governed by France, it was legal and not uncommon. Then there are the stories of prosperous white men, on and off the plantations, who had a legal wife who was white and a common-law wife who was Black. Louisiana's most prominent Jew in the nineteenth century, Judah Touro, never married but had a child with a free woman of color named Ellen Wilson. Sybil Haydel Morial, a Creole whose husband and son were both mayors of New Orleans, is a direct descendant of the white family that owned Whitney plantation, which now operates as a museum devoted to the horrors of slavery. The way she heard the origin story of Victor Haydel, her great-grandfather, the son of Antoine Haydel and a slave named Anna, was that Anna had been raped, "since a slave girl could not have resisted a white man's advances."

Creoles were a tightly self-contained group, situated apart from the two main racial categories, until the Civil War. Then they were recategorized and most of what they had— their freedom of movement, their property—was taken away; Louisiana was racially reorganized into two castes, and the previously indistinct line between Black and white became a very firm one, at least officially and legally. Louisiana noted your race on every official document, and there were only two choices. If you were a DeCuir or a Bajoie—devout Catholics with large families—there was considerable skin-color variation even within one household, which meant that some family members had the option of passing as white and others did not. "Jumping the fence" was always easier to bring off if you moved someplace far away—and, if it worked, you might have to arrange for your visiting relatives from Louisiana to meet you at a restaurant, rather than risk your white neighbors seeing how multihued they were. Back home, evidence of just one Black great-great-grandparent was enough to put you across the color line. There were government officials whose job was to reclassify white people as Black, after investigating, if somebody chose to challenge their status. One of my early stories as a journalist was about such an official, who worked at City Hall in New Orleans—in 1973! Winston DeCuir said that when he arrived as a student at LSU law school, the person next to him at the welcoming assembly turned to the students seated nearby and told them that he heard that the school had been integrated, with only one student—not recognizing Winston as that student. After word got around that it was him, when he'd sit down at a table in the dining hall, the other students would get up and leave.

There were Black-owned restaurants and nightclubs in Black neighborhoods that catered to a well-paying white clientele who were seeking a taste of the exotic, and so wouldn't serve Black customers, unless they came to the kitchen door. There were vacations taken in California, Mexico, or even farther afield, because you had to leave the South to get a taste of real freedom. There were segregated schools where decent textbooks had to be smuggled in, if they were available at all, and hidden under the desks when inspectors from the state education department came by. There were off-the-books interracial liaisons, voluntary from the white point of view, forced or transactional from the Black point of view. The Bajoie brothers told a story about a female relative of theirs who had called home in the middle of the night: her prominent white lover had had a heart attack and died in bed. The family had to organize a group of men to come to the house, load the man's corpse into his car, and drive it into a ditch, so it would look like that was how he had died.

In Donaldsonville, the Bajoies said, a white woman had tried to seduce a Black man. Terrified, he resisted, so she claimed he had raped her. He was lynched and his body hung from a railroad trestle so everyone in town would get the message. Stories like this were pervasive in the Black South but since it was forbidden for them to be officially recorded as they had actually happened, they had to have the status of legend. That didn't diminish their power. The way it came down to the Bajoies was that this incident, in the 1920s, caused Donaldsonville to be put under a curse, which explains its deteriorated condition today.

In 1838, two years after Jacob Lemann arrived in Louisiana, Georgetown University sold 272 enslaved Black people, who lived on nearby tobacco plantations in Maryland owned by the Catholic Church, to help pay for its operations. Where they wound up exemplified the old saying about being sold down the river—both literally and in the sense of being consigned to much harsher circumstances. The largest group within the 272 went to Chatham plantation, which is in Ascension Parish just a few miles north of Donaldsonville. Their new owner was Henry Johnson, a member of the U.S. House of Representatives who was also a former governor of Louisiana and a future U.S. senator. Chatham plantation sat at the northern border of the parish, on the west bank of the Mississippi River. The next significant plantation downstream was Mulberry Grove, which is still standing—a white columned building with a full-length second-story balcony and large live oak trees in front, just like Quercus, the house in New Orleans where I grew up. Then there is a stretch of small farms, and then the McCall plantation, whose scion, Jonathan McCall, was Father's closest friend in his last years. The small farms are the home ground of Donaldsonville's most consistently prominent Black family, the Juliens, who can trace their roots in Ascension Parish back to 1820.

The Juliens operate a bar called the Sportsman Lounge, which sits back a short distance from the road that runs alongside the levee. It's a converted chicken coop—a dark, warm, comfortable place, long and narrow, with, as you're moving from the front to the back, a polished wooden bar, then some tables, then a small dance floor, then a stage. Outside sit three worn-out retired tour buses, the remains of one of the family's former businesses. I arranged to meet Leonard Julien Jr., at eighty the current patriarch of the family, and as many of his relatives as he could gather, one day at the bar. In Leonard's generation there were eleven siblings, eight still alive today. Five of them were at the Sportsman Lounge when I arrived, and during the time we were talking, several more Juliens from Leonard's generation and the one below it drifted in and out. From the torrent of stories they told me, I could get a sense of what was possible for a strong, deeply rooted Black family in Donaldsonville, and also of where a family like theirs would encounter the impenetrable upper limit of what was possible.

One of the Juliens had brought a carefully produced family tree to the bar. That was the visual aid the family used to give their history in Ascension Parish, which went this way: Rosemont Julien, born in 1820, lived on Germania plantation, just up the road, which was one of three plantations owned by a German immigrant family named Reuss. Two of the plantation houses have vanished; Mulberry Grove is the third. Rosemont was one of thirteen children, all born into slavery. Rosemont's son Etienne, also born into slavery, somehow got favored treatment from the plantation owner's wife. He had learned to read and write even before emancipation. During the brief period before the full flowering of Jim Crow when Black people could hold office, he was the local postmaster. Etienne's son Anthony, born in 1870, stayed on the plantation, like his father a member of a favored category among the Black workers. He was educated at a Black school in New Orleans called Straight College. At Etienne's insistence, Anthony learned bookkeeping. When he returned to the plantation, the owners, by that time not especially competent Reuss descendants, put him to work in the office. Anthony kept the plantation books in such a way that he was able to skim off some money, which he used to buy parcels of land from the increasingly strapped owners. That was how, among his eight children, who included Leonard Julien Sr., Leonard Jr.'s father, several wound up owning forty-acre plots of farmland along the river; where the U.S. government didn't deliver, they found another way.

Leonard Julien Sr. married a white woman named Alyce Gaudin, whose father was a moonshiner and bootlegger who had moved to Louisiana from Nova Scotia. Actually she wasn't exactly white, though her documents said she was—her mother was Native American, and when her parents married, their parents disowned them for violating one of the many stipulations of the color line. Then, when she married Leonard Julien, her parents did to her what had been done to them. They wouldn't come to the wedding. Despite all the interracial marriages, the Juliens weren't Creole, because in Ascension Parish they had always been Black, rather than having been transferred into that status, and had been enslaved. In their family, if children asked their parents what they'd heard about what life was like during slavery and Reconstruction, they'd be told, don't ask about that. And if elements of the old system were still obvious in the present, you weren't supposed to ask about them either. Just down the road, at a remnant of one of the Reuss plantations, the Julien children would see an old man who'd agreed to let his wife become the planter's mistress in exchange for favorable treatment, but she hadn't agreed. Instead she ran away. He didn't. There was always some evidence of what life used to be like, or of how things hadn't really changed, no matter how much you tried to focus on a supposedly bright future.

In Leonard Jr.'s generation, people were old enough to have seen as children what they remembered as the heyday of Black Donaldsonville, back in the 1940s and '50s, when there was a Black doctor, a Black pharmacist, a Black theater, Black restaurants, Black churches, and a working-class Black neighborhood that, at least in their memory, was crime-free. Ascension Parish spans the Mississippi River. The principal town on the east bank is Gonzales. As the Juliens told the story, after the Civil War, the whites in Gonzales—then a newer, rawer town, which is now more prosperous than Donaldsonville, less evocative of the plantation past—ran the Black people out of town; Donaldsonville was not as hostile, partly because it was already multiethnic on account of the Jews and Italians who lived there. Donaldsonville's schools integrated relatively early and nonviolently. Black customers were allowed to try on clothes at Lemann's store. I asked the Juliens about the lynching story the Bajoie brothers had told me—no, they said, ever loyal to their hometown, that didn't happen in Donaldsonville, it was in Labadieville, a few miles down Bayou Lafourche. The way they heard it, a white woman was pregnant by her uncle, and rather than tell the truth, she explained it by saying she'd been raped by a Black man—so a Black scapegoat was found and lynched, and his dead body put on display.

In 1964 Leonard Julien Sr., a sugarcane farmer and a self-taught inventor, developed a machine for planting sugarcane. It replaced a much more laborious by-hand method that the plantations had been using forever. He found a local engineer to fabricate the machine and staged a successful demonstration on his place, which was called New Africa Farm. He arranged for Lemann's Farm Supply to sell it. There was an article in *Ebony* magazine touting the invention as an example of Black achievement. Only a few dozen sold, though, and before long there were enough cheap bootleg copies circulating that, as a commercial venture, the cane-planting machine was dead. Over time the Juliens' farming business soured. Leonard Julien Jr. joined a large, long-running lawsuit by Black farmers against the U.S. Farmers Home Administration, charging that its white-dominated local boards had denied them credit for years. The Black farmers won, but by that time the Juliens were not farming anymore. All these setbacks offered the same lesson: somehow, no matter how hard you tried, they'd find a way to put an insurmountable obstacle in your way.

The Juliens gave me a less cheerful account of Donaldsonville in the present than of Donaldsonville in the past. The chemical plants had a reputation for being unfriendly to Black job applicants. The Black farms were gone. The plantations were using Mexican immigrant labor—just a few days after my visit, the Sportsman Lounge was going to have a Cinco de Mayo celebration. Commerce had moved across the river, to Gonzales. A lot of the town's Black youth don't have anything to do. The deal sugar country offered Black people after emancipation was: work in the fields, or maybe in white people's houses, or fend for yourselves, because this society is not prepared to invest in creating better opportunities for you. Today you can find homemade videos online in which young men in the poor part of Donaldsonville show off their guns and drugs. Some of them are surely going to wind up in Angola, the state prison.

The only remnant of the Juliens' dream of building a business empire around the sugarcane-planting machine is a large, angular, rusted metal hulk that sits under a tarp on an empty lot in the Black part of Donaldsonville. Years ago a brother and sister, Darryl and Kathe Hambrick, established the River Road African American Museum in Donaldsonville. They had moved back home, after years in California, when a relative who owned a funeral home in Gonzales died. Now Darryl runs the Hambrick Family Mortuary and the two of them run the museum. At first it was located on the grounds of a nearby plantation. Then they moved it into what used to be a Black doctor's house in town.

The museum is full of home-brew exhibits about the past: one on Pierre Caliste Landry, the first elected Black mayor in the United States, who presided over Donaldsonville immediately before Marx Schoenberg; one on jazz musicians who grew up in and around Donaldsonville; one on cooking; one on Louisiana-born Madame C. J. Walker, the early-twentieth-century cosmetics queen, who lived in Indiana but whose products were ubiquitous in the Black South. Gradually, over thirty years, the Hambricks have expanded the museum through the neighborhood. The museum owns several small old artisans' houses. It operates a community garden. It hauled into town, from where it sat rotting out in the country, and restored one of the thousands of Rosenwald schools for Black children that were built all over the rural South through a partnership between Julius Rosenwald of Sears, Roebuck and Booker T. Washington of the Tuskegee Institute. It took over the Episcopal Church of the Ascension, originally built with a gift from Henry Johnson of Chatham plantation, and turned it into a monument to the 272 Georgetown slaves. It bought True Friends Hall, long abandoned, built at the advent of the Jim Crow era in 1886 as a Black mutual aid society and dance hall, and has plans to restore it. Sprucing up the Julien cane harvester and putting it on display is another future project. The museum's slogan is "More than just a slavery museum," which is a mild dig at Whitney plantation, thirty miles downriver, the plantation my friends from New York visit when they're in Louisiana. Here the message is that Black people in sugar country, facing the worst possible headwinds, did more than just suffer and endure—they persisted, they built, they stuck together.

GENERATIONS

Ten years after the Lemanns had returned to Donaldsonville with the close of the Civil War and reestablished themselves in business, the family store on the town square burned down. What makes it obvious that things were going well for them was that Jacob and Bernard immediately hired James Freret, one of the leading architects in New Orleans, French trained, to design a considerably larger version of the store on an expanded parcel of land. It was the tallest commercial building in Donaldsonville, with floor-to-ceiling windows running across the block-long façade facing the river, and thin iron columns supporting a wide second-floor balcony in front of another row of tall windows. Bernard's name was painted on the cornice above the corner of the building, just above a pair of tall arched windows that, my Donaldsonville cousins believe, were designed to recall the stone tablets bearing the Ten Commandments that Moses brought down from Mount Sinai. Within a few years, Myer Lemann, Bernard's younger brother, who'd been sent away to be educated in New York and Germany, returned to Donaldsonville and joined the family

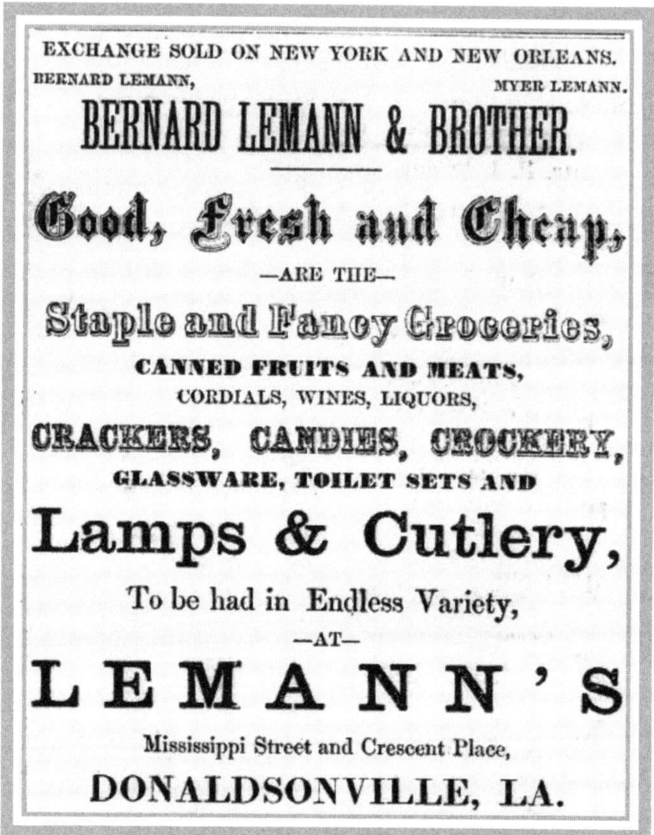

An advertisement for B. Lemann & Brother,
the family store, 1870s.

business; the store became B. Lemann & Brother. I used to visit on my childhood trips to Donaldsonville. The store was well worn, comfortable, and clean, with an unmistakable feel of the nineteenth century. My relatives

The emblem used for decades by
B. Lemann & Brother.

kept exotic items from the old days—buggies, frock coats, molasses jugs, barrels of nails—on display alongside more contemporary goods.

By now it was forty years since Jacob had arrived alone on the New Orleans docks. He was in his late sixties. The adult lives of the next generation, his and Miriam's children, were taking shape. Bernard and Myer were in Donaldsonville running the family business. The third surviving child, Coralie, at the age of nineteen, married the Alsatian-born Lazard Kahn at Bikur Cholim, Donaldsonville's newly built synagogue, a solid two-story wooden building with a double-height entrance that lent it a touch of small-town grandeur, proudly located on the main commercial street. Rabbi Isaac Leucht, who'd married Bernard and Harriet, came up from New Orleans to officiate. Lazard had come to America alone at the age of fifteen with forty francs in his pocket, and had spent lonely years living in a series of rural towns trying to establish himself. Marriage seemed like a distant dream. During this time he wrote to a friend, "From present indications I don't think I will ever find any one who cares enough for me to be my own + I have therefore given up all hope of ever succeeding." Now success had finally come. In the Ascension Parish courthouse there is an official marriage contract between Coralie and Lazard, executed the day before the wedding—the secular companion to their *ketubah*, the religious marriage contract—in which Jacob promises to pay Lazard a dowry of twenty-five thousand dollars.

Coralie and Lazard spent their married life in Cincinnati, which had become the de facto capital city of the German Jews who lived in the United States between the coasts, the home of Hebrew Union College, the Reform seminary. Lazard wound up founding a successful stove-manufacturing company. In 1886, in New Orleans, Myer married sixteen-year-old Carrie Abraham, the daughter of Henry Abraham, another German Jew who'd come to America alone as a teenage boy, and who was now the New Orleans partner of Lehman Brothers, the financiers who had come from Germany to Mont-

Jacob Lemann's grave, Walnut Hills cemetery, Cincinnati.
DANA HERMAN

gomery, Alabama, and then relocated to New York. Whether or not these marriages were love matches, they cemented the Lemanns' place in a high-functioning German-Jewish business and financial network that supplied them with much of the credit, farm supplies, and dry goods that they needed to run their businesses.

In the summer of 1878, on a vacation in the Blue Ridge Mountains of Virginia, Miriam Lemann suddenly died. It was her wish that Rabbi Max Lilienthal, who had performed her religious remarriage to Jacob in New York, also preside over her funeral. Lilienthal had moved to Cincinnati shortly after Miriam and Jacob's wedding, so Miriam was buried in Cincinnati, in the Walnut Hills Jewish cemetery. I've visited the grave, a perfectly maintained stubby stone monument on a hilltop, surrounded by old trees and other venerable, comfortably worn gravesites; when it was built, the cemetery must have been a significant site in the sturdy little civilization the German Jews had created in the United States. Jacob died considerably later, in 1887, at the age of seventy-eight. Rabbi Leucht came up from New Orleans to conduct the funeral. Afterward, there was a grand procession from the house to the railroad depot, where Jacob's coffin was put on a train bound for Cincinnati, so that he could rest next to Miriam. Max Lilienthal had died by then, so the rabbi who presided over Jacob's interment was Isaac Mayer Wise, the founder of Hebrew Union College and leader of American Reform Judaism. So ended Jacob's long project of going forth from his native land.

As soon as Jacob had died, Harriet Lemann moved back to New Orleans with her children, so that they could be educated at above the level that was available in Donaldsonville, and perhaps also because she preferred city life (she was a regular operagoer, at a time when New Orleans, like every other substantial American city, had an opera house). Bernard usually spent the working week in Donaldsonville and weekends in New Orleans, something that the advent of trains and paved roads had made easier than it was in the days when Donaldsonville was accessible only by steamboat. After a few years the family built a spacious wooden house in Uptown New Orleans, on St. Charles Avenue. This house was still standing when I was a boy—it was a music school, with high ceilings and large, gloomy, barren rooms. After high school the boys were sent to Tulane and the girls to its women's college, Sophie Newcomb; Ferdinand, the oldest child, went on to Harvard, to be followed there by three more sons of Bernard and Harriet.

Throughout Bernard's copiously self-documented life, he was frequently ill. The way he described his diseases, when he was inclined to do that, and the modern list of maladies we have now don't intersect, so it's impossible to figure out what was wrong with him. New Orleans in the nineteenth century was subject to frequent epidemics of yellow fever and other terrible diseases; also, what we'd call anxiety, depression, or stress (and people back then called neurasthenia) would have been understood and treated differently. In any event, both Bernard and Harriet died, by our standards, relatively young— she in 1897, at forty-six, and he in 1899, at fifty-eight. The *Don-aldsonville Chief*'s account of Bernard's demise has the impenetrable opacity the past can so easily take on. I know that in most ways Bernard was more like me than not, but the language about his death creates a barrier, a foreignness. He died at Touro Infirmary (where I was born), as "the result of a severe and delicate surgical operation performed several days before." The *Chief* has him undertaking this mysterious procedure despite knowing about its "almost invariably fatal character." He gathered his children beforehand to say goodbye and to urge them to maintain a strong family bond after he was gone.

So now, as the nineteenth century ended, the first two generations of the Lemanns' American life were gone. The family had adeptly maneuvered its way through the violence and chaos of the Civil War and built a successful business from scratch. They had educated themselves, married, reproduced, and achieved some status in Donaldsonville and New Orleans and even farther afield. They had found a way to reestablish the Jewish life that Jacob had abandoned when he left Germany. They were American citizens, but they lived socially and economically within a distinctly Jewish world—German-Jewish. And they were also Germans. It was obviously important to them that emigration not entail breaking all ties to their mother country, the birthplace of most of the people they were close to in America and, to their minds, the empyrean seat of culture and civilization in the world. Jacob and Miriam visited Germany regularly, their daughter had been born there, their sons had both lived there for long stretches, and all three of their children-in-law were German, or, in the case of Lazard Kahn,

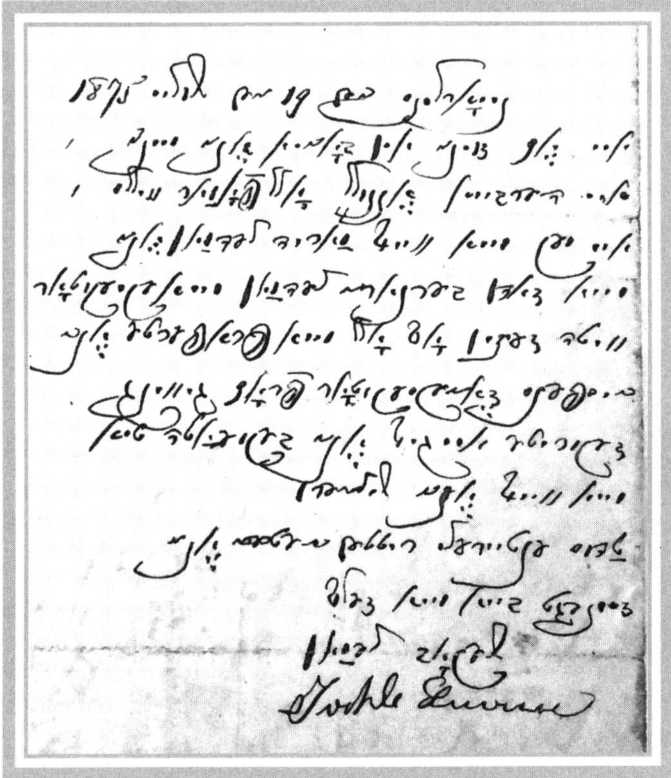

Jacob Lemann's handwritten will, rendered
in Hebrew characters, 1875.

German-adjacent. All writing that Jacob left behind is in German,
rendered in Hebrew characters. He probably thought in German.

For decades, a wine merchant in Mainz named Johann Harth
functioned as Jacob's agent back home. He regularly shipped Rhine
wines to Donaldsonville. He also supervised the housing and education of Myer Lemann during the time he spent in Mainz as a
teenager, bought and sold parcels of land for Jacob, and arranged
for Jacob's contributions to local charities and synagogues. Just after
Miriam's death, in 1878, Jacob took his two younger children, Myer
and Coralie, on a long trip to Mainz (Bernard was married and a
father by then, and running the business, so he couldn't go). That

turned out to be his last visit, but up to the very end of his life he was constantly in touch with Harth.

An elderly woman in a village outside of Mainz named Jeannette Weiss had gotten in touch with Jacob to say that she had helped his mother raise him—remember that Jacob's father had died when he was three—and had since then become destitute. Jacob arranged, through Harth, to send her a modest monthly stipend. In return for this, she promised to look after his parents' graves. As the years went by, Jacob's payments sometimes lapsed. When they did, he'd get a stern letter from Jeannette Weiss reminding him that his mother had promised her she'd always be taken care of, and then the payments would resume. Another frequent German correspondent of Jacob was his cousin Frederike Mayer (remember that back in the early nineteenth century, Jacob's father had taken the last name Lehmann but his siblings had named themselves Mayer). She had an unmarried daughter, and she attributed this misfortune to the dowry's she could afford to offer being insufficient. Jacob arranged for 4000 Deutschmarks to be put into an account that Harth could dispense for this purpose. After some time, Harth wrote: "Miss Mayer had several opportunities to get engaged to sincere men, but the dowry of 4000M is too small. 6,000–8,000 Mark is necessary. Would you be willing to give more?" Months before he died, Jacob added 500 marks to the account; I don't know whether that was enough to do the trick.

In 1894, Bernard and Harriet took a long trip to Europe, partly in the hope that some time spent at a spa would help with whatever Harriet's health problem was. They went to Paris, Vienna, Antwerp, Amsterdam, Warsaw, Frankfurt, and Berlin. I read their accounts of this trip intensely aware of what they couldn't have known: that in just fifty years there would be almost no Jews left in these places. In the manner of spectacularly unaware characters in a novel whose readers are in on the secret they haven't discerned, to them Jewish life in Europe looked serene and well established. Whatever lines there were between the Jewish and non-Jewish world were permeable. As in Bernard's travels in Europe three decades earlier, they toured the major secular and Jewish sites wherever they were, and went to services at synagogues on Saturday morning. In Antwerp, Bernard noted, he had a guide named David Abas. "When I asked him about the Dutch cakes I used to eat, called Bolus, he said, 'That's the kind the Juden eat.' I said 'O, yes!' And he said 'Are you, sir, a Jehovah?' And when I said yes he was delighted, took off his hat, shook my hand, and said, 'Sholom Alechem.' . . . He showed us the old Church and the steps where the Pilgrim fathers set sail for Leyden, Southampton, and then by *Mayflower* for America." In Warsaw, "the Polish Jews with their corkscrew curls and long coats and boots are very queer and quaint looking and they are very numerous here and seem to attract but very little attention, although I always look at them rather more than politeness would warrant."

Bernard and Harriet made a point of seeing their relatives—Bernard's in Mainz, Harriet's in Lambsheim, Germany, and Lazard Kahn's in Ingwiller, France, both towns not far from the Rhine. Maybe it's retrospective wisdom, but I think I can detect the family's German ties growing fainter by this time. In looking for Harriet's cousins, they first went to the wrong house, before finding the right one and staying for services and a Sabbath lunch. The same thing happened in Ingwiller: a false start, then a long, warm visit. They got some information about cousins of Harriet who lived in Paris, Frankfurt, and Mainz, one of them a prominent rabbi. It was the end of their trip; they would have to visit these other relatives next time, when, they'd naturally have assumed, these large, established, observantly Jewish families would be pleased to welcome them. But there wasn't a next time.

In America, the late-nineteenth-century Lemanns were part of a newer Jewish civilization that was just as evidently confident as the one they encountered on visits to Europe. In the end it too was unexpectedly perishable. Its main idea was that Jews could be Jewish in ways that would not strike non-Jews as strange and threatening—that we could join the wider world without being penalized for being

Jewish, and without penalizing ourselves by giving up too much of what we were. Harriet's and Bernard's funerals took place at Temple Sinai, New Orleans's first Reform congregation. It had been organized in 1870, and its grand, twin-towered headquarters at the edge of the New Orleans business district opened in 1872. It was designed to be as impressive as the large Catholic churches that were all over the city but a little more architecturally exotic. It had pairs of narrow, arched, tablet-resembling windows, like the ones on the Lemann family store in Donaldsonville that was built a few years later. Temple Sinai's first rabbi, James Gutheim, arranged in 1884 to purchase a tract for Temple Sinai within Metairie cemetery, the resting place for the New Orleans elite, just outside of town. This was a step. Jews had always been buried in Jewish cemeteries. In Donaldsonville, Congregation Bikur Cholim had its own cemetery, with only Jewish graves. Jacob and Miriam are buried in a Jewish cemetery in Cincinnati. Jacob's parents' graves in Germany are in a Jewish cemetery.

But in Metairie cemetery it's a Jewish neighborhood, not a Jewish cemetery. The first grave there is occupied by Gutheim himself, who died shortly after having made the arrangement with the cemetery. He liked to be called Reverend Gutheim. His tombstone refers to him that way, and bears as an epitaph a quotation from a prominent Presbyterian minister, carved into the stone just above a few words rendered in Hebrew. A short distance away is the eternal residence of most of my relatives. The original Lemann tomb is a stone obelisk memorializing Harriet, Bernard, a number of other Lemanns, as well as one of Miriam's Catholic relatives from Thibodaux, Emma Berthelot. Behind it is a second plot that our family acquired long ago to handle the overflow, which by now includes Mother's and Father's graves. Nearby, under group tombstones for their families, rest many Hymans (Father's mother's family), Newmans (Father's grandmother's family), and Godchauxs (along with Jacob, the other major post–Civil War Jewish sugarcane plantation owner), along with most of the rest of my grandparents' circle. It's a synecdoche of the tight, prosperous world Father was born into, including its experiment in detribalization, in venturing partway into the non-Jewish world around it.

I've spent some time looking for clouds on the Lemanns' horizon, beyond the illnesses and deaths that afflict every family. In sugar country, after Reconstruction, there was a good deal of labor unrest, more so than on Southern cotton plantations where the workforce were sharecroppers, not paid employees. This culminated in a major strike, organized by the Knights of Labor, which ended with a white militia gunning down dozens of Black plantation workers in Thibodeaux, Miriam Lemann's hometown, on the morning of November 23, 1887. But I see nothing about strikes, or even unrest, in the copious records of the Lemann plantations during that period. I doubt that means they were impassioned champions of workers; accommodating would probably be more like it, because no matter what the situation, that was always our inclination.

The white South's overwhelming obsession was race, but every so often its malign attention went beyond Black people, and when it did, the next place it often went was to Jews. After a severe financial panic in 1893, followed by a long depression, there was another outbreak of militia violence in Mississippi. A group of white terrorists, one of a long line in the South in the post–Civil War years, who called themselves Whitecaps, were notable for being not just racist like all the rest, but also antisemitic. Their complaint was that Jews who owned stores and also farmland had preferred access to Black labor, because they could offer farmhands credit at their stores, while straight-up farmers—who themselves had often mortgaged their land to Jews—could not. "Pauperized Jews are imported here who use every damnable idea conceivable to obtain possession of our lands," one Whitecap manifesto said. The Whitecaps' fervent wish was "that we may tend the soil under white supremacy, and under no circumstances will the negro be allowed to cultivate a Jew's or syndicate's land." If peaceful means would not achieve these goals, then it would be necessary to use violent ones—in the case of Jews, "force them to abandon our country and confiscate their lands for the benefit of the white farmers."

All this was happening not so far away from Donaldsonville. Surely it did not escape Bernard Lemann's notice. I'm noticing it now especially because the Whitecaps were active in the town of Summit, Mississippi, where Father's mother's family came from (and, of course, they owned a store and lent money). One of the Whitecaps' chief targets was a man named Hiller, a Jewish immigrant from Alsace who had acquired a string of small farms through mortgage foreclosure. He was my relative by marriage. The Whitecaps burned down twenty-seven workers' houses on his farms, which sent a message to the rest of the workers that they'd better leave. Most did. Hiller sold out to a Gentile and moved to New Orleans. Of course Bernard couldn't have known about this direct family connection, which lay far into the future, past his time.

The German Jews in the United States knew that, with the formal unification in 1871 of all the German states and principalities into a single modern nation-state, Jews in Germany finally were fully emancipated—given the unimpeded rights as citizens they'd never had before. All the long centuries of special taxes, occupational and residential restrictions, and, regularly, much worse might finally be done with in the modern world. What Bernard saw on his visits to Germany was Jews thriving—as Jews. They were proudly observant, and they also were beginning to participate in the wider world. This was how he had lived his own life, for decades: the Sabbath, and then the opera; the Torah, and then George Eliot (who was herself, as her life approached its end, becoming fascinated with "the hitherto neglected reality that Judaism was something still throbbing in human lives"). All over the United States, all over Europe, doors were opening, and Jews were gaining wider renown without having to renounce anything.

But for the Lemanns, and other German Jews, Germany was becoming more an idea and less a real place. We'd been in America for more than half a century. Our ties to our relatives abroad were weakening, our visits becoming less frequent. That made it easier not to notice more ominous developments in Germany, which, if you know what was coming, are retrospectively impossible to miss. In 1878, the year Jacob Lemann died, Adolf Stoecker, court chaplain to Kaiser Wilhelm I, founded Germany's first explicitly anti-Jewish political party, the Christian Social Party. Shortly afterward, Heinrich von Treitschke, a highly respectable German historian who was also a member of the Reichstag, began popularizing openly anti-Jewish rhetoric, such as the slogan "The Jews are our misfortune." Wilhelm Marr, a German journalist, introduced the term *antisemitism*, as his suggested stance for Germans who saw their hatred of Jews as racial rather than religious. These views, which emerged almost instantly after the long-hoped-for arrival of Jewish emancipation, attracted a substantial following. This was not the Germany my relatives chose to see. It wasn't a harbinger of any Jewish future they believed in.

When you have ten children, as Bernard and Harriet did, you have to think of a lot of names. Most of their children seem to have been named after recently departed relatives, which is the Jewish custom. The first child born after Miriam died was Miriam. The first child born after Jacob died was Jacob. But they took some liberty with other names. Child number five, born in 1879, was named Walter Herz Naphtali Lemann. That would have been a tribute to Naphtali Herz Wessely, one of the most prominent German Jews of the eighteenth century, a close associate of the most celebrated of all German Jews, Moses Mendelssohn, and an impassioned advocate of secular education for Jews, even as he produced many works of learned Jewish scholarship.

Child number eight was my grandfather, Montefiore Mordecai Lemann, born in Donaldsonville in 1884. His first name was in honor of Moses Montefiore, the British financier, official liaison between British Jewry and the crown, philanthropist, abolitionist, and proto-Zionist whose hundredth birthday that year was celebrated by Jews all over the world—even in remote Donaldsonville.

His middle name commemorated the hero of the Book of Esther and therefore of the Purim holiday. Montefiore Mordecai Lemann was born in early April, just after Purim. Remember that Bernard had been the first president of the Purim Association in New York and that he and Harriet had met at the Purim ball in New Orleans. Although these names would read to us as most definitely Jewish, they are not traditional Jewish names, of the patriarchs or of family members. Montefiore and Wessely were Jews who became prominent on the larger stage of the modern, secular world, but most definitely as Jews, not members of an ethnically blended German elite. Jewish progress, Jewish pride; Jewish loyalty, recognition on a wider field—these seemed to be their parents' dreams for these children.

There was so much of this history that I hadn't known when I was growing up—and when, all those years ago, I set my course as a person who investigates things that are not immediately visible—that form an unexcavated structure underlying the life I live. I hadn't known anything about my family's life in Germany, about the way we rose in antebellum Louisiana: my relatives' direct participation in slavery, their careers as midlevel financiers. I hadn't known about their relocation to New York, their reengagement in Jewish life, their temporary return to Germany during the Civil War, or how they had acquired a string of plantations. What I knew was Palo Alto and the old B. Lemann & Brother store in Donaldsonville, and our deeply rooted but only faintly Jewish lives as members of a prominent many-branched family in New Orleans. I suppose you find out whatever you need to know in order to take the next few steps.

What I can see now is that my relatives—our family's patriarchs and matriarchs—made what they probably understood as a practical decision to return to Louisiana, which wound up determining the way all of us who came from them have thought of ourselves down through the generations. We were Southerners first, Jews a distant second. That was what I was as a child and as a young man during the second half of the twentieth century. Then, over time, something made me reverse the order. Learning more about our history was part of it. Another part is harder to explain. I think it's the idea that, no matter what the circumstances, being Jewish has a way of pushing itself to the fore: because of how people who aren't Jewish think and act; because of how strongly it imprints itself, unbidden, irresistibly, on our consciousness; because of what it offers, including both extraordinary treasures and a feeling of perpetual unease. In that last sense, it has a good deal in common with the way that, as an adolescent aspiring to a life as a reporter and writer, I conceived of being Southern. But as I've learned about my family's history, I can see that it took quite some time for our decision to become Southerners to penetrate my relatives' self-conception fully, because for decades, like most Jews who have ever lived, they were still primarily Jews.

Part Two

———

ARRIVING

ON PREVIOUS PAGE
St. Charles Avenue in the early twentieth century.
The house belonged to Father's great-uncle,
Isidore Newman.

IF OUR FAMILY'S HISTORY WERE A STANDARD AMERICAN FABLE, IT would seem appropriate for the first two American generations, Jacob and Miriam and then Bernard and Harriet, all dead by the end of the nineteenth century, to have big plans for the next generations, the ones who would make their lives in the twentieth century. Jacob had come here as an immigrant, alone and with nothing, become a big success, and established his family as the seigneurs of a prosperous Southern town. Like many immigrants, he had a primary tribal identity. But wouldn't that be bound to fall away, as his descendants became more acculturated, educated, and secure? Somewhere back in the mists of time, the aristocrats of Burden's Landing surely had been humble frontiersmen, not aristocrats—but in the present of *All the King's Men* they were governors and judges, dignified and high-minded, members of no particular group except the upper class (although there's always something). Wouldn't one expect the Lemanns to have such aspirations?

When I was coming of age, I would have found this fable persuasive. That's why *All the King's Men* resonated with me. We lived surrounded by people who were at least locally prominent, many of them the children and grandchilden of plantation owners as we were, enacting their lives in the upper reaches of New Orleans rather than in sugar country. But now, having investigated more closely, I doubt that's what my nineteenth-century relatives thought was coming. They knew what it was to rise, but not to de-identify. Their direct experience would have impressed on them how new, how utterly unfamiliar, the idea of Jews participating as full members of society was. Had he been just a few years older, Jacob would have been born without a last name, and even at the end of the great distance he had traveled in his life, he lived as a member of a Jewish enclave. In all of the sweep and variety of Jewish history, very few Jews had ever lived any other way. It would have been astonishing to expect that to stop being so, for success to bring an end to Jewish distinctness, in the new century. That's why I doubt they did expect it.

So I suppose what actually happened would have come as a surprise: we did move from the Jewish world into the wider world, as pioneers in a historically new and unfamiliar Jewish project. And yet, for Jews maybe even more than everybody else, there's always something: a tug in two opposing directions, an inescapable calculus of cost and benefit for life on the outside, losses that offset whatever has been gained. Nothing has been simple or straightforward. We of the successor generations should have understood this—I should have—because all of it would have become clear from studying the very beginning of the project.

THE JEWISH QUESTION

What would happen if a Jew wanted to live outside of the strict confines of an enclosed Jewish world? That would have been a completely hypothetical question for most Jews, almost all of them, in 1800, or even in 1900, when my family began exploring it. At least in the part of Europe my family came from, Jews were, to use the language of medieval times, a corporation, or an estate: a legally separate entity. And for most non-Jews, too, it would have been exceptional to be able to live as citizens, with rights and no restrictions. It was the Jews' fate to be subjected periodically to horrific savagery—something that never came entirely as a surprise—but most Jews, most of the time, were still in a better situation than most peasants. Jews were sometimes given special access to the wider society by kings and princes. This took the form of a bargain, in which we would provide some higher skill, usually involving handling money, in return for privileges outside of the *Judenstrasse*. It was nothing approaching full membership. *Schutzjuden*, Jews who got special privileges in return for paying a special tax, lived better than most Jews. Court Jews, a tiny group, lived best of all.

In the eighteenth century, with the Enlightenment, came the early versions of ideals that are familiar to us, like citizenship, rights, and democracy—and the appearance of a few non-Jews who called for the emancipation of the Jews. But even for them, there was always what people called the Jewish question: it would be unthinkable to accept Jews as they were, so we would have to be reformed, made more normal. Christian Wilhelm von Dohm, author of *On the Civic Improvement of the Jews* (1781) and the first prominent German intellectual to position himself publicly as an advocate for the Jews, argued that the Jews' repellent traits—our proneness to usury and other varieties of greed, our peculiar understanding of religious faith in terms of an insanely detailed set of rules—were the malign result of centuries of oppression. They weren't innate, they could be fixed. As such ideas progressed, especially after the French Revolution, they became the basis of policies. Jews would learn to speak the dominant language, not just a variant of Yiddish. Jews would be educated in state schools, not just their own *cheders*. Jews would be barred from their traditional occupations, like trading, peddling, and lending; perhaps they could become farmers. Jews would take last names. Jews would no longer be governed by Jewish courts and Jewish legislatures; the national government could, for example, rule the Jews through new entities, such as the consistories that Napoleon created in France, headed by a special kind of Jewish official who would organize and control the Jews for the benefit of the state. My grandfather's namesake, Moses Montefiore, was for forty years head of the state-sanctioned Board of Deputies of British Jews.

The idea of being emancipated, freed from being subjected to overt prejudice and often also to violent oppression, is automatically appealing—in today's world, you don't have to explain why. But when you look at it more closely, thinking as one might have at that moment, it's a complicated blessing, because it can't be enacted without painful sacrifices. Traditional Jewish life in the Diaspora may have been, as even sympathetic non-Jews believed, a maladaptation to the outside world's restrictions—or it may have been a separate, glorious, painstakingly constructed, astonishingly durable and fecund civilization. Jews had power (over themselves, at least), they had rules to live by, they had powerful community bonds, they had a language and a literature, they had a scholarly tradition, they had holidays and rituals and customs, scripts for the proper handling of food and sex and love, birth and death and marriage, that formed a sturdy armature structuring everyone's life. Jews looked out for one another. How much should we care that everything about us is repellent to everyone who isn't us? The Jewish historian Salo Baron, in a 1928 essay arguing against the "lachrymose theory" of Jewish history before the Enlightenment, with its emphasis on the constancy of Jewish suffering, wrote this memorable line about traditional Jews' sense of the loss that their emancipation would entail: "There were locks inside the Ghetto gates in most cases before there were locks outside."

It's usually a fault of storytellers to present history in individual terms, but for my people, the German Jews, the history of assimilation actually does begin with one man, the philosopher Moses Mendelssohn. The son of a *sofer*, a ritual scribe who hand-letters copies of the Torah onto parchment scrolls, in the small city of Dessau, Mendelssohn arrived in Berlin on a donkey in 1743, at the age of fourteen. He entered, as Jews were required to do, by the city gate reserved for livestock. He became one of the first Jews to get a first-rate secular education and to publish important works that were not on Jewish themes. He accomplished this largely through the patronage of Gotthold Ephraim Lessing, a leading figure in German theater, who was, like von Dohm (another friend of Mendelssohn), one of the rare German intellectuals who was a public champion of Jews. Lessing's play *Nathan the Wise*, written in 1779 though not performed until 1783, after he had died, was set during the Second Crusade, but its hero was based on Mendelssohn. Nathan, the lightly fictionalized Mendelssohn, was one of the first favorably portrayed Jews in a work of literature not written by a Jew. One scholar calls it "the Magna Carta of German Jewry." It was widely popular during the nineteenth century; Bernard Lemann saw it during his travels in Europe as a young man.

Mendelssohn was always an observant Jew, who was confident that other Jews could follow his path into the mainstream without any loss of Jewishness. His confidence underlay a series of acts that were departures from traditional Jewish practice—beginning with his calling himself, when he was in the non-Jewish world, by something other than his Jewish name, Moshe ben Mendel. In the early 1780s, toward the end of his life, he translated the Torah into German—rendered in Hebrew characters, like the standard Torah. He urged German Jews to learn to speak German. He advocated for religious tolerance in a secular society, so that Jews would be free to practice Judaism while also complying with the laws of the principality where they lived. But every time Mendelssohn resolved one problem in connecting Jewishness to Germanness, another problem presented itself. Did he believe that the Torah was the revealed word of God? If so, did he really believe that Christianity was just as valid religiously as Judaism, only different? These were questions that drew him into controversies that were never fully resolved. And then there was the question, less profound philosophically but perhaps more immediately challenging, of how strongly to keep oneself bound to the all-encompassing practices of daily Jewishness after it had become possible not to. Of Mendelssohn's six children, four converted to Christianity. The possibility of acceptance, it turns out, turned Jews into Christians far more effectively than the more brutal methods of medieval Crusaders and Inquisitors did.

All through the nineteenth century, in Germany and in the United States too, many former small-town Jewish peddlers who had prospered found Mendelssohn and everything they thought he represented deeply attractive. It looked like a way of having everything that being Jewish, and also everything that not being Jewish, had to offer, all at once. Although in his own life Mendelssohn was what we would call Orthodox, German Jews in America took—actually mistook—his success in the wider world as an implicit endorsement of Reform Judaism, which had become, maybe more by happenstance than by a conscious decision, Bernard Lemann's religious affiliation by the time he died. On the test that I flunked at the Temple Sinai religious school, the one that made Father think I wasn't being educated properly, one of the questions I couldn't answer was the date of the consecration of the grand Reform temple in Hamburg. We children of Temple Sinai were meant to think of this as a turning point in Jewish history, signaling the first-ever real solution to the Jewish question.

In Germany and the United States, a series of Jewish liberalizers proposed a series of loosenings of the bonds of Jewish law. Each of these could be seen as an example of bringing down the curtain on a silly, outdated, even barbaric and offensive practice, the latter-day equivalent of the animal sacrifices that long passages of the Torah are devoted to prescribing in detail. Or, like the embrace of secular education, they were ways of making a happy fit between Jewishness and the wider world more possible. Or perhaps they were merely attempts to imitate the goyim, in sincere admiration and the hope of winning their approval. In Frankfurt, a group of Reform rabbis drafted a set of principles entirely rejecting the legal authority of the Talmud over every aspect of Jews' lives; they even considered making circumcision, the fundamental practice sealing the Jews' covenant with God, optional. In the United States, Reform temples experimented with using organs and choirs, as high-church Protestants did; with moving the Sabbath to Sunday; with replacing the bar mitzvah with a Protestant-style confirmation ceremony (Father had one of these); with banning *kippot* and *tallitot*, the traditional Jewish headgear and prayer shawls; and even with putting the Torah scroll into storage because Reform services no longer required using it.

A traditional Jewish service usually struck outsiders as peculiar, because the people there prayed individually in Hebrew, often while swaying vigorously, and otherwise wandered around and chatted. In a Reform service, the impeccably dressed congregants sat quietly in pews and listened as a rabbi led the service, and they couldn't speak or read Hebrew. In a traditional service, the Torah scroll was treated reverently, paraded around the room so that the people there could symbolically kiss it, and then carefully unfurled so that the week's portion could be read aloud by the congregants, taking turns, in a special incantatory rhythm. In a Reform temple, the rabbi would read one paragraph aloud from the pulpit, possibly in German or more likely in English. Reform Jews dropped the use of Hebrew names and the custom of not naming children after living relatives (I have a cousin named Harris Hyman IV). They often found it uncomfortable, as Father did, even to say the word *Jew*, which sounded rather raw, preferring *Israelite*. Many Reform temples downplayed or abolished Purim, the holiday that had played such a large part in Bernard and Harriet Lemann's lives, because the celebration was too nationalistic in spirit and too raucous in style.

The Enlightenment was supposed to take religion out of the controlling position in the world. For individual people, at least if they were educated, reason would become more important than faith. For governments, law would take the place of theology; no longer would it be legitimate for rulers to have people killed because of their religion. Jews who had the luxury to think capaciously about their lives could choose to see this as the end to long centuries of limitation and suffering, because they understood antisemitism as motivated fundamentally by religious prejudice. Imagine how thrilling it would have been to contemplate life without inquisitions, disputations, expulsions, forced conversions, crusades! It would be natural to assume that downgrading religion would lessen antisemitism. The non-Jewish world would become safe for Jews. It was the idea that religion, in the post-Enlightenment, had been decoupled from danger which led Reform Jews to adopt the slogan that I was raised on: "We are a religion, not a race." We would be on an equal footing, from the standpoint of the law and of public opinion, with the other religions (especially after we had made a few religious adjustments to make ourselves seem less strange). We would no longer be a tribe, a people, a separate society—unlike others, set apart. In 1885, the Reform Jewish movement held a convention in Pittsburgh that produced an official platform, which became known as the Pittsburgh Platform. It made these crucial adjustments to modernity: Reform Jews no longer believed they were in a unique relationship with God, as his chosen people; Reform Jews no longer saw the Torah as revelation, or the laws derived from it as binding; Reform Jews no longer had national aspirations, especially about the return to Palestine that is so central to the narrative of the Torah.

But whenever Reform Judaism asserted its confident presence, there was a strong counterreaction. Because Reform began in Germany, so did the counterreaction. In 1851, not long after the temple in Hamburg had opened, Rabbi Samson Raphael Hirsch, who like Mendelssohn had both a Jewish and a secular higher education, took the leadership of an Orthodox synagogue in Frankfurt, built in disapproval of the advent of the Reform movement there. Even earlier, in the 1840s, another leading German rabbi, Zacharias Frankel, had founded an early version of the Conservative movement, also as a rejection of Reform. The cheerleading version of German Reform Judaism that Temple Sinai tried to teach me to the contrary, Reform, and also the allied movement in Germany that called itself Liberal, never had the allegiance of more than a small minority of German Jews—even of Jews who lived in the big cities. In the United States, Rabbi Samuel Isaacs, the man to whom Jacob and Miriam Lemann sent Bernard, their firstborn son, to receive his Jewish education in New York, relentlessly attacked the American Reform movement in the pages of *The Jewish Messenger*, the paper where Bernard worked as a teenager, in passages like this: "the Reformer is not progressing, but throwing aside all the landmarks of Judaism." This put him at odds with Isaac Mayer Wise, the Reform rabbi who presided over Jacob Lemann's burial in Cincinnati. When Hebrew Union College in Cincinnati, under Wise's leadership, graduated the first class of

American Reform rabbis in 1883, the celebratory banquet following the ceremony was notoriously non-kosher. Many rabbis were so outraged that they began working to establish the American Conservative movement, which wound up surpassing Reform in membership.

In Germany, in one of his fusillades against the Reform movement, Samson Raphael Hirsch wrote: "Judaism is not a religion, the synagogue is not a church, and the Rabbi is not a priest. Judaism is not a mere adjunct to life; it comprises all of life. To be a Jew is not a mere part, it is the sum total of our task in life." That got across how profoundly different, new, and offensive the innocuous-sounding idea that Judaism is a religion was, when it emerged, to most Jews. Jews didn't think in terms of "believing in God" so much as of living a God-commanded Jewish life, defined in every aspect by Jewish laws and practices and by membership in an enclosed community. What the Reform movement was proposing was daring, unfamiliar. It rested on the idea that Jewishness could be stripped of its ritual and tribal aspects and still survive and thrive, and that, under the right circumstances, Jews could be accepted by non-Jews, as they had only rarely ever been.

Is it God who likes to play cruel tricks on the Jews, or is it fate? In Germany, the Enlightenment did reduce the power of religion, but one of the forms of science, or pseudo-science, it empowered was race science. The advent of German nationalism led to full Jewish emancipation, but also to the idea that being German meant being Aryan, a category that excluded the Jews; in pre-Enlightenment times, Jew haters offered conversion as a way to save your skin, but now that Jews were a race, there was no way out. The title of the most popular pamphlet by the pioneering antisemite Wilhelm Marr, *The Victory of Judaism over Germanism*, conveys his message that Germany's small Jewish minority posed a dire threat to the entire newly united nation, the most populous and powerful in Europe. In 1881, Eugen Dühring, a highly respected and prominent German philosopher, published a book called *The Jewish Question as a Racial, Moral, and Cultural Problem*, calling for the "murder and extermination" of the Jews. In 1882 there was a Congress of German and Austro-Hungarian Anti-Semites in Dresden. Houston Stewart Chamberlain, a British-born intellectual and son-in-law of the composer Richard Wagner, who immigrated to Germany during this period and enthusiastically absorbed such views, provides the direct personal link between these early stirrings of anti-Jewish race-hatred and Adolf Hitler—whom, in old age, he met in 1923.

But perhaps it would be too much to ask of the Jews who sat at services in the grand, new, immaculate Reform temples of Hamburg, Frankfurt, and Berlin, with their soaring ceilings, their elaborate ornamentation, their hushed dignity, to foresee what was in store for them. They were the children of peddlers, and now they owned department stores, practiced medicine, taught at universities, published books. They or their children went to university. They lived in comfortable bourgeois apartments with heavy furniture, books, silverware, thick draperies. They were not just Jews, they were also Germans. What now seem like ominous early warnings might not have been the obviously loudest sound in the political and intellectual cacophony of late-nineteenth-century Germany, especially if they were exactly what you most didn't want to hear.

In America, intellectual and political antisemitism was especially distant, and there was an automatic reverence for Germany among German Jews. Bernhard Felsenthal, the German-born rabbi of a Reform congregation in Chicago, who conducted services in German, offered this florid statement of what was a standard sentiment: "We must not distance ourselves from German Judaism and its influences. As in medieval times the sun of Jewish *Wissenschaft* [learning] was shining on the Spanish sky, this sun is now shining on the German sky, sending out its light to all Jews and Jewish communities, who live among the modern cultured peoples." Even when I was growing up, in the second half of the twentieth century, wisps of sentimentality about Germany clung to the life of our household: German wines at the dinner table, German words sprinkled into our conversations. We avoided what would have been the obvious topic about Germany. I take that as a sign of how deeply it contravened the way we preferred to think of ourselves.

Even in the early, optimistic days of American Reform Judaism, it would have been hard to argue that our dream of a genuine German-Jewish culture had been realized. It was more a matter of German Jews simply becoming less Jewish and more German, not of our having somehow synthesized the two cultures into a distinctive and durable new one. Can the Jewish question ever be solved? I don't think so, but I would guess that my relatives at the turn of the twentieth century might have thought so. They were still proudly and distinctly Jewish, but they had made miraculous progress outside the Jewish world in just a few decades. The third American generation was coming of age, with every opportunity open. As is usual with immigrant families, their once intensely close ties with friends, relatives, and business associates in the old country were loosening as the years passed, so in the early decades of the twentieth century they were no longer in a position to receive automatic updates on the situation in Germany. They could rest assured that all was well there.

OUT OF DONALDSONVILLE

My grandfather, Montefiore Mordecai Lemann, was intellectually precocious. He entered Tulane as a freshman at age fourteen, graduated at eighteen, and then got two degrees from Harvard, a second undergraduate degree in 1903, and a law degree in 1906. At some early point in his life he shortened his heavyweight moniker to Monte M. Lemann, but Father always called him Pop and trained me to do the same, so that's what I'll call him here.

Pop graduated fourth in his class of five hundred at Harvard Law School. His rank meant that he also worked on the small staff of the *Harvard Law Review*. This put him into a tight network in which he maintained membership until the end of his life. Some of the members of the network became founders of large, prominent business-

The staff of the *Harvard Law Review*, 1906. In the second row down, Pop is second from left and Felix Frankfurter is at the end of the row on the right.

law firms, but the most important member to Pop, continuously for more than half a century, was the person who was first in the class, Felix Frankfurter: a short, bespectacled, high-domed, bright-eyed, Vienna-born Jewish immigrant who became a leading liberal intellectual, a law professor, and a Supreme Court justice. The network in general, and in particular his close connection to Frankfurter, meant that Pop was a lifelong member of what Frankfurter's biographer calls the liberal establishment (which he credits Frankfurter with helping to create).

In the third generation of the Lemann family, almost everybody remained in Louisiana, but not everybody stayed in the family business. Pop had positioned himself for entry into a wider world, beyond the Deep South, but I can't find any evidence that he ever considered that. It looks as if he wanted to operate on a stage larger than Donaldsonville and the plantations and the store, but closer to home than New York or Washington—and that's what he found. New Orleans in those days was a rising city with a busy port, a

Father at the front door of the determinedly old-fashioned
Monroe & Lemann office, circa 1970. ELLIS LUCIA

place where civic monuments (statues, parks, museums, office tow-ers), signaling optimism, were being constructed. He moved back there, joined a law firm, and taught part-time at Tulane Law School. He became law partners with J. Blanc Monroe, the son of the chief justice of the Louisiana Supreme Court—who, if it needs to be said, was not Jewish. Their firm, Monroe & Lemann, represented banks, insurance companies, utilities. It eventually took in Pop's two sons and Mr. Monroe's two sons, along with other partners.

Visits to the Monroe & Lemann office, on the fourteenth floor of the Whitney Bank building, a steel-girdered cathedral of provincial finance that was made to appear as if it were built of solid stone, were a regular occasion of my childhood. Well into the 1970s, Father and his partners made sure it looked and felt like a law office from the 1920s. You'd pass through a building lobby full of well-polished marble and brass, where the bankers, whom we knew as family friends, sat on a platform serenely shuffling through documents, and then you'd ride upstairs in a hand-operated elevator. On the door of the firm were the partners' names, painted onto pebbled frosted glass. At the receptionist's desk there was an old-fashioned switchboard, where an incoming call would be properly directed by plugging a thick black wire into the proper hole. The offices had dark wood paneling, rolltop desks, ceiling fans, spittoons, and manual typewriters. Monroe & Lemann was open for business six days a week; in acknowledgment of the weekend, on Saturdays the lawyers wore bow ties. From this perch Pop functioned for decades as, in effect, the liberal establishment's Deep South bureau chief, a man who could be put on a national board or commission without the risk that he'd function as a Confederate bitter-ender, as so many other New Orleanians at his level might have done. The diversity he provided wasn't only geographic: there weren't many more Jews than Southerners who were as fully eligible for membership in the liberal establishment as Pop was.

Back in 1892, Ferdinand Lemann, Bernard and Harriet's eldest child, the first member of the third generation of the family and Pop's much older brother, fired off a thirty-page letter to his parents. He was a student at Harvard, the first of a long procession of Lemanns to go there. He had taken a course called Political Economy, where he had encountered the laissez-faire views that were coming to the fore in the brand-new American economics profession. Full of righteous passion, Ferdinand informed Bernard and Harriet that a new age was dawning in which protectionism would meet the end it deserved and free trade principles would prevail. This was anything but an abstract proposition for the Lemanns: Ferdinand was planning to join the family business. Tariffs had been part of the lives of sugar planters since the late eighteenth century—a life-and-death cause, economically speaking, that they were accustomed to fighting for. But to Ferdinand sugar tariffs were a way of protecting lazy planters from the Darwinian rigors of the marketplace, and of placing an unfair tax on consumers of sugar, who might be able to buy more of it if it cost less. Also, he felt, it was ridiculous for Louisiana sugar planters to be in two businesses at once, farming and manufacturing. Instead they should establish a great centralized sugar-processing factory and ship their harvested cane there. That would permit them to switch from a wage system to a sharecropper system, as the cotton planters had. Such modern techniques would enable them to fend off competitors, like the Cuban sugar planters and the new sugar beet industry, without the aid of tariffs. "The planters must arouse themselves to action, intense action," he declared.

Not many years later, in the first decade of the twentieth century, with Bernard and Harriet dead and Ferdinand running the business with his uncle Myer, the Lemann plantations were in economic crisis. When you think of plantations, your mind would go first to their dependence on the pervasive racial ordering of the Jim Crow system, by then firmly established and unchallenged even by white liberal reformers outside the South. But there were many other variables, starting with the eternal one in agriculture, the weather. In 1903 Congress substantially reduced the tariff on imported sugar, supposedly on its way to instituting the free trade policy that the young Ferdinand had dreamed of. That brought a flood of Cuban sugar into the United States. In 1913, when Woodrow Wilson, a former academic instinctively sympathetic to free trade, became president, he announced that he was going to eliminate sugar tariffs entirely, permanently. (He didn't; there are still tariffs on imported sugar.) Independently of tariffs, sugar prices fluctuated on the world market, and in the early years of the twentieth century they were declining. In 1907 there was a global financial crisis that made business activity contract severely, followed by another financial crisis in 1914. There were floods. There were blights. There were bad crops. And the American Sugar Refining Company—the sugar trust, maker of Domino sugar, created in 1887, the year Jacob Lemann died, and operated by Horace Havemeyer out of a headquarters in New Jersey—by the early twentieth century controlled 98 percent of the nation's sugar refining, which meant that planters were forced to sell into a market with only one bidder. One year the trust refused to buy any Louisiana sugar at all.

Pop was only twenty-three in 1907, when the crisis arrived in full force, a young lawyer newly returned to New Orleans and starting his practice. Even so, he was deeply caught up in trying to save the plantation business. This was a time when the German-Jewish economic network was at its peak—though that turned out not to be enough to forestall the fate that was coming for the Lemanns' business. It's striking to see how financially interconnected the German Jews were then, often through marriage. Pop's uncle Lazard Kahn, in Cincinnati, who had consulted constantly with Bernard about the business, was writing long letters of advice and also lending money. Two of Pop's siblings had married the children of German-Jewish businessmen in Cincinnati, named Hirsch and Freiberg, regional barons in the outer orbit of the German-Jewish business-financial system. Both of them also loaned the Lemanns money. So did Henry Abraham, Myer Lemann's father-in-law. And through people like him and Lazard Kahn, the family was able to seek more substantial help from the country's most important German-Jewish banking firms, like Lehman Brothers and Goldman Sachs. In 1907, Lazard wrote Pop, just before the official news of a loan extension arrived, "Mr. S. of G.S. Company said a great many pleasant things personal to Uncle Myer and myself and seemed rather to make the impression that these personal considerations were the prime incentive for their friendly attitude."

I have the impression that the reason Lazard was writing Pop was that he didn't believe Myer and Ferdinand fully grasped the gravity of their situation. They were too casual in their dealings with creditors. They were exploring unrealistic expansion plans with neighboring planters—the Godchauxs, the Kocks, the McCalls—in the vain hope that they could grow their way out of the crisis. Pop, a lawyer and a sober young man, physically close by in Louisiana, might be able to impose some discipline on his relatives, to make them understand how the business world worked in the twentieth century (that is, rapidly and unsentimentally). In 1914, well into a second wave of the crisis, with the plantation business in receivership, Pop wrote a stern letter to Ferdinand: he'd had a visit from a "credit man" from Swift and Company, the giant Chicago meatpacking company, a crucial supplier of goods to the family store and of feed to the plantations. Swift hadn't been paid, and its representative obviously hadn't gotten the attention he'd expected from the Lemanns in Donaldsonville—so he went to New Orleans to see Pop, who wasn't yet thirty. In the letter, Pop lectured his older brother: "I consider it important to pay them their account even two or three days before it is due if possible." He also wrote the Swift man a long letter promising that from now on the Lemanns would pay promptly, and asking that the family's troubles be kept strictly confidential.

The tide that was running against the family plantations couldn't be reversed. In the spring of 1919, the formerly buoyant Ferdinand wrote to the youngest of his siblings, Jack: "The winter was a very hard one and conditions very difficult and unfavorable for planters—it rained almost incessantly from middle of November until end of February. Plantation roads became not only impassable but actively *impossible*—in worst condition ever known." Ferdinand was writing from New Orleans, where he'd gone to have doctors look at a mysterious stomach ailment. Less than two weeks later he was dead, at the age of forty-eight. During the Lemanns' forty-year heyday in the plantation business, people called Donaldsonville "Little Jerusalem," because the town was completely encircled by one Jewish family's landholdings. Now, one by one, the plantations were sold off, leaving Palo Alto as the remnant; the store in town continued to operate. My cousin Bubs, who lived at Palo Alto and ran both businesses when I was a child, wrote a short memoir about his father, one of Pop's younger brothers, who had spent his life in Donaldsonville. "A sugar cane plantation during his lifetime must have been one disappointment after another," Bubs wrote, "and he, like his brothers and sisters, no doubt suffered to see the holdings that their grandfather and father acquired shrink a little more each year. It was to this, however, that he devoted his life."

Of Bernard and Harriet's eight children who survived to adulthood, three, all boys, spent their adult lives in Donaldsonville and worked in the family businesses. The other five moved away. In group photographs they all appear formal, serious; they look straight at the camera, neatly dressed in dark suits and heavy dresses that must have been stiflingly uncomfortable in Louisiana's sticky, moist heat. Seven of the eight children married Jews. During the time of the plantation economic crises, there was also a religious crisis, because, in 1914, Pop's younger brother Arthur, the subject of the poignant description that I just quoted, married Mary Lee Landry, a member of Ascension Parish's leading Catholic family. According to family lore, Arthur's brothers and sisters, all more or less observant practicing Jews, stayed up all night with him trying to talk him out of intermarrying, fruitlessly. Arthur wound up having eight children, all raised as Catholics. Mary Lee, in addition to being a Landry, was also a descendant of the Ayrauds, the family that had owned Palo Alto before the Civil War. As the story was handed down to me, their marriage was a Romeo and Juliet drama in reverse: whatever lingering bad feelings there may still have been over the Lemanns taking the plantation, and whatever contemporary bad feelings there were over the mixed marriage, love triumphed, and they lived together for many evidently happy decades, with the two streams of family heritage behind Palo Alto united.

Jacob Lemann had come to America knowing that he would be immediately unable to function as a practicing Jew. He had intermarried. Over the decades, through a great deal of effort on his and Miriam's part, he had been able to establish a Jewish life for his large family. A few days after he was born, Arthur, like his brothers, had been the star attraction at a bris, a celebratory public circumcision to mark a male child's entry into the covenant. Now the Lemanns were dividing into two categories: those who remained in Donaldsonville, who became Catholic, and those who left, who remained Jews. One by one, the other Jewish families in Donaldsonville left too. Like many small towns in the South—and for that matter, but for different reasons, in Europe—Donaldsonville for years had an official last Jew, a small, gray old man. His name was Irv Birnbaum, and he tended Bikur Cholim cemetery until he died in 2004. When I met with the Julien family at the Sportsman Lounge, they objected to the idea that there were no Jews left in Donaldsonville. What about the Lemanns? By one standard, fair enough, but loyalty to Donaldsonville had entailed leaving organized Jewish life behind. And Jewish life is organized; it has to be, by Jewish law.

The Lemanns who remained in Donaldsonville had launched an unfamiliar project, living as non-Jews. The Lemanns who left, like Pop, had launched a different unfamiliar project of their own, living as mainstream Americans. Pop's grandparents had gone to a lot of trouble to avoid the Civil War, but Pop, along with two of his brothers, served in the First World War, which the United States entered when he was in his midthirties. He worked as a lawyer for the U.S. Shipping Board in Washington. In his letters home, he complained about how hard he was working, but it was a propitious assignment—as one family member put it, "he is deriving considerable benefit from meeting and knowing big men who are doing things." He renewed his friendship with Felix Frankfurter, who also had a wartime government job and was living in the "House of Truth," a Washington townhouse that functioned as the capital's leading salon for rising liberals. Pop went to Yom Kippur services. He dined with Herbert Lehman, then on leave from Lehman Brothers to work for the army, later to become governor of New York, "who seems to be a very nice chap." Twice, during visits to the theater, he saw President Wilson, looking "very old and worn," and his "pretty buxom" wife, Edith. Wilson, almost three decades older than Pop, was an unreconstructed child of the Reconstruction South, dedicated to white supremacy. Pop was not, but he disapproved of Wilson for other reasons. Why was the President spending his evenings "entirely as a successful business man rather than as a man of letters, a scholar and a statesman would"—at the theater rather than in gatherings of "the sparking brains of the country" that he had convened at the White House? Such judgments are evidence of a scope of ambition that no previous Lemann, going back infinitely through the generations, would have been able to harbor.

Though not always at the same impressively high level as Pop, other Lemanns in those early years of the new century, like Reform Jews back in Germany, were getting university degrees, entering the professions, and finding work in institutions that were not Jewish. Through the previous decades of the family's rise that had not happened. The Lemanns had been in family businesses that most of the time operated through close connections to other German-Jewish family businesses. The overwhelming main line of Jewish history up to that point was one of separation from non-Jews, economically, socially, legally, ritually, thanks to some combination of choice and exclusion. If, indeed, the gates to the ghetto had been locked from both the inside and the outside, what would a Jew who ventured outside the gates encounter there? What would need to be given up? What could a Jew offer to the world that would turn the world's historic and customary revulsion into a warm embrace? These questions had never been entirely absent, but now, for Jews like us, they were becoming primary.

COURT JEWS

As it does on all big questions, the Torah has a good deal to say about these—or, rather, it has stories to offer, whose meaning and application it's for us to figure out. Before we are even out of the Book of Genesis, we have encountered a long, complicated, unforgettable account of a Jew who operates at a high level in a non-Jewish society: Joseph, who becomes the vizier of Egypt, at the behest of Pharaoh. He is hardly the only Jew in the Torah who has extensive adventures outside of the confines of the tribe, as the Lemanns began to do in the twentieth century. Moses, the Torah's main human character, was raised, his identity disguised, inside the Egyptian court. Like Joseph, he married a non-Jewish woman. Outside of the confines of the Torah, in other canonical Jewish writings, Daniel, in the Book of Daniel, and my grandfather's namesake, Mordecai, in the Book of Esther, both served as the right-hand man to non-Jewish rulers—a series of Babylonian kings in Daniel's case and Ahasuerus of Persia in Mordecai's. Joseph and Daniel were elevated from their previous status at the very bottom of society on the strength of their ability to interpret the ruler's dreams.

Not just Scripture but real Jewish history, and for that matter the Jewish present, offers a long procession of Jews who have served in high-level advisory roles out in the big world. The Jew has something to offer, some expertise, and is awarded special privileges in return. Yes, it was a Jew who wrote *The Interpretation of Dreams*, but that's more often the canonical ticket to these roles than the real-life one. The most famous European court Jew, probably, was Mayer Amschel Rothschild, who provided financial services to Prince Wilhelm of the German state of Hesse-Cassel—not far from where my family comes from—and founded his family's bank. Jews have a reputation for understanding about money. Jews can communicate across national boundaries. Jews are doctors and scientists. Jews are adept with words and ideas. Jews can plan. Jews can organize. Powerful people who need these special skills and can't find them any other way install Jews in high positions. But there are always conditions, aren't there?

Sometimes in Scripture, and surely far more often in real life, the ruler may be unaware of the court Jew's tribal identity, which makes disguise a condition of elevation and revealing the truth a risk. King Ahasuerus made Mordecai's adopted daughter Esther—a distinctly Jewish name now, but then a camouflaged one (in Hebrew Esther means "hidden"; she was really named Hadassah)—his concubine and then his queen because he didn't know who she really was. Pharaoh knew that Joseph, whom he first encountered as a slave who had been imprisoned as a falsely accused rapist, was a Hebrew, but it was only after Joseph had been a miraculously successful administrator for more than a decade that he sought Pharaoh's permission to import his Jewish family, numbering seventy people, to Egypt to live there. Both Joseph and Esther began their rise in the world as slaves whose physical beauty attracted their owners to them. Joseph, Esther, Mordecai, and Daniel all wound up being gorgeously garbed in magnificent non-Jewish raiments as an aspect of their new roles at court. Joseph was given a new, Egyptian name. We are never even told Mordecai's Hebrew name. Except for Daniel, all the biblical court Jews abandoned the Jewish dietary laws at court.

If the Rothschilds are the best known court Jews, the most memorably rendered artistically is probably Joseph Süss Oppenheimer, court Jew to Duke Charles Alexander of Württemburg in the early eighteenth century. Mayer Rothschild, born more than forty years after Oppenheimer, looks almost modern, balding, with large clear eyes and white side-whiskers; the bewigged, crudely rendered Oppenheimer is a figure from another age. Oppenheimer, a banker who, like Rothschild, came from southwest Germany, has been the subject of two novels, two films, and several biographies. Like his biblical forebears, he rose quickly on the basis of his special skills. He lived outside the ghetto, ostentatiously and gorgeously dressed. And when his noble patron suddenly died, he was hanged, following a flurry of accusations of lechery and financial impropriety. What put Oppenheimer in the spotlight in the twentieth century was the German writer Lion Feuchtwanger's popular novel *Jud Süss*, published in 1925. In Feuchtwanger's version of the story, it emerges that Oppenheimer was secretly not Jewish but, instead, the illegitimate son of a nobleman, and that, rather than his being a rapist, his daughter had been raped. On the gallows, he is offered the opportunity to reveal all this and to convert to Christianity—a venerable life-saving opportunity offered to imperiled Jews—but he refuses. Instead, defiantly, he recites the *Shema*, the brief and most essential Jewish utterance, and dies.

Pop was an exact contemporary of two famous Jews, Feuchtwanger, the German novelist, and Leo Frank, the German-Jewish manager of an Atlanta factory who was lynched in 1915 by a mob that believed he had raped and killed a young white girl who worked for him. Feuchtwanger was, along with the Austro-Hungarian visionary writer Joseph Roth, one of a cohort of ardent early warners about Adolf Hitler and the Nazis—in his case, beginning in the early 1920s. As soon as Hitler came to power, Feuchtwanger fled Germany. After a series of daring escapes, he arrived in Los Angeles in 1941, quickly becoming a leading member of the colony of artistic German refugees in Los Angeles, along with Thomas Mann and Bertolt Brecht. Leo Frank's lynching took place just as Pop was rising in the world. It landed heavily with German Jews in America, not merely as an injustice but also as a reminder that our new status was anything but secure—that the mob was always waiting for us somewhere just out of view, obsessed with our supercharged greed and sexuality, waiting for a pretext to strike.

In *Parade*, the musical about Frank by Alfred Uhry (an Alsatian-descended Jew from Atlanta), the final scene has Frank reenacting the ending of Feuchtwanger's *Jud Süss* by reciting the *Shema* on the gallows just before the curtain falls. In real life that didn't happen; Frank merely said that he loved his wife and his mother. The German Jews in America, with some exceptions, took pains to be careful, muted, not defiant. We may not have known many Eastern European Jews, but we knew the stereotypes about them—loud, vulgar, radical—and we designed our self-presentation with the aim of seeming different. There was nothing to be gained by calling attention to yourself, by ardently advocating for the tribe.

Even the uncharacteristically strident Feuchtwanger, who had been raised Orthodox, had internalized the idea of an implausibly binary distinction between ordinary Jews and court Jews, at least in the way he imagined life in late-medieval Germany. There was a sharp, irreconcilable gulf between the two categories. In the ghetto, he wrote, "their men slunk with bowed heads, their women faded early; of every ten children whom they bore, seven died. They were like dead brackish water, cut off from the free-flowing life outside, dammed off from the language, the art, the spirit of others." But if you were anointed as one of the lucky few, everything changed: "On the door of the Jew with money no watch was set; the Jew with money stank no more, and no magistracy clapped a ridiculous, pointed cap on his head. The princes and great lords needed him, they could not make wars and levy regiments without him, they allowed him to spread himself in their sunlight and to grow great and magnificent." Feuchtwanger didn't have to add: temporarily. There's no opportunity for a full Jewish life in such a choice, is there?

The biblical court Jews had it easier than the real-life ones. All of them wound up not only ably serving the ruler but also, and more significantly, helping Jews to escape whichever of the terrible fates that are periodically visited on us was lurking at that moment. (One reason the German Jews in America became so uncomfortable with Purim was that in the Book of Esther, Mordecai leads a merciless revenge on the enemies of the Jews, which we are commanded to celebrate joyously forever.) The Book of Genesis ends with the peaceful deaths of Joseph's father Jacob, the last of the patriarchs, and then of Joseph himself. The Book of Exodus begins—as if anticipating the plot of *Jud Süss*—with the ascension of a new Pharaoh "who knew not Joseph." It's Pharaoh's failure to realize the advantages of Jews, especially court Jews, that sets off the great drama of mass enslavement, oppression, and escape from Egypt. Joseph didn't have to see that. Looking for lessons in his story, I see that, in contrast to many real-life court Jews, he never forgot who he was, and that, when he had the chance, he used his power to serve his people. He advocated not only for his large family but for the whole Hebrew tribe, for whom, as vizier, he secured the fruitful land of Goshen as an Egyptian home.

The scriptural court Jew is never vain. Joseph didn't imagine, and never said, that his special skills were the product of his own abilities, rather than of his covenanted relationship with God. "Not I!" he tells Pharaoh, who has asked Joseph to explain a dream he has had. "God will see to Pharaoh's welfare." Later, he forgives his brothers for having sold him into slavery and telling their father that he was dead; he puts the higher principle of reunion above the option of cutting them off, which the combination of his high status and his understandable bitterness would have made possible. Through the whole story, he adapts, but he doesn't assimilate. For centuries learned rabbis have scratched their heads over why Joseph had his father and then himself embalmed, and, in his father's case, why Joseph staged a grand funeral procession from Egypt back to the land of Canaan, where Jacob was buried. These are profound violations of Jewish burial law. But the point is that Jacob, and later Joseph, were both buried back home, with their people, not in Egypt. The result—solidarity—and not the means of achieving it that circumstances dictated, is the point.

EXCLUSION

Very near the end of his life, when he was in his midnineties and no longer able to leave Quercus, Father wrote my sister and me to ask whether we'd like him to propose us for membership in the New Orleans Country Club, which drew the same kind of people as the elite Mardi Gras krewes. Pop, he explained, had been a founding member of the club when it was organized back in 1914 and he was a thirty-year-old rising lawyer, but some time after that it had adopted a policy that no Jews were allowed to join—as far as Father knew, he, having been admitted on the principle of inheritance, was the only Jewish member. We all knew he didn't have much time left. Perhaps he could seize the moment and get us in, also on the inheritance principle. Otherwise it would be too late. We had gone to the club occasionally for my whole life, including for holiday meals long after I had moved away. These presented a tableau of undiluted Southernness: long tables of rich foods, candied yams and pecan pies and roasts, in silver dishes spread over white tablecloths, presided over by uniformed and elaborately deferential Black people. Large, elegantly dressed extended families (the men in blazers, the women in pearls, the boys wearing jackets, the girls dresses) sat at long tables. People greeted one another jovially. As I thought about it, Father had a point: I couldn't remember ever seeing any other Jews there.

At about the same time, I ran across an article in *The Journal of Negro History*—I'll explain the racial connection later—that said Pop's closest friend in New Orleans, Edgar Stern, two years younger, a fellow German Jew and Harvard graduate, had been offered membership in the Boston Club, which was even more elite, and more firmly forbidden to Jews, than the New Orleans Country Club. "Stern asked if the invitation included his life-long friend Monte Lemann," the article said. "The membership committee expressed regrets and Stern politely declined membership." I showed this to Father, who followed these matters of Jewish exclusion very closely, though never with the intention of openly protesting them. He said indignantly that it couldn't possibly be true: if the Boston Club were going to admit only one Jew, it would have been Pop, not Edgar Stern. The larger context was similar to what it was at the New Orleans Country Club, and also the Mardi Gras krewes: Jews had been admitted to the Boston Club until some time in the second decade of the twentieth century, and then the doors had closed, firmly and forever.

Back in 1879, Pop's Alsatian-born uncle Lazard Kahn, not yet thirty but already a rising and confident businessman in Cincinnati, soon to marry Jacob and Miriam Lemann's daughter Coralie, wrote a letter to Thomas Nast, the famous cartoonist for *Harper's Weekly*.

"My esteemed sir," he began, in a strong, assertively calligraphed hand, and went on to suggest that Nast turn his satirical and moralizing attention to some recent highly publicized incidents in which Jews had been denied admission to fashionable hotels in New York. These had resounded widely in German-Jewish America. The best known of them had one of the leading German-Jewish bankers, Joseph Seligman, turning up in 1878 at the elegant Grand Union Hotel in Saratoga Springs, New York, a resort some hours north of New York City where people would go to take the waters, and being told that henceforth no Jews could stay there. The story has an alternate explanation, which is that the hotel's owner, Henry Hilton, was a political enemy of Seligman (Hilton was an ally of the Tammany Hall political machine, Seligman a reformer) and had merely used antisemitism as a pretext. Nonetheless, as Lazard Kahn noted, other hotels soon followed suit. So did high-society subdivisions, resorts, apartment buildings, and clubs—and, even more consequentially, prestigious employers like banks, industrial corporations, law firms, universities, museums, and publishing houses. A new age of Jewish exclusion in the United States was beginning. Thomas Nast did not produce a cartoon; indeed, a few years earlier, during the 1873 financial panic, *Harper's Weekly* had published a cartoon that showed hook-nosed bankers profiting from the crisis.

This business of not being admitted to hotels was ancient. In *Jud Süss* there is a scene in which Oppenheimer, the court Jew, arrives at an inn, in the early 1700s, in the company of a traditionally dressed Jewish companion; Oppenheimer is admitted, his companion is turned away. Perhaps the ongoing progress of the modern world would finally bring an end to all this. Was that too much to expect? Or would admission be reserved for the more acceptable Jews and denied to the rest, so that court Jews would have to distance themselves from their coreligionists in order to enjoy their privileges? In any case, these hotel incidents profoundly violated the German Jews' preferred version of their progress in America. There had been signs everywhere of their increasing acceptance: their children were beginning to go to the leading universities, members of the group were entering the professions. Could this really be ending so quickly? It's much clearer now where things were going than it was at the time: inclusion, briefly, followed by exclusion.

Bernard Lemann had occasionally stayed at the Grand Union Hotel during the 1860s, when he was living in New York. (Joseph Seligman himself had been a regular guest, before he was turned away.) In 1883, vacationing in Saratoga from Donaldsonville, Bernard groused to his brother Myer about being consigned to a boardinghouse and noted that the Grand Union seemed to have lost most of its business. We were in a strange equipoise, as we moved into the wider society. Everything went magically well, and then, at not completely predictable moments, the door would close. In 1902, Ferdinand, Bernard's eldest son, on his honeymoon, having heard that President Theodore Roosevelt welcomed visits from Harvard graduates, arranged for his bride and himself to be received at the White House—at least according to family legend—by the President himself. In New Orleans, Pop, along with being a founding member of the New Orleans Country Club, was welcomed as the second-named partner in Monroe & Lemann. But, balanced against these triumphs, he couldn't have lunch with Mr. Monroe. Instead he, Edgar Stern, and one or two other German-Jewish friends would eat at Kolb's, a venerable German restaurant downtown, deeply cured in generations of its patrons' cigar smoke, that endured, with tuxedoed waiters serving schnitzel and potato dumplings under ceiling fans powered by a system of rubber transmission belts, into the late twentieth century.

In New York the leading German Jews did not react to the crisis that the Grand Union Hotel incident represented by appealing to the humanitarian impulses of Gentiles, in the manner of Lazard Kahn's letter to Nast. Instead, many of them came to see their new and unexpected troubles as the result of the mass emigration of Jews from Eastern Europe that was just getting underway—so the way to combat anti-Jewish prejudice would be to do something about them, not to do something about prejudice. Before 1880 there were 300,000 Jews in the United States, most of them German. Between 1880 and 1920 another 2.5 million Jews arrived, overwhelmingly from Eastern Europe. They weren't just far more numerous than the German Jews, they were more observant, more concentrated in urban slums, and much poorer.

In 1891, three leading German Jews—a Schiff, a Seligman, and a Straus—asked President Benjamin Harrison to send a delegation to Russia to persuade the czar to adopt more lenient policies toward the Jews, and to stanch the rising incidence of pogroms, so Russian Jews wouldn't feel they had to immigrate to the United States. Another German-Jewish project was the Galveston Plan (1907–1914), funded by a Schiff and endorsed by an act of Congress, which aimed to steer Jewish immigrants away from New York and other big cities, where there were highly visible Jewish slums. A third initiative was funding the Jewish Theological Seminary, for Conservative Jews, in the hope of steering the Conservative movement in a direction that would strike Gentiles as academically respectable. Another was establishing a Yiddish-language newspaper called the *Jewish World*, funded once again by Seligmans, Schiffs, Strauses, and the like, as an alternative to the unmannerly homegrown press, which was both sensational and socialist, at least to the German Jews' way of thinking. Still another was funding settlement houses near the Lower East Side slums. Funding the early Jewish agricultural settlements in Palestine for Eastern European Jewish refugees aimed to provide a destination that wasn't New York.

Surely there was compassion in these efforts—maybe even the enhanced compassion you would feel for people who were like you in some way. But it didn't extent to actual mingling. As a son of the German-Jewish financier Felix Warburg wrote about his father, who contributed millions to the aid of Jews in distress, "He disliked almost everything about the Jews except their problems." At least in cities bigger than New Orleans, German Jews established their own social organizations, which excluded Eastern European Jews in the same way that Gentile social organizations excluded them. As the advent of Jim Crow had recategorized the Creoles of Louisiana in the minds of whites, identifying them with the poor masses of their race, emigration from Eastern Europe had recategorized the German Jews in the minds of Gentiles—but, not having to confront an impediment as legally impenetrable as the color line, the German Jews imagined that they could maintain their own category. The evidence was mounting that the intra-Jewish distinction that was so obvious to them wasn't to the non-Jewish world.

In France in the late nineteenth century, as antisemitism was stirring in Germany, a Jewish army captain, Alfred Dreyfus, was put on trial on false charges of treason. Dreyfus's sensational case turned him into a public enemy, and made it clear that France, site of one of the earliest programs of Jewish emancipation, was not friendly to Jews either. Dreyfus could have been a member of my family: he was the son of an Alsatian peddler who had made himself into a textile manufacturer. Theodor Herzl, the journalist who founded the modern Zionist movement, was converted by the Dreyfus case from a typically assimilated, secular Western European Jew into someone who believed the time had come, only a few years into full emancipation, to declare the Diaspora a failure and create a Jewish nation. This did not appeal, to say the least, to German Jews in America. No idea was more threatening to our subtribe at the turn of the twentieth century than Zionism. We wanted to blend in, to be unobtrusive, to be accepted. Zionism was loud, insistent, separatist, tribal. Zionism called attention to the unsettling reality that millions of Jews in Europe wanted to leave—many, no doubt, for America rather than Palestine. Reform Judaism's slogan was that we were a religion, not a race. Zionism was a secular movement rooted in Jewish identity: race, not religion. Zionism demanded solidarity, not keeping a distance from the sorrows of the Jewish mass.

Just as America's carriage-trade institutions were systematically excluding Jews, the German Jews' Reform institutions systematically excluded or expelled Zionists. Their script and our script were fundamentally inconsistent. Kaufmann Kohler, the German-born Reform rabbi who in the mid-1880s had convened the gathering that produced the Pittsburgh Platform, became the president of the Reform movement's Hebrew Union College in Cincinnati in 1903. He purged all Zionists from its faculty; he also would not let Zionists speak there. Judah Magnes, a rabbi at the grandest of all Reform houses of worship, the palatial Temple Emanu-El on Fifth Avenue in New York City, was forced out in 1910 after he'd delivered a Passover sermon calling for bringing back the bar mitzvah and other Reform-banned elements of traditional observance. (Magnes, who was also suspect for being, by Temple Emanu-El standards, too Zionist, wound up relocating to Palestine.) In 1918 the Central Conference of American Rabbis, the national Reform organization, issued a statement condemning the Balfour Declaration, the British government's official recognition of the Jewish people's right to a homeland in Palestine—holy writ to most Jews. "The ideal of the Jew is not the establishment of a Jewish state— not the reassertion of Jewish nationality which has long been outgrown," the statement said.

SOUTHERN REFORM

What were Pop and Edgar Stern doing in *The Journal of Negro History*? They were among the founders of Dillard University, the historically Black school in New Orleans that succeeded Straight College, where some of the Juliens in Donaldsonville had gone. Pop was a trustee of Dillard for more than forty years. I have a hazy early memory of being taken to a celebration of his seventy-fifth birthday there in 1959, just a few months before he died, when I was four years old. I have a copy of the program, which evokes the spirit of schools like Dillard in places like New Orleans in those days: the university choir first sang a series of classical choral pieces, by Bach and others, and then "five Negro spirituals." Afterward there was a debate between the Dillard and Harvard debating teams (topic unrecorded) in Stern Hall.

Edgar Stern was a cotton broker, a member of a prosperous family of New Orleans German Jews. The local branch of Lehman Brothers, after it was called Lehman and Abraham, was called Lehman and Stern. In 1921 he ascended to a much higher economic plane when he married Edith Rosenwald, the daughter of Julius Rosenwald, who as head of the giant retailer Sears, Roebuck was one of the richest men in America. In the early twentieth century, German Jews were among the very few prominent and established white people who publicly supported Black causes. Their positions on racial matters were a long way short of what would be acceptable today, and there was always a measure of cynicism in Black America about their involvement: they were promoting an end to prejudice partly in the hope that if prejudice ever did end, that would benefit them too. Still, they were willing to go in a direction opposite to the way the tide was running.

Recall that Rosenwald had formed a partnership with Booker T. Washington, head of the Tuskegee Institute in Alabama and one of the most celebrated Black men in America—though he isn't so celebrated today, because of his willingness not to challenge the Jim Crow system as long as he felt it was possible to improve Black people's situation within it. Rosenwald and Washington together built more than five thousand modest, solid, wooden schoolhouses in the South, with matching funds contributed by Black people locally, to replace the existing system of one-room windowless shacks, or no schools at all. Louisiana's first Black chief justice, Bernette Joshua Johnson, who was born in 1943 in the all-Black hamlet of Lemannville, a few miles south of Donaldsonville, got her early education at a Rosenwald school.

In Edgar Stern's papers there is a composition he wrote when he was a student at Harvard, on the question of whether the Fifteenth Amendment to the Constitution, guaranteeing Black people's voting rights—ratified three and a half decades earlier, then nullified through the federal government's acquiescence to white terrorism—should be repealed. He had trouble making up his mind: you get a sense that the standard views of whites in New Orleans had a strong hold on him. He was "firmly convinced that the negro voter (in La. at least) is more often than not merely the tool of unscrupulous politicians," although, on the other hand, "I have no prejudices on the subject beyond the common, and I think natural, antipathy of the Southern white man to the negro as a social equal." (His instructor wrote at the bottom of the page, "You need to be extremely careful of prejudices.") Perhaps in part because of his marital connection to Rosenwald, Stern over the years became one of the leading local white champions and funders of Black causes, though never departing from Booker T. Washington's idea of promoting racial progress without going all-in on racial integration. Edith Stern, his wife, a small, slender, impeccably elegant woman, whom I knew growing up as someone with an air of absolutely confident authority that was terrifying to a little boy, was a notch or two more liberal than her husband.

In the same year that Edgar and Edith Stern married, 1921, Pop married Nettie Hyman, a daughter of another rich Jewish cotton broker in New Orleans. Photographs of them in those days show Nettie, thin and angular, in fur-collared coats and short brown hair done up in the neatly marcelled waves that were stylish in the twenties; Pop, just as well tonsured, in silk ties and double-breasted suits, his small eyes looking out at the world in a steady appraising gaze. Nettie's father worked for a family business called Hiller/Hyman—that's the same Hiller who was driven out of Summit, Mississippi, by Whitecaps—and her mother, Clara Newman, came from yet another large family of German-Jewish cotton brokers.

What I know about the life of this extended clan comes mostly

Monte M. Lemann in the 1920s,
around age forty.

from a short memoir that Nettie's younger sister Lillian wrote in old age, with the help of her grandson. From this you get a plummy picture of stone mansions on St. Charles Avenue, small armies of servants (hairdressers, dressmakers, upstairs maids), large heavy multicourse meals, evenings at the New Orleans opera house, long summer trips to Europe to visit spas in the hope of curing unspecified illnesses. Surely these relatives of mine didn't have as much money as the great industrialists and financiers of New York and Chicago, but being in a caste system enabled them to live almost as luxuriously, as if they were rajahs in India.

The memoir is full of small, well-remembered slights. The Newmans, who came from the same part of Germany as the Lemanns, looked down on the Hymans, because they came from Poland. But then there was some kind of business scandal at the Newmans' brokerage—H. and C. Newman, known colloquially, I always heard, as Hook and Crook Newman—that couldn't be discussed openly at home but that diminished the family's status. (There was a two-paragraph story about it in *The New York Times* in 1902, under the headline "NEW ORLEANS COTTON BROKERS EXPELLED." The *Times* said, "The affair has created a

tremendous sensation.")
According to Lil-
lian, Isidore, the third
Newman brother after
Henry and Charles,
founded New Orleans's
leading private school,
which is named after
him, in order to restore
the Newman name. I've
seen a few artifacts from
those days: ponderous
amber cut-glass wine
goblets, dinner plates
rimmed in gold leaf,
photographs of long
dinner tables populated
by moustachioed, portly
men and women in ruf-
fled dresses.

Nettie Hyman Lemann in the 1920s,
around age thirty.

Nettie, in Lillian's telling, was always the favorite. Lillian was given a string of pearls by their parents, only to find that Nettie had been given a more valuable string of pearls. Lillian was taken to a Paris couturier, but she was told that she couldn't have the dress she most wanted because it was too similar to the dress Nettie had chosen. Nettie was sent to a Swiss boarding school, then returned to New Orleans to make her debut, then was sent to a girls' finishing school in New York called Miss Finch's. Father's version of her life story was that when she returned to New Orleans and encountered Pop, the rising and serious young lawyer, she was worried he would think she was too flighty and insubstantial. So she went to nursing school and became a surgical nurse at Touro Infirmary, a bloody job that wouldn't have been a standard occupation for a Jewish debutante. Father had a copy of her application letter, which of course doesn't mention Pop but otherwise matches his version of her life story. Nettie wrote the nursing school:

> My home surroundings have been of the most pleasant, and, perhaps, luxurious kind. My parents have given me everything in their power to further my happiness. They have given me great educational advantages, having put me in a boarding school in Switzerland where I might learn French, and also in schools in the East, where I might put the "finishing touches" on the education acquired at High School. Since finishing school I have merely amused myself, having never sought or desired an occupation until this time. My father's occupation is that of cotton brokerage, and his position has made me free from domestic responsibilities and from the necessity of being a contributor toward the support of my family.

Another result of Nettie's choice of career besides the marriage, most likely, was that she contracted tuberculosis, another of the diseases that life in Louisiana visited on our family through the years. Her life with Pop looks to me now like a blend of luxury and suffering. The drugs that cure tuberculosis hadn't been invented. In photographs, as the years pass, Nettie is ever thinner and more drawn, and ever more elegantly dressed. Family letters are full of talk about setbacks, trips to hospitals, gruesome-sounding experimental treatments that don't quite work. In the 1930s the Sterns built what must have been the grandest house in New Orleans, at the outer edge of the city. It was designed to look like a Palladian villa from the front and a Louisiana plantation house from the back, and was surrounded by elaborate formal gardens. After the Sterns died, Father went to a great deal of effort to have it made into a museum open to the public. The Lemanns were there constantly, and they lived in a large and elegant house of their own in Uptown New Orleans, right around the corner from the house on St. Charles Avenue where Pop had spent the later years of his childhood.

I have the sense that the way of life that had emerged among the German Jews in New York by the early twentieth century took some time to reach distant, provincial New Orleans. In Lillian's memoir, she describes a childhood of de rigueur attendance at Sabbath services, both on Friday night and on Saturday morning, followed in each case by a holiday meal for the extended family. There was a Passover seder, preceded by days of scrubbing the house to remove any trace of *chametz*, bread. When a son was born, a wide circle of family and friends came to the house for the bris. When Lillian's grandparents, in small-town Summit, Mississippi, celebrated their fiftieth anniversary, they reenacted their wedding ceremony with a rabbi presiding. I don't think a similarly situated German-Jewish family in New York would have done all this. The two institutional associations of Bernard Lemann's youth in New York City, the gaudily celebratory Purim Association and the anti-Reform *Jewish Messenger*, went out of business in 1902 and 1903, respectively. They'd become too Jewish for the German Jews.

It's even more striking that the rabbi at Temple Sinai, Maximilian Heller, the man who gave Pop his boyhood Hebrew lessons, was possibly the leading vocal Zionist in the entire American Reform movement. This would not have been tolerated at Temple Emanu-El, and indeed it wasn't: in 1903 Heller, fifteen years into his tenure at Temple Sinai, made himself a candidate for the rabbi's job there. He wrote to a friend that he was "heartily tired of New Orleans" and eager to leave. The friend told him he'd have to play down his Zionism if he wanted the New York job. We don't know what happened in his job interview, but he wasn't hired, and he wound up serving for another quarter century at Temple Sinai, where his views hadn't yet become as unacceptable in the community as they were in New York. Heller had been brought up in the Jewish ghetto in Prague as what we'd now call Orthodox, but in the United States he wound up being trained at Hebrew Union College in Cincinnati.

A loyal protégé to Isaac Mayer Wise, the very Reform head of the seminary (and the officiant at Jacob Lemann's funeral), Heller waited until a year after Wise had died to reveal publicly his Zionist views. The Reform movement may have renounced the kosher laws in their entirety, but it was not so relaxed on all topics; Zionism was strictly *treyf.* Heller also spoke out in favor of the immigration of Russian Jews, whom he called "the Hebrew of the Hebrews," the people who might restore the magic of traditional observance that the Reform movement had cast aside in the vain hope of acceptance. He denounced pogroms in Eastern Europe. He defended Leo Frank (who wrote him a thank-you note). He was also a public champion of civil rights for Black people. W. E. B. Du Bois quoted him in *The Crisis.* Du Bois's archrival, Booker T. Washington, invited him to be the commencement speaker at Tuskegee.

Heller finally retired in 1927, the year after Father was born, and soon after that Temple Sinai moved to a large new home in Uptown, designed by Moise Goldstein, Pop's friend and regular lunch companion at Kolb's, right across the street from the house Bernard Lemann had built at the end of the nineteenth century. It's still there, a large square pile of pale brick and stone and cement with decorative embellishments meant to read as "Oriental," with a seating capacity of more than a thousand and, more in the manner of a church than a synagogue, an organ and a place for a choir (discreetly concealed). Heller had presided over the temple for forty years, since it was only a few years old, and had built it up into a preeminent position in the South. Perhaps that, plus his eminence in the wider world, plus the goodwill he'd built up through the hundreds of weddings and funerals he'd performed, gave him leeway to depart from the majority views of the community.

But it was also true that, at least when he was first appointed, German Jews in New Orleans were not only more free to be openly Jewish than they would have been in New York, they were also, at least as Father handed down the story to me, more fully accepted by the Gentile gentry. According to Father, Henry Abraham, the local representative of the Lehman brothers and father-in-law to Myer Lemann, was a member of the most prestigious of the Mardi Gras organizations, Comus. And there was the famous example of the first Rex, the king of Carnival, having been a Jew. If you accept the thinking of the German Jews in New York, it may have been that because New Orleans was the destination for many fewer Eastern European Jews than New York, it could be a safer haven for German Jews. It's hard to think of a leading business-law firm in New York in the early twentieth century that had one Christian and one Jewish name partner, as Monroe & Lemann did. Surely Mr. Monroe was happy to be in business with someone who was as bright and well connected as Pop, and Pop must have been essential in acquiring the firm's important clients who were Jewish, like the Sterns, or J. Aron and Company, a coffee importer that many years later was bought by Goldman Sachs, or Sam Zemurray, a rough and unlettered, but very successful, immigrant Jew from Moldova who was on his way to becoming the king of the banana business.

Outside of New Orleans, as Jewish immigrants from Eastern Europe kept arriving, they—indeed, collectively, Jews—became increasingly upsetting to the better sort of American Gentiles, and those who put their sentiments into words often resorted to the new vocabulary of race science that was becoming part of the lingua franca of their class. Because we are so accustomed to thinking of racism as unacceptable, it's jarring to encounter its pervasiveness among those who thought of themselves as the better, more progressive sort of people, little more than a century ago. And it's also jarring to see that among the principal targets of racism back then were people we now think of as white, but who weren't thought of that way then. Jacob Riis, anything but a voice of conservatism, took the readers of his fiery reformist book *How the Other Half Lives* (1890) to New York's Jewish Lower East Side, which he said was the most densely populated square mile in the world at that moment: "Thrift is the watchword of Jewtown, as of its people the world over. It is at once its strength and its fatal weakness, its cardinal virtue and its foul disgrace. . . . Money is their God. Life itself is of little value compared with even the leanest bank account. In no other spot does life wear so intensely bald and materialistic an aspect as in Ludlow Street." Others who made these journeys into the ghettos came away with similar exotic, disgusted impressions. Poor Jewish immigrants were part of an undifferentiated flood, a swarm, a tide, devoid of individual humanity. Henry James, visiting the Lower East Side a few years after Riis, compared its crowded fire escapes to "a little world of bars and perches and swings for human squirrels and monkeys." The historian Frederick Jackson Turner found Boston's North End to be "fairly packed with swarthy sons and daughters of the tribe of Israel."

When, somehow, a Jew escaped this environment and became prosperous, that didn't make him any less repellent—if anything, the opposite. He was vulgar, flashy, corrupt, powerful, able to change the whole nature of society for the worse. The aristocratic historian Henry Adams, who began focusing on the Jews after the 1893 financial panic, wrote to a friend, "For the first time in history, the blood is vitiated. The Jew has got into the soul. I see him—or her—now everywhere, and wherever he—or she—goes, there must remain a taint in the blood forever." Edith Wharton's fictional characters Simon Rosedale, in *The House of Mirth*, and Julius Beaufort, in *The Age of Innocence*, neither explicitly Jewish but both with certain familiar traits (financial expertise, mysterious background, ambition for an undeserved place in high society) are usually assumed to be based on August Belmont, the Rothschild representative who was one of the few Jews who got into range of Wharton's social world. When F. Scott Fitzgerald, in the 1920s, sent Wharton a copy of *The Great Gatsby*, with its cameo appearance by a heavily accented Jewish gangster named Meyer Wolfsheim, who wore cuff links fashioned from human teeth, she wrote him, "It's enough to make this reader happy to have met your *perfect* Jew." Even the extremely rare public intellectual who wasn't actively antisemitic usually felt, as the pioneering Jew-friendly Christian Wilhelm von Dohm in eighteenth-century Germany had, that there was something wrong, something unacceptable, about the Jews one encountered in the mainstream of society. Randolph Bourne, writing in *The Atlantic* in 1916 as a brave and lonely voice in favor of what we'd now call muliticulturalism, said, "It is not the Jew who sticks proudly to the faith of his fathers and boasts of that venerable culture of his who is dangerous to America, but the Jew who has lost the Jewish fire and become a mere elementary, grasping animal."

A decade or two into the twentieth century, these attitudes arrived in New Orleans, and when they did, they stuck. Doors that had almost miraculously opened to Jews who aspired to operate outside the confines of the community began to close, after just a few years, and soon the doors to the United States itself substantially closed with the passage of the Johnson-Reed Act, a strict immigration restriction that Congress passed in 1924. In the South, racial ordering was overwhelmingly aimed at Black people, and since it was essential to everything about the operation of society, it was particularly pervasive and entrenched. Other ethnic groups were collateral damage. The largest mass lynching in American history took place in New Orleans in 1911—of eleven Italian immigrants who had been accused, but not convicted, of murdering the chief of police. (Lynchings of Black people were far more numerous, but typically individual.) New Orleans's German Jews, too, became a little less white than they had been. When you look at Mardi Gras, when you really think about it—its origins during the time Reconstruction was being overthrown and Jim Crow instituted, its heavy use of mystical-nationalist symbolism, its self-conscious adoption of titles of nobility, its cherished custom of parading men through the streets on horseback dressed in hooded robes—it's hard to imagine how it could have avoided excluding us sooner or later. Like the Louisiana Creoles, only with far milder consequences, the German Jews were being joined to the much larger, poorer, and more obviously visible mass of their ethnic group. With exceptions like the immovably fierce, prophetic Rabbi Max Heller, they responded to this more often through self-isolation than solidarity. And this order lasted in New Orleans far longer than it did in the rest of the country, well into the time when I was growing up. I've come to think of this as a gift, in a way: it put me in closer touch with the totality of Jewish experience than Jews who grew up in friendlier circumstances in postwar America were.

"A SUPPLICANT AT MANY GATES"

In our world, the Pharaoh who knew not Joseph was the grave, lavishly moustachioed Boston Brahmin Abbott Lawrence Lowell, who became president of Harvard in 1909. Lowell's long-serving predecessor, Charles William Eliot, had not erected barriers to keep Jews out of Harvard, but Lowell did. I came across a letter one of the New Orleans Sterns, a member of the Harvard class of 1922, wrote just after he had graduated to Louis Marshall, a New York lawyer who functioned as the de facto secretary of state of the established American German Jews, about the situation there. He told Marshall, "The clash is between the Jews of the New England towns and the scions of the blue blooded New England aristocracy of which President Lowell is so splendid an example. The Jews of New England are for the most part sons of poorer families or those who are wealthy are often unnecessarily ostentatious." These Jews were seen as being, on one hand, excessively studious, unathletic, and not well rounded or companionable, and on the other unethical and oversexed. There had been some unfortunate incidents that young Maurice Stern had helped to keep from becoming publicly known—for example, some Jewish boys had been caught with girls in their rooms, and then expelled.

Now, "it is evident that Harvard is willing to keep out some Jews though it will never attempt to keep out all Jews. . . . You may be certain of this that the Jew will be limited in the number of representatives he will have at Harvard. It may be admitted that the Jew is less socially desirable than the non-Jew." All this left Stern feeling deeply concerned about being grouped with people he felt were so different from himself, and whose presence had made life difficult for him. "Thirty percent of the Jews in the class of 1922 are immigrant Jews almost entirely from Russia," he told Marshall. "They are products of their environment. They bring that environment with them. Is it Jewish or Russian? . . . Can I be a Jew and an American at the same time in the same way I can be an American and a Catholic? Must I always be an hyphenate? Am I when I am born in America and my parents worship in a synagogue an American Jew or an American-Jew?"

That same year, one of the most prominent German Jews in America, Walter Lippmann—Harvard class of 1910, already a celebrated journalist and intellectual, advisor (or court Jew, one might say) to presidents, and a close friend of Felix Frankfurter—wrote an article in a Reform publication called *The American Hebrew*, arguing that "the rich and vulgar and pretentious Jews of our big American cities are perhaps the greatest misfortune that has ever befallen the Jewish people. They are the real fountain of anti-Semitism. When they rush about in super-automobiles, bejeweled and furred and painted and over-barbered, when they build themselves French chateaux and Italian palazzi, they stir up the latent hatred against crude wealth." Lippmann's friends called him Buddha, because of his round face and serene manner, but the Jewish question roused him out of his customary calm. His early writings about Jews display a deep physical revulsion, a conviction that antisemitism was fully justified by Jewish behavior and curable only by Jews' de-Judaicizing themselves. Lippmann surely understood that to get where he wanted to go in American society, he had to show that he wasn't one of *those* Jews, but his adoption of elite loathing of Jews was more than a conscious stance, it was something he fully shared.

Consulted privately by Harvard about whether it should institute a Jewish quota, as it soon in fact did, Lippmann drafted a letter considering the idea seriously and finding merit in it, though he ultimately opposed a strict numerical quota. "I do not regard the

Jews as innocent victims," he wrote. "They hand on unconsciously and uncritically from one generation to another many distressing personal and social habits." He went on to say forthrightly, "my sympathies are with the non-Jew. His personal manners and physical habits are, I believe, distinctly superior to the habits and manners of the Jews." In 1933, Lippmann wrote a column downplaying the importance of the antisemitic policies Adolf Hitler had begun instituting in his first months as chancellor in Germany, and calling him "the authentic voice of a genuinely civilized people." Felix Frankfurter, formerly a close friend, stopped speaking to him for several years. In all his copious writings during the midcentury peak of his career as a columnist, Lippmann never mentioned the Holocaust.

My family hadn't risen high enough, and wasn't yet far enough from its religious roots, to have become actively antisemitic like Lippmann. Instead, what I see among my relatives is something more poignant, a yearning for the wider world to embrace the Jews, to consider Jewish causes to be the causes of all morally aware people. It was thrilling to most Jews that President Theodore Roosevelt publicly condemned the Kishinev pogrom, a four-day killing spree in a Moldovan village that had begun on Easter Sunday 1903 and was the most publicized incident of collective violence against European Jews until Kristallnacht. Lazard Kahn, Pop's uncle, composed an indignant letter to a newspaper writer who had speculated that Roosevelt had done this to curry favor with Jewish voters. No! He was merely making the czar aware of "civilized international opinion." A wrong done to Jews was a wrong done to humanity.

Lazard Kahn lived for another twenty-five years after he wrote this. In 1926, not long before he died, he read a book that greatly disturbed him: *Israel*, by Ludwig Lewisohn, a German-born Jewish intellectual who had become a Zionist. Lewisohn treated America's Reform, assimilationist German Jews—people a couple of steps up the social ladder from Kahn—with vicious contempt, which surely stung all the more because he wasn't completely ignorant about the Jews he was condemning, as most critics of Jews were. Lewisohn offered a lurid picture of Jews longing for an acceptance that would never arrive, cutting themselves off from their heritage piece by piece in the vain hope that each successive casting off would finally propitiate the Gentiles, adopting an elaborate, overripe admiration for anything not Jewish and a matching hypersensitivity to whatever flaws might be attributed to anything identifiably Jewish. Hence the Reform Jew: "He is a generation or two removed from ritual or religious observance; he does not know his ancestral tongue or the history or legends of his people; his children are not permitted to hear even those scraps of colloquial Hebrew that persist longest. He is an American, an *American!*"

Traversing the Jewish world, Lewisohn found the situation in Germany comparable, or maybe worse: "Here, if anywhere, the Gentile invitation to assimilate, to become part of the nation and of the national culture was accepted. Here was the classical land of assimilation. And in this land arose the modern anti-Semitic movement and the theory which, for the obvious purpose of excluding Jewry from the work and the councils of the nation, substituted the Aryan or Nordic for the old-fashioned Christian State. Between the fear that the Jew will damn the Christian soul and the fear that the Semite will contaminate the Aryan mind the difference is small." Either way, "the Jew of Germany and of America is a supplicant at many gates; he treads up the weary stairs of others . . . the stairs wind up and up. There is no end." But when Lewisohn visited Vilna, which to the minds of upper-class German Jews was the most tribal and deprived Jewish ghetto imaginable, he did not find the same impulse to self-erase: "Amid the inconceivable squalor of this place, from the crooked, crippled, crazily winding alleys of its noisome Ghetto, arose again and again the dignity of learning and the authority of scriptural power." But that was only a better alternative to assimilation, not a fully satisfying one. The real place for Jewish life, for the Jewish future, was Palestine.

All this was too much for Lazard Kahn. There must be a better way for the Jews than to bind together and remove themselves from the society they had struggled so mightily to join, and instead to emigrate again, this time into self-exile. Instead, Jews and Christians could explore their commonality, their potential for cooperation. Such optimism is understandable in someone born into primitive, impoverished conditions in an Alsatian ghetto, who was now a rich and respected American citizen. "If such associations were sincerely established and maintained," he wrote, "if they were free from intolerance and prejudice and founded on mutual respect, they would soon demonstrate the hollowness of current Gentile accusations against Jews."

Let's not be too quick to award the match to Lewisohn, who devoted the last half of his book to describing a promising present and a utopian future for the Jews in Palestine that today seems no more realistic than German Jews' dreams of complete acceptance in Germany and the United States. In Palestine the Lewisohn who had detected the structure, even the grandeur, in Eastern European ghetto life has forgotten himself and gone into a swoon over the new Jew, the farmer in Palestine. The new Jew was bronzed, muscular, shirtless, hatless, clean-shaven, confident (if male); buxom, with luxuriant wavy hair and loose peasant blouses and skirts (if female); equally conversant in modern agricultural methods, folk dancing, and the landmarks of Western thought, committed to social justice, relatively secular. The Zionist paradise would bring the long centuries of Jewish self-expression in inelegant Yiddish to a close, in favor of the higher languages of Hebrew, English, and German. There would be no formal apparatus of a state, no military, no use of force, no colonization (even though the new Jews referred to themselves as colonists). Although, in truth, "the Arab cannot by any possibility reach the level of our economic and political thinking," Jewish-dominated Palestine would nonetheless also zealously protect Arab rights. This kind of thinking dominates the writings of liberal Zionist American Jews who found their way to Palestine in the 1920s. Max Heller, after retiring from Temple Sinai, spent a month there—his first and last trip—in 1927, and came back similarly exhilarated, convinced that the Jews were building a modern, peaceful society in what he managed to persuade himself was an empty, uncivilized land.

In the way that Lewisohn presented his Palestinian fantasy, one can see that he hadn't escaped the grip of the Jewish question any more than have the assimilated Jews he discussed with such contempt. Even for him the true Jew, the *ur*-Jew, the money handler, the obsessive text studier, needed to be improved, rather than being accepted as is; this was why "the transformation of the Eastern Ghetto Jew into the free and erect Palestinian will tend to clear and heal one of the festering wounds of civilization." But didn't this assume that there was something irreparably damaged about the dominant Jewish culture of the Diaspora, and that Palestine had to be constructed as a kind of gesture, a riposte, aimed at people who didn't like Jews, rather than a straightforward and authentic manifestation of Jewish culture? "The Anti-Semite who speaks of a nation of hucksters and exploiters and middlemen and commercial nomads ought to be finally silenced," Lewisohn announced. That doesn't say much for Jewish life up to this point, does it? And why must Jewishness reorganize itself as a response to the critique of its enemies, rather than being what it actually is?

Some years before Lewisohn's book was published, Coralie and Lazard Kahn, along with another Jewish couple from Cincinnati, made a trip to Palestine. Lazard kept a detailed diary that he sent to their children. Although Lazard and Lewisohn were both born in Europe, Lewisohn grew up postemancipation in an assimilated urban family; Lazard was the product of a religiously observant village *Judenstrasse*. You can see some of the difference this makes in Lazard's openly awed and reverential reactions to his first in-person encounters with holy sites. At the port of Jaffa he thought of the precious minerals and rare woods that had arrived there by ship, to be sent on to Jerusalem to build the Temple, and of Jonah's departure on the sea voyage on which he was swallowed by a whale. At his first glimpse of Jerusalem from the road, "imagine our emotion when beholding it, the center of adoration of myriads of people." At the Temple Mount, where Abraham had offered up Isaac as a sacrifice to God, he was thrilled to be standing in the most sacred spot on earth. He gathered a handful of dirt there, intending to bring it to his relatives back in Ingwiller.

Palestine in the early 1920s was a desperately impoverished, hungry, disease-ridden place, where most improvement efforts were funded by Jewish philanthropists from abroad who saw themselves as creating a kind of spread-out settlement house aimed at helping, in the language of the time, poor unfortunates who were fleeing Eastern European barbarism. The Kahns toured the Jewish Quarter in the old city, where they saw poor and exotic Jews studying Torah and Talmud. They visited the Children's Jewish Orphan Asylum, some of whose residents were freshly arrived survivors of Russian pogroms that had claimed the lives of their parents. Lazard found all this deeply moving, but he ended his account by rejecting Zionism: "because of the rivalry, if not hatred, between Arab and other nationalities now there, it can never be the home of the thousands and millions which our Zionist friends would like to make it, without causing more misery perhaps than exists now." Better, instead, simply to support further modest charitable efforts aimed at improving the condition of the Jews who were there, along, perhaps, with encouraging them to adapt to the modern world.

A hundred years later, we know so much that it takes a determined act of will to try to understand the way these German Jews saw the world—including their dismissal of Zionism. Jews in this privileged subcategory stood apart from the Jewish majority, in Europe and in the United States, where by now they were far outnumbered by Eastern European Jews. The fuel driving Zionism was the constant oppression, poverty, and physical danger in the lives of Jews in Eastern Europe, far more than the empathetic concern of a small cohort within the assimilated Jewish minority. Most German Jews in the United States retained a deep conviction, even after Germany had officially been their enemy during the First World War, that Germany was the seat of Western civilization—of scholarship, of philosophy, of modern statecraft, of science, of literature, of progressive business practices, of music. To their ears, German was a beautiful language.

New Orleans, with the smallest Jewish population of any significant American city—about 1 percent—and the only one where the community was majority Reform, was even more attached, and for longer, to this optimism about Germany than the rest of the Jewish United States. Elsewhere, the pogroms drew more alarmed attention, and so did the 1924 immigration restrictions. After Max Heller died in 1929, there was no strong voice about these matters in Reform Jewish New Orleans. Underneath their pleasant and genteel self-presentation, Jews in New Orleans were surely aware that episodes of ethnic violence weren't so unfamiliar in Louisiana, and that it might not be wise to poke a slumbering beast by calling attention to such episodes elsewhere. But nationally, when Hitler came to power in Germany in 1933, the Reform movement, or at least its rabbinic advance guard, began to change. In 1937, a year before Kristallnacht, the movement produced a new platform that retreated a good deal from the highly assimilationist Pittsburgh Platform of 1885, especially in giving Zionism a qualified endorsement and being more approving of traditional religious observance. Probably the most prominent Reform rabbi during the 1930s and '40s, the Budapest-born, ardently liberal Stephen S. Wise of New York, was an outspoken Zionist.

A few Jewish writers in Germany, who had been watching the Nazis' rise for years, became appropriately alarmed early. Lion Feuchtwanger, the author of *Jud Süss*, and Joseph Roth, the Austrian-born journalist-novelist, both left Germany in 1933. Even the more perceptive—meaning, the less sanguine—American Jews, especially if they were Reform Jews, were slower to wake up. Jacob Rader Marcus, the founder of the Reform movement's American Jewish Archives in Cincinnati, brought out a book in 1934 called *The Rise and Destiny of the German Jew*. On the cover is a picture of a swastika with a large question mark superimposed over it. This level of concern would have put Marcus at the forefront among Reform Jews, but he still imagined assimilation as the worst threat to the Jew in Germany—because, in response to antisemitism, "his tendency was to cling, not to his Judaism, which he had all too often left behind him, but to his newly gotten and dearly gained Germanism." This, to Marcus, could best be remedied through a renewed embrace of Judaism, not through Zionism. For all the depredations already being visited on the Jews by the Nazis—ancient, newly revived techniques like special taxes, confiscations, attacks by thugs, and restrictions from occupations, which Marcus catalogued in some detail—"German Jewry will be safe physically." He was aware that, officially, the Nazis were in favor of exterminating the Jews, but he could not conceive that such a thing could actually happen. The rest of the world would not allow it.

A SENTIMENTAL JOURNEY

It was possible to be much less concerned than Marcus, especially in New Orleans, especially from a position at the pinnacle of the Jewish world, where, if everything is collapsing, if the situation is morally urgent, it calls into question the assumptions underlying the excellent, public-spirited, and comfortable life one is living. I am holding a beautiful object, a leather-covered, gold-accented, hand-bound book called *A Sentimental Journey Through France and Italy (and Other Countries)*. In 1936, when Edgar Stern, Pop's close friend, turned fifty, his wife gave him the gift of a sabbatical. They placed their three children in a Swiss boarding school and spent the year traveling. When they returned, Edith Stern had Edgar's letters home from the trip, accompanied by elegantly composed and printed hand-tipped photographs he had taken, turned into the book I'm holding. The title is a joking reference to Laurence Sterne's novel from 1768. Only fifty copies were printed, given to the Sterns' closest friends and relatives in 1938. Pop and Nettie got one, which they passed on to Father, and which I have now. I remember once seeing it on a shelf in Father's warm, comfortable library at Quercus, being curious, taking it down, and paging through it for a few minutes. But when I did, I saw something that I felt I wasn't supposed to see, so I closed the book and put it back on the shelf. Regularly at Quercus I had the sense that there were things I shouldn't know, things I shouldn't ask about, things that would not comport with the enveloping grace and beauty of our home. In this case, a quick surreptitious glance was enough to tell me that what one would want an educated and concerned American to have seen on a tour of Europe in 1936 wasn't going to be there. I didn't open the book again for many years.

In the summer of 1936, the Sterns and the Lemanns attended the elaborate ceremony in Cambridge marking the three hundredth anniversary of the founding of Harvard University, and then, separately, sailed for Europe. Father told me that he and his younger brother, Stephen, had gone on this trip with their parents, traveling on an ocean liner called the S.S. *Rotterdam*. Edgar Stern noted that the two families had spent "a joyous, giggle time" together in Stockholm, Copenhagen, and London, and that "Monte seems to have gotten a tremendous kick out of the trip." He was well aware of the great sadness that Nettie's ever-worsening illness had visited on the Lemanns. Then the Lemanns left and the Sterns began their *Wanderjahr* in earnest.

By that time, it wasn't just left-wing German writers like Feuchtwanger and Roth who were warning the world about the situation in Europe; American journalists like Dorothy Thompson and William Shirer were too. There had been widely publicized, though unsuccessful, attempts to organize a worldwide boycott of the 1936 Olympics in Berlin, which Hitler tried to close to Jewish and Black athletes. American German Jews like the Sterns were liberals, hardly sympathizers with fascism like many right-wing Americans, but they were also deeply averse to alarm. They lived in a world that combined security, because of their wealth and position, and precar-

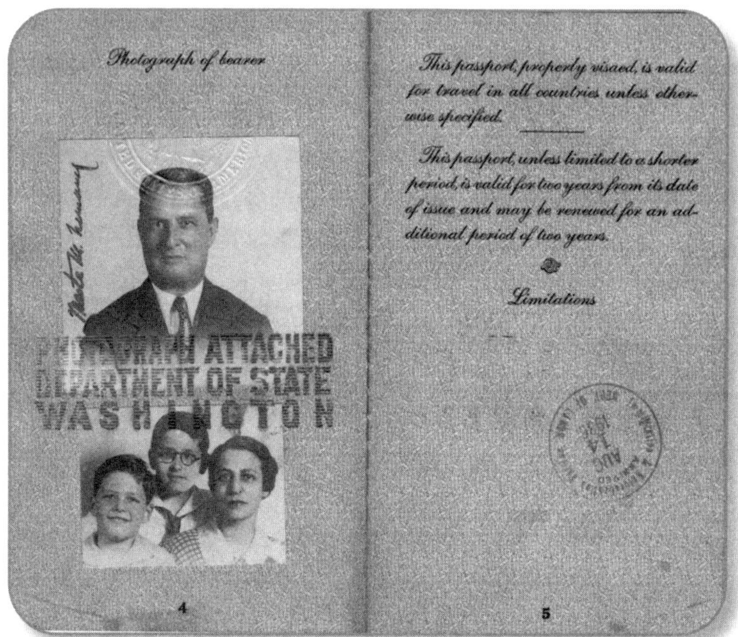

The passport the Lemanns used on a trip to Europe in 1936.

ity, because they were members of a category most of whose members the world found repellent and threatening. In that situation, people develop a thick protective casing, an enforced limitation on perception, a reality-excluding calm and optimism.

Wherever he went on his sentimental journey, Edgar took notice of the situation for Jews, and he usually found reason to be surprisingly sanguine about it. At Harvard, which by then had a firm Jewish quota, he wrote, "It struck me that they went out of their way to recognize the Jews"—part of the evidence being that Pop was given a special honor as an outstanding member of his class. Across the Atlantic, "one of the many pleasant things about England is the apparent absence of any feeling about Jews." In Hungary, "there seems to be comparatively little anti-Semitism, with some Jews holding noble titles." In Romania, "there is quite a large Jewish population in Bucharest, who look comparatively clean and prosperous, and most of the large stores have Jewish names." In the Soviet Union, which Edgar, to his surprise, found very impressive—"America has much to learn from what the Russians are doing"—one could be optimistic about the future of the Jews, because "there is absolutely no consciousness of difference in any phase of life between Russians and Jews, or any other minority races." All this is testament to the overwhelming power of choosing to see only what one wants to see.

Even in Germany, where the Sterns spent a few days and had an audience with the American ambassador, William Dodd, another pessimist, Edgar did not see a cause for maximal worry. His attitude toward the Nazis was closer to revulsion than to grave concern. Edgar and Edith happened upon some goose-stepping soldiers passing in review. They refused to offer the troops the stiff-armed Nazi salute, and they were pleased that nobody criticized them for that. During their time in Germany, they only once heard a person greet someone else on the street with "Heil Hitler!" Edgar had brought one of his relatives over from Hamburg to England to brief him on how his own relatives in Germany, with whom he had fallen substantially out of touch, were doing. He didn't get a happy report. The Nazis had ruined this man's business; other relatives had left for Palestine, with a little financial help from Maurice Stern in New Orleans. In person in Berlin, however, Edgar found a less dire situation: "We saw very few of the red signs in shop windows, indicating that this was an 'Aryan' shop, and we walked through the big Wertheim department store, as well as another store called Rosenheim, and both these Jewish stores were relatively well filled with customers. We saw quite a few Jewish faces in the restaurants." A few months later, the Nazis ordered that these stores be Aryanized, meaning that their Jewish owners had to transfer their ownership to people the government considered to be real Germans.

The only place in Europe where Edgar got the feeling of a Jewish crisis was in Warsaw, and that was not because of antisemitism, but because of the way the Jews themselves had chosen to live. At his request, his guide took him to the section of town occupied by traditional, unmodernized Jews, the kind of people he'd never actually seen but who occupied a large space in the consciousness of German Jews in America because our incomprehensible association with them was so threatening. He was profoundly shocked: nothing in his life had prepared him for this encounter; nothing could have upset him more. To let him tell the story:

> I never thought I would see Jews so foul, filthy, and degraded as these people whom we saw by the thousands. They are literally so filthy on their persons that I would have shuddered to touch them, and their homes and shops wide open to the street, were unbelievably sordid. . . . You might conclude that I have had a strong injection of anti-Semitism, but I was filled, not so much with annoyance, as with disgust, shame, horror that *any* Jews could sink so low. . . . And here is the worst of the story: There people, practically every one of them, men, women, and children, looks less like human beings, with the minimum of dignity and decency which we like to associate with the "higher animal," than like some sort of lower animal with half a brain and less than half a soul. They swarmed around us, bent, crooked, misshapen creatures, with grimacing distorted faces, and they gibbered and squawked and shrieked inquiries whether we were American, Spanish, etc. There was a suggestion from a few that we might be "judisch," by the crowd but a great majority voted that down, and for the moment I was glad to abide by the opinion of the majority. At that instant I was almost ashamed to be a Jew, or at least, I was horrified, aghast, and immeasurably saddened that any group of this race could sink to the very bottom of the pit of human existence.

As people who greatly disapprove of something often do, Edgar wanted to see more. He had the guide take him to a *cheder*, an airless room crowded with black-clad men and boys wearing *kippot*, *tallitot*, and *tefillin*—small black boxes containing a scrap of paper inscribed with a few words of Torah, strapped to the forehead. They were swaying back and forth, mumbling prayers to themselves. Edgar reminded himself that Max Heller, the rabbi he'd grown up with at Temple Sinai in New Orleans, had told him that such Jews were admirable for their religious devotion and learning, but Edgar was having none of it. They were merely primitive fanatics, nothing more. Still, repulsed as he was, he was unable to stay away. He returned to the Jewish quarter once again for Friday night services. Then he tried to draw some conclusions from what he had seen. First, he fully appreciated how much of a heroic venture the advent of Reform Judaism had been, for lighting a path out of this unacceptable way of life. Second, "If I were a Pole, I wouldn't want that kind around me, and neither Jews nor Gentiles would want them around in America. So they should get out of Poland and find another place to live." Third, "There are too many Jews in Poland and I fear there will be trouble if a substantial number can't be moved out." One of the philanthropic ventures of Edgar's father-in-law, Julius Rosenwald, who had died a few years earlier, was funding the establishment of agricultural colonies for Eastern European Jews. Edgar and Edith had visited some of these, in Ukraine, and had been impressed. The director of the program had told the Sterns that he was in touch with the Soviet government about establishing a new Jewish Soviet republic in Siberia, and he was optimistic that this might happen. In that case, additional Jews from Poland, Lithuania, and Romania could be sent there.

A few weeks later, the Sterns went to Palestine, where they had the opposite of their experience in Warsaw. They had set up the trip only because they felt philanthropically obligated to keep themselves apprised of efforts to establish colonies, like the ones they'd seen in Ukraine, for the more needy and distasteful Jews. But they found themselves deeply impressed, even moved, by the beauty of the country and by the work they saw the Jews there doing. Because of who the Sterns were, their visits were mainly to symphony conductors and university presidents rather than to collective farmers.

They shared with earlier American visitors the feeling that in Palestine a new kind of Jew had been born, who evoked very different reactions in a visitor from the poor Jews of Europe. The disturbing qualities of those Jews had disappeared. The Jewish question had been solved. Ordinary Jews in Palestine were clean-shaven, healthy, proud, secular. They were normal, not freakish. Israel seemed even to have successfully addressed the bedeviling problem of the tasteless Jewish parvenu, which was, from the point of view of German Jews like the Sterns, so often an unfortunate step on the road to full assimilation. Even the more prosperous Jews they encountered in Palestine were not grasping or vulgar. They were Jews whom Jews like the Sterns could be proud of, could regard as peers. Although Edgar wasn't quite ready yet to declare himself a Zionist, everything he had seen on his trip had left him far more open to the idea, and perhaps more willing to acknowledge the true nature of the situation for Jews in Europe, than he had been beforehand. In Europe whatever realistic assessment may have been possible for him was put out of reach by his visceral, ineradicable need to distance himself from the Jewish majority.

On their way home, the Sterns gathered up their children from boarding school and together attended the coronation of King George VI at Westminster Abbey in London, a glorious, grand affair that offered a reassuring picture, not so long before Britain came under Nazi bombardment, of a civilized and safe traditional social order, with a dignified royal family cheered by throngs of its adoring subjects. "There was every evidence of cordiality toward these peers and peeresses as they drew up to the Abbey, magnificently clad in red velvet and ermine capes, carrying their coronets," Edgar wrote. "In spite of the tremendous changes in the world, it may fairly well be said that every Englishman loves a lord!" A few days later they embarked for New Orleans, where a team of architects and landscape designers imported from New York was working with them to superimpose a layer of elegance—their splendid new house and its gardens—over an expanse of Louisiana's wet, fecund soil.

"I HAVE BECOME A MYTH"

Most of the world doesn't have royal courts anymore. Even in Britain the court is mainly symbolic. The term *court Jew* sounds archaic. And yet, Jewish history, Jewish life, is full of patterns that begin in Scripture and somehow keep recurring. When I look at the lives of Pop and his friend Felix Frankfurter, I see court Jews transposed to the twentieth century. Both of them, especially Frankfurter, rose to a very high level, transcending the boundaries of the Jewish world, and they were both constantly aware of being not just prominent people, but prominent Jews. They were seen, and treated, differently because they were Jews. Their high status was conditional, vulnerable both to expulsion from court and to the rage of the mob that so often seems to be waiting outside the castle walls. They always had to think about where their primary loyalties lay, with their people or with their patrons.

It may be a sign of the never-ending fascination with the court Jew as a type that in 1934 a British studio, the Gaumont-British Picture Corporation, made a film version of *Jud Süss*, Feuchtwanger's novel about an eighteenth-century court Jew in Germany, with Feuchtwanger himself as one of the screenwriters. The film—released in Britain as *Jew Süss*, and in the United States as *Power*—was meant as an anti-Nazi gesture, a work of philosemitism. It is faithful to the novel in ending with Süss's martyrdom. Today it looks as if making the film must have been a challenging project, because having Süss read to 1930s audiences as Jewish (so as to maintain the impact of the revelation at the end that he actually wasn't) required presenting him as off-puttingly exotic and foreign. He looks different, big-nosed and sallow, he has special abilities wielding money and political influence that are the basis of his special status but that automatically arouse suspicion and hostility. Even to their friends, Jews in those days weren't quite normal; or, if they were Jewish and came across as normal, it was because they concealed their Jewishness.

Exoticizing of Jews as the film was, it infuriated Joseph Goebbels, the Nazi propaganda minister, who retaliated by producing his own version of *Jud Süss*, released in 1940. In the Nazi film it's Süss himself who is a rapist, rather than being falsely accused of rape. His death on the gallows at the end is treated as a joyous occasion, a liberation of the Gentiles from his insistent grasp. The Nazis' film was a much bigger hit than the British one. It has been banned for decades, like Hitler's *Mein Kampf,* but occasionally a snippet pops up briefly online, before an algorithm discovers it and takes it down. From that you get a sense of the gravamen of the film, and it's a familiar one: the cunning, greedy, lustful, misshapen Jew, who has a supernatural power to twist all of society to his and his people's malign purposes.

When I was ten years old, Father took me to visit Justice Frankfurter in Washington. It was only a few months before he died. What I remember is a small and very old man sunk into a soft, enclosing armchair in the living room of a dark apartment. Everything Father communicated about the visit gave me the impression that this old friend of Pop was a very important, or formerly important, man, but I didn't understand how. Now that I've read the hundreds of letters he and Pop wrote back and forth for decades, I have a better grasp of who both of them were and of how, individually and together, they managed the always present tension between being Jewish and being at court. Frankfurter had come to America as a twelve-year-old boy, when his father moved the family here from Austria in the hope of a big business success, which eluded him. Compared with Pop, Frankfurter was in much closer touch with Jewish life in Western Europe, where most of his family still lived, and in the Lower East Side tenements, where he had grown up. By the time he was in his midthirties, he was an ardent Zionist, and also a socialist. Pop was neither. Frankfurter was much more intensely ambitious than Pop to be at the center of the great events of his time. He knew everybody and wanted to be a part of everything; he combined an ardent desire to be at court with equally ardent views that weren't acceptable at court. The provincial life that Pop had chosen had no appeal for him. He relentlessly pushed Pop to join him on the big stage, sometimes successfully.

Only once was Pop in an obviously more prominent public position than Frankfurter. That was when President Herbert Hoover appointed Pop as one of the eleven members of a national commission to review law enforcement in the United States. It was five months before the 1929 stock market crash; Hoover, an engineer celebrated for his work organizing relief efforts, was still a national hero. There's a stiffly formal group portrait of the members and Hoover in front of the White House, with Pop looking self-conscious in a heavy, double-breasted suit. The commission's nominal mission disguises what was really at stake, and what put the commission at the center of attention: it was supposed to assess whether Prohibition, the country's brief, disastrous experiment with a national ban on alcohol, was working. It would help Hoover, a teetotaler, if the commission reported that it was—but it wasn't; illegal drinking was ubiquitous, and because it was also illegal, Prohibition was a gift to organized crime.

Frankfurter, then a professor at Harvard Law School, was raptly attentive to the commission's doings. Because one member, Pop, was his close friend, and the commission's staff director, Max Lowenthal (also Jewish), was one of his legion of protégés, Frankfurter knew a great deal about the commission's deliberations. And he was already a constant informal advisor to the presidentially ambitious governor of New York, Franklin Delano Roosevelt, who had no stake in Prohibition, which was far more a Republican cause than a Democratic one, and would not have wanted it endorsed by a prestigious commission. Frankfurter quickly became convinced that the commission was up to no good. Pop had confided to him that its private deliberations were amateurish; he'd been expecting to take part in a scientific inquiry, and instead it was merely political.

What should a court Jew do when things are going awry at court—keep quiet, or speak out at the risk of losing his high position? Pop told Frankfurter he was thinking of resigning. Frankfurter,

The newly appointed National Commission on Law Observance and Enforcement in front of the White House, 1929. Pop is standing second from left. President Herbert Hoover is sitting third from right.

acting out of some combination of friendship and his own political interest, instead urged Pop to stay on and become a public dissenter. He barraged Pop with sympathy, encouragement, ideas for potential strategies, and sometimes even flattery. His idea was that Pop should spend much more time in Washington, a long train trip from New Orleans, and battle the other commissioners at every point. It wound up that Pop protested less than Frankfurter wanted him to, but more than the other commissioners did. He issued a personal dissent from the commission's main report on Prohibition. Drinking was unstoppable, he wrote, and everybody knew that even Prohibition's official supporters (except for Hoover) were ignoring it. Therefore, "I see no alternative but repeal." That was in January 1931. The Great Depression had begun. In 1932, Roosevelt defeated Hoover in the presidential election, and Prohibition was on the way out.

Now, with Roosevelt's election, Frankfurter became far more of a court Jew—the brainy, cosmopolitan essential advisor to the ruler—than Pop had ever been, even though for years he held no official position. Frankfurter's boundless energy and his willingness to insert himself into situations, and Roosevelt's informal way of conducting White House business, made for a perfect fit. Frankfurter was constantly suggesting that his allies, including Pop, be given high-ranking government jobs. He was frequently in Washington and when he wasn't he was writing long letters to Roosevelt. All Pop's episodes at court—top-level national politics, anyway—came to him via Frankfurter.

One Sunday evening in 1935, Frankfurter and Roosevelt were sitting on the White House balcony, drinking rum cocktails. Roosevelt mentioned that Huey Long, the dictatorially powerful populist senator from Louisiana, was maneuvering in a way that suggested that he might stage a challenge to Roosevelt, from the left, for the 1936 Democratic presidential nomination. What did Frankfurter think? Frankfurter told Roosevelt that he didn't know enough about Long to answer. But he should ask Monte Lemann, in New Orleans. As Frankfurter remembered it years later, Roosevelt said, "There is a telephone. Call him and ask him to come see me." Frankfurter called. Pop, whom I picture hastily packing a suitcase and jamming a straw boater on his head, booked passage on the first available train and went to Washington.

In the downtown business world where Pop worked, hatred of Long was nearly universal, except among a handful of men who had allied themselves with Long in exchange for economic favors. As Pop knew well, the sugarcane business wasn't what it used to be, but Louisiana still had an extractive economy—if not sugar, then oil and gas, or rice, or sulfur—that made a few people rich but didn't support much of a middle class. Even an electorate that didn't include the state's Black population, which had been disenfranchised, was mainly poor, and strongly attracted to Long's slogan, "Share our wealth," and his roaring, fearless attacks on business interests. Pop had confided to Frankfurter that he was so upset about Long's steamrolling of Louisiana's political institutions that he was thinking of moving away, so that his sons would not have to grow up in the Long regime. (For centuries, in many places and many guises, populism had regularly made a special target of Jews.) What made Pop unusual among Long-haters was that he was also an enthusiastic supporter of the New Deal. Roosevelt's core voting constituency in Louisiana was the same as Long's, poor whites, and it adored him for the same reason, that he was on their side and used government aggressively to make their lives better. Roosevelt didn't have a lot of allies in Louisiana who were also anti-Long.

During the period when Frankfurter was old, sick, and retired, Father's brother, my uncle Stephen, went to see him in Washington and got him to tell the story of Pop's visit to the White House, which he still remembered vividly. Together, Frankfurter and Pop went to Roosevelt's private study. There they found, along with Roosevelt himself, a group of Southern senators—tough, canny, long-serving, segregationist allies of Roosevelt—who were worried that Long was going to recruit populist opponents to run against them, as Long was himself planning to be the populist opponent of Roosevelt. The senators wanted Roosevelt to threaten to cut off federal funding for their states, unless Long ended his political rebellion. Pop said that was a bad idea—it would only strengthen Long's hand by making him look like a lonely crusader against established interests.

Frankfurter, perhaps out of fondness, made it sound as if only Pop's eloquence in making his case could have persuaded the Southern senators to stop pressuring Roosevelt to punish Long. We'll never know whether Long would have made good on his insurrectionist plans, because not long afterward, the son-in-law of one of his political enemies (recast in *All the King's Men* as the brother of one of Willie Stark's mistresses) shot him in the lobby of the Louisiana state capitol as he was emerging from the legislative chamber. Long's bodyguards fired a fusillade at the assassin so intense that you can still see pockmarks from their bullets in the lobby's wall; Long himself had enough life in him to run down a corridor to safety, but after a day of agony in a hospital, he died, at the age of forty-two. Two hundred thousand adoring Louisianans lined up to see him lying in state in an open casket. In 1936 Roosevelt, having adeptly avoided any other challenges, was reelected in one of the most lopsided presidential votes in American history: he carried forty-six of the forty-eight states, won 523 of 531 electoral votes, and had the support of large majorities in both houses of Congress. He had as much political power as any American president has ever had.

For Pop, the Long episode was his only moment as a court Jew inside the White House; for Frankfurter, it was one of what must have been dozens of incidents when he demonstrated his value to Roosevelt. After Roosevelt was reelected, Frankfurter had to confront one of the moral dilemmas that present themselves to people in such positions. It's the essence of the court Jew's position that he's not just another courtier. All courtiers have to decide whether to tell the king when he's wrong, knowing that might bring their heady role to an end. Jewish courtiers also have to decide how much to stand up for their own people, knowing that to do so may imperil their standing even more, because of the special hatred Jews attract. At that moment, anti-Jewish passions were rising everywhere, not just in Germany. Frankfurter, on non-Jewish matters, was willing to trim. On Jewish matters, he stood firm.

Not long after the 1936 election, Roosevelt, intensely frustrated by an aging Republican majority on the Supreme Court that had ruled several of his main initiatives unconstitutional, proposed an expansion of the Court's membership, from nine members up to a maximum of fifteen. The liberal legal world that Pop and Frankfurter inhabited was horrified: this was a gesture worthy of Huey Long, a first step in the direction of dictatorship. During Roosevelt's first term, Frankfurter had turned down an offer to become chief justice of the Massachusetts Supreme Court, which Pop had urged him to accept, and also an offer from Roosevelt to become the nation's solicitor general. It was obvious that he had a higher post in mind. Now Roosevelt told Frankfurter that he intended to nominate him to the Supreme Court. Roosevelt was surely clever enough to realize that their conversation would lead Frankfurter to drop his usual outspokenness, at least about the court-packing plan. If Frankfurter opposed the plan, that might annoy Roosevelt enough to scotch his appointment; if he supported the plan, that might make him a pariah in the legal establishment, whose strong opposition would also scotch his appointment. So he remained conspicuously quiet.

One of the leaders of the opposition to Roosevelt's plan was a law school classmate and close friend of Frankfurter and Pop, a patrician corporation lawyer in New York named Grenville Clark. He persuaded Pop to sign a public statement opposing the plan; evidently Pop was undeterred by Frankfurter's regular reminders of government appointments he might get—even a Supreme Court appointment. Then Clark went to work on Frankfurter, though without ever directly accusing him of being motivated by ambition. Frankfurter responded with a series of long, tortured letters to Clark explaining his silence. He used a number of arguments: His close and confidential relationship with Roosevelt required his discretion on all New Deal policies. He was merely an academic, contemplating public affairs from the sidelines, and he wouldn't want to create the impression that Harvard Law School was a political institution. And there was this: "Fundamentally, because through circumstances in the making of which I have had no share, I have become a myth, a symbol and promoter not of reason but of passion. I am the symbol of the Jew, the 'red,' the 'alien.'" Clark was having none of it—but perhaps that was because it was inconceivable that such accusations could be flung at him. Frankfurter, whose relatives in Europe were forced to think about their survival and whose position in the United States was nowhere near as secure, was in a far different situation, and his frequent presence in the White House did not protect him.

Frankfurter mailed a series of jousting letters between Clark and himself to Pop, perhaps hoping for sympathy, adding private letters of his own. And he spent these months being especially attentive to their friendship. He sent a long handwritten letter of sympathy to Nettie about her latest round of medical setbacks, mentioning his own wife's series of nervous breakdowns and her other health problems. Evidently Pop, in return, let Frankfurter know that he wasn't being judged as harshly by his coreligionist in New Orleans as he had been by Grenville Clark. Frankfurter ended one letter by saying, "It comforts me much to know that you approve of my silence."

Within a few months, the opponents of Roosevelt's plan had organized a vast campaign of letters, petitions, and scholarly essays; the coup de grâce came when the Senate majority leader, Joe Robinson, one of the Southern senators Pop had encountered on his visit to the White House, who was the chief legislative steward of the plan, died of a sudden heart attack. Roosevelt dropped the plan. Frankfurter's Supreme Court chances were undiminished. But there were far more consequential and distressing developments in Europe and even at home, which were soon commanding Frankfurter's attention, and also Pop's. The Nazis' drive to absolute power, their ambition to conquer Europe, and their all-consuming hatred of Jews had become impossible to ignore—and yet many Americans, including some of the most prominent German Jews, had chosen to ignore it, or at least to downplay it. In the United States, the reaction to antisemitism abroad was not the revulsion you might expect, but a notching upward of antisemitism at home. The times, which were approaching a level of Jewish peril that would have been familiar from the Torah but not yet from the direct experience of people of Frankfurter and Pop's generation, presented American Jews who had achieved a position of influence outside the Jewish world with a choice. They would put their unusual and hard-won positions at risk if they spoke out. They would be moral cowards if they did not.

Frankfurter was deeply involved in the creation of the University in Exile in New York, a refuge for mostly Jewish scholars fleeing the Nazis. He enlisted Pop in this campaign. In 1937, Pop hosted a fundraising lunch in New Orleans for the university's director, Alvin Johnson, and he also persuaded his two richest Jewish clients, Edgar Stern and Sam Zemurray, to contribute. And Frankfurter consistently, though unsuccessfully, lobbied the State Department to admit more Jewish refugees from Europe. He wasn't worried about the fate of Jews only in Europe. In 1936, he wrote to Pop: "In connection with the deeper national aspects of the emergence of the Jewish problem in this country, you may be interested in the exact terms of a recent 'Anglo-Saxon' bequest to Yale (which you may have spotted in the New York Times), and as to which I made some references at the dinner recently held in New York to promote the work of the University in Exile." This was a gift from an insurance company executive, who left a million dollars to Yale in his will, to be used for scholarships restricted to "the sons of white Christian parents of Anglo-Saxon, Scandinavian or Teutonic descent."

In 1938 Frankfurter invited Pop to a highly confidential dinner for a handful of prominent Jews, to discuss a new survey of American antisemitism—"It will not surprise you to learn that the findings are very disquieting." Pop made a trip to Washington, where he met with eighty-one-year-old Louis D. Brandeis, at that point the only Jewish Supreme Court justice, and a New Deal lawyer named Ben Cohen, both of whom were very close to Frankfurter, to discuss the survey. Once Pop was back in New Orleans, he wrote a dispirited letter to Frankfurter, complaining that all these high-placed Jews could suggest was an educational program. But what if "the forces which were responsible for increases in prejudice . . . emanated from educated circles"? Pop and Frankfurter had both become familiar with the deep antisemitism of many of the non-Jews who ruled America's most prominent institutions. Harvard, Yale, and America's other great centers of light and learning were hardly leading the way toward greater acceptance of Americans Jews and sympathy for European Jews.

The Anschluss, the Nazis' unresisted conquest of Austria, Frankfurter's native country, took place in March 1938. Within hours German troops had arrested Frankfurter's elderly uncle, Salomon Frankfurter, the librarian of the University of Vienna, in his apartment and put him in a prison reserved for politically suspect people. Frankfurter adored his uncle, and he pulled every possible string—in his case, that was a lot of strings—to get him transferred first to a hospital and then back to his apartment, where he lived under house arrest until his death, at the age of eighty-four, in 1941. Pop wrote Frankfurter a letter of condolence. Frankfurter wrote back: "About half-past two in the morning of the day that the Nazis entered Vienna, they pulled my uncle out of bed and put him in a concentration camp. His only crime was that his eminence as a scholar made him a prominent Jew in Vienna. From that day until the end his external life was made miserable. But his was man's greatest achievement—self-mastery—and so he lived his inner life with dignity and serenity until his death. I appreciate your kind words."

A few months after the Anschluss, Kristallnacht, the vast, coordinated Nazi rampages against Jews, took place all over Germany, including the part of southwest Germany the Lemann family came from. Much of the rest of the world was horrified, including Roosevelt, but the President resisted entreaties to loosen the country's severe immigration restrictions so that more of Germany's Jews could find safety here. Britain created a program, the Kindertransport, to bring endangered Jewish children from Europe across the English Channel to safety. In the United States, Senator Robert F. Wagner, of New York, proposed a similar program that would allow an additional twenty thousand German children to come to the United States. Eleanor Roosevelt publicly endorsed it. Franklin Roosevelt declined to take a position.

In the spring of 1939, Pop went to the capital to testify in favor of the bill, which prominent members of Louisiana's congressional delegation were opposing. He began his testimony by mentioning his two children, Father and Stephen. He imagined what they would be going through if they were in Germany. It was true, he said, that there were poor, undernourished children in Louisiana who needed help, but the situation of the German children was different: "What I think of is the mental torture that these people are subjected to, treated as the lowest form of animals, and what that means to them and their outlook upon life." The bill, he argued, shouldn't be thought of as presenting merely a practical question of whether the country should devote its limited resources to native-born Americans or to children in Germany. Members of Congress should be guided by the feelings in their hearts. This would have to lead them to open the country's doors to the German children.

The bill never came to a vote, because it had nowhere near the support it needed. It wasn't just the members of Congress who at that moment were overwhelmingly isolationist, hostile to immigration, and unmoved by sympathy to the plight of the Jews. Polls showed that most Americans shared these views. The children the bill would have admitted were most likely murdered, along with their families, everyone in their neighborhoods and villages, and most of the rest of the Jews of Europe.

During the summer of 1938, Justice Benjamin Cardozo died. (Pop was one of the speakers at his memorial service.) So far in his second term, Roosevelt had nominated two Supreme Court justices, and it must have upset Frankfurter to see those prizes go to other men. But Cardozo was Jewish, so that opened up a "Jewish seat" on the Court. Everybody knew that Frankfurter was a leading candidate, and not everybody was happy about it. Among his behind-the-scenes opponents were two of the country's most prominent and influential German Jews, Arthur Hays Sulzberger, the publisher of *The New York Times*, and Henry Morgenthau Sr., a real-estate man and the father of Roosevelt's treasury secretary. They considered Frankfurter to be too liberal and too Zionist, and they were comfortable with the idea of a Court that would have no Jewish members after Brandeis's obviously imminent retirement. It was typical of the American German-Jewish culture that what was supposedly a relaxed, confident position—Jews were now fully American, so why was it necessary to have a Jew on the Supreme Court?—actually displayed an intense awareness of the pervasiveness of antisemitism. A Jew like Frankfurter might draw too much malign attention, might reinforce prejudices that were always ready to reassert themselves. It would be better for the Jews to try to go unnoticed.

Just after New Year's Day 1939, nine months before the Second World War began in Europe, Roosevelt announced that he was nominating Frankfurter to the Supreme Court. (A month later, Brandeis announced his retirement.) Pop immediately fired off a congratulatory telegram and then a letter. "I do not know in what capacity I am most happy about it—as friend, classmate, lawyer, Jew, American citizen," Pop wrote. "But it is great enough to fill me up in every capacity. How proud you both should be in your souls! What a record for an immigrant Jew, unaided save by his own extraordinary quality!" The Senate confirmed Frankfurter unanimously. He did not treat his elevation to the Court as an opportunity to withdraw from the world, even though his outside activities would now have to be conducted with more subtlety. And he knew that Pop would be a partner he could trust to be discreet—we'll see more examples of that soon. Their close friendship continued. Part of their bond, it seems, was a shared commitment not to let their unusual high status (for Jews) nudge them into quiescence, as it had for so many others, on matters of life and death concerning their people.

COUSIN JULIAN

Not long after Pop testified before Congress in support of the bill that would have brought Jewish refugee children to the United States from Germany, an ocean liner called the *St. Louis*, carrying more than 900 German Jews, set sail from Hamburg for Havana, Cuba. Although the passengers had been issued Cuban visas, it wasn't allowed to land. The *St. Louis* sailed to Miami, where it stood in sight of the harbor while passengers cabled the White House and the State Department, asking for emergency permission to enter the country. These got the same response as the bill in Congress had:

no. The *St. Louis* returned to Europe. Some of its passengers managed to repatriate outside of Germany. The rest, more than 250, perished in the Holocaust.

Such was the attitude of the United States on the eve of the Second World War. Louisiana was surely less sympathetic to the plight of Jews in Germany than the country as a whole, and the Jews of New Orleans were less inclined to raise their voices on behalf of their coreligionists than Jews nationally were. If Rabbi Max Heller had still been alive, he would have prodded the community. Its new leader at this crucial moment did not.

In 1936 Julian Feibelman arrived as the new rabbi at Temple Sinai. He wound up holding the job for thirty-one years, and so being the main direct religious authority of both Father's childhood and mine. In 1938 he married one of the Lemanns, which made him, to me, Cousin Julian. Julian had grown up in Jackson, Mississippi, when it was a town of five thousand people, without paved streets. Only a small handful of Jews lived there. Julian had no childhood religious education: he didn't know any Hebrew and never studied Talmud. His father, who like most of the other Jews in town owned a store, had the family eat matzohs during Passover and take the day off on Yom Kippur, but that was the extent of their observance. They also celebrated Christmas and Easter as secular holidays. Julian went to a Methodist college in Jackson where daily chapel attendance was compulsory—as he told an interviewer when he was an old man, "I knew the Methodist hymns before I knew the Hebrew hymns. I listened to the Bible reading from the Old and New Testaments and I knew mighty little about Moses in those days." Born in 1897, he grew up during the height of the Lost Cause period in Mississippi, where many people refused to celebrate the Fourth of July because that was the date when Vicksburg had fallen to Ulysses Grant. He was educated at the Robert E. Lee School, reflexively loyal to the Confederacy.

The Feibelman family's roots were in the same part of Germany that my family came from. Julian liked to boast that he could trace his lineage back to the 1200s, and that it included several court Jews; this may account for the stately way he carried himself when I knew him. Julian's German-born maternal grandfather had been widowed. Feeling unable to take care of his daughter, Julian's mother, alone, he acquired a mail-order bride from Berlin. But it evidently wasn't a real marriage—she arrived in Jackson, quickly took Julian's mother back to Berlin for a few years, returned to Mississippi for a short time, and then relocated to Berlin permanently by the time Julian was born. Like many American German Jews, Julian was raised with the idea that Germany was the seat of civilization. The wonderful presents he regularly got from his step-grandmother in Berlin reinforced the impression. While growing up, he later wrote, "I heard no sorrowful living experiences of uprooted homes or persecuted individuals fleeing from pogroms, Cossack knouts, or from bedeviled anti-Semites." He insisted that he had never experienced antisemitism growing up.

Not wanting to take over his father's store, Julian enrolled in law school at the University of Mississippi. He didn't like it, so he left and entered the training program for Reform rabbis at Hebrew Union College in Cincinnati. There, he encountered a kind of Jew who was unfamiliar to him: "Lots of them were born in Eastern Europe. Since four years of age they had studied Hebrew. By the time they got to college they were already reading the Talmud. They could argue with the professors." That made him only more determined to resist this kind of Judaism, and in those days the seminary would not have insisted otherwise. He wound up spending the first ten years of his career as the number-two rabbi at a large, prosperous Reform temple in Philadelphia, where the services were on Sunday, where there was no thought of obeying the dietary laws, and where the custom was that gentlemen should remove their hats when they were indoors, not put them on.

There was a fierceness to the determination of German Jews of Julian's generation, especially if they were from the South, to separate themselves from the way of being Jewish of most Jews in Europe and, by now, in the United States. They were the *real* Jews, the Jews who had answered the Jewish question. The main challenge that fate had dealt them, they felt, was not the crisis in Europe, but the aspirations of the *Ostjuden* to be understood as representing Jewish authenticity in religious practice, in culture, and in politics, in ways that put the German Jews' entire project at risk. The idea of holding back a dangerous and threatening tide had hold of their minds, which ought to have been on other things.

While he was in Philadelphia, Julian enrolled in graduate school in sociology at the University of Pennsylvania. He wrote his dissertation after he had moved to New Orleans: "A Social and Economic Study of the New Orleans Jewish Community." Reading this today generates a full-on emotional re-creation of the ruling assumptions of the Jewish world I grew up in, which otherwise is hard to explain to most Americans who grew up Jewish. There's a capitalized headline breaking up the text of the dissertation: "JEWS ARE NOT A RACE: That Kind of Thinking Is for Nazis." New Orleans, Julian reported, had not even two thousand Jewish families—educated, secure, established, Reform. Fortunately by Julian's lights, it was spared the mass migration of Eastern European Jews, "which caused such congestion in New York City, overran the lower East-Side, and subsequently produced the social problems of the vicious sweat-shops and tenements." These Yiddish-speaking immigrants "brought with them the habits that long years of restriction and fear had inculcated." More recently, he averred, New Orleans had spared itself another set of problems because it was the destination of very few refugees from Nazi Germany.

It was of paramount importance to Julian to dismiss the Conservative movement, then growing, as a temporary phenomenon that was sure to pass. He saw no purpose in it except to criticize Reform. Thankfully, it was nowhere to be seen in New Orleans, where "instead of the strict Mosaic laws of the Pentateuch," the Reform movement "emphasized moral and social consciousness." The rabbi was, appropriately, more like a minister than an interpreter of the myriad Jewish laws. As fully as all this seemed like progress—modernity—to Julian, there was one crucial aspect of it that he found frustrating. The New Orleans Reform Jews of Temple Sinai would not participate in even the relaxed version of religious observance that was all the temple asked of them. Julian would walk out to the pulpit on a Friday night and see only a few people sitting in the temple's vast fourteen-hundred-seat main sanctuary. "My heart usually sank, my brain would be devoid of content, and my spirit would drain out. I would steel myself to go ahead and do my best."

His frustrations built up over the years and then produced a crisis. In 1941 the local chapter of the National Council of Jewish Women scheduled an event on a Saturday morning. Julian wrote an editorial in the local Jewish paper criticizing it. Then the local Jewish country club—which was for the Jews who, unlike us, were barred from the New Orleans Country Club—held a dance on a Friday night. Julian wrote another chastising editorial. Not long afterward, he was called before Temple Sinai's board and given a ten-point memorandum outlining ways he'd be expected to improve his performance as rabbi. One point was that he should not write editorials like those without first getting the approval of the board. Another was that his sermons—we didn't have D'vrai Torah, the venerable explications of scriptural texts, at Temple Sinai—should be shorter, no more than fifteen minutes, and should be "on more up-to-date subjects": "Sermons based on Biblical texts are considered pointless." Julian came home and told my cousin Mary Anna, his wife, that he wanted to look for another pulpit. She said no: she was a New Orleanian and she wasn't leaving.

It's easy for me to see from this distance why the variety of Reform Judaism Julian was practicing, and his congregation was practicing even less, didn't last. If you try to demystify and deritualize any religion, with the aim of making it completely normal and rational and up-to-date and unproblematic, then it winds up losing its hold on people. For Reform Judaism in particular, the idea of dropping everything that might strike outsiders as racial, or tribal, so that Jewishness could emerge in a purified form as a religion that could be practiced without any friction between it and the Gentile world, was fruitless. You wound up with nothing of the essence of it left. Then there was a layer that was Southern. Here we were, a tiny, often hated group living in a supposedly relaxed, charming, easygoing, tolerant, fun-loving city. But we had to be aware, or at least to sense, that our society rested on a very strict and inviolable set of rules about how every group should stand in relation to every other group, and that when that was put off center, bad things happened—usually to Black people, but not always.

The manner we Temple Sinai Jews adopted was casual, wry, offhanded, unexcitable, and never overwrought, except when it came to anything obviously Jewish, in which case a high wall of absolute unacceptability went up. Standard-issue Jewishness went against everything we stood for. It raised the possibility that we might lose everything we had. It was terrifying, threatening. It stood our whole life upside down. Our territory within Jewish America was shrinking, and as it did, maintaining ourselves required shutting out more and more that didn't fit our cherished and fiercely held assumptions— things that were religiously, culturally, politically uncomfortable; things that were close by and things that were far away.

Everything about the picture of the world and our place in it that we had constructed for ourselves made it almost insuperably difficult to absorb, let alone confront, the destruction of the German Jews in Germany. It was like a violation of natural law: it required believing that what seemed impossible in Germany was possible; that an all-encompassing Jewish solidarity had become necessary; that Zionism might represent the only realistic future for many, even most, Jews. The opposite of each of these was a core assumption for German Jews. It's a sign of our fondness for Germany and our optimism about the Jewish future there that Julius Rosenwald, who was the son of German immigrants, named his firstborn child (born in 1891) Lessing, after Gotthold Ephraim Lessing, the first prominent German philosemite, friend and champion of Moses Mendelssohn, and author of *Nathan the Wise*. As an adult, Lessing Rosenwald worked for some years at Sears, Roebuck, his father's company, and then retired to devote himself to good works. He lived in Philadelphia and belonged to the Reform temple where Julian Feibelman had worked before coming to New Orleans, and of course he was Edith Stern's brother.

Events forced Lessing Rosenwald to abandon whatever optimism about Jewish life in Germany he'd had; he transferred it to the United States. In the early 1940s, he became the president and chief funder of an organization called the American Council for Judaism, which was devoted to preventing the establishment of a Jewish state. (He had earlier been a member of the America First Committee, which opposed the United States entering the Second World War.) It had a council of rabbis; Rosenwald's rabbi in Philadelphia, William Fineshriber, was a member, and Julian Feibelman was another. Julian still had many relatives in Germany, including his much-loved step-grandmother, and he had constant personal reminders of how desperate the situation there was. He'd get pleading letters from German Jews he'd never met who were also named Feibelman, saying they were his relatives. Could he help? Could he rescue them? Something in him made it impossible for him to receive these entreaties sympathetically. (From 1938: "Dear Cousin: We are very disappointed and troubled of not yet having an answer to my letter that I have directed to you Oktober of last year." From 1941: "Please, Julian, try and try again, there is no time to lose anymore.") He told himself that the writers had just picked his name out of a phone book, and in any case, he couldn't imagine what he could do. If the larger implication of the individual cases was Zionism, he found that impossible too. He firmly did not believe that establishing a Jewish state in Palestine would help the Jews. "I never wanted to see a nation," he told an interviewer, decades later. "I don't have any faith in nationalism whatsoever, whether it's Jewish, German, Russian, Chinese, or what."

Word was beginning to leak out about the Nazis' plan to exterminate the Jews en masse. In the summer of 1942, a secretly anti-Nazi German businessman who'd dined with Heinrich Himmler, just after Himmler had made an inspection tour of the Auschwitz death camp, told a Jewish banker in Switzerland what he'd heard. The news went from hand to hand among the leadership of Jewish organizations. Gerhard Riegner, an intelligence official for the World Jewish Congress, put it into the form of a telegram addressed to Stephen Wise, the head of that group. The telegram passed among various government officials in Switzerland, England, and Washington before it finally got to Wise at the end of August. A formidable, proud man, zealously liberal and ardently Zionist, Wise was like Frankfurter in having a carefully maintained direct relationship with Franklin Roosevelt and other high American officials. Unlike Frankfurter, his relationship with Roosevelt was mainly confined to Jewish matters, which led to a particular version of the court Jew's dilemma: Do you press hard, and risk losing access, or be cautious, and keep the doors open?

Wise, choosing to play the insider, gave the telegram to a high State Department official, who asked him to keep Riegner's report confidential until he could check it independently. Two consequential months went by, when there was no time to lose. Finally the State Department told Wise that it was true: the Nazis had a plan to murder three or four million Jews through industrial processes that surpassed in pure purposeless cruelty anything the world had ever seen. There would be no government announcement of this, but Wise could tell the world himself. He held a press conference, which got only moderate public attention. One can retrospectively chastise Wise for not being more aggressive—but for contrast there is Julian Feibelman's reaction, which was probably closer to typical among American German Jews, certainly in New Orleans. A few days after Wise's press conference, Julian devoted his column in the *New Orleans Jewish Ledger* to criticizing Wise, and not because he thought Wise hadn't acted quickly enough. He found Wise's story implausible—it wasn't so much that the Nazis would not have such intentions as that they would not be able to carry them out. He remembered that "the horrible atrocities of the First World War were proved false later." This could well turn out the same way.

To Julian nothing about Wise's account was plausible. Why would Germany, in the middle of a vast offensive against the Soviet Union, divert precious men and matériel to killing "poor and actually harmless Jews," when that would not help them win the war? Also, Wise had said that one of the Nazis' methods of killing Jews was to inject air bubbles into their veins, at the rate of up to one hundred per hour, but a doctor in New Orleans told Julian that this was impossible. Who knew what other wild exaggerations Wise had chosen to believe? It bothered Julian, too, that Wise had chosen to announce what he had heard directly, when it might have been more appropriate for the announcement to come from the State Department. Of course the State Department hadn't and wouldn't make such an announcement, but it was one of the core convictions of anti-Zionist Reform Jews like Julian that Jews should not advocate on their own behalf, that the advocacy should come from others, who were more neutral. That way it wouldn't enhance the perception that Jews are pushy, loud, and aggressive. Julian ended his editorial by asking, "Would it not have been far better for Dr. Wise to have refrained from adding his name to these accounts?"

Wrath immediately came down on Julian's head—first from a Zionist Reform rabbi in New York named Louis Newman, then from Stephen Wise himself. Both of these rabbis were already furious about the formation of the American Council for Judaism, at just the moment when the Nazis were putting into place the mechanisms of the final stage of the Holocaust. (Another vocal opponent of the council was Rabbi Max Heller's son James, who had become a Zionist Reform rabbi in Cincinnati.) Why, Newman wrote, would Julian choose this of all moments to give the world reason to doubt that the horrors unfolding in Europe were actually happening? Why would he lend his voice in opposition to the efforts to find a place of refuge for whatever Jews were able to survive? Julian wrote back, staunchly maintaining his commitment to anti-Zionism: "I can see no future for the peace and security of our people unless they can enjoy these privileges throughout the world." (That sounds like an awfully big project.) Julian's letter, understandably, made Newman only angrier—he wrote again, pointing out that Julian had put himself "in company with Goebbels" by disputing Stephen Wise's alarming report. And Wise's letter to Julian was even harsher: "I am sorry for you. I pity you. I consider your attitude disgraceful in every sense. Instead of lifting a finger to help your people, you traduce one who has sought to do everything within his strength in order to touch the conscience of the American people and to avert further Hitler crimes against his people."

In the summer of 1943, a few months after Wise's press conference, a member of the Polish resistance named Jan Karski came to Washington to give the still evidently unbelieving American officialdom another report on the Holocaust, then in its peak period of factory killing. Karski, disguised, had managed to visit the Warsaw ghetto and the Bełżec extermination camp. He then made his way to London and told the Polish government-in-exile what he had seen. From there he was sent to Washington. He secured meetings with, among others, President Roosevelt and Felix Frankfurter. Four decades later, in Claude Lanzmann's film *Shoah*, Karski reenacted his meeting with Frankfurter. In his telling, after he had laid out his terrible story, Frankfurter rose from his seat and declared, almost shouting, "I don't believe you!" It's a resonant moment in the film—but what did Frankfurter mean? Karski's idea was that Frankfurter wasn't accusing him of lying; nor was he reacting in the manner of Julian Feibelman, by implying that things in Europe couldn't be awful on that scale. Instead, Frankfurter meant that what he had heard went beyond the bounds of what he'd been able to consider possible, in a long life of crusading against injustices. How could one live after learning this? Could it be put out of mind?

After the war, Julian joined a delegation of American dignitaries on a trip to Berlin. The city still lay in ruin, filled with piles of rubble and ghostly, half-destroyed buildings that had not been demolished yet. These conditions shocked and horrified him; he thought the United States should not have demanded an unconditional surrender from the Nazis, so that the war might have ended earlier and with less destruction. Just before he left, he stopped by the office of the Joint Distribution Committee, an organization devoted to helping Jewish refugees, to ask whether there was any news about his step-grandmother and his other German relatives, from whom he had heard nothing in years. As he told the story, the people in the office promised to try to find them. It would have been possible, I suppose, for Julian to pursue his search for his missing relatives more doggedly, running down every possible lead, but he hadn't chosen to do that during the war either. It wasn't who he was. He never heard back from the Joint Distribution Committee. He returned to New Orleans and resumed his old life at Temple Sinai. With the establishment of the state of Israel in 1948, he resigned from the American Council for Judaism, though without endorsing Zionism.

I grew up in the penumbra of the American Council for Judaism. Father was not a member, probably because he knew Pop would not have approved, but he and most of the other Jews in New Orleans whom I knew shared its perspective. That was what I knew as normal. It was only when I left New Orleans that I realized how profoundly different, in fact opposite, the council's views were to what most American Jews believed, and also how widely despised, for being an organization of Jewish traitors, the council itself was. At every point in the standard story most American Jews told themselves about who they were and the progress they were making in America and in Israel, the council had an alternate story.

The director of the council was an energetic Reform rabbi named Elmer Berger, who was an old friend of Julian. To him, President Harry Truman's early recognition of the Jewish state in 1948 was not a great human rights advance, but a cynical gambit to pander to a bloc of voters so as to improve his chance of being reelected in 1948.

The capture of Adolf Eichmann, one of the architects of the Holocaust, by Israeli intelligence agents in Argentina in 1960, and his subsequent public war crimes trial in Jerusalem, which most Jewish Americans cheered, was to Berger a disaster, legally and morally indefensible. (In Berger's view, it was Theodor Herzl, the father of modern Zionism, who had given the Nazis the idea that Jews should be removed from Europe.)

When American Jews, by the postwar decades prosperously middle class, began to expand the network of Jewish summer camps and day schools, which were meant to keep traditional Jewish religious culture and practice strong into the next generation, Berger tried to launch a campaign of resistance, because he saw these institutions as examples of Jewish self-segregation. Integration should be the Jewish ideal; the council had a program devoted to producing alternate Jewish educational materials that touted assimilation. When Jewish aid organizations launched campaigns to help Jews in Romania and the Soviet Union immigrate to Israel—another popular cause throughout Jewish America—Berger saw it as just a self-interested financial scheme, insisting that actually those Jews were quite happy where they were. When Leon Uris, the son of Eastern European Jewish immigrants who became a popular novelist, published *Exodus* (1958), his sentimental bestseller, beloved among most Jewish readers, celebrating the birth of Israel, Berger started a back-channel conversation with the Hollywood producers who were going to make the movie version, to get them to tone down the novel's glorification of the Jewish state. The central concern that pushed Berger to do all this was not primarily Palestinian rights—the word *Palestinian* was not in his vocabulary—but changes he found alarming in the way American Jews chose to define themselves. They had to be persuaded to resist the tribal impulse.

Berger and his colleagues at the council regularly had quiet conversations with people they thought could be their allies. Another article of faith in the Jewish mainstream was that the career diplomats in the State Department were unfriendly to Israel. From the standpoint of the American Council for Judaism, that was quite true, and a good thing, so they conducted regular off-the-books meetings at the State Department to explore the possibility of weakening American support for Israel. In 1959, when *The New Yorker* published "Defender of the Faith," by Philip Roth, a brilliant young short-story writer, about an unsavory Jewish army private appealing to his Jewish sergeant's tribal loyalty, it was condemned by rabbis across the country—bad for the Jews. But an official of the American Council for Judaism invited Roth to lunch and offered to support his future work financially. (Roth declined the offer.) Elmer Berger's long run at the council finally ended in 1967, after Israel's victory in the Six-Day War over the armies of the countries surrounding it. That was another event that played very differently inside the council than among most American Jews, who regarded it as a triumph to be celebrated: it indicated that the shaky new state could survive and that Jews could successfully defend themselves. Even Lessing Rosenwald and the council's other German-Jewish patrons, who were becoming less worried that coming across as too Jewish would lead to exclusion, were not upset about Israel's victory. But Berger, on behalf of the council, called the war an unwarranted act of aggression and the Israeli victory a tragedy. The board of directors pushed him out.

CIVIL RIGHTS

Somehow Julian Feibelman came out of the war years prepared to take a moral stand. Perhaps he was atoning, even subconsciously, for not having done that earlier. He chose a non-Jewish cause, but nonetheless, one result was that he was subjected to a torrent of antisemitic abuse. In New Orleans in those days—and maybe still today—everything was about race. It would be hard to find a white person whose racial views would be acceptable by today's standards. Among the whites who held what we might consider painfully cautious and moderate racial views, which in that time and

place entailed some genuine risk of being exiled from the full acceptance of other whites, Jews were heavily overrepresented. In 1949,
a liberal organization called the New Orleans Committee on Race
Relations invited Ralph Bunche, the chair of the political science
department at Howard University, a member of the cohort that had
founded the United Nations, and the chief negotiator of an early
peace treaty between Israelis and Palestinians—in other words an
immensely prestigious and respectable figure, at least outside the
Deep South—to give a public lecture.

Where would it take place? Because Bunche was Black, and
because he insisted that the audience for the lecture be integrated,
this was not an easy problem to solve. All the big downtown hotels
said no. Tulane University said no. The local civic auditorium
said no: it was prohibited by law from holding integrated gatherings. Touro Synagogue, the second German-Jewish neo-Moorish
Reform temple on St. Charles Avenue, said no. But Julian was able
to persuade Temple Sinai's board, by a split vote, to agree to host the
lecture. Just before the event was to begin, somebody called Julian,
not giving his name, and told him that all the temple's stained-glass
windows were going to be smashed that evening. He had every reason to be terrified as the hour of Bunche's lecture drew near, but
somehow, magically, everything went perfectly. Nobody smashed
the windows. Bunche drew the kind of full house that Julian had
so much trouble attracting for religious services. The board members who'd opposed inviting Bunche apologized. The New Orleans
Times-Picayune published Bunche's photograph on the front page,
breaking from its usual practice of publishing pictures of Black people only if they were entertainers or criminals. Publications all over
the country praised Julian—even the Yiddish-language *Jewish Forward* in New York. It was the high-water mark of his career, deeply
gratifying for someone who yearned for prestige as deeply as Julian
did. The next year, Bunche was awarded the Nobel Peace Prize.

Julian kept among his papers an essay he'd written as a
twenty-year-old college student, at a time when he'd never lived any-

where but Jackson, Mississippi. What he wrote will sound shocking; I'm quoting it because it demonstrates where Julian started out on race. It's also typical of the kind of thing I'd hear from adults in New Orleans when I was growing up. Julian, like most other whites I knew, though of himself as a paternalist ("the white man of the South loves the negro"), not a racist. But there's nothing benign about paternalism, because it entails a strict, abiding, supposedly deserved rank ordering, which lay at the heart of Julian's youthful thinking. "Only a little more than half a century removed from the yoke and shackles of abject serfdom the negro of the South has made a progress that has startled civilization as well it might," he wrote. "Two centuries from the jungle where primal law ruled, where brute lust took the place of wedding vows, where his metaphysics and philosophy was the metaphysics and philosophy of the wild creature, where his Gods were physical objects, where hope there was not and light had never dawned, he stands today at the very beginning of his career as a national entity."

Nothing Julian left behind indicates that he ever had a definite racial conversion. I wonder whether he was unaware that language like that had often been used by outsiders to describe his own people—or maybe he knew but thought the Jewish objects of prejudice were from the poor Jewish masses, utterly different from him. His own racial prejudices were never directed at dignified, educated Black people like Bunche, whom he thought of as the Black equivalent of himself. Whatever it was that motivated him to host Bunche at Temple Sinai, he should get credit for doing it when nobody else in the city would. The success of the event, and the acclaim that followed, encouraged whatever limited racially liberal impulses he had developed since he was a college student in Jackson. A few years later, he got a more sustained chance to oppose the local racial order when the New Orleans school board, in response to the 1954 Supreme Court decision that declared legally segregated public schools unconstitutional, hired a lawyer to help it devise ways to resist the decision. Along with a handful of allies, Julian appeared at a public meeting of the school board in 1955 to urge it to drop the lawyer it had hired and to comply with the decision.

Immediately he received a substantial pile of hate mail. He saved a lot of it—and it makes clear that his abusers never failed to highlight his Jewishness. Anonymous callers phoned him at home, including one who said, "We Nazis will get you Jews this time!" There were telegrams, also anonymous. One said, WHY DON'T YOU JEWS AND DISSATISFIED BLACK START A PILGRIMAGE TO AFFRICA, YOU ALL WILL NEVER BE HAPPY IN U.S.A. It was signed OLD BLACK JOE. A letter, signed "Old S.S. Trooper," said, "If you think a pogrom cannot happen in the land of democracy wait a few years you misbegotten son of an Arabian ass. . . . You and yours are in vogue now. In years to come the only style will be you and yours used as soap. So get out your petitions. We'll burn you with them later."

The New Orleans establishment, including the Jewish establishment, would not have been so crude, but it was by no means willing to support Julian's stance on school integration. He hadn't cleared his activities with Temple Sinai's board, one of whose members also was a member of the school board. The temple board was furious. Without telling him, the board hired an armed guard to stand inside the temple, at the door to the sanctuary. Several board members chastised him for going too far and endangering the Jews' position in New Orleans; often in the South, any Jewish organization's endorsement of civil rights produced an organized boycott of the local Jewish merchants. Julian remembered one member of the congregation coming up to him after services and saying, "We've gotten along nicely in New Orleans, now don't spoil it." The following year, a federal judge in New Orleans named Skelly Wright ordered the integration of the schools. Two elementary schools went first, and most white families immediately withdrew their children. The new Black students at the schools had to be escorted to the front door every morning past a gauntlet of jeering white protesters. There was one white family that continued sending its daughter to one of the schools; she had to be escorted too. Julian went to see the local U.S. attorney, who ran the integration effort through federal marshals, and volunteered to escort the white girl one day. When he did, the anonymous calls immediately started again. He assumed that a disloyal federal marshal had reported what he had done to the white protesters. Soon the family of the white girl Julian had escorted moved out of town. And Judge Wright, who lived on the same block we did when I was a small child, had it far worse than Julian. A few years later, he got a judicial promotion, specially arranged so that he could serve on a higher court in Washington, rather than remain in New Orleans.

It would be a mistake to see Julian as having become an all-out civil rights crusader. Something, maybe conscience, had called him out of the safe zone where most people he knew remained, but his zone had its boundaries too, not all that much wider. He always insisted that if he had been a small-town rabbi in the South, he wouldn't have done what he did in New Orleans, and there were limits to what he was willing to do in New Orleans. When the public transportation system in New Orleans was considering ending its version of the Jim Crow system—Black customers forced to sit in the back of streetcars and buses—Julian worked with a group of ministers to prepare a statement asking the people of New Orleans to "be reasonable, comply with the over-all law, and accept the change and decision with moderation and decent compliance." The head of the transportation system, a friend of his, called him and asked him not to release the statement. He didn't. In 1960 Dorothy Zellner, a young woman from New York who had come to New Orleans as a Freedom Rider, came to see Julian in his office at Temple Sinai. She would surely have struck Julian as an alien creature: the daughter of crusading, left-wing, Yiddish-speaking immigrants, she was slight, intense, informally dressed, self-consciously radical. Julian would have struck her as an alien creature too. She was militantly secular, but she assumed that anybody who was Jewish would be committed to social justice. She asked Julian to organize Jewish support for the Freedom Riders' sit-ins at segregated lunch counters. He told her that the New Orleans Jewish community was in far too insecure a position to feel it could safely support public acts of civil disobedience. She left Temple Sinai disappointed and puzzled: who were these Jews who prioritized building a grand temple over a commitment to what she thought of as the real meaning, the moral meaning, of being Jewish?

On Jewish matters even more than on race, Julian was never comfortable identifying with crusading, confrontational reformers. After Julian made his appearance before the school board, he got a letter from Justine Wise Polier, a judge in New York who was the daughter of his old combatant, Rabbi Stephen Wise, congratulating him on his courage. That was gratifying, but when she followed with an invitation to give a speech on desegregation to a national Jewish women's organization, he declined. He may have felt uncomfortable about the prospect of speaking to a roomful of ardent Zionists, or perhaps he knew how poorly his playing the role of the liberal hero before a Northern audience would go down back home. In his last years, the middle and late 1970s—years when I remember him sunk into a soft armchair at home, soaking his aching feet and reading news reports about a world that was going in directions that disturbed him—Julian became disillusioned about the results of the civil rights activities he'd participated in. He was just as disturbed about Jewish developments in the late 1960s and early 1970s, because the sort of proudly particularized ethnic Jewishness he'd hoped the Jews could transcend now seemed to be transcendent itself. The Holocaust, the advent of the state of Israel, and Eastern European Jews' rapid progress out of the slums had changed the atmosphere among American Jews, in ways that had ended the reign of old-line Reform Judaism as the dominant strain. Jewish children were being taught Israeli songs and dances. Jews had begun to say "Shabbat" instead of the more dignified, less particularist "Sabbath." And now Black people were following the same misguided path, toward nationalism. In 1973, in an interview with the *Times-Picayune*, Julian said, "The Negroes wanted to be integrated—now all they want is to separate, to vote in a bloc, to wear Afro hair-dos and declare that 'black is beautiful.' . . . This is not a responsible use of freedom."

During this period, Julian, an intensely proud and loyal alumnus of Hebrew Union College in Cincinnati, was invited to lecture there. He was thrilled and accepted eagerly, thinking he'd be appropriately honored in old age by the institution that had launched his distinguished career. But then the president called, embarrassed, to say that the students had protested the invitation. The ambient prejudices at Hebrew Union were the opposite of what they'd been half a century earlier. Then, James Heller, Max Heller's son and later a harsh critic of Julian's anti-Zionism, hadn't been permitted to give a Zionist talk there. Now, in the new American Jewish world, it was anti-Zionists who were not welcome. To spare Julian the embarrassment of being directly confronted by protesters, the invitation had to be withdrawn. Like so many people who are the product of a strong and particular set of circumstances that feel as if they will last forever, but don't, Julian ended his life bewildered by a world that had abandoned most of what he held dear.

POP'S APOTHEOSIS

After the war but before the establishment of the state of Israel, the minority of European Jews who had survived were hardly able to resume their old lives. Their villages had been destroyed. Their businesses had been expropriated. Many returned home to find that somebody else had taken possession of their house and would not leave. Most of them had no money. In some parts of Eastern Europe, pogroms—the traditional kind, spontaneous rather than state-sponsored—resumed. Many Jews lived in displaced-person camps, from which it was very difficult to immigrate to another country, because most countries, including the United States, were reluctant to accept them. It was in this context that Jewish organizations in the United States launched large fundraising campaigns to resettle Jewish refugees in Palestine, where they also weren't warmly welcomed, either by the Palestinians or by the British, who were then in the waning days of their three-decade rule there and had officially renounced the Balfour Declaration, their commitment to Jewish statehood.

For decades, Pop kept up an almost daily correspondence with his brother-in-law, Alan Steinert, a businessman who lived in Cambridge, Massachusetts, and was married to Nettie's youngest sister, Claire. In June 1946, Alan wrote Pop to complain that he hadn't been invited to a big Jewish fundraising dinner at a Boston hotel, which had raised the astonishing sum of $1.4 million. To be invited to the dinner in Boston, you had to have given $3500 to Jewish charities the previous year—but Alan and Claire made it their practice to give half of their contributions to Jewish charities and half to non-Jewish ones, so they didn't make the cut. Alan grumbled to Pop, "I am amazed at the financial devotion being expressed by the Jewish community toward a couple of million Jews in Europe whom they don't know and with whom they have, for the most part, no practical ties." Fifty years earlier, prosperous, assimilated German Jews in America, the equivalent of Alan and Claire, would have felt an automatic kinship with German Jews of similar status in Germany, even if their personal ties had become faint. But now there were no such people.

A small exception to America's strict immigration restrictions had been made for agricultural laborers in places where there were shortages; oddly enough, this led to one family of Jewish refugees from the displaced-person camps winding up in the care of the Lemann family at Palo Alto plantation. The great Black migration to Northern cities was underway, and there weren't enough field hands in Louisiana sugar country. Bubs, Pop's nephew who ran the family businesses in Donaldsonville, requested that five families from the camps be relocated to Palo Alto, where they would move into the cane workers' cabins that stood in a long row behind the main plantation house. When the first couple arrived, Bubs was annoyed to learn that they were actually a doctor and a teacher, who had claimed to be agricultural workers because before the war they had owned a small farm in Lithuania that they used as a weekend home. That was their best option for getting released from the camps. Like the Black workers whose jobs at Palo Alto they had filled, they immediately began looking for better opportunities in the North. They left after six weeks. Bubs cancelled his request for more families from the camps.

The Jewish majority, in America and in Europe, presented the German Jews in America (a remnant, though we didn't think of ourselves that way) with a difficult, though also unavoidable, test of loyalty. American German-Jewish culture was built around strict separation from the Jewish mainstream; everything about typical Jews—their consciousness, their practices—was alien to us, even repellent, threatening. And yet, we were eternally unable to persuade non-Jews to accept this categorical distinction that was so obvious to us. To them (up to and including the Nazis), we were all, simply, Jews. And it was true, we *were* all Jews. And the Jews who weren't like us were in dire need. Could they attract special concern and attention from us, based on solidarity?

Something made Pop feel a closer connection to suffering Jews in Europe, and also more sympathetic to Zionism, than most German Jews in the United States did—including his own relatives. He replied to Alan Steinert's letter by reminding him, gently, that his family, if their luck had been different, could have been among the Jews living in Europe when the Nazis came to power. Pop was himself actively fundraising for Jewish refugees. He was also helping to start a local chapter of the American Jewish Committee. He always attended the much smaller New Orleans version of the Boston dinner Alan wrote him about. He made modest contributions to Hebrew University in Palestine, and he facilitated large contributions to Zionist causes from his rich client Samuel Zemurray, who had been born in Kishinev, three decades before the famous pogrom there.

That Pop took this stance is something of a mystery; he lived his own life fully inside the German-Jewish culture. He was himself far less religious than his parents had been. He was a loyal member of Temple Sinai but he went only once a year, on Yom Kippur, and he sometimes confessed to close friends that he couldn't confidently say that he believed in God. But it was easy for him to be Jewish without being religious. All his social friends in New Orleans were like him, secular German Jews. During the summers when Father was a boy, the Lemann family—meaning women, children, and servants—would relocate to the blessedly cool resort town of Charlevoix, Michigan. (The men would come for two weeks, arriving by train in their business suits.) There, the Lemanns and the Steinerts lived in a two-block-long enclave on Michigan Avenue, inhabited by German Jews from Cincinnati, St. Louis, Chicago, and other cities. A short distance away was the Chicago Club, a private community of charming, rambling old houses with broad porches: restricted, meaning no Jews were allowed, including German Jews. And the German Jews on Michigan Avenue, emulating the Gentiles who shunned them, had arranged matters so that no Eastern European Jews could live there.

I think his friendship with Frankfurter must have had something to do with Pop's departure from the German-Jewish norm. Frankfurter had been actively Zionist for decades. He was born and partly raised in Europe. He had kept up closely with the rise of European antisemitism through his relatives who lived there. As a sitting Supreme Court justice, he had to be quieter about his political maneuverings, but he didn't abandon them; one was doing what he could to get the United States government to recognize the new Jewish state, over the objections of the State Department. Because of his Zionism and his other political stances, Frankfurter had been regularly attacked at the controversial moments of his career for being a Jew with radical, foreign, threatening beliefs. He had never participated in the German-Jewish culture; it's impossible to imagine him finding a comfortable Jewish identity through sitting in a pew at a Reform temple, listening to the choir singing hymns. Anyway, the truth was that anybody who was Jewish, even very fortunate people like Pop and Frankfurter who operated at the highest possible level, knew that someone who claimed to believe there was no antisemitism in the United States (as many German-Jews did publicly) had to be either disingenuous, self-deluded, or willfully ignorant. The best-off Jews, let alone ordinary Jews, still could not stay in fancy resort hotels, could not buy real estate in many neighborhoods, could not be hired at many companies, and had strictly limited access to the leading universities and to the professions.

A couple of years after his exchange with Alan Steinert, just as the state of Israel was officially declaring its independence, Pop told Frankfurter that he found it impossible to agree with the standard insistence of the Reform movement that Jews are a religion, not a race. One didn't have to stray into the territory of Nazi race science to believe that Jews were at least an ethnic group, recognizable to one another and usually also to outsiders. More than the high-Protestant denominations that the Reform movement aimed to emulate, the Jews had their own network of organizations and their own social life. And, despite his having grown up in a well-established family, Pop had experienced antisemitism himself, beginning in childhood—though not nearly as much as Frankfurter had. For Pop, less Zionist than Frankfurter but distinctly more tribal than most German Jews, I think his being a Southerner also helps explain the way he thought of himself, and his activities, Jewish and non-Jewish. His life took place entirely within the confines of the Jim Crow system. How could you be enveloped inside a society where every aspect of life, down to casual social interactions on the street, was determined by the racial order, and not be overwhelmingly aware that the world operates by hard-edged human categories, which people put themselves in and are put in by others? Being a Jew was Pop's category, but in New Orleans, being Black or white was most people's dominant category. Living there as a Jew, being in some ways set apart, being strange, would make you more aware of the larger form of apartness that prevailed in that place and time. Maybe that explains why Pop, often in partnership with Frankfurter, spent the final years of life being pulled, as if by a strong tide, into the race question, even more than he was into the Jewish question.

Pop's life beginning in his late middle age looks in retrospect like an endless procession of honors. He'd done a lot to deserve it, and also, the country needed a totemic native Southerner who was prominent and respected at home, but who had fully put the Civil War behind him. Pop was one of a limited number of people who could fit the bill. And there was his friendship with Frankfurter, who almost addictively promoted the careers of people in his network. Pop was constantly being offered important government jobs, often through Frankfurter's efforts. There was a flurry of letters between the two of them about a federal judgeship in 1938, and another flurry, about another judgeship, in 1942. In 1943 Pop wrote down some notes about a call he'd gotten from Dean Acheson, the under secretary of state and another intimate friend of Frankfurter, who wanted him to serve on "a commission for the purpose of making recommendations as to government of liberated regions between the end of hostilities and the setting up of new self-governments."

Pop turned all these offers down, explaining that Nettie's terrible and worsening health made it impossible for him to take on anything new. Her life during those years sounds like a nightmarish succession of long stays in sanatoriums, experimental surgeries, heavy doses of opiates, and painful injections through the back of her rib cage into her lungs, among other tortures. Through the mid-1940s she wrote dozens of long, perfectly typed letters to Father, always downplaying her own afflictions and focusing on him with an intensity that must have been both gratifying and worrisome. Father told me that she had been so sick for so long—it's all he had ever known—that he had assumed her condition would be somehow, magically, permanent. In the summer of 1946, back from the war, he was in Charlevoix, feeling it was safe to be carefree, when he got the news that Nettie had died of a sudden heart attack, at the age of fifty-two. He rushed home and sat with Pop and Stephen for hours, weeping.

One of Edgar and Edith Stern's myriad projects in New Orleans, with Pop and Nettie working at their side, was starting a small, private, progressive "country day" school just outside the city; founding such schools was a vogue among patrician liberals in the 1920s. Father and Stephen went there, and so did my sister and I. In the early years there were only a few students and everybody knew everybody else. In 1948 Pop married Mildred Lyons, a widow who had been in charge of the school dining room for years. She lived to be ninety-five, well into my adult life; she was the beloved grandmother I knew growing up. On weekends she'd drive up to Quercus in her Oldsmobile, wearing white gloves, and whisk Nancy and me away to the zoo, or the park, or a meal at the Camelia Grill. We'd spend Mardi Gras at her house because it was near the parade routes and because her sister—to us, Tantine—had a background in the local theater and knew how to get us set up in costumes and makeup. Nettie's death, and his remarriage, took Pop at least a step away from the heart of German-Jewish New Orleans, which was what Nettie's large extended family represented.

Pop's honors continued. In 1949, *Fortune* magazine published his picture as part of an article about the leading practicing lawyers in the country. Harvard appointed him to visiting committees for the law school and the Department of the Middle East, twice nominated him to its board of overseers, and, after he wasn't elected, gave him an honorary degree. In 1953 Frankfurter wrote Pop an excited note saying, "If by any chance you are asked to become Solicitor General, don't you dare turn it down." In 1956 Frankfurter gave a small dinner in Washington to welcome a new liberal justice, William Brennan, to the Supreme Court, insisting that he wouldn't set a date until he was sure that Pop could travel from New Orleans to be there. That same year, Pop wrote a letter to John Foster Dulles, the starchy, ardently anti-Communist secretary of state, regretting that he would have to decline another, unspecified proffered appointment. My guess is that this was meant to counter the bitter attacks on the State Department by anti-Communists like Senator Joe McCarthy, who considered Dulles to be too soft. Pop was a regular signer of statements opposing loyalty oaths and other anti-Communist excesses.

THE EYES OF THE WORLD

Felix Frankfurter's exalted place on the Supreme Court did not diminish his close friendship with Pop, or his penchant for political maneuvering. His maneuverings beginning in the 1940s actually enhanced his and Pop's dealings with each other, because Frankfurter's attention was moving into a new realm, race and civil rights, where Pop could function as his man on the scene. In 1945, a sixteen-year-old Black teenager in St. Martinville, Louisiana, named Willie Francis was charged with murdering his boss, a white pharmacist named Andrew Thomas. He was tried, convicted, and sentenced to death, a sentence that in those days was administered by a crew that traveled around the state with a portable electric chair. On the day of the execution, in the spring of 1946, the electric chair malfunctioned. The crew administered a lethal shock that left Francis still breathing; they readministered the shock, and again he was still breathing. At last they gave up and left St. Martinville, and Francis returned to his jail cell.

As the liberal world got wind of what had preceded the failed execution—Francis's court-appointed lawyers had tried to prevent him from pleading not guilty, had not called any witnesses, and had not appealed his conviction—the case began to attract attention. New lawyers, including the future federal judge Skelly Wright, took on Francis's case. They petitioned the Supreme Court to ban a second attempt to electrocute him. The Court heard the case, but it decided that it was up to Louisiana to decide what to do. Officially, Frankfurter should have done nothing else. Instead he wrote Pop privately to ask him to lobby the state parole board to prevent Francis from being executed. "I realize that the eyes of the world are in a sense upon us in this case," Pop wrote the board, adding that an unnamed prominent lawyer—obviously Frankfurter—had told him that "it would be a serious blot upon our State if Francis was permitted to be executed." His entreaties didn't work: in 1947 the portable electric chair returned to St. Martinville, and this time it functioned properly and Willie Francis was killed.

From the present day, you might wonder why any reasonably sympathetic and aware white person in Louisiana wouldn't choose to support civil rights. But almost none did, especially if they had grown up in Louisiana. The conceptual tools we have most readily available to understand this are the idea that they were racist, or that they were afraid to speak out. Besides these, there is the power of familiarity. The bloody battles that preceded the birth of Jim Crow had faded from memory, or had been purposefully erased through the creation of a powerful white mythology about the end of Reconstruction. The Southern caste system was familiar. It was the way things were. People are not naturally inclined to question basic arrangements, especially ones that work to their advantage. But that raises the question of why Pop was inclined, and willing, to break ranks. His position was secure enough that support for civil rights did not put him at risk. More than most New Orleanians, he moved in a wider liberal world that was finally beginning to awaken to racial injustice. What I can't completely answer is why being raised on a plantation, in an overwhelming atmosphere of white supremacy, didn't produce in him the same convictions it produced in almost everybody else who was white and was raised that way.

Whatever motivated him, Pop kept participating in early civil rights stirrings in Louisiana, often after prodding from the president of Dillard University, Albert Dent. Pop wrote to the mayor and the chief of police, complaining that the New Orleans police force almost never hired Black officers even when they got high scores on the civil service exam (at the time, there were only two Black men in the city police department) and, when it did hire someone

Black, would not put him in uniform. He wrote again when two Dillard students were arrested, taken to a police station, and not permitted to make phone calls. He congratulated Loyola University for opening up its track to a star Black athlete who had been barred from running on the track in a city park. He protested to one of the local newspapers for referring to a Black woman who had been killed in an automobile accident as "the Blouin woman," which was "an expression usually reserved for prostitutes," when if she had been white she would have been "Mrs. Blouin." He urged the editor of another newspaper to investigate a report he'd heard that more than half of New Orleans's Black doctors had chosen to relocate to other cities, where there was less discrimination. He chastised Edgar Stern, who by then owned one of the local television stations, after seeing an article in the local Black newspaper, the *Louisiana Weekly*, "complaining that after a young colored girl was the winner of a prize on a WDSU program, WDSU declined to carry her on the screen because she was colored." He also accepted an invitation, which Stern had declined, to join an effort to integrate New Orleans's public libraries. He attended a fundraising dinner for Adlai Stevenson, twice the Democratic presidential nominee in the 1950s, which had to be held on Loyola's basketball court because there were Black guests seated at the same tables as whites; none of the downtown hotels would permit Blacks to be at an event like that, unless they were waiters. He wrote to President Truman himself, asking that he pardon a Dillard faculty member who had been sentenced to a six-month prison term for being a conscientious objector to military service.

Pop was well aware that the institution most likely to produce meaningful racial progress at that moment was the Supreme Court, because the political system was so resistant. The Democratic Party was dependent on the South, and the South, where most Black people still couldn't vote, was completely opposed to civil rights; the Democrats' very small movements in that direction had led Louisiana to vote Republican, for the first time ever, in the 1956 presidential election. Pop's close friend was a Supreme Court justice, who was thinking more and more about race. A stage was being set. In 1953, Pop wrote to Alan Steinert, after he'd attended a grandly staged public event in New Orleans that included a military parade: "It moved me to see the Negroes marching in the front line with the white standard bearers." That had happened as a result of Truman's having integrated the armed forces a few years earlier. Pop went to Dillard to hear a speech by Thurgood Marshall, the tall, elegant, fearless head of the NAACP Legal Defense and Education Fund, who had spent years painstakingly pursuing a legal strategy aimed, ultimately, at getting the Supreme Court to declare segregated public education in the South unconstitutional. This would be a huge step, because it struck at two of Jim Crow's foundational assumptions: that the federal government had no right to tell the South what to do, and that integrating schools would inevitably lead to the violation of the taboo against free social contact between Black men and white women that lay at the heart of the Southern caste system. In 1952 Pop wrote to another member of his close circle of liberal lawyers who didn't live in New Orleans, Charles C. Burlingham: "If I were on the Supreme Court I think I might well hold that segregation is per se a denial of equal treatment under law and allow a period of perhaps ten years for the states to arrange for its elimination in the public schools."

In 1950, one of Thurgood Marshall's long string of lawsuits, on behalf of a Black student who had been denied admission to the University of Texas's law school, went to the Supreme Court, which ruled unanimously against segregation. The obvious next step, but a much more consequential and difficult one, would be a challenge to segregation in ordinary public schools. Frankfurter believed that the chief justice, Fred Vinson, who'd grown up in a small town in Kentucky and who had no evident objection on principle to legal segregation, would not be able to lead the court to a clear decision on schools. He also didn't want the court to agree to take any school cases, let alone hear and decide them, during an election year. So he successfully persuaded the other justices to combine five separate school cases into one, and then to delay considering that case until after the 1952 election. In 1953 Vinson died of a heart attack; this led to a famous remark of Frankfurter's that "this is the first solid piece of evidence I've had that there really is a God." He meant that it was now plausible to hope for a unanimous decision in the school cases that are now enshrined as *Brown v. Board of Education* and that were heard after Vinson's death in 1953 and decided in 1954, a few months before I was born.

Frankfurter worked furiously to produce a unanimous decision. Court records show that he had eleven private meetings with Vinson's successor as chief justice, Earl Warren, a former governor of California who understood politics but had no previous experience as a judge, during the two months before the Court's decision was released. He also lobbied the most skeptical justice, Stanley Reed, a Kentuckian like Vinson, until Reed was comfortable joining the majority decision. He persuaded the Justice Department, which officially he wasn't supposed to talk to about active cases, to file a brief supporting Thurgood Marshall's position in the case. And he kept in close touch with Pop, his closest friend in the South, about whether it might be possible to keep the former Confederacy's rage about the decision under control.

In May 1954, the decision—probably the most obviously consequential in American legal history—was announced. Reactions were immediate and copious. Black groups cheered. Liberal groups, including Jewish groups, cheered. President Dwight Eisenhower was notably cautious, urging compliance but not endorsing the decision. Southern politicians vowed to defy the Supreme Court, which would test the legitimacy of the American political system. Pop undertook a campaign to persuade a group of prominent Southern lawyers—people who had taken an oath committing themselves to the legal system—to support a stance more like Eisenhower's, by signing a statement calling for compliance. Officially, he got the idea for this from Will Alexander, a white liberal who had been president of Dillard before Albert Dent, but it strikes me that Frankfurter must have been involved; Pop certainly was keeping him closely posted. There's a draft of the statement in Pop's files, filled with crossings-out and rewordings as he struggled to produce something that he believed his professional peers might sign, but that wasn't so watered down as to amount to a call to delay endlessly implementing the decision. His anxiety almost rises off the page. Probably because he thought it might be too strongly stated, Pop removed even this innocent-sounding sentence: "It is at this point, we believe, that members of the legal profession have a special responsibility to help clarify the role of the judiciary in our society." Once he was done, he sent the statement to a long list of lawyers and law school deans he knew whom he thought might be sympathetic—his own law partners not among them. Some of his letters went unanswered, even though the recipients knew him well. Only three people agreed to sign, and only two of the three were living in the South; the third was a man from Arkansas who had recently become dean of the law school at New York University.

Some of those who declined to sign the letter told Pop it would do more harm than good, by stirring up even more resentment of the Supreme Court than there was already. Some said they were worried that having Black students in class would slow down the progress of the white students. Some brought up what most Southern whites thought they knew about Black people's sexuality, and wondered whether integration would corrupt the moral purity of the white students. With infinite patience, Pop answered these objections. He assured one man that if he signed, other white people would not ostracize him. To another, he offered the thought that poor Black families so greatly value education that their students would surely excel in integrated schools. To another he insisted that the idea of Black people as a sexual threat was a relic of a day that had long since passed. But in the end he decided not to release the statement because its having only three signatures would send the opposite of the message of support he'd hoped for.

He did send the responses he'd gotten to Frankfurter, who showed them to the other justices. Earl Warren, whom Frankfurter saw in those days as his protégé, ready to be educated by him, sent a written response. In August 1954, Frankfurter sent it to Pop, "solely for your eyes and no one else's ears." Warren, perhaps trying to please Frankfurter, perhaps showing his naïveté about the South, chose to see the letters to Pop as cause for optimism. If Monte Lemann was willing to support the *Brown* decision, how far behind could other prominent Southerners be? His actions said more than the other Southern lawyers' discouraging words: "I feel certain that even a comparatively few men like him can do much to help the situation which I cannot believe is as bad as his friend Tunstall"—a lawyer in Norfolk, Virginia, who had declined to sign the statement—"believes it to be," Warren wrote.

By this time both Frankfurter and Pop were in their seventies and had been close friends for fifty years. Frankfurter was becoming more conservative. Like many people who start out on the left and move in that direction, he insisted that he hadn't changed, the world had; he'd always believed in judicial restraint and he still believed in it. It bothered him that the tidal wave of liberal praise for the *Brown* decision was mostly directed at Warren, who wasn't a first-rate legal thinker by Frankfurter's lights. The world didn't know how large a role Frankfurter had played in the case. In 1955, when a second set of cases, about how the *Brown* decision would be implemented, came before the Supreme Court, Frankfurter put on the brakes. He persuaded Earl Warren to insert a phrase from a 1911 decision by Justice Oliver Wendell Holmes—"with all deliberate speed"—into the Court's unanimous decision. The NAACP's preferred language for the enforced timing of desegregation was "forthwith." Frankfurter was keenly aware, partly through Pop, of the deep opposition to the decision. He was worried that the South simply would not comply, provoking a crisis over the authority of the Supreme Court—but the result was that the South didn't proceed with any speed at all. For the same reason, also in 1955, he persuaded his fellow justices not to agree to hear a Virginia case that challenged the Southern states' laws against "miscegenation," interracial marriage. The Court finally declared antimiscegenation laws to be unconstitutional in 1967, but Frankfurter was gone by then.

Soon Frankfurter began publicly distancing himself from the justices he had, not so much earlier, believed should decide civil rights cases unanimously. In 1958, the Supreme Court went into special session to decide whether the state of Arkansas had the right to keep Little Rock Central High School segregated, in violation of the *Brown* decision. This produced yet another unanimous decision, against Arkansas, but by now there was a publicly visible gap between Frankfurter and the four most liberal justices. He insisted on issuing his own concurring opinion, a week after the main decision was issued. The decision had told Arkansas that it must bow to the superior authority of the Supreme Court, but actually, Frankfurter wrote, the justices should be understood merely as "depositories of law." The Court was not the higher authority; the law and the Constitution were. From here Frankfurter progressed over time into a dyspeptic, all-encompassing disapproval of the justices, especially the liberal ones, as being merely officeholders, politicians, not real jurists. In 1963, after Pop had died and Frankfurter, disabled by a stroke, had retired, Father went to see him in Washington. Afterward he reported to his brother: "He is still bursting with passion, most of which consisted in venting his spleen at Warren and Brennan"—liberal justices whom Frankfurter had mentored when they were appointed—"and most of the rest of the Court, who he complained are not lawyers at all." Frankfurter told Father that he wished he, rather than Warren, had written the *Brown* decision, so that it could have made the argument he made in the Arkansas case.

Nobody ever accused Pop of being a radical—that was the younger Frankfurter's reputation, not his. But during the years after the *Brown* decision, to judge by their correspondence, Pop had moved to the left of Frankfurter on racial issues. In 1958, Learned Hand, an eighty-six-year-old federal judge from New York who was a member of Pop and Frankfurter's legal inner circle and the object of great veneration, gave a series of three lectures at Harvard Law School criticizing the Supreme Court for overreaching, with the *Brown* decision as the primary example. It's easy to understand the white South's opposition to the decision, which was a direct assault on its racial order—but Hand, whose square head and massive eyebrows made him look like a heroic sculpture of a judge and who'd come of age politically as a member of Theodore Roosevelt's Progressive Party, was an impeccably credentialed liberal. "For myself," he said in the third lecture, "it would be most irksome to be ruled by a bevy of Platonic Guardians"—the supposedly benign aristocratic ruling class in *The Republic*—"even if I knew how to choose them, which I assuredly do not." What's perhaps more shocking than his opposition was how unshocked the legal world was by it. Frankfurter, already heading in the same direction as Hand, was mainly enthusiastic about the lectures. Pop was skeptical. They wrote dueling letters about Hand's lectures to their friend Charles Burlingham, Pop stoutly optimistic that in 1954 the Court had "blazed the trail" for the post–Jim Crow era that was sure to arrive one day, Frankfurter upset about what he saw as the Court's new conviction that it could simply nullify any law it disapproved of.

For many decades, the Jim Crow system had seemed unassailable, partly because so many white people didn't think it was wrong, and partly because the Democratic Party's success nationally depended on its keeping the support of the South. Now, the *Brown* decision, along with the growing strength of the civil rights movement in the South, was producing breaches in the castle walls. Every new development reinforced the disharmony that had opened up between Pop and Frankfurter. In 1957, Congress passed the first civil rights law since the dismantling of Reconstruction more than eighty years earlier, aimed at beginning to reestablish the Black voting rights that the advent of Jim Crow had taken away. It had to be watered down considerably to get enough Southern support to pass. One amendment mandated a jury trial for those charged with obstructing

Black voting—which, because Southern juries were all white, meant that getting a conviction would be impossible. Pop, seeing that the amendment would make voting rights unenforceable in the South, signed a letter opposing it. Frankfurter, who wasn't supposed to get involved in legislative politics, once again couldn't restrain himself; he made it known that he supported the jury trial amendment. Why not compromise? He wrote Pop: "I thought that the feeling aroused by the proposal to have a jury in a case of criminal contempt was absurdly out of proportion to the significance of the issue."

Frankfurter continued to retreat and Pop to charge forward. After reading reports that Senator James Eastland of Mississippi had convened a secret meeting of Southern elected officials to discuss flouting the *Brown* decision, Pop helped form a national group of lawyers who produced a public statement of stern disapproval; this one was successfully published, though with few Southern signers. He wrote a "memo to the file" noting with exasperation that although the state college in Lafayette had integrated, there were still no Black students at Louisiana State University in Baton Rouge. He wrote Senator Russell Long, Huey's son (but, Pop believed, not cut from the same cloth) to chastise him for signing the Southern Manifesto, a pro-segregation statement that got the support of all but a few senators from the former Confederate states. Another letter scolded one of the local television stations for refusing to show a documentary by Edward R. Murrow on the South's resistance to school integration. Pop even wrote Ralph Edwards, host of a popular national television program called *This Is Your Life*, a faraway celebrity whom he couldn't possibly have known, suggesting that he devote a show to New Orleans's most prominent Black journalist, Orlando Taylor.

THE END

Old age can be cruel. Frankfurter's wife, Marion, whom he'd met back in the 1910s in Progressive-era activist circles, was by now an invalid, afflicted with crippling physical and mental ailments. The

Frankfurters, childless and with no connection (in his case because of the Holocaust) to relatives, hard up financially after a lifetime of being completely indifferent to money, were living a more isolated life than they were used to. Felix was intensely conscious of the irony of his political situation: a lifetime of political crusading, with the *Brown* decision as one of its culminating achievements, had helped bring into being a new world in which he found himself increasingly uncomfortable with the liberal mainstream. "We have ceased to be a Court," he grumbled in one of his dispirited letters to Pop. In Pop's letters to Frankfurter, beginning in the mid-1950s, there's an unmissable impulse to cheer Frankfurter up. Pop's own life lacked the grandeur of being a Supreme Court justice, but he was happily remarried, deeply rooted in his community, and surrounded by family and friends. His sons, Father and Stephen, had come home to New Orleans and joined Monroe & Lemann.

Still, Father told me, Pop had periods of depression in his later years. I see signs of this, too, in his letters. The deaths of old friends and close family members seemed to hit him very hard. He worried incessantly about his sons, especially Stephen, who was kicked out of a succession of schools for poor grades, and then, temporarily, out of Harvard College, before finally graduating and going on to law school. (Father was always a stellar student.) When Nettie died, Louisiana's civil legal code dictated that Father and Stephen immediately inherit her money, and this gave Pop something new to worry about: were they, especially Father, becoming lavish livers? This wasn't what Pop, who liked to tell people he was the grandson of a peddler and a French peasant, thought of as the proper way for Lemanns to comport themselves. Perhaps as a form of therapy for Frankfurter, perhaps because he wanted to take advantage of Frankfurter's being less personally reserved than he was, Pop would regularly enlist his old friend to act as a kind of backup father to his sons. They'd visit the justice in his chambers to get a lecture, usually meant to steer them away from whatever might distract them from joining Pop's law firm; Pop himself didn't feel he should offer those urgings himself. Or Frankfurter would write Father and Stephen letters of advice. Or he'd write Pop, assuring him that he need not worry so much about his sons.

By this time, German Jews (I'm counting Frankfurter as one, though he was Austrian) were losing their dominant position in the American Jewish world. They hadn't been demographically dominant for a long time, but by the 1950s most of the children and grandchildren of the Eastern European Jews—the people we called "Russian Jews"—had found their way out of the slums and into the middle class. The Conservative movement was bigger than the Reform movement. Although by today's standards antisemitism was shockingly widespread in the United States, it would be hard for members of the Eastern European Jewish majority to feel utter despair. For them doors were opening, not closing. Large, solid new synagogues and Jewish community centers were being built all over the country. Eastern European Jews were leading Jewish organizations. The establishment and early growth of the state of Israel, as a refuge of a kind that had never been available, was to most American Jews, if not to German Jews, an inspiring, joyous development.

Pop didn't have much, or maybe any, direct contact with this part of Jewish America. It's clear from his letters that he was acutely aware of the doors that still hadn't opened. (In the late 1950s, he noted in one letter, Massachusetts General Hospital, in supposedly enlightened Boston, had no Jewish residents or interns.) To him it looked as if they would never open. The German-Jewish culture that had been strong through most of his life was beginning to fade. German Jews were converting, or intermarrying, or dropping religion entirely. Their long-running search for a universalist version of Jewishness was running up against the natural limit of how universal Jewishness can ever be. (I can't imagine anyone I knew growing up asking the familiar question "Is it good for the Jews?," because we were supposed to be only for things that would be good for everybody.) It couldn't have brightened the picture that he had lived so recently through the time of the worst yet in the endless series of Jewish disasters. Like Mordecai, his biblical namesake, he had refused to bow down or to disguise his identity, and he had nonetheless been admitted to court and given a measure of wealth and power. But unlike Mordecai, he had been unable to aid in the saving of his people from disaster. He dutifully participated in Jewish causes. He maintained his membership in Temple Sinai, but he hardly ever went and drew no real sustenance from it. The elaborate Passover seders and other joyous Jewish celebrations of his and Nettie's childhoods were long forgotten. He lived well in his highly restricted, small, and comfortable milieu. I don't get the feeling that he knew where the saga of the Jews was headed.

Similar logic may also explain Pop's racial optimism, which one wouldn't expect from a Southern liberal in the 1950s. Pop had grown up in Black-majority sugar country, in a racial order that was not so far removed from slavery. The post-Reconstruction denial of rights to Black people was fully underway, and white America, even outside the South, seemed blind to the injustice of it. He'd had a candid view of what really went on in the plantation South, behind its concealing scrim of gentility: the utter domination of every aspect of Black life, including even sexual life, by white people. During his adult life in New Orleans, Pop saw a general strengthening of Black institutions, a rise in Black education, political activity, and expectations generally, and some increase in white sympathy for civil rights—all from a very low baseline. The *Brown* decision looked to him like the beginning of something. "We are moving along and cracks are appearing in the ice," he wrote to his friend Charles Burlingham a few months after the decision.

But it's impossible for me to make myself understand Pop's racial stance without also relying on his Jewishness as a good part of the explanation. He himself, in his letters about race, frequently made this connection. To a member of the extended Monroe family who had become a civil rights advocate, he wrote: "I greatly admire your character and courage. Belonging as I do to a minority group, I am

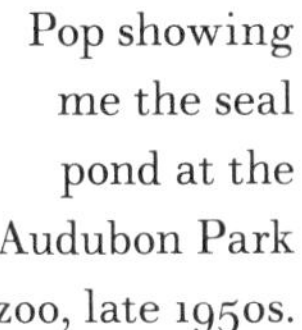

Pop showing me the seal pond at the Audubon Park zoo, late 1950s.

always conscious that in issues of this sort my influence is not to be compared with that of persons in your position, but I think everyone knows how I feel." To Frankfurter, by way of putting a positive light on the situation in the South since the *Brown* decision, despite all the resistance, he wrote: "We can never hope to eliminate all bigotry. (Look at the experience of the Jews for 5,000 years.)"

I was born in August 1954, four months after Pop's seventieth birthday. There are photographs showing him playing with me in a backyard, and taking me to the seal pond at the zoo in Audubon Park. He looks old: not much hair left, his face deeply creased, its features less sharp than they had been. My clearest memory of him is as an old man in pajamas, slippers, and a smoking jacket, sitting in a chair in a kind of home library—a desk, books, leather—on the second floor of his house, the house where Father grew up, emanating the kind of crinkly warmth that children are looking for in the elderly people they encounter.

In the spring of 1957, in Shreveport, Louisiana, to try a case, Pop had some kind of heart problem that landed him in a hospital there for several days. From then on, it's impossible to miss an overwhelming worry pervading all the family correspondence, a sense that his secure place in the world and at the center of the family had become precarious, for the oldest and simplest reason, mortality. When he returned to New Orleans, doctors put him on a restricted regime that kept him at home as much as possible. He reported to Frankfurter that he was on a heavy cocktail of drugs and in nearly constant pain from an old injury—but "it is not terrible however and will not kill me." Sometimes, not often, he went downtown to his dark, premodern office at Monroe & Lemann, a preserved shrine to his prewar commercial heyday, and he kept up his practice and his other activities as much as he could. Father, Stephen, or his secretary would bring him papers to sign and take them back downtown. Affairs were wound up. Commemorations of his achievements were planned. Arrangements were made for him to sit for a portrait.

It must have been clear to everyone that seventy-five—April 3, 1959—would be his last milestone birthday. That was the occasion for the event honoring him at Dillard that I remember attending. At the end of May he returned to Dillard, though he found it taxing to leave the house and travel to a different part of town, to hear the thirty-year-old Martin Luther King Jr. give the commencement address. ("He is a remarkable man," he reported to Frankfurter.) In late August, his closest friend in New Orleans, Edgar Stern, had a sudden heart attack while on a cross-country train trip and died in a country hospital in a small town in the Utah desert. For Pop this was a devastating blow from which he had a hard time recovering. Hearing distressing reports about the shape Pop was in, Alan Steinert, his brother-in-law in Cambridge, decided to fly down to New Orleans to check on him and to try to cheer him up. Alan arrived on a Thursday. By Saturday he felt that Pop's mood was improving. That night Pop was able to come downstairs for dinner and converse, as if he were almost back to normal, although it was obvious that he would never return to the full life he'd been living a few years earlier. Perhaps a period of being a comfortable semi-invalid, receiving a few visitors and answering some letters, was in store.

Alan, thinking Pop had successfully come through his crisis, was planning to take a midday plane back to Boston on Sunday. Early that morning, Mildred woke him up with the news that Pop was having trouble breathing. She administered a portable oxygen supply that was kept next to his bed and called the doctor. Within half an hour Pop was dead from, according to the autopsy, a blood clot that had formed inside his heart. "The end came so fast that there was no evidence of infarction of the heart, and he suffered no pain at all," Alan wrote Frankfurter.

The next day there was a funeral at Temple Sinai, just around the corner from the house where Pop had died. Julian Feibelman delivered a long, flowery eulogy that I think would have embarrassed Pop, elevating him almost to prophetic status: "When he spoke men became silent; when he advised, they were prone to heed; where he led they followed." I suppose a casual visitor to the service, seeing the temple's soaring marble sanctuary packed with the great and good of New Orleans to mark the passing of the grandson of an immigrant peddler who had risen to a high place out in the big world, would have thought Julian's grandiose message was fully justified. That would have missed the provisionality, the in-betweenness, that was a less obvious part of the lives of New Orleans's prosperous German Jews—as it is, intermittently, of all Jews everywhere. We stood at a distinct remove from the local gentry, and also from the Jewish majority. Our conviction that we shared a transatlantic culture with people in Germany who were just like us had been obliterated; this was so unimaginable that we found it difficult even to acknowledge that it had happened. We were intensely uncomfortable with the prevailing response, Jewish nationalism, so we had trouble acknowledging that too. We wanted to be Jews of whom Jewishness demanded very little, benign white Southerners in a social, economic, and political order that was being challenged, full members of an American culture that wasn't sure it wanted to admit us. The architecture of Temple Sinai signaled arrival, permanence—but historically, Jews have had to live lightly on the ground, to make ourselves transportable. Our physical monuments have more often than not wound up representing misplaced confidence. Perhaps what we had built for ourselves in New Orleans was not as solid as it looked.

RETURNING

ON PREVIOUS PAGE

Father with Nancy and me on a trip to Europe,
early 1960s.

IN THE YEARS AFTER Pop's DEATH, THE EARLY 1960s, FATHER often spent Sunday afternoons taking me around to visit our elderly relatives. This didn't require much travel. Dozens of them, it seemed, lived in Uptown New Orleans, within a few blocks of Temple Sinai and of the house on St. Charles Avenue that Bernard and Harriet Lemann, my great-grandparents, had built in the late nineteenth century, when they were half relocating from Donaldsonville to New Orleans in order to educate their children. Aunt Minnie— Miriam Lemann, Bernard and Harriet's last surviving child—lived on Walnut Street, next to Audubon Park. She was, Father liked to remind me, the matriarch of the family, a position of great honor that one achieved merely by remaining alive. I remember her as small, round, warm, with an unruly bob of frizzy hair, presiding over a sitting room that on Sunday afternoons was filled with a large brood of family members, there for a heavy supper. Also on Walnut Street, two or three blocks away, was a brick house with one apartment upstairs and one downstairs. Julian and Mary Anna Feibelman, the rabbi at Temple Sinai and his wife who was one of Father's many cousins, lived downstairs, and Mary Anna's mother, Alice Lemann Fellman, an eternally coquettish aging Gibson girl, lived upstairs, often in the company of her ne'er-do-well son, John. Mary Anna was her mother's opposite: plainspoken, plainly presented, her apartment devoid of decorative frills, perpetually unhappy with her financial situation, which was far more constrained than that of her mother upstairs.

Stella Lemann, the widow of one of Pop's brothers, lived on St. Charles Avenue. She would greet us in a room with a bearskin rug that I found terrifying, because the bear's head was still attached. Her house had an elevator that went from the first floor to the second floor, and she had trouble remembering who we were. John Lemann, another of Father's cousins, lived on Palmer Avenue, in a house designed as a smaller replica of Palo Alto. Mildred, Pop's widow, lived around the corner on Marquette Place, until she surrendered the house to Stephen, Father's brother, and his wife, Shirley, and moved to a smaller place not far away. Then there were the relatives from Nettie's side of the family, who had more money: Uncle Junior (whose obituary had the headline "HARRIS HYMAN JUNIOR, SPORTSMAN-INVESTOR") and Aunt Helen-Aimee, Cousin Teddy and Cousin Barbara, Aunt Mimi, and so on. There seemed to be no end of them.

In the generation above Father's, most of the relatives we'd visit were widows—women who in their late teens or early twenties had married considerably older men, who had then died, usually of heart attacks, in their fifties. Photographs of their late husbands—olive-skinned, olive-shaped, moustachioed, formally attired—adorned the mantelpiece or the top of the piano. Often these women were widowed for longer than they'd been married. We'd sit with them in dark living rooms with heavy furniture, the curtains drawn against the heat, the long Sunday afternoons slowly drifting by, reviewing the doings of our (to my boy's way of thinking, anyway) limitlessly large extended family and of the German-Jewish families in New Orleans that were one step away from ours: Cahns and Cohns, Sterns and Steegs, Blums and Blooms, Wolfs and Weils. Births, deaths, and marriages were enumerated, children's accumulation of educational credentials proudly noted, discords and the troubles of family businesses lamented. We were a tightly bounded Jewish subtribe, a cultural cul-de-sac: deeply conventional, provincial, cautious, devoid of radical or bohemian impulses, and also nowhere near being a high-society elite. Father, in his Sunday uniform of khaki trousers and white bucks—Tommy, to the relatives we'd visit, pronounced *Taw-mee*—was polite, solicitous, loyal: the young father and husband who had done the family and the community honor by coming back home, joining the family firm, and pulling his oar on behalf of worthy local causes. As impeccably loyal as he was, I can see that he had some impulse to find a less constrained life for himself, though of course without leaving the neighborhood.

To me as a boy, nothing could have been as secure, as serene, as likely to last forever, as our environment. Sometimes Father would take me downtown. We would go to an oyster bar called the Pearl, where he had lunch most days, perhaps partly because he was banned from the Boston Club—unless the shucker caught his eye, gave a short horizontal chop with his hand, and muttered, *"Pas bon, pas bon"*: the oysters weren't good that day. Or he would take me to Mr. DiStefano, his barber, at the old St. Charles Hotel, built in 1896, across the street from the Whitney Bank building where Monroe & Lemann had its offices. Or to the office of the William B. Reily Company, coffee importers and clients of the law firm, where men in white linen suits sat around a big round rotating table arrayed with small piles of beans placed next to cups that they'd taste from, and then send the mouthful of coffee flying into a spittoon on the floor. Once or twice a year, a red-faced, out-of-breath man, a traveling salesman from Brooks Brothers, would take a suite at the St. Charles that we'd visit, so that we could order shirts chosen from books of swatches he'd brought to New Orleans in trunks. If it was the holiday season, Father would distribute fresh, expertly palmed bills to the attendant at the parking lot, the elevator man, and the people who kept the Whitney building clean. This may not sound like anybody's standard idea of life in the 1960s, but New Orleans does not swiftly embrace change. Even the other big cities of the South are hurried by comparison.

My life was designed to be an exact replica of Father's. We both had hair cut so short that it didn't need to be combed. We both wore round tortoiseshell glasses. Father went to the local country day school, as I've said, and before that to a progressive nursery school that had also been founded by the Sterns, so I went to both of them

Thomas and Stephen Lemann, brothers and law partners,
at Monroe & Lemann, 1980s.

too. In the summers I went to a camp in North Carolina, founded
at about the same time as these schools and along the same progressive lines, where Father had gone as a boy. In all these places, I was
one of a very small number of Jewish children, because the alternatives that were the standard for most Jewish families were too Jewish
for Father's taste, too shackled inside an inescapable ethnic prison.
Father had been sent to the Sunday school at Temple Sinai—and so
was I, until the breach over Cousin Julian's letting a few mentions
of the state of Israel slip through kept me from being confirmed,
as Father had been. In ending my Jewish education, Father was
not rejecting the familiar, he was objecting to the temple's moving
away from what was familiar to him—the unadulterated Pittsburgh
Platform—in a direction that struck him as too tribally Jewish.
What was familiar usually seemed right to him. Within days of my
birth letters were circulating in the family about the certainty that
I would go to Harvard, like Pop and Father, and after that it was just

as certain that I would go on to Harvard Law School and then move back home and join Monroe & Lemann.

"I KNOW HIS KIND"

It's a standard trope in depictions of assimilated Jews to open with a scene built around a Christmas tree. That's how Tom Stoppard's *Leopoldstadt* and Alfred Uhry's *The Last Night of Ballyhoo* begin, and also Ian Buruma's memoir about his grandparents, *Their Promised Land*. The idea is, as soon as you show that, you've got the audience's full attention, especially if it's a Jewish audience, because it's so peculiar. When I was growing up, the idea that it was peculiar wouldn't have occurred to me—all the Jews in New Orleans, at least the ones we knew, celebrated Christmas, though we did so a little more enthusiastically than the others. In both *Leopoldstadt* and *The Last Night of Ballyhoo* there is an intrafamily debate about whether to crown the Christmas tree with a five-pointed or a six-pointed star, but that was not a question we would have considered: six-pointed was too particular, too limiting. Weeks in advance, we would choose our tree, haul carefully preserved boxes of beautiful and fragile ornaments out of the attic, summon an attitude of mixed reverence and joy for trimming the tree, and place wreaths and other decorations around the house. On Christmas Eve we would sing all the standard carols and Father would solemnly read out loud Clement Moore's poem "A Visit from St. Nicholas." On Christmas morning my sister and I would arise at dawn and sit impatiently in front of the tree, waiting to open the dozens of presents that had come in from across the Lemann family's expanse of relatives, friends, and legal clients. Once or twice Father went to a good deal of effort to arrange to have a grandly presented roast suckling pig, which is about the most unkosher dish imaginable, instead of a turkey as the main course at our Christmas dinner. I can see that one might read this and ask, Why not just convert? Part of the answer is that in

New Orleans, at least our New Orleans, everybody knew everybody else, going back for at least two generations. So if we had tried to tell people that we weren't Jewish, it wouldn't matter—everybody knew we were. Father's preference was to redefine the meaning of Jewishness, as it applied to us, to suit his preferences.

As I got older, I began to have a sense that there was a different American Jewish life out there somewhere. Father's taste in reading in those years, unconsciously echoing that of Bernard, his grandfather, in the mid-nineteenth century, ran to Trollope, Thackeray, and Sir Walter Scott, but Mother had novels by Philip Roth, Saul Bellow, and Bernard Malamud on her bedstand, which I would sometimes look at when nobody was around, in the same way that I would read the copy of *Lady Chatterley's Lover* that Mother and Father kept hidden in a closet. Or, though it was rare in those days, there would be a television show or a movie with a character you were meant to read as Jewish (let's say, a Catskills comedian making an appearance on a talk show), who looked and spoke like nobody we knew in New Orleans. I went off to college never having tasted any of the suite of familiar Jewish foods: bagels, lox, kugel, matzoh, gefilte fish, latkes, babka, and so on. Many of the foods of my childhood, like gumbo and jambalaya, which still exert an inescapable tug, are triply *treyf*, because they use pork, shellfish, and butter all in the same dish.

I had never been to a bar mitzvah or a bris. We never lit Hanukkah candles. Once we went to another family's Passover seder, because the host was a federal judge Father admired, but usually we marked that season with an Easter egg hunt—with adorable dressed-up children scouring the bushes for pastel-colored eggs we'd dyed and hidden for the occasion—in the backyard at Quercus. I wonder, looking back, whether we were keeping everything overtly Jewish out of range, so resolutely that I didn't even realize that we were doing it, or whether we just weren't aware of Jewish things. Either way, they simply didn't exist. I can't remember Israel ever being mentioned in our house, including during the 1967 war that commanded the full attention of most American Jews. Is it possible that the Holocaust was never mentioned either? It seems hard to believe, but that's the way I remember it. When you build a view of the world and your place in it, and something happens that utterly, horrifyingly upends it, you have the choice of simply shutting out the destabilizing new information. Once when I was still attending Sunday school at Temple Sinai, a teacher—who, like most teachers in synagogues, was more religious than the students' families—showed us Alain Resnais's short documentary film about Nazi concentration camps, *Night and Fog*, which was made in 1956 and contained a few of the now (but not then) familiar images of stacked-up corpses and skeletal survivors. She was shocked that, as far as she could tell, none of us in the class had been told there had been concentration camps, and not so many years earlier.

The obvious question is, how did we get this way? It's very difficult to answer that from a child's point of view, because in that case things just *are* the way they appear to you and you don't need to understand their origin. The way we were as Jews seemed normal, it had no particularized origin requiring an explanation. The playwright and memoirist Lillian Hellman, probably the most famous child of German-Jewish New Orleans, halfway in age between Pop and Father, was "a Jewish Southerner whose religion was held in abeyance," as her biographer puts it. She grew up going sometimes to temple, sometimes to church. During her decades as a *grande dame*, Hellman had a companion and chronicler named Peter Feibleman, who was another product of German-Jewish New Orleans (there were the Feibelmans, Julian's family, my relatives, and the Feiblemans, who had owned a small department store in a formerly Jewish, later Black, neighborhood at the edge of downtown and were Pop's and Father's clients). In a memoir about their friendship, he wrote, "For most of her life Lillian had displayed an unfortunate tendency to separate all food that didn't please her into one of two categories: goy dreck and kike dreck. Baked Alaska was the epitome of goy dreck, beef Wellington was kike dreck."

What strikes me about this now is that anybody who'd ever been within range of Eastern European American Jewish life would know, as I'd guess Hellman didn't, that beef Wellington is non-kosher: milk and meat in the same dish. But what Peter Feibleman noticed was the epithet, which Hellman was using because she liked to shock people and wanted to demonstrate that she wasn't one of those Jews who's reflexively pro-Jewish. Our quest to classify Jews as a religion, not a race, had wound up exactly reversed: all race (though renounceable as an identity) and no religion. We indulged ourselves in the majority's antisemitism—but then, inevitably, we ran up against it ourselves. In Hellman's first memoir, the only authentically Jewish moment comes when she goes to Germany to study in 1929, in the earliest stages of the great disaster, and is invited to join a Nazi youth group, "no dues for foreigners if they had no Jewish connection." She aborts her plans and leaves the country. By her lights it was antisemitism, and only antisemitism, that makes one Jewish; therefore antisemites, not Jews, get to define what being Jewish means.

Father and Mother left enough material behind for me to trace how they individually arrived at the version of Jewishness I remember from my childhood. That's more interesting, more poignant, than just noting that it was typical. Father graduated from Metairie Park Country Day School in 1943 and then enrolled at Harvard. During his freshman year he turned eighteen, and at the end of the year he enlisted in the army. Historically, extremely long terms of required army service were one of the special punishments often visited on Jews in Europe. It occurs to me that a resulting visceral aversion to being drafted may help explain Bernard Lemann's departure from the United States during the Civil War. But in the next generation, the family had become Americanized, and the U.S. army didn't single out Jews for bad treatment. Just as Pop served in the First World War, Father served in the Second World War (a few years later, his brother, Stephen, was a Marine during the Korean War). Father's letters home indicate that he may not have been enthusiastic about it, but he would have been drafted anyway, and he saw it as the obligation of a loyal American.

During basic training he was given a standardized mental test. The result—probably an unusually high math score—got him assigned to the Signal Corps, the part of the army in charge of communications. He spent most of his time in the service at a base in the Philippines, encoding outgoing messages that were sent out all over the Pacific theater. It was technical desk work; he was in a protected environment made up of young men who'd been judged to be more valuable to the war effort for their brains than their bodies, and who didn't see combat. I have a photograph of a crude desk Father had set up for himself in the tent where he lived: many books arranged in neat rows, a light suspended from a wire, a couple of bottles of liquor stashed in a corner. Other pictures show a group of bespectacled, skinny, shirtless young men standing outside a tent, and young Filipino boys who evidently roamed the base, smoking cigarettes the soldiers had given them.

The most dutiful of sons, Father wrote many long letters to his parents, some of which arrived in New Orleans scissored into scraps by military censors. They were mainly devoted to the standard concerns of an enlisted man, laid out in insistent detail: the irrationality of the military bureaucracy, the inedibility of the food, the endlessness of his tour of duty (Father didn't get to come home until eight months after the end of the war). I can't picture him committing the usual misdeeds of soldiers. In camp, loudspeakers played jazz constantly, to keep up morale, but it didn't keep up Father's. He preferred classical music or silence. Short, underweight, studious, with thick glasses, he developed the habit of reading as copiously as Bernard had when he was far away from his family at the same age. Father read novels by Thomas Hardy, D. H. Lawrence, Emile Zola, Anatole France, and Thomas Wolfe (who was his favorite among living writers), plays by William Shakespeare, George Bernard Shaw, and Eugene O'Neill, poetry by Dante and Boccaccio, philosophy by Bertrand Russell. He read Richard Wright's *Black Boy* and

Booker T. Washington's *Up from Slavery.* ("Wright is probably the more brilliant, the more sensitive of the two, whereas Washington is the more stable, the more hardworkingly sober, the less exciting a person.") He told Pop and Nettie that he'd been thinking about becoming a writer himself.

In one letter home, in early 1946, Father said that he had been reading and thinking about religion. He had absorbed the Old and New Testaments, the Qur'an, and the works of many writers on the subject. On the base he had spoken "to Christian Scientists, Orthodox Jews, and members of most other Western faiths about their religion and I have tried to get their different points of view." He went on: "I don't want to discuss the subject here, only to tell you that it is a big one for me and one which I'll be thinking and talking about a lot when I get back." This struck me because I have trouble picturing Father as a searching young man, looking for answers to life's most profound questions and hoping to find guidance in theology and literature. He read copiously well into his nineties, but, for as long as I can remember, this wasn't connected to a search for meaning in any way that I could detect. His passion in life wasn't searching, it was protecting what was familiar and pursuing eccentrically specific topics that had piqued his interest.

In another letter that caught my attention, he told his parents about a friendship he'd struck up with Herman Weintraub, "a Brooklyn Jew who is thirty but looks forty-five." In *The Last Night of Ballyhoo*, set in Atlanta in 1939, the action revolves around the appearance of Joe Farkas, also a Brooklyn Jew, whose presence in a German-Jewish Southern milieu causes intense anxiety. Father was raised to react that way, but now, in 1946, he was surprised to find that he might feel differently. What initially drew the two of them together was a shared hatred of the jazz that the base loudspeakers played. Herman acted as a kind of older brother to Father, which he appreciated; Father wasn't used to being around people who came from a wide range of backgrounds, and Herman was. On the other hand Father knew more about culture than Herman did. He lent Herman his copy of Dreiser's *Sister Carrie* ("a beautiful book, Tom"). They discussed Mozart. The pleasure Herman took in these things was moving to Father. He was also struck by Herman's socially crusading impulses, which on the base took the form of distributing condoms to Filipinos and lecturing them on the disadvantages of having large families. In the end, though, Herman was too far outside Father's known world for him to allow their relationship to go past a certain point: "I know his kind. He'll never amount to anything, in spite of his sensitivities and worthwhile ideas, but he has a warm and generous nature and would be a good friend."

MOTHER AND FATHER

Mother—Barbara London during these years—was in college at Wellesley, which represented a big step up for somebody from her middle-class neighborhood in Perth Amboy. Her letters home, though not nearly as copious as Father's, show her as being almost deliriously happy. She was smart and funny, and also physically striking, blonde with green eyes and a broad, full face. She was one of the best students in her class, elected to Phi Beta Kappa in her junior year. Boys evidently found her irresistible, to judge from the references in her letters to the dates she went on incessantly, and she also had a close circle of female friends. She decided she wanted to be a psychologist. She was admitted to a graduate program at Harvard, which she entered the year after Father had returned from the service to finish his college degree.

The one obvious problem in Mother's life was that she had severe rheumatoid arthritis, which had first manifested itself when she was a toddler. She'd inherited the condition from her mother, who evidently worried about its limiting her life more than Mother herself did. "Mother darling," Mother wrote from Wellesley, "please, please don't feel that you have inflicted on me a serious handicap." She struck a pose of insistent optimism, which I think was probably more what she thought she wanted her mother to hear than what she really believed.

Thomas Lemann in the late 1940s,
his early twenties.

Mother was a child of the Depression, which had left the Lemanns in New Orleans completely untouched, and she felt a deep tug toward the secure, the respectable: life a safe distance away from any precipices. But nobody was more aware than she of what lay behind appearances. She was dark, sarcastic, a gifted mimic, an amateur diagnostician of emotional and physical maladies. "See that couple?" she'd say when we were eating in a hotel dining room. "They'll be divorced in two years. And that one? They're not married, they're having an affair, but she's not as serious about it as he is."

During the time when Mother was in college, medical scientists discovered what seemed to be a cure, or at least a great relief, for Mother's condition: cortisone. Her father, being a doctor, was able to secure an early supply of cortisone for Mother (this was at about the same time that John F. Kennedy, the future president, was also put on cortisone). She kept taking it, in ever heavier doses, for the rest of her life. Nobody could have known at the time, when the discovery of cortisone was winning medical awards, that it would wind up being not so miraculous, because of its terrible long-term side effects. There's a long list of them, including weakened muscles and bones, mottled, bruised skin, and emotional instability, all of which were fully on display in Mother's later years. But in those early days, from what I can tell, only Mother's parents saw her as someone with a serious handicap. Certainly her suitors didn't. She particularly relished telling me about the most pathetically ardent of them, an irrepressible young Jewish doctor in Newark—a pediatrician, just like her father—with the Philip Rothian name of Nathan Zukerberg. Mother wasn't the only person for whom constant worshipful atten-

Barbara Lemann in the late 1940s, her early twenties.

tion isn't entirely attractive, though she did save his importuning letters for the rest of her life. Among them I found, for example, a Valentine's Day telegram: DARLING TERRIBLY IN LOVE AND VERY HAPPY STOP WANTED AS SOON AS POSSIBLE ONE CLINICAL PSYCHOLOGIST STOP BLONDE BEAUTEOUS BRILLIANT STOP.

Reading the letters now, I have an impulse to counsel this love-sick young man: wrong approach! Mother likes somebody with a bit of an edge, someone who isn't such an easy conquest and who doesn't adore her to a greater degree than she adores herself. But I suppose it wouldn't be a good idea to steer Nat away from a course that wound up producing me. Early in her graduate school years, Mother wrote her parents, "Nat is pretty unexciting. There are things about him that appeal to me tremendously—wisdom, humor, gentleness, kindness, patience, understanding, and unswerving stability & loyalty—*but* he lacks sparkle, restlessness, curiosity. He's smart, but he doesn't have the kind of mind that explores and likes to play around with ideas. He doesn't question things any more, doesn't kid around enough, and is too damned content with the status quo in general. I cling to a blind faith that life holds greater fullness and excitement for me." Finally there's a letter from Nat in May 1949: "It is with a great deal of sorrow that I concede defeat."

Mother must have encountered Father, who was out of the army and back at Harvard, by then. I picture them being in a class offered by the Social Relations Department and somehow spotting each other: both Jewish when that wasn't so common at Harvard, both assiduous note-takers (I know because I have their notebooks) and probably question-askers. I can imagine each dazzling the other. Father was not accustomed to women who ventured outside the confines of official, though often disingenuous, passivity that was standard in his New Orleans. Mother may never have met somebody from as luxurious and prominent a background as Father's, or who knew so much about so many things. I can imagine them being witty, teasing, with each other. Father had the qualities Nat Zukerberg lacked, the sparkle and curiosity. And, not to be too psychologically facile, he had recently lost his mother, who also had had a career as a healer and a serious health condition of her own.

Well into my middle age, after the advent of the internet, I came across an article by Father in a scholarly journal called *Sociometry*. "Group Characteristics as Revealed in Sociometric Patterns and Personality Ratings" was the lead article, published when he was barely out of college; it must have been a version of his senior thesis, but he had never mentioned it to me, perhaps out of modesty, or perhaps because it was evidence that there was another life, as professors in a university town somewhere, that he and Mother could have lived instead of the rooted, rock-certain one they did live in New Orleans. Father had surveyed the social relations of students at Radcliffe, Harvard's women's college, and subjected the results to what to me are a dense and incomprehensible set of statistical formulas. What did they reveal? That being noticed, which you'd think people would want, was actually perilous. Students who were more noticed were more likely to be disliked than liked. Students who were more obscure were also regarded more favorably. The lesson would seem to be that if you want to avoid being disliked, you should keep your head down.

Surely this was a scientific finding, but it also comported with what Father was seeing all around him. Harvard still had a Jewish quota, and barely concealed antisemitism was everywhere. Being noticed as a Jewish student couldn't possibly have felt safe. Jewish issues in the world, like what was becoming known about the Holocaust, the fate of the Jewish refugees in Europe, and the conflicts leading up to the creation of the state of Israel, made Jewish obscurity more difficult. At Harvard, Father encountered Jews whose family roots were in Eastern Europe and who had a different, less constrained, way of being Jewish than he did—including Mother. Was he like these people? It was something he had to think about now, as he hadn't growing up. Father had two Jewish classmates from Country Day School, both children of prominent families: Philip Stern, son of the rich and philanthropic Edith and Edgar, and Edward Heller, grandson of Max, the rabbi at Temple Sinai during most of its early decades. I have some letters that circulated among the three of them in the 1940s, full of immature, sex-obsessed high spirits. All three of them appear to have had the Jewish question on their minds. Philip liked to write in what he imagined to be an Eastern European Jew's accent. Father appended to one of his letters a "Seal of Israel," which said, "Happy Yom Kippur. Scholom Alechem. Baruch ataw Adonoy Elohaynu Melach Hawolom. Bray Pree Hagofen! Amen." They were being naughty, even consciously offensive—playing with the forbidden.

But it was becoming more difficult to joke about Jewish matters, to avoid making choices and taking sides. In 1947, Edward Heller, at that point newly enrolled at Harvard Law School, wrote a letter to his parents reporting that he and Father had been discussing Zionism. Father, Edward wrote, had friends and roommates "who are all violently pro-Zionist," and who believed that the United

States was becoming so antisemitic that the Jews would all soon be deported. They would have no choice but to settle in Palestine, but that wouldn't be a terrible fate, since Jews are meant to live there and not in the Diaspora. Father and Edward both found these ideas upsetting, radical, but what surprises me now is that Father even knew any Zionists, given how resistant to Zionism I knew him to be. Harvard in those days assigned all Jewish students to Jewish roommates. This policy may have produced his Zionist social con nections, since it's hard to imagine that there wouldn't have been any Zionists even among the limited number of Jews at Harvard then. Edward tried to persuade Father that not all Zionists were like the ones he had encountered—some Zionists were moderates, who believed that Jews had a plausible future in America as well as in Israel. But Father seemed to be coming to the idea that any degree of Zionism at all is perilous, because it would indicate that Jews didn't really belong in America. He quoted to Edward from an encyclopedia that listed a series of prominent Jews—Mendelssohn, Einstein, Disraeli, Brandeis—who had succeeded in what it referred to as their "foster countries," which Father took to mean that to the compilers of the encyclopedia, they didn't really belong there. This was proof that non-Jews were always ready to understand Jews as aliens—so let's not give them another opportunity by talking about a Jewish homeland.

Bear in mind that Edward Heller was the grandson of one of America's most prominent and forceful Zionists, and that at that moment both his father, a lawyer in New Orleans, and his uncle, a rabbi in Cincinnati, were traveling around the country speaking on behalf of the creation of a Jewish state in Palestine. Edward's mother was even more ardently Zionist than his father was. And here Edward and Father were, at the moment a Jewish state was finally, and violently, aborning, struggling to see whether there might be any way to make Zionism into a tamer, less alien and threatening ideology—Father more so than Edward. How did he, who recently had been gingerly befriending a Brooklyn Jew and promising to contemplate religious questions deeply, become so uncomfortable with Zionism so quickly, and, as matters played out, eventually become the man I knew as a child, who stoutly stood guard against any mention of Israel, at Temple Sinai or in his own house?

GENTLEMEN

To answer, I think, entails doing the imaginative work of finding our way back into the Jewish world Father entered at Harvard and then reentered after the war. To say that there was still a Jewish quota doesn't begin to capture the situation. You might think Harvard's reaction to the Holocaust's demonstration of where antisemitism could lead would have been officially forswearing antisemitism. Instead, the deeply rooted exclusionary customs continued unabated. They may even have intensified, because the uncomfortable truth of what had happened in Europe was impossible to incorporate into the ordinary life of the university. The reminders of it had to be pushed away. Harvard didn't have a chapter of Hillel, the national organization for Jewish college students, until 1944. There were very few Jews on the Harvard faculty, and none of the senior administrators was Jewish. The standard employers of Harvard graduates usually would not hire Jews, unless they were specifically Jewish firms. Father had a sweet spot—maintained for more than half a century—for Alice Sedgwick, a child of a venerable New England family whom he had met when he was at Harvard. If Father had ever been tempted to think of Alice as somebody he could ask out, he had to know that this would have been something akin to the still-on-the-books Southern crime of miscegenation.

Where could one get a rich, novelistic picture of the situation for Jews at Harvard in the 1940s? From a novel: *Remember Me to God*, by Myron S. Kaufmann, published in 1957, a bestseller at the time, now almost completely forgotten. Kaufmann was a member of the Harvard class of 1943—he graduated a few months before Father arrived as a freshman. The hero of *Remember Me to God* is the thor-

oughly loathsome Richard Amsterdam, the unaccountably blond
and tweedy child of an Eastern European Jewish family in Boston,
who comes to Harvard from a public school and quickly develops
an ambition to be fully accepted, as Jewish students almost never
were. He wages a lengthy campaign to join the Jew-barring Hasty
Pudding Club. He acquires a brainy, assimilated Jewish girlfriend—
when he brings her home, she doesn't understand his grandmother's
Yiddish—but he leaves her to take up with a sweet, vapid, blonde
girl named Wimsy Talbot, who has family connections to Boston's
Gentile aristocracy. It's Richard's half-conscious hope that this liaison will help him to be admitted to the Hasty Pudding, but few
people are so obviously cynical; he convinces himself that he loves
Wimsy and they become engaged. Along the way he encounters
more obviously Jewish Jews than himself. Some of these are liberal
crusaders—for example, students who were in favor of American
entry into the Second World War, which was not the standard position of Harvard students at the time. Others are also trying to penetrate the main Harvard social milieu and want Richard to advocate
for them out of a sense of tribal solidarity. That won't be possible, he
decides, unless they scrub from their self-presentation anything that
might read as Jewish, as he has tried to do. He decides to write an
instructional manual for his coreligionists, called "How to Become
a Gentleman."

Richard's romance with Wimsy inevitably begins to run afoul of
the antisemitism that pervades her world. She brings him to church;
mystified by the collection plate (Jews are forbidden to handle money
on the Sabbath), he puts in a five-dollar bill and makes change for
himself, attracting hostile stares. Wimsy asks him if he loves Christ.
He temporizes. It gets worse when Wimsy brings Richard home to
meet her father. Trying very hard to be supportive, he insists that
Richard convert to Christianity as a condition of his blessing the
marriage. "Your people have for centuries been driven by a feeling of
unsatisfied longing, because they haven't accepted the Saviour. And
it's that feeling of longing that drives them and makes them the way

they are—their genius, and always trying to get money, dabbling in radicalism, and migrating from country to country in search of a peace they can't find." Richard is persuaded. But the minister he goes to see to start the process of conversion refuses to help, because he doesn't think Richard's motives are sincere. Then what was meant to be a cordial first meeting between Richard's and Wimsy's parents goes horribly awry, and Wimsy's father drops the mask: "You never loved my daughter, you conniving schemer," he tells Richard. "I never liked you. I never liked you and I never trusted you. Your ambitions and your maneuvering." Soon Richard joins the army. His letters to Wimsy are returned unopened.

What's upsetting about *Remember Me to God* isn't just the precision of its rendering of the endless, pervasive manifestations of antisemitism, subtle and unsubtle, at Harvard. It's also the quality it re-creates of being trapped in an airless space from which there is no escape. The novel's official stance, exemplified by a few of the minor characters, is that there is a good and right and comfortable way to be Jewish, which is to be politically liberal and culturally nonassimilationist. But Richard's consciousness is what dominates. The familiar term *self-hatred* is too bland to do justice to the all-consuming task of trying to remove from one's self-presentation, even from one's thoughts and one's soul, anything that would read as Jewish to someone who finds Jews repulsive. And then there's the necessity of distancing oneself from other Jews, lest one be tainted by the association. Everything obviously, openly Jewish is threatening, terrifying, requiring strict avoidance. But the harder Richard tries to make his life not be about being Jewish, the more his life is about being Jewish. (Myron Kaufmann went on from *Remember Me to God* to write a series of widely spaced and little noticed novels. I met him once, when he was in his seventies and I was in my thirties; we served as judges for a literary prize together. He was surprised that I knew who he was.) It's heartbreaking for me to think about Father—as eager, as sensitive, as idealistic, as protected, as he was—being thrust into such an environment, at a university that he had been raised to think of as an unsurpassable beacon of light and learning.

Harvard did not stand out as different in its attitudes toward Jews from the country as a whole. Glorious Jewish-American institutional achievements—Macy's and Bloomingdale's, *The New York Times* and *The Washington Post*, Metro-Goldwyn-Mayer and Warner Bros., Random House and Simon & Schuster—took pains not to present themselves as Jewish. Jewish movie stars, like Lauren Bacall and Kirk Douglas, were renamed and deracinated so that it would be possible for the public to adore them. Even the rare efforts in mainstream American culture to condemn antisemitism now seem rather restricted. The year after Father returned to Harvard from his army service, an earlier sensational bestselling novel about antisemitism was published, *Gentleman's Agreement*, by Laura Z. Hobson. It soon also became a hit movie. Its aim was to blow the whistle on the prevailing mores of the genteel precincts of American society—things everybody knew about but nobody talked about, like the barriers to Jews in white-collar jobs, in resorts, in real estate, in clubs. Perhaps after the war these would seem more patently wrong than they had in the prewar world depicted in *Remember Me to God*. To make its case, *Gentleman's Agreement* gave up a lot of ground. The device Hobson, the child of Yiddish-speaking Russian immigrants, used to engender sympathy for Jews was to have an impeccably non-Jewish hero experience antisemitism. He is an aristocratic magazine writer named Schuyler Green (played in the movie version by the non-Jewish Gregory Peck—impeccably tall, slim, dignified, and restrained, with no presenting trace of anything that would read as "Jewish"), who persuades his editor to let him write an article called "I Was Jewish for Three Months." Under cover, he reenacts the familiar drama of being turned away from a fancy hotel, like Joseph Seligman back in 1878. His young son is taunted in school.

Hobson was clearly calculating that only by showing a non-Jew experiencing antisemitism could she get other non-Jews to register the wrong of it—otherwise, in every instance it would be some Jewish trait, some misdeed, that explained and justified the way Jews are treated. And it was also necessary for Jewishness to be deracinated for the message to get through. Green's young son asks him, "What *are* Jews, anyhow?" His father explains that, well, there are Catholics, who go to Catholic churches, and then there are Protestants, who go to Protestant churches, "and there are others who go to still different ones, and they're called Jews. Only they call their kind of church synagogues or temples." And that's it—there's no troublesome Jewish culture to deal with, no tribalism, no ritual, no laws. Hobson makes a point of having the one phenotypically Jewish character in the book, a brilliant physicist named Joe Lieberman, renounce Zionism and Jewish observance, as if that was the only way to make it possible for readers to see prejudice against him as pure and therefore unjustified, rather than as an understandable reaction to his views and his practices. Such were the times when Father and Mother were entering adulthood.

COMPROMISES

After Father died, I found a thick stack of letters his mother had written him when he was in the army. It must have been at the same time gratifying and also suffocating to have the amount and intensity of attention Father got from Nettie, and his awareness of her constant physical suffering surely put extra emotional force into the way he received her letters. "I don't believe I ever wake up that you are not the first thing in my thoughts," she wrote, "no matter how many times a night I do wake up, and, as I told you, your Daddy and I spend hours talking about you and speculating about you." How could that not make you nervous? And Nettie's missives were not entirely encouraging. She worried about Father. His copious reading habits seemed excessive, not quite normal. Intellectuals were a tricky category. "When all is said and done," she wrote, "there is a certain something—and I don't think it can be definitely defined—that makes you think, or rather, that gives you the impression of effeminacy." He ought to avoid that. Why didn't he get more exercise? Couldn't he play tennis on the base? But as long as he was reading so much, why wasn't he reading in French? Or memorizing poems by Rudyard Kipling?

Sometimes in these letters I saw evidence of how well a parent can know a child, to the point of being uncannily able to see what lies in store, which the child can't see himself. After Father had written one of his long letters home full of headstrong ideas about the kind of life he intended to lead, Nettie responded: "I am very interested in what you wrote about your thoughts for your future. But, my dear, how on earth can you get in all you are thinking about? And then, if you should marry, what about your wife? You can't marry a person and expect her to do *just* what you want. You will have to take part in her interests too (share). Marriage, certainly, is a compromise, a give and take. I think all you can do is plan what you'd like to do *most* and let the other things take care of themselves. You don't seem to even consider that one of your pleasures may be doing things with your wife, and just wanting to be with her." Something about this must have bothered Father, because he scribbled indignant denials of his mother's analysis of his character in the margins of the letter. He didn't like being told that he was the kind of person who insisted that things be done his way. He preferred to see himself as being unusually polite and considerate, and that was the way most people saw him. It stung to have his mother challenge his version of who he was.

It was during the summer of his first postwar Harvard year that Nettie died, and it was in the aftermath of this devastating loss he fell in love with Mother. Mother told me that she had sat Father down for a serious talk early in their relationship to tell him about her arthritis, with a warning (contradicting what she'd written to her mother) that he should know that her condition seriously limited her life. Having recently lost someone who'd had a far more serious condition for as long as he could remember, Father assured her that he didn't mind. Whether he was just overwhelmingly smitten, or was used to living in proximity to illness, or was drawn to that without being aware of it, they moved onward together.

During those years, Mother was a student at the Harvard Psychological Clinic, which was directed by a patrician and overpowering and peculiar man named Henry A. Murray. The clinic was in an old wooden clapboard house. Murray had someone make up a flag bearing an image of the white whale from *Moby-Dick*, and mounted it above the clinic's front door, as if to send the message that the study of ungovernable urges and obsessions had a home here. Projective tests, meant to reveal the unconscious mind, were an important part of Mother's training. In partnership with his lover, Christiana Morgan (who had previously been involved with Carl Jung), Murray had developed one of them, the Thematic Apperception Test, which Mother occasionally administered to me when I was a boy: a box of shadowy, expressionist black-and-white drawings on stiff cards showing people in distress, designed to evoke revealing stories. Mother had always told me that when Father proposed to her, she had told him that she could not give him an answer until after he had submitted to a different projective test, the Rorschach (inkblots), administered by her.

Sometimes Mother yielded to the impulse to improve what had really happened so that it would make for a better story, but after Father died, going through old papers, I found evidence supporting most of her credulity-straining anecdotes. Could Nat Zukerberg have been quite as desperately in love with her as she said he was? Yes, or maybe even more so. Another wonderful story of Mother's was that at the height of her courtship with Father, he went on a trip to Europe with Stephen, his brother, and sent her frequent, but completely emotionally opaque, postcards, wildly in contrast to Nat's letters. Really? But now I have them in front of me—the output of the same young man who had poured his heart out to his parents in his letters home from the Philippines, just a few years earlier. No salutation, no sign-off. From Grenoble: "We spent a day here visiting several old buildings and monuments." From Biarritz:

An image from the Rorschach test Mother administered to Father to help her consider his marriage proposal, circa 1950.

"We spent the day here and found it much too crowded." And did Mother really subject Father to a prenuptial Rorschach test? Yes, I have the actual test. Father felt that most of the inkblots resembled the map of a country. One looked like Turkey, another like Yugoslavia, another like Scotland. Could this have been the degree of psychological projection Mother was looking for? Nat may have been overavailable, but did Father's unavailability seem like a warning sign to somebody as psychologically astute as Mother? Evidently not, because Mother accepted his proposal.

Now that they were engaged, it was time for Mother to visit New Orleans. That happened during the holiday season at the end of 1950. In those days the city was in a moment of postwar optimism. More people lived in New Orleans then than do now, the port was booming, new buildings were going up downtown and new houses in the suburbs. There was the idea that, rather than being finally unable to escape the grip of its plantation past, New Orleans was going to become the commercial gateway to Latin America and the Caribbean, embracing progress without losing its exotic charm. But it didn't strike Mother that way. Her stories of that first visit fully called forth her skill as a raconteur. By that time Pop was married to Mildred. Mildred had two children: a son, Lucien, who'd been killed in the war, and a daughter, Tite (her real name was Mildred—Tite was short for Petite Mildred). Tite was tall, pale, beautiful, a presence. A few years earlier, she'd gone to Los Angeles hoping to become a movie actress. Even in New Orleans she had connections to the local version of show business, the nightclubs in the French Quarter and at the downtown hotels. I remember her greeting with joyous shrieks her theatrically extroverted friends when they'd visit: Honey! Baby! Lambie! Now she was back in New Orleans, married, but frequently separated from her husband—whom she had married at an open-all-night courthouse at five in the morning at the end of their very long first date—and mainly living with Pop and Mildred.

None of this was like anything Mother had experienced before. As she was leaving for college, her parents had finally been able to move into a single-family house in blue-collar Perth Amboy, a city of factories, oil tanks, and enclosed neighborhoods populated by white ethnics from Eastern Europe. Now she was in a grand, many-roomed mansion with formal gardens and a large cadre of uniformed servants. In Perth Amboy she lived in a Jewish neighborhood where some families were Orthodox (one such family engaged her to come over on the Sabbath to turn the lights on and off). Now, thanks to Pop's remarriage, she was in a mixed-religion household. There was a Christmas tree surrounded by gifts, a formal, heavy Christmas dinner, and an endless round of collateral parties where she was introduced to the Lemanns' large circle of friends. In the Lemann house, every day at five, Mildred and Tite, sometimes accompanied by Mildred's widowed sister and mother, whom we called Tantine and Muz, would change into brightly colored floor-length satin dressing gowns and begin to drink. Mother, in a wool skirt, a sweater, and penny loafers, her hair pinned back in barrettes, coming from a home where I remember a small display of unopened liquor bottles meant to signal arrival into the upper middle class, went into a kind of cardiac arrest of the soul. She'd gotten engaged to a young intellectual, known to come from a distinguished family, but what this actually brought her, evidently, was entry into a life of cocktails, gossip she didn't understand, and household management. She returned to Perth Amboy and collapsed weeping into her mother's arms, sure that she'd made the wrong decision. But her mother told her no, every woman had to make adjustments and she'd better get used to it.

As in a nineteenth-century novel, this was a propitious marriage for Mother—maybe that explains everything. Certainly it meant a great deal to her parents that she was marrying up, that whatever trapdoor might open and send them tumbling back to the slums would now be sealed shut forever. Mother and Father were young, brilliant, attractive, optimistic. Why couldn't everything just work out somehow? It's facile, unfair, for me to watch them from this great distance and identify their mistakes—but it's also impossible to resist. Father graduated from Harvard College in 1949 and entered Harvard Law School that fall. Mother began working on her dissertation, which entailed interviewing the children of war veterans to surface and analyze their fantasies. There was talk in those first years of their marriage about possibilities other than moving back to New Orleans. In the fall of 1951, Pop, speaking about Father, wrote Frankfurter: "Whether he will decide to return to New Orleans to practice I do not know. I think Barbara has somewhat cold feet about living in the South, and I emphasize that this is a decision for them to make." Mother, that tells me, wasn't disguising her feelings, even from her father-in-law.

But if the question hadn't already been settled by then, it was soon. A few decades later, mores had changed, and a young couple like Father and Mother would have stayed at Harvard until she finished her dissertation. It had also become rare for graduates of Harvard Law School to go into practice with their fathers. But in those days men and women didn't get equal votes, and, as Nettie noted in her letter to Father during the war, even as an adolescent he had a way of being inflexible, of insisting that his own sense of his life control the arrangements. He graduated from law school in 1952 and then took an additional year at Tulane Law School to learn Louisiana's distinctive legal code, a legacy of its past as a French colony. Then he joined Monroe & Lemann. His brother joined him there a few years later. I've tried to picture us living in Berkeley or Ann Arbor or Evanston—Father in a sports shirt, grilling steaks in the backyard of a modest suburban house, Mother mixing martinis in the kitchen, the guests gossiping about sociograms or the Hawthorne effect—and I just can't do it. New Orleans was so pervasive— where else, how else, could we have lived out our family's life?

Still, Mother found ways to resist. She got the idea that they could re-create a small version of Cambridge in the Deep South. In the 1950s they bought a big old house on a corner lot in what Mother imagined to be a racially integrated neighborhood, tore it down, and created a small curated subdivision made up of four new midcentury-modern houses. They lived in the house on the corner and three deans at Tulane, handpicked by them—the dean of admissions, the dean of the drama school, and the dean of the architecture school—lived in the other three, surrounding us with a protective academic layer of people who gave the sense of being connected to a faraway liberal world that was ordinarily not evident in New Orleans. Mother in those days was an apprentice child psychologist with a caseload of kids who wouldn't speak, wouldn't eat, wouldn't get out of bed, their maladies recorded meticulously by her in spiral notebooks. She'd coax them into the world, and I can see how she did it: the way she looked (green eyes, a broad moon face, hair in a sensible blonde bob) made a sympathetic impression, and she was funny, intimate, charming, indiscreet. It was easy to form a warm connection to her. She often complained to me about life in New Orleans, which was too anti-intellectual, too conservative, and too social. Once her younger sister, who lived in Milwaukee, came to visit and caused a minor stir by sitting in the back, the Black section, of the St. Charles Avenue streetcar. Mother was going to build a different life for us.

But over time her rebellion flagged. Father had developed ever more luxurious tastes, which Mother and even Pop didn't approve of. Pop himself was hardly an ordinary middle-class American—at the height of the Depression, when Mother's family was struggling in their modest apartment in Perth Amboy, Father was being driven to Country Day School every morning in a Packard by a chauffeur—but he enjoyed thinking of himself as a simple country boy from Donaldsonville. Using his inheritance from Nettie, Father began collecting Cuban cigars and expensive wines from Bordeaux, and driving European sports cars. "Mr. Rockefeller Lemann the other night reminded me that he has quite definitely decided to purchase a Jaguar," Pop wrote Alan Steinert when Father was just starting at Monroe & Lemann. "I thought this seemed like putting on the dog, but he claims that it was not much more expensive than an Olds, which relatively humble people drive. A Chevrolet would be more down my alley." And then there were the monthlong trips to Europe that they began taking while they were still in their twenties, which Father would elaborately plan for months, poring over each year's *Guide Michelin* for newly anointed three-star restaurants and five-tower hotels where he could make far-in-advance reservations. I can't imagine Mother, especially in those early years of their marriage, going in for that sort of thing.

Mother was never very good at discretion. She must have complained to Father about her new life in New Orleans. She certainly complained about it to me when I was little, though parents are usually supposed to hide their dissatisfactions from their children. I see her life in those days as a struggle, not obviously resolvable, against the time and place to which fate had consigned her, and against Father's genteel stubbornness. One letter to a relative of Father's, pushing to the edge of how candid she could be with her husband's family, said: "We are in the land of Charm. People worry not about how to get the most work accomplished but how to celebrate most uniquely and efficiently. Needless to say, an old Puritan like me (and T., though he is loath to admit it) finds this a little foreign and heady." That was surely an understatement—she really meant something closer to repellent. I can see that she tried to make the best of things. She joined the local chapter of the National Council of Jewish Women. She insisted that our household help include students at New Orleans's Black colleges, Dillard and Xavier—King Wells, Eloise Johnson, Geraldine and Jacqueline Lastrapes, Faustina Aryee, all of whom went on to become first-generation Black professionals—so that my sister and I would be exposed to educated Black people who were closer, though not all that close, to being our social equals. She talked about finding a way to write her dissertation, though that wouldn't be easy because there were no doctoral programs in clinical psychology in Louisiana.

Father, however, kept moving in the other direction. Perhaps it was a result of inheriting money at an early age, perhaps of being back in New Orleans after years away, or perhaps it was just his nature—but the questing liberal youth on display in his letters home from the army was fading from view. Pop had lived comfortably with the cognitive dissonance that being a wealthy business lawyer in a seigneurial city in the Deep South, and at the same time a crusading liberal, entailed. His son Stephen was roughly the same way—for decades he was a trustee of Xavier, as Pop had been a trustee of Dillard, and supported whoever was the most liberal plausible candidate for local public office—but Father's ideas and his tastes became roughly what you'd expect of somebody in his position. At Monroe & Lemann, it was the custom for the lawyers to send one another memoranda and notes, typed on thin yellow paper with a hole punched in the upper right corner, asking for a reaction to something. A few months before he died, Pop sent his sons one of these, asking them to comment on a more-in-sorrow-than-anger treatise on the inherent genetic inferiority of Black people, of a kind that circulated regularly through the white New Orleans households of my childhood, accompanied by a letter to the editor that *The New York Times* had published saying pretty much the same thing. Stephen, the liberal son, wrote: "This letter is no better than most other diatribes on the subject, and is characterized by the same sort of sloppy thinking. . . . I find this pseudo-goodwill toward the Negro sickening." I'm sure that pleased Pop. Father wasn't so sure. It was true, he wrote, that "the use of intelligence tests to prove differences in racial intelligence has been condemned by most psychologists," but "it will probably take a long time for the Negroes to become absorbed—look at the Jews after 300 years."

Late in his life, Father told me a couple of stories about his early years at Monroe & Lemann that make it clear what he meant about the Jews. Once he was given the task of managing Mr. Monroe's correspondence when he was away on vacation. He saw that Mr. Monroe had nominated a Jew named Sam Israel, a coffee importer and trader who was a business partner of the Reilys, clients of the firm, for membership in the Boston Club. There were seconding letters from other impeccable members of the club—but still he was blackballed. (In retrospect Father wondered whether Israel had engaged in sharp business practices; whatever these practices were, he always thought Jews should take special pains to avoid them, since we were always being watched for signs of greediness.) Monroe & Lemann ordinarily did not handle divorces, which were inconsistent with its gentlemanly legal practice, but it made an exception in the case of a businessman who was an important client. One day a senior partner came back from lunch, where, as downtown lawyers in New Orleans often did in those days, he'd had a few drinks. He stopped by Father's office to chat about how awful it was that the firm had to handle a divorce case. It wasn't just the case itself that was unsavory, he told Father, it was also—here he was perhaps forgetting himself because of the drinks—that he'd had to have lunch with the client's wife's "Jew lawyer." Father knew who the Jew lawyer was: a man named Saul Stone, who was a protégé of

Pop and the head of a leading law firm in New Orleans. This is what you saw when you got a peek behind the curtain.

About race, of course, respectable downtown lawyers' attitudes were even less openhearted. Some Jewish lawyers had achieved a precarious place in the major New Orleans firms; any presence of Black lawyers there was inconceivable. Some years after the *Brown* decision, Stephen wrote one of those punch-holed memos to Father and to Mr. Monroe's two sons, who had joined the firm. (Pop had died a few months earlier.) Someone from the Justice Department in Washington had called, asking him to become a member of the Louisiana advisory committee to the U.S. Commission on Civil Rights, to help push the South past its post–*Brown* decision stasis. Thus far, no prominent citizens had been willing to join, except for the president of Dillard, a Catholic priest, and a Baptist minister. Stephen's request to his partners has a gingerly tone. Though he was a very junior member of the firm, I imagine that he would have wanted to accept the offer; he would have enjoyed doing something on the national stage. But the answer came back, stated in a gentlemanly manner: Better not. The community won't accept it. You would be ostracized.

CAMELOT

As I look back at this period, I get a picture of Mother in a kind of pressure cooker, with the pressure constantly increasing. She was being drawn deeper and deeper into an environment about which she'd had doubts that she'd tried to put to rest, but it turned out they were fully justified. She had two small children. Pop was gone, which freed Father to continue unimpeded in the direction he was already headed, as someone who self-consciously belonged to a class of aristocratic gentlemen. She had set her professional ambitions aside. A round of distinctly New Orleanian obligations that didn't satisfy her—supervising servants, going to the parties that were the essential activity in the land of Charm, having her hair sculpted into a blonde helmet—took up her time. Mother wasn't especially good at keeping the lid on whatever was roiling her. What became her standard resort was taking pills, in three categories: steroids, amphetamines, and barbiturates. She was a genius at charming and cajoling doctors in order to get open-ended prescriptions, and in those days people were less aware than they are now of the bad effects of drugs. Once in a while, Mother would quietly disappear to some kind of treatment program. I don't remember how this was explained to us—not very well, if at all. Then she would come back.

It was during those years, when we were living in the constructed colony of modern houses, that Mother and Father's marriage had its great crisis. I don't know how I know what I know about it; we weren't a family that talked about things that were unpleasant. A whispered comment here and there over the years, a scrap of paper found in a drawer—from a few such things, I developed a sense of what had happened. I didn't probe as deeply as I could have, because I'm not sure I wanted to know everything, and also because I thought that wouldn't have been Mother and Father's preference. The idea I have now is that Mother went off to a psychiatric hospital in New York. While there, she had an affair with one of the doctors, maybe the doctor who was treating her. This would be high on the list of things about Mother's and Father's lives that would be considered shocking today, but seems not to have been then; I would guess that it was she (the adulteress), not the doctor (the abuser of a patient), who would have set off the louder alarm. Without any real evidence, I imagine him to have been more emotionally expressive than Father, more liberal, more comfortably Jewish. For a time they were officially in love, planning to marry. Then, as had happened after Mother's first visit to New Orleans, her mother laid down the law. She had to break it off and go back to Father and New Orleans. People like us don't get divorced. It's messy, unrespectable.

It seems as if my sister and I were sent off to live with Mother's parents in New Jersey for a time, while negotiations took place.

We must have been there for quite some time. I remember walks through Perth Amboy's redbrick downtown, trips to Bamberger's department store in Newark and to the beach club where my grandparents rented a small wooden structure where you could change into your bathing suit. I have some letters that my sister and I wrote from Perth Amboy, in the summer of 1961, addressed to "Dear Father." The wording indicates that Mother was elsewhere. Both of us mentioned being taken to see *Camelot*, then in its original run on Broadway. It's funny how memory works. I was just short of seven years old, but I still have a vivid picture in my mind of Robert Goulet, the other man who was making Richard Burton miserable, on stage in a glittering white doublet. What has lodged *Camelot* in American mythology is Jacqueline Kennedy's invocation of it in the first interview she gave after her husband's assassination. It stood for a glamorous court that had vanished, a short-lived, gracious, noble place where everything was perfect. What lodged in my mind was that hundreds of people would crowd into a theater for a story about a man who had lost his wife's love, something that, as far as I was consciously aware, didn't actually happen in the world. Another scrap I came across, after Father died, was one of his wartime letters to his parents, reporting on his reaction to Goethe's *The Sorrows of Young Werther*, the tale of a sensitive, artistic young aristocrat's tragic, unrequited, and ultimately fatal love for a beautiful young woman of a different class. Father found he couldn't connect to the story. "Maybe because I've never been in love I can't conceive of any sane human being killing himself when his woman marries somebody else," he wrote. "I can understand temporary unhappiness, even temporary despondency, but never so deep that it would induce me to take my life, and never so lasting that I would never get over it." But when something like that happened in his own life, I don't think he ever did get over it.

Mother must have come back, because I don't remember her ever being away, but things between Father and her had irrevocably changed, and each of them had changed too. Mother had lost the standing to assert herself, and Father's thinking had become harder edged, more self-contained. People make bargains that they're not always fully aware of. The first house Mother and Father built, the one surrounded by the homes of deans at Tulane, looks to me now like an explicit exchange: Mother would agree to move to New Orleans and Father would agree to let her make their living arrangements. I doubt Father consciously saw these as a concession. But after Mother's return, it was decided that we would leave our small simulacrum of Cambridge and build a much larger new house, only a mile away but in a much more straightforwardly elite neighborhood, one with no academics and no nearby Black homes, stores, or churches.

I remember years of elaborate planning for the new house. An interior decorator, whom I remember as wearing a cape, flew in from New York, and a landscape architect from San Francisco. Construction took years. Mother and Father would go to Europe in the summer to look at houses and gardens they might use as inspiration and to buy art and furniture. Mother, making what may have been a brave show of enthusiasm, threw herself into their new, all-consuming architectural project. On their long summer trips to Europe, which became ever more elaborate, they would visit villas looking for inspiration, and go to the Venice Biennale and to the South of France to buy art for Quercus. Mother was in charge of the paintings (large, abstract, with bright colors and bold shapes) and Father was in charge of the sculptures (small, smooth surfaced, dark, precise). After they had returned, large wooden crates containing works of art, and also giant olive oil jars, stone wellheads, and bas-reliefs would arrive and be put into storage until the house was ready to receive them. Finally, in 1967, we moved in. In New Orleans in those days, it seemed as if no one ever made arrangements with strangers; Mother and Father sold our old house to the family of Edward Heller, Father's classmate beginning at Newcomb Nursery School.

The summer trips, which continued for many years after we

had moved into Quercus, occupied a central location in Father's mind. He meticulously planned every detail, months in advance: the hotels, the restaurants, the (to use one of his favorite words) excursions. On the way home he and Mother would stop in Zurich so he could buy Cuban cigars—banned in the United States since 1961—and in London so he could order custom-made shoes and umbrellas. In the evenings on their trips, Father would dictate detailed journals into a mechanical gadget, to be typed up by his secretary, a tall, efficient, prim woman whom he addressed formally as Mrs. Burst, when he and Mother got home. Then he'd mail the journals to a long list of friends and relatives. For his eightieth birthday I had a book made up of excerpts from these, so I read through decades' worth of them all together. It brought home both Father's astonishing ability to speak in flawless prose and the endlessness of his highly particular obsessions. Topiary—plants elaborately pruned into distinctive forms—caught his interest, so he'd find out where the outstanding examples were (as long as they were in Europe), and then plan his trips around visiting them. Or, on other trips, it would be baroque plaster medallions set into the ceilings of palaces or venerable government buildings. Or reliquaries, holy (Christian) relics that may or may not have been genuine, carefully set into obscure nooks of cathedrals—I remember Father's being particularly fascinated with the holy prepuce, Jesus's foreskin, which a number of cathedrals claim to hold. Father also traveled with an array of instruments for measuring the altitude, the humidity, and the barometric pressure, which it was essential for him to know and which he'd carefully enter into his journals, partly so that he could compare previous years' readings with new ones when he visited places he'd gone before.

I'm thinking about the Rorschach test Mother administered to Father after he proposed marriage, and about his uninterpretable responses to the inkblots. It's difficult to resist the impulse to think about Father's eccentric pursuits as a gateway promising admission

Mother and Father on one of their European vacations, 1960s.

to his subconscious. Surely Mother thought about that. As with the Rorschach test, though, Father didn't have much to offer to people pursuing that kind of inquiry. It was hard for me to tell whether he was actually interested in all his peculiar topics, or merely pretending to be interested. He liked being teased about them. Was it all an elaborate prank? Who knows. He may not have known. He must not have been entirely feigning his interest in the things that interested him, or he wouldn't have put the effort into them that he did. What was important was that he was able to—had to—live in his own world, where he made the rules, freed from having constantly to adjust to whatever the changing mores and concerns of the moment were. His journals are filled with bemused complaints, delivered in a tone of possibly feigned outrage, and scenes of him grilling hapless minor officials about the substandard, indefensible policies they had adopted. The quality of service at the Gritti Palace had declined. Restaurants had begun to restrict cigar smoking. Grammatical errors were going unnoticed.

Mother was left to apply her analytic inclinations to others, rather than to Father. Objects fascinated Father, people fascinated Mother. In the evenings, in the dining rooms of elegant hotels, she would make up entertaining and plausible stories about the other guests whom one could see at other tables. During the hours before dinner, Mother, officially because of her arthritis, usually let Father pursue his distinctive inquiries alone. Father's copious photographs from these trips mostly show whatever attracted his interest, but occasionally he must have persuaded a concierge or a headwaiter to take a picture of the two of them, showing a glamorous, well-dressed young couple sitting at a table or standing in front of a statue. Mother would be dressed tastefully, but in vibrant colors, with a scarf and big sunglasses, tanned; Father, in well-worn khakis or shorts, projected innocent boyishness, his face unlined and untroubled.

Back at home, Mother dropped her professional activity—seeing patients as a child psychologist—and her plans to finish her dissertation. She and Father both became pillars of the community, generously involved in every conceivable civic cause (but Jewish causes, only minimally) and widely admired for that. Mother went from being, at least with me, relentlessly critical of New Orleans, when we lived in our village of modern houses, to permitting no dissent from the prevailing local mores, after we had moved into Quercus. We took up a life as, by Father's lights, unhesitant members of the local aristocracy. In the evenings, Father instructed me to greet him, when he came home from Monroe & Lemann, by shaking hands and saying "Good evening, sir." Then, a little later, the butler, Melvin Major, a short, deeply cordial (possibly naturally, possibly as a protective stance) Black man, would come into the library and solemnly announce, "Dinner is served," and we would go to the dining room. After dinner, Mother would go to bed and read—I remember contemporary literary fiction and *The New York Review of Books*— and Father would retreat to a desk built into a corner of the library that functioned as a kind of command post, where he sat surrounded by files, piles of books, and small beautiful objects that had attracted his admiration.

The magical world that Father had built for himself was entrancing to those invited to enter it, especially children. They'd be quizzed about the fine points of grammar, asked to solve one of the topographical puzzles he collected, given a small stack of memoranda on those yellow punch-holed sheets of paper and asked to respond. If a child couldn't solve a puzzle, he'd affect shock—it was so simple! If she could solve it, he'd affect astonishment—it was so difficult! The person on the witness stand would be asked to defend some indefensible practice, like the use of *which* to precede a restrictive clause; if they couldn't, he'd invite them at least to join in his shock and indignation. On Sunday afternoons, we'd go on one of his excursions (at that point, a convertible dark blue Porsche had succeeded the Jaguar), not only to visit relatives but also to see things that had aroused his curiosity, such as trees with unusually large girths—he had invented an adapted tape measure for this task.

I'm aware that one of the odd things about my family was all the things that, by today's standards, we should ideally have talked about and didn't. During the height of the civil rights movement, which was all-consuming in Louisiana and had been a major cause of Pop's, it didn't come up in our highly specific dinner table conversations directed by Father. (I do remember, in those years, hearing the sound of spirited conversations in the kitchen; curious, I'd open the door, and everyone would instantly fall silent.) Of course we didn't discuss the major events in Jewish life, in America or in Israel, either. It was inconceivable that we would have frank conversations about the careful bargains that underlay Father and Mother's marriage. I don't remember our household as being cold, or lacking in intense mutual love that we all felt. It was more that somehow the condition of all the accommodations we'd made was that life had to be what we said it was, what we wanted it to be, not something that was out of our control and constantly changing, or that demanded ongoing reactions and recalibrations from us.

I'm looking at a few documents Mother and Father left behind. One is a photo album memorializing an event Father staged some time in the early sixties, which he called a levee—according to the dictionary, "a reception held by a person of distinction on rising from bed." The invitation has three young couples—from the highest rank of New Orleans society (meaning of course not Jewish), except for Mother and Father—requesting the pleasure of your company at a garden party in honor (that's "honour") of the tenth wedding anniversary of George and Anne Montgomery. George was Father's close friend; his father and Pop had both been close associates of Samuel Zemurray, the Jewish immigrant who had come to New Orleans from Russia as a young man and who wound up inventing the banana-importing business, and also the practice of staging U.S. government-assisted coups d'etat in Central America to ensure that governments hostile to American banana companies would not remain in power. Anne Kock Montgomery came from the family that had owned the sugarcane plantation next to Palo Alto. (The Civil War skirmish that still draws souvenir hunters to Palo Alto is called the Battle of Kock's Plantation.) The party was in Audubon Park, which long ago had been the plantation where Etienne de Bore had demonstrated that sugarcane cultivation was possible in Louisiana, an event that not so indirectly accounts for my being here today. Ancient, gnarled live oak trees draped in Spanish moss evoked the park's origins. The photographs in the album, obviously taken by a professional engaged for the occasion, show men wearing top hats and cutaways, women wearing flowered dresses, long white gloves, and broad straw hats, holding parasols, and guests being ferried around the park in horse-drawn carriages with liveried drivers. The one picture of Mother, who must have been newly returned from her temporary escape to New York, presents her standing with the other hosts, a tight pearl choker around her neck, flashing what I imagine to be a self-conscious, pasted-on smile.

Then there's a set of beautiful color sketches on tracing paper, accompanied by a handwritten letter in French, evidently from an expert Father had located in Europe, proposing various heral-

Father, Mother, and their cohosts—the Montgomerys and
the Walmsleys—at a "levee" in Audubon Park, early 1960s.

dic shields that could represent the possibly noble lineage of the
Lemann and Berthelot families—who were itinerant peddlers and
fur trappers, from what the documentary record shows. And I have
a letter from Father to Julian Feibelman, from 1963. If you belong to
a synagogue, you'll know that every year you get a form letter from
the rabbi, reminding you of an approaching *yahrzeit*, the anniversary of the death of a parent, and hinting that in addition to the customary prayer you might want to say on this occasion, a memorial
contribution might be in order.

Observing *yahrzeit* connects you to the past. It reminds you that
you are a link on a chain that extends very far backward. It is a practice that Father's grandparents and great-grandparents had scrupu-
lously followed, but when he got one of these letters from Julian, he
wrote back: "I believe this matter arose once before and we replied to
you that, while we are aware of the anniversary, it has been a tradi-

One of the heraldic shields
my father had someone design.

tion in our family to celebrate births rather than deaths on the theory that it is the birth for which we give thanks, rather than the death." From this same period, there is a letter from Stephen, who lived just as lavishly as Father did, to Julian complaining that Temple Sinai's dues were too high. Many years later, I found out that Stephen's wife, Shirley, had been raised in an Orthodox home in New Orleans, something that nobody ever mentioned during my childhood. It was part of moving up, moving on, to sever the limiting connection to the past and begin anew, on very different terms that weren't Jewish in the same all-encompassing way.

In our part of New Orleans, everybody had known everybody else for generations; many of Father's closest friends were the children of close friends of Pop, whom he had known since his days at nursery school. We all lived in the same neighborhood, and it wasn't unusual for a family to have lived in the same house through two or three generations. There wouldn't have been any point to our pretending not to be Jewish, because everybody thought of us as Jewish and that would never change. We *were* Jewish, and, beyond that, we were conspicuously different from most people we knew in New Orleans in ways that comported with what people thought Jews were like. We had rooms full of books in our house, we had more money, we had modern art instead of hunting prints on the walls, we didn't drink much by New Orleans standards. What Father wanted was for being Jewish to mean what he remembered it as meaning when he was growing up, before the Holocaust, before Eastern European Jews had become dominant in American Jewish culture. He wanted it to be elegant, comfortable in the wider world (especially the upper-class world), free of imposed restrictions, not too conspicuous. What he wrote to Julian about *yahrzeit* he said to me many times, about a wide variety of Jewish customs and practices that over the years became part of my adult life. Why did Jews wear "headgear"? Why did they wear prayer shawls? Why did they eat smoked salmon, when everybody knows that's Scottish, not Jewish? All these at heart were variants of the same question: Why couldn't things still be the way they were at Temple Sinai in the 1930s?

Thinking back to Mother and Father's formative years in the 1940s and early 1950s, when they made their way from their separate corners of the Jewish world to Cambridge, met, fell in love, decided that their two sensibilities could be successfully united, and moved to New Orleans, it looks to me one of those recurring times of abrupt divergence in Jewish life. Like the German Jews who went through emancipation in the nineteenth century, they convinced themselves that they were seeing the advent of a newer, more hopeful way of being Jewish. Most American Jews were ardently embracing Zionism, which because of the Holocaust and the establishment of the state of Israel had gone from being a long-running but not so immediately consequential preoccupation among Jews to being a palpable, ever-present, undeniable reality. Zionism made Father and many other German Jews in the United States (there were no more German Jews in Germany, except in displaced-person camps) intensely uncomfortable. It was, simply put, too Jewish, requiring incessantly reminding the world of our disruptive presence as a distinctive people. Fortunately, by his lights, another path was available, the one he and Mother chose, which represented a kind of hyper-*Haskalah* for the late twentieth century, in which you'd persuade yourself that all the main sources of oppression of the Jews over the centuries—religion, nationalism, ethnicity—would now finally yield to modernity and rationality, thanks to advances in science, especially the kind of social science Mother and Father were studying, and a collective determination never to relive the horrors of the war. Why should we cling to the superstitions and the tribal loyalties of the past, when they were on the way out?

INVITATIONS

In New Orleans Father took on the project, to be carried out with exquisite delicacy, of getting our family admitted into New Orleans's highest social rank. His parents had lived through the period when this had become impossible: his mother had been a debutante, but now there were no Jewish debutantes, and his father had been a founding member of the New Orleans Country Club, but now its doors were closed to Jews. Father aimed to reverse these reversals. His partner in this effort was George Montgomery, who, as much as anyone, was the master arbiter of New Orleans high society. George was a sharp-eyed, witty, convivial man with a broad ruddy face, whom I can't picture without a cigarette in one hand and a drink in the other, bursting with some juicy piece of information that he was eager to convey. He exemplified the New Orleans principle that social status was a separate domain, not connected to one's professional life as it is in most places in America; he was so supremely an insider that he could indulge in the luxury of making fun of what was ridiculous about his domain, even as he ruled over it. Every year on Mardi Gras day the Rex parade would stop at the home of George's wife's family, the Kocks, on St. Charles Avenue, so that the king could offer a toast. This was an honor accorded no other private citizen.

Father's fiftieth birthday party was a black-tie dinner at Quercus held in 1976, the house blazing with light, the walls filled with Father and Mother's collection of modern art, servants in uniform passing heavy-duty drinks, the murmur of the guests' conversation occasionally interrupted by a shriek of hilarity (New Orleanians aren't especially restrained). At the crucial moment, George stood up and said, with tears in his eyes (and Father's too), "The most Christian man I know is a Jew, Tommy Lemann." The absolute security George felt about his own social position, plus some liberal impulse stirring within him, led him to want to take down the Mardi Gras krewes' barrier against Jews, or at least against the Lemanns. Because Father's parents had been invited to the Montgomery family's annual party at noon on Christmas day, where there would be crustless duck sandwiches—the fruits of the labors of the hunters who made up the majority of the men at the party—and eggnog and hearty exchanged greetings of "Merry Christmas!," we were invited too. Most of the members of Temple Sinai went to an all-Jewish Christmas party hosted by one of the members, with Julian Feibelman in attendance. Somewhere in New Orleans there must have been Jews who didn't celebrate Christmas at all, but they were unknown to us.

One year George arranged for Father and Mother to be invited to one of the leading Mardi Gras balls, Atlanteans. It was Mother who first reported the news to me; Father treated matters of that level of gravity with discretion. (I would guess that George had also been responsible for my eighth-grade invitation to the Squires ball.) I think Mother was less excited by the prospect of going to the ball, and more by its being something that we could have fun discussing, because of its forbidden quality. But when the evening of the ball arrived, neither of them could hide where they were going, because it required dressing up—white tie for Father, some kind of pale floor-length gown for Mother. Afterward Mother gave me a report. The male members of Atlanteans were masked. Their wives and female guests were not. They sat in the balcony until they were invited to dance with the members. George's generosity extended to the unmissable gesture of seating Mother next to Anne Kock Montgomery, his tall, regal, Roman-nosed wife. Father's role was to act as a kind of assistant to the members, conveying their invitations to the dance floor and escorting the women to them, but, as a mere aide in a metaphorical mating ritual, not being permitted to dance himself.

What did everybody think about the Lemanns being there? It was hard for Mother to tell, because of the masks. The men who had asked Mother to dance were obviously the ones who approved, but they were not supposed to identify themselves to her. Who were they? She could only guess. And who, behind his mask—surely it would be somebody Mother and Father saw constantly in other circumstances and knew well—was scowling over this gross violation of tradition, this insinuation of Jews into a place where they weren't welcome? And, afterward, how had Father and Mother done? Had they slipped up and acted in some way that could have been construed as Jewish, which is to say, unacceptable? I don't know, but that evening seems to have brought Father's Mardi Gras ambitions to a close. I don't remember their setting off for any balls again.

It now looks to me as if no matter how hard Father tried, somehow, at least in the eyes of others, our Jewishness kept reasserting itself, just as it had in the utterly different environment of Cambridge in the immediate postwar years. The most obvious ways were through the social antisemitism of the clubs and krewes, or the occasional taunts that would be directed at my sister and me at the overwhelmingly non-Jewish Country Day School: someone would roll a penny up the aisle past my desk, to demonstrate that as a Jew I loved money too much to be able to resist pouncing on it. I had a friend at Country Day whose parents were divorced, which was rare in that time and place. His father had moved away and none of us had ever met him. His mother remarried and his stepfather—one of us, a German Jew—began proceedings to adopt his stepsons formally, which would entail changing their last name from Thomas to Freiberg. One day my friend's father turned up at the school and asked to see his son. This was to give him a lecture about how he didn't want to go through life with a Jewish last name. He was young, he had no idea of what a fearsome price he'd pay—of how much would be closed off to him. Think of the jobs you wouldn't get, the clubs you couldn't join, the girls you couldn't ask out.

These glimpses indicated that there was a more extensive conversation about us going on out of our sight and hearing. What was it like? Who among the familiar constellation of people we knew spoke about us as vulgar or greedy or strange, and how exactly did they put it? Would it ever end? And on the other hand, I think of Mother and Father as yearning for a comfortableness that people on the other side of the American Jewish cultural divide, the less assimilated side, could get through Jewish means, but that were unavailable to them because of the path they had chosen. Quercus had two libraries, a public one for entertaining guests and a private one for Mother and Father. Their large collection of Jewish books was kept in the private one. Father studied ancient texts in their original language with a teacher every week, as many observant Jews do, only the texts were by Homer, the language was ancient Greek, and his teacher was a Catholic priest who was a professor at Loyola University. He had a strong interest in the archaeology of the ancient world, which he expressed by supporting a Harvard project in Turkey; he never went to Israel, which would have marked him as being too Jewish. He always noticed, but always privately, when someone Jewish ascended to a prominent position, and he also wondered whether concealing or downplaying their Jewishness had contributed to their ascent. A critique of Jews by non-Jews was eternally playing in his head. Perhaps this critique also functioned as a test he thought we ought to apply to ourselves, so that we could extirpate from our self-presentation, even from our private thoughts, anything that people who didn't like Jews regarded as Jewish.

In his last years, when he was well into his nineties, on a feeding tube, and confined to Quercus, Father, skeletally tiny and frail, maintained his characteristic fierce energy and curiosity to an astonishing degree, but sometimes he would offer me a moment or two of open self-reflection, which hadn't been customary for him. I noticed which topics were available for this and which ones weren't. He spoke often about his not having been elected to the *Harvard Law Review*, as Pop had been, when he was a young man. This may have been a sign that the life of a business lawyer was not a perfect role for him; his sense of himself didn't rest firmly enough on his ability to perform legally in a driven, superior way. (Monroe & Lemann went out of business in the 1990s, and Father spent the rest of his career as a much-loved senior counsel at a newer and less patrician firm.) He'd tell me that he had been able to live so grandly because of his inheritance, not the income from his legal practice.

But these conversations never strayed into a full-blown wish that he had become an academic instead. That was something that I had thought about more than he evidently did, partly because the topic of his stellar undergraduate research, social network theory, was very much in vogue during his old age. The alternate life I imagined for him, being in on the very beginnings of a revolutionary development, would have entailed leaving the small territory within New Orleans that he had always inhabited, which was inconceivable, and also dealing with people who were very different from his circle of relatives and lifelong friends. Father would talk sometimes, obliquely, about the old troubles between Mother and him, again without taking the conversation into speculation about other possibilities they might have considered. He also never expressed any regret about the kind of Jewish life he had chosen, even though he realized it had represented inhabiting an island whose landmass was steadily decreasing. Our life in plantation-descended New Orleans—everything about it, the way it looked and felt, the heavy moist air, the smell of sacks of coffee and rained-on asphalt, the pace, the vast enveloping network of acquaintanceship, the determination to focus on pleasure and camaraderie and ease—made any other way of being Jewish seem impossible.

When I was growing up, we didn't go to Yom Kippur services at Temple Sinai, because Father preferred to go on Thanksgiving. The endlessly long services where you would find me now culminate in a brief ceremony called *Neilah*, which means the closing of

the gates. In the Temple in Jerusalem, the gates were closed and
locked at the end of the holiday; in a synagogue, it's the doors of
the ark, the cabinet that holds the Torah, that are closed, in a final
burst of especially fervent prayer, as Yom Kippur ends. That sym-
bolizes the cessation of the special, exalted access to holiness that
we have on the holiest day of the year—and even as the gates are
about to close, we, weak from hunger, swaying, beating our chests
with a closed fist, overcome from a mixture of exaltation and
exhaustion, pray to God to open them. The special connection is
too precious to lose. And sure enough, not so long afterward, in a
more ordinary way, the gates reopen for morning services. I think
of the life Mother and Father chose to lead as a kind of permanent
Neilah: the gates would close, never to be reopened. What had
gotten her family and his family, through countless generations, to
the point where the two of them were able to join together would
now be shut down, in the name of a form of optimism, a sense of
new opportunities, an allegiance to a quite different tradition. It
was easy to close the gates. There were no portentous signs and
wonders. Nothing happened.

THE END OF EXILE

Among the Torah portions we read during services every week,
there are the more glamorous ones, recounting the revelation at
Sinai or the flight from Egypt, and the more mundane ones, like
the long stretches devoted to the precise details of religious practices. I don't think I'm alone in reading these on Saturday morning
with a mixture of boredom and a sense of duty. Somewhere in there
is profound wisdom, which gave meaning to the lives of centuries'
worth of people I came from. Can I summon the patience, the separation from my ordinary secular life in the present, to discover it
and extract meaning for myself? Can I enter a different space? This
is even more of a struggle when I encounter one of the many passages of the Torah that are intensely discomfiting to our sensibilities

today, for the many ways in which they violate our sense of right and wrong about, for example, sexual practices, revenge, animal rights, slavery, and concubinage.

One of these would be chapter 25 of the Book of Numbers, which comes in the Torah portion called *Balak*. It tells us that, in a place that would now be part of Jordan, Jewish men were found to be "whoring" with the women of another tribe, the Moabites, who then tempted them into worshiping their god, rather than God. It that really so terrible? Well, it is to God. He instructs Moses to find the ringleaders of these activities among the Jews and have them publicly impaled, so that all can see their mangled corpses; also, as a collective punishment, he inflicts an unspecified plague on the Jews, which takes twenty-four thousand lives, including, presumably, those of many Jews who weren't whoring. Pinchas, a grandson of Moses's brother Aaron, steps up to begin carrying out God's orders. Encountering a Jewish man and his non-Jewish companion, he "stabbed both of them, the Israelite man and the woman, through the belly." God is pleased. He ends the plague, grants Pinchas's descendants priestly status in perpetuity, and orders Moses to make war on the Midianite tribe to which the woman Pinchas killed belonged.

How am I supposed to fit this kind of bloodthirsty ethnocentricity into my life? Can I possibly find guidance, or even inspiration, in this repellent story? Shouldn't I instead condemn it as inhumane and unacceptable? But there it is in the Torah, from which one isn't permitted to pick and choose, keeping only the parts that comport with contemporary standards. There's a useful lesson in humility here: if this supremely long-lasting and widely read book seems out of date in so many places, doesn't that indicate that some of what we know today as moral certainties will one day seem just as dated? Reading Torah can be an exercise not just in finding something of use in what initially appears useless, but also in trying to understand how people in the past could have made what strikes us as obvious, unforgivable mistakes and misjudgments. People are incorrigibly fallible. The standards of any moment can later become abhorrent. Everything deserves reexamination.

The proscription on intermarriage has always been difficult for Reform Jews because it so completely violates the Reform movement's founding principle that Jews are not a race. One of Julian Feibelman's successors as rabbi at Temple Sinai, briefly, was Roy Rosenberg, who liked to boast that he had performed more intermarriages than any rabbi in Jewish history: he claimed, implausibly, that his lifetime total was five hundred thousand. In 2001, while driving between officiating at one intermarriage and officiating at another, he had a heart arrythmia, crashed into a tree, and died. Was that by the hand of God? When Mother and Father were coming of age, intermarriage, at least to another member of their social class, would have been inconceivable, more because of the antisemitism of Gentiles than the tribal loyalty of Jews like them. In my generation, Mother and Father (once Mother had entered her militantly pro–New Orleans phase) were thrilled whenever there was an intermarriage between a member of our German-Jewish cohort and a member of the New Orleans social elite: a Heller and a Denegre, a Moses and a Dupuy, a Weiss and a Wisdom. Maybe we had finally arrived, broken down the last remaining obstacles. But here the Torah ought not be impatiently waved away. There must be some relationship between its operatically harsh treatment of intermarriage and the improbable long-term survival of the Jews as a people. How could there not be?

One can also look to Scripture on the question of what happens to court Jews in the long run. For my family, that has been a not merely theoretical question through several generations, including, as it has turned out, my own. Let's explore it by turning to two linked canonical texts that aren't in the Torah itself but in the larger collection of ancient writings called the Tanakh: the Book of Ezra and the Book of Nehemiah. One of the worst of the never-ending series of tragedies that have been inflicted on the Jews was the destruction of the first Temple in Jerusalem, in 586 BCE, on the orders of King Nebuchadnezzar of Babylon. Afterward many

Jews lived in Babylonian exile. Nearly half a century into the exile, after Cyrus the Great had conquered Babylon, God instructed him to permit the Jews to return to Jerusalem and rebuild the Temple. More than forty-two thousand went. One can picture them, as in an old Hollywood epic, trudging through the desert in a stretched-out column, dressed in robes, the men with long beards, accompanied by crude wagons and pack animals. Then, Scripture's familiar combination of Jewish backsliding and the successful scheming of the Jews' enemies caused the building project to stop, through the reigns of several Persian kings, until King Darius ascended to the throne and the Jews persuaded him to let the work on the Temple resume. It reopened in 516 BCE to great rejoicing, accompanied by the ritual sacrifice of one hundred bulls, two hundred rams, four hundred lambs, and twelve goats.

Court Jews keep reappearing in the story of the Babylonian exile. Even the evil Nebuchadnezzar couldn't get along without court Jews, Daniel and three of his friends. Other Persian kings had court Jews too. Nehemiah was the cupbearer to King Artaxerxes. Ezra was a priest—a descendant of Aaron and Pinchas—and high-ranking enough to be commissioned by Artaxerxes to travel, well provisioned, from Babylon to Jerusalem to establish regular religious practices in the reopened Temple and in the city and countryside around it. When he arrives in Jerusalem, Ezra discovers that the Jews have fallen into sinful practices once again: Jewish men have married (which, in context, probably means had children with) women from other tribes. Ezra weeps, he rends his garments, he prays. Then he summons all the Jews to the Temple and orders the men who had intermarried to send their non-Jewish wives into exile. Righteousness returns, but only briefly, until the usual happens: Jerusalem, though some combination of Jewish sinfulness (this time we were too lazy to keep the city's walls in good repair) and other tribes' attacks, falls into ruin. Word of this reaches Nehemiah, back in Babylon; he obtains the king's permission to lead a Jewish repair mission to Jerusalem.

In Jerusalem, Nehemiah organizes a great collective effort to rebuild the walls around the city, overcoming the Jews' enemies' repeated attempts to stop the work. When it is done, Ezra, the priest, reappears and establishes the still familiar basics of Jewish religious practice: Torah reading, the cycle of holidays, Sabbath observance. In a way all this is odd. Why go to all the trouble of rebuilding the Temple and then introduce religious practices that don't require the presence of a Temple? It seems to foreshadow the future of Judaism in the Diaspora, after the just-completed Temple has been destroyed again, by the Romans, never to be rebuilt (so far, at least). After twelve years in Jerusalem, Nehemiah returns to Babylon. Not long afterward, he learns that the Jews have descended into wickedness yet again. He rushes back to Jerusalem and restores order: "I censured them, cursed them, flogged them, tore out their hair, and adjured them by God," focusing especially, once more, on ending intermarriages.

The Book of Nehemiah leaves it unclear whether, on completing this last mission, Nehemiah is going to return to being a court Jew in Babylon. But what is clear is that, like all the scriptural court Jews, he has a primary commitment to his people; being a court Jew is a role, not an identity. The model of a Jew who gives up his tribal loyalty in exchange for acceptance or for power may have become familiar later, but I don't find it in the Hebrew Bible. And, for those biblical Jews who choose to devote their lives to the project of building a Jewish nation in the Holy Land, fierce illiberal tribalism is a sine qua non, represented by an extreme, repeated punishment of intermarriage. If you're looking for relief from Scripture's unremitting ethnonationalism, not so many pages away from the Book of Ezra and the Book of Nehemiah is the Book of Ruth, the heroic story of a Moabite (which is to say, non-Jewish) woman who marries a Jewish man and, after his death, decides to throw in her lot with his family and the Jewish people. Among the descendants of Ruth's intermarriage were King David, who made plans to build the first

Temple in Jerusalem, and King Solomon, who actually did build it. I'm mindful that I'm here because a young woman of another tribe, the Cajuns, decided to marry a Jewish man and to live as a Jew.

One of Felix Frankfurter's biographers referred to him as a court Jew, meaning the accusation to be devastating: Frankfurter had put his relationship with Franklin Roosevelt, and his seat on the Supreme Court, ahead of primary loyalty to his people at their time of greatest peril. This seems awfully harsh to me. Yes, it's easy to imagine Frankfurter constantly wondering how hard he could push Roosevelt on Jewish matters without seeming to be so much a special pleader that he would no longer be welcomed at court. Still, he was far less guilty than many of the most prominent American Jews of avoiding any advocacy on behalf of his people. He met with the Polish Gentile Holocaust witness Jan Karski, after all, and I'd guess he had a hand in arranging for Karski to see Roosevelt, for all the ambiguity of those meetings. Pop was far less proximate to power than Frankfurter. I don't see him longing for either influence or acceptance by non-Jews, but he was able to find a life outside of our declining family business by providing essential expert services to powerful people outside the confines of the Jewish world, his law partners and clients. That's a venerable role for a court Jew.

Father's own legal practice was mainly as a trust and estate lawyer. I would sometimes come to his office and find him encircled by the members of one of New Orleans's wealthy families, people he'd known all his life and who had come to him for advice in drawing up wills and arranging for philanthropic gifts. They were surely aware that they were hiring someone to do this who wasn't merely a trusted friend but also a Jew, somebody who understood legal intricacies especially well (they may have thought: because he was a Jew). So Father was also a kind of court Jew, but one who aspired, at least for a while, to join the court as a full member, or to lay the groundwork for me to join it. Reading Scripture makes it impossible to avoid thinking about long-running intergenerational succession. I think Father hoped that in my life, I could end the court Jew phase of our family's history, because the question of balancing my loyalties might not arise for me. There might be no court Jews because Jews would no longer be members of a special category. I would take my preordained place in the upper reaches of New Orleans without any restrictions. Father and Mother set up my life with that in mind.

When I was growing up, it wouldn't have occurred to me to look to religious texts for guidance, but I do now. How should a Jew, how can a Jew, live in the non-Jewish world? What's gained and what's lost? That's the Jewish question, and it's easy to read back into the texts, even though the term hadn't been invented when they were written. Jews are constantly made to negotiate the complications of living in non-Jewish environments, constantly tempted into non-compliance with God's law, constantly attacked by their enemies. These difficulties can't be resolved simply by exiting membership in the tribe, which isn't desirable and may not be possible—even today. Through all the scriptural stories, the aspiration for a nation, a homeland, is constant. Diaspora is always troublesome, never entirely workable. It always has an element of unfulfilled longing. On the other hand, nationhood entails never-ending risk and severe, intolerant, racialized limitations on the people who inhabit the Holy Land. There's no end to the Hebrew Bible's preoccupation with purifications and categorical separations. They may seem obsessive and beside the point, but without them, would we still be here? My people, the Reform Jews, dreamed that the Jewish question could be made to go away. It never did. That was partly because of the unending resistance of non-Jews and partly because there is no way completely to normalize Jewishness, to the point where it comfortably conforms with the standards of the outside world, without its losing most of its richness, maybe even most of its real meaning. It's never simple or easy to be Jewish. It's always complicated—externally and internally. That's what I've had to struggle with as I have spent my adult life trying to return to it.

INVESTIGATIONS

One day when I was a senior at Country Day School, somebody posted on the main school bulletin board a two-page spread from an underground newspaper, the *Vieux Carre Courier*, about the leading Mardi Gras organizations. This got my attention right away. In those days all mentions of these organizations—the krewes of Comus, Momus, Rex, Atlanteans, and the rest—in the main daily newspapers, whose publishers were members, were written in the kind of deferential and opaque prose that one might find in *Pravda* or *People's Daily*. This article wasn't exactly an exposé, but it did discuss the specific reputation of each krewe in an irreverent tone. I was amazed that it was possible to be this candid in public. It wasn't that inside information about the krewes wasn't a constant topic of conversation. (Who would be king and queen this year? If a krewe had leading members whose fathers were known to have been supporters of Huey Long forty years earlier, did that mean it wasn't quite so prestigious as the others?) It was that these conversations were reserved for private settings. The article had the feeling of samizdat publishing. It obviously hadn't been posted by our school's administration, and I remember its having disappeared from the bulletin board after a short time.

I'm not sure what made me interested in journalism. Mother and Father didn't really know any journalists; none of my friends had parents who were journalists. Back then, at least in New Orleans, it was a raffish, underpaid trade. But journalism caught my interest starting when I was quite young. Perhaps it was that newspapers and magazines were made to be engaging to ordinary people, not professionals or experts, or that they brought you into at least notional intimacy with a world much less enclosed than the one where our family lived, or that, as in the article posted on the bulletin board, they were permitted to say what people usually didn't. At that point I hadn't encountered Jack Burden yet, but now I can see in myself some of the same impulse to find a role outside the strict boundaries of my upbringing.

By the time I was in high school at Country Day, I would tear through all the publications that Mother and Father got at home, then go to one of New Orleans's few newsstands and buy whatever was there that seemed interesting, then go to the library at Tulane and look through the stacks for back issues of the publications I liked best. Decades later, my high school girlfriend (a daughter of one of the high-society couples that had cohosted Father's levee in Audubon Park) published a novel about our lives during this period. There's an implicitly Jewish character named Nathan Kentor, child of an eccentric brainy couple, who's a kind of proto-journalist, claiming to understand everything that's going on in New Orleans; the head of the school calls the heroine in and warns her that there's something different about Nathan, he's not safe to be with.

Not long after the miraculously candid article was posted on the bulletin board at Country Day, I found out where the *Vieux Carre Courier*'s office was, worked up my courage, and went there. The office was on the second floor of an ancient mustard-yellow building at the back of the French Quarter, beyond the usual ambit of tourists. I walked up a long, steep, barren flight of stairs and found myself in a large, shabby open room, full of boxes and stacks of paper, where seven or eight people in their twenties were working at desks. I asked to see the editor, and then asked for a reporting assignment. We wound up making a deal: in turn for being allowed to try being a reporter for the *Courier*, I would agree also to go to the printer every week, load up the *Courier*'s Datsun station wagon with stacks of the new issue, drive around the French Quarter unloading the previous week's paper and containers full of quarters from coin boxes and refilling them with this week's edition, and bring the returned papers and a cloth sack full of quarters back to the office.

That was the beginning of my real life. I hadn't encountered Quentin Compson yet either, but I definitely did not hate the South, and I especially didn't hate New Orleans. I wanted to find a different way of being there than the way that Quercus represented. The *Courier was* different. The 1960s arrived late in New Orleans; this was probably the height of it, in 1972. The French Quarter was home to underground newspapers, head shops, teenagers who had run away from home, vegetarian restaurants. The *Courier*'s staff was a kind of squabbling family, more or less located within the local bohemia, such as it was: self-consciously Southern writers, gay activists (as opposed to the handful of undoubtedly gay "confirmed bachelors" who were part of my parents' social circle), antidevelopment preservationists, hippies, jazz historians, convivial drunks, nude-rendering painters and photographers.

That part of it wasn't consistent with everything that happened to me afterward in journalism, but what was consistent was that we got to gossip and complain relentlessly, something frowned upon at Quercus, and that it was our job to be actively curious to the point of intrusion—to know, or try to know, or pretend to know, everything that everybody in the city was up to. How did real-estate interests get permission to build incongruously tall buildings in the French Quarter? Who'd set a fire, killing dozens, in a gay bar called the Upstairs Lounge? Where were there vestiges of the Jim Crow system, a few years after it had officially ended? The thick fog of politeness, of surface-dwelling conviviality, of things unspoken, that usually settled itself over everything had lifted. The second job I acquired during this period, interviewing the elderly veterans of *The Double Dealer*, led me to a man named William B. Wisdom— scion of one of the leading antebellum sugarcane plantation families and a collector of material about the Southern novelist Thomas Wolfe. He wore a white linen suit and had a similarly white goatee. A few days after I had interviewed him, he called me and asked whether I was the same person whose byline he'd seen in the *Vieux Carre Courier*. Yes. "Son," he said, in his elegant Southern accent, "I knew your grandfather. I know your father." Pause. He had registered that what, to his mind, the Lemanns represented in New Orleans and what the *Courier* represented were completely inconsistent. "Son, you are a traitor to your class." Exactly.

It wound up that most of my friendships, most of my romances, most of my decisions about where to live, and most of what I undertook to learn about have been connected to journalism. Just about every serious undertaking has been end-point punctuated by my publishing something. Over the years I moved from working for outsider publications to working for established ones. I began to spend my time with people who were like secular high priests, or maybe even court Jews, in the sense that we were not formally, securely in control of anything, but we knew what was going on, we were able to get in touch with anybody who was important, and we were confident about our ability to dispense wisdom on every conceivable matter. We had inside information about who was going to get which major job, and confident opinions about what course they should follow once they got it. We had the self-conferred right to decide what books and ideas mattered and which did not. We were unconstrained, at least consciously, by having a point of view particular to our circumstances or by having to dwell in the mundaneness, the quotidian detail, of making everyday things work properly. As journalists we were, as I was raised to be, a religion (of the public interest), not a race (of people who belonged to an inescapably delimited subcategory of humanity). This way of defining oneself was supposed to fulfill every need, every doubt, every longing, and for a long time it did.

In college I had my first encounters with Jews from the American Jewish mainstream. Harvard had changed from the time when Father was there. There was never a press release to announce it, but it was clear that the Jewish quota was gone. The *on dit* was that Harvard in the 1970s was one-third Jewish; the grandchildren of Jews who'd fled Eastern European pogroms and wound up in America's urban slums and whose children had miraculously progressed to middle-class suburban neighborhoods were now possibly closer to being the typical Harvard student than were high-Protestant graduates of New England boarding schools. All these years later, it strikes me that many of my Jewish classmates were overconfident that their new acceptance was complete and permanent. Somehow being a Jew in the wider world, which had always been complicated, was going to be uncomplicated from now on. It looked as if all the old barriers had fallen, without any modulating or disguising of one's Jewish identity being part of the bargain. Even Harvard's most elite undergraduate social club, the Porcellian, which always occupied a large space in Father's mind, accepted one of my classmates as its first Jewish member.

Today, I think of the way I was brought up as a kind of advantage-in-reverse, because it taught me never to be completely sanguine in my estimate of how much the rest of the world loved us, but back then, encountering pure Jewish confidence for the first time was intoxicating. I found that I felt unaccountably comfortable around Jews, even though I'd been raised to feel uncomfortable, unless they were New Orleans Reform Jews of a kind it was difficult to find anywhere else. Jews were lively, funny, smart, voluble. They were free to talk—constantly, obsessively—about being Jewish, in ways that I might have wanted to, because I thought about it, but that felt dangerous in our house in New Orleans. They seemed to lack the earnestness that so many other people had. They came at life from an oblique angle. They didn't obediently accept situations as they were presented.

Feeling comfortable wasn't the same as simply joining up, though. I told people I was Jewish only sometimes, and when I did, they often seemed surprised. I didn't fit their idea of what Jews were like. When one went beyond their manner and got into specifics, my Jewish friends were a font of unfamiliar touch-points. I didn't know any Yiddish expressions, even *oy*. I had never eaten at a delicatessen. I had never lit Hanukkah candles. I wasn't aware of knowing anybody who had ever been to Israel. I had never been to a bar mitzvah, and I was mystified by some of my Jewish friends' custom of calling each other by the Hebrew names used at their bar mitzvahs— Shmuel ben Yitzak, and so on. One of these people, someone whose parents had fled Europe in the 1930s, used to greet me with a taunt: "Here comes Finzi-Contini." This was a reference to the Italian novel (published in 1962) and film (released in 1970) about an assimilated, well-connected Jewish family that thinks it's safe, but winds up being deported along with all the other Jews. I was beginning to get the picture that Jews like us, German Jews, had a lot to answer for, in the minds of the American Jewish majority—we had not welcomed the arrival of the Eastern European Jews, and most of us had been actively anti-Zionist, even during the period when the establishment of the state of Israel was an urgent necessity. At that moment, the last thing I wanted to do was watch *The Garden of the Finzi-Continis*. I didn't want to see my family attacked, via comparison to a similar family. When I finally did watch it, not so long ago, I was surprised to see a scene where the Finzi-Continis are conducting a solemn and joyful Passover seder, wearing *kippot*. We'd never have done that.

Once, I remember, Harvard's Polish-born, *kippah*-wearing Hillel rabbi, Ben-Zion Gold, a grave-looking man who was the only member of his family not to have been murdered by the Nazis, appeared in the newsroom of *The Harvard Crimson*, where I was usually to be found, and asked for me. Somebody must have tipped him off. He asked me if I wanted to come to services. I said I was too busy being a student journalist, but that was just an excuse. The picture his invitation conjured up was of students with whom I had nothing in common, doing things (like praying in Hebrew) that I didn't know how to do, and probably also talking about Israel. It felt as if I would be out of my depth, and I also had a deeply bred-in instinct that if I were the kind of person who was a regular at Hillel, it would somehow disqualify me from whatever it was that I wanted to do that was not explicitly Jewish—not just at Harvard's social clubs, but even at the *Crimson*.

Another time, a younger friend of Pop, a federal judge named Charles Wyzanski, an elegant, magpie-bright man who walked around Cambridge in a bespoke suit and a fedora, carrying a polished wooden walking stick that, according to Father, had once belonged to Lord Byron, turned up in the *Crimson* newsroom and invited me to lunch at his house. That was more like it. There, I heard the kind of confidential talk about the doings of prominent people that used to fill Pop's correspondence, and that represented, roughly speaking, the world that my Harvard friends and I aspired to enter. I found out later that Judge Wyzanski's wife, Gisela Warburg, of the famous banking family, was a German-born refugee from the Nazis and a prominent Zionist, but I don't remember any of that coming up at the lunch—instead, what I left with was a sense of the allure of prominence, of insiderness, that would have stood in contrast to what I imagined that being in the overtly Jewish environment of Hillel represented.

I remember once getting a call from Mother in the *Crimson* newsroom. I was sitting at a desk surrounded by other people at other desks, so they could hear only my end of the conversation, which covered (let's say) whatever was the latest controversy in the literary and intellectual world, how my classical archaeology course was going, my reaction to her armchair-psychological analysis of the travails of this or that New Orleans family, and what I thought of some mid-1970s movie of the moment that everybody was talking about—*Nashville? Last Tango in Paris?* After I'd hung up, a Jewish friend asked me who I'd been talking to. My mother. Your *mother?* The person asking me couldn't believe it. No badgering, no guilt, no irrational fears, just a witty, emotionally contained adult conversation? Was such a thing possible?

It was, but at the same time Mother had become an ardent advocate of my taking up my destined place at Monroe & Lemann. I think this represented some combination of trying to please Father by being more aggressive than he'd want to be in stating their shared view that I should come home, and the ingrained conviction of middle-class Jewish parents of her generation (a category that included her but not Father) that their children should become lawyers or doctors, because anything else was either too risky or not open to them. After they both had died, I came across a letter Mother had written me after I'd told her I had gotten a postgraduation job at a new, low-paying liberal political magazine in Washington that was becoming known for launching promising careers in journalism. Mother must have thought better than to send me the letter, or else why would it have been among her things? "I feel like the victim of an anti-personnel bomb," she wrote. "Congratulations on the high-paying job. But move out, whoosh. I feel a great sense of loss. Perhaps it is strange that a mother should enjoy the presence in the menage of her 20-year-old son but indeed I do and indeed I will feel deprived if you live elsewhere. Of course I will let you and accept it but it is a wound." Even now, I feel a stab as I read this, a feeling that I had betrayed her and Father by choosing to leave New Orleans. But I can see that there may also have been some impulse on Mother's part, the impulse that left the letter unmailed, not to try to stop me from living the life she'd chosen, and may have regretted choosing.

The founder, owner, and editor of the magazine, the *Washington Monthly*, was Charlie Peters, who had been a young politician in West Virginia, joined John F. Kennedy's presidential campaign, come to Washington to work in the Kennedy administration, and then started the magazine. Officially, and up to a point actually, we were devoted to evaluating the effectiveness of government programs, but the charge of working there came from believing that from our small, shabby, hard-up offices we were going to be able to change the course of history. Isn't that the eternal dream of people who do this kind of work? People who wrote for us would get influential government jobs. Our staff members would go on to run major institutions in journalism. We belonged, I suppose, to the later and more establishment-oriented cohort of the sixties generation. Journalists had recently toppled the President of the United States; now we would help to devise a new liberal order, harnessing the wild energies of the civil rights and antiwar movements to replace the aging political system represented by the New Deal.

I suppose Charlie was my Willie Stark, powerful to the point of being dominating by force of personality, which is especially impressive in somebody who isn't actually powerful. He was a small, round, hard-drinking man who spoke in an intimate Southern accent and had an uncanny ability to charm people, especially young people, by making them believe they had joined a sacred cause. He earned the adoration of his staff partly through his limitless interest in custom-tailoring the big futures we hoped were in store for us. In my case an essential part of this entailed Charlie's openly confirming a message I'd imbibed implicitly for my whole life. "What's great about you is that you're a Jew, but you're not a Jewy Jew," he would say jubilantly, meaning, my ascent would not be blocked as it would have been if I'd been in the latter category. Embedded in this formulation was the idea that it wasn't completely okay to be Jewish, that the rough edge of it had to be sanded off. Explaining further, he told me that everybody important needs "a little Jew in the back room," some-one who might not be clubbable but who could master the details of highly complicated subjects for them. Senator Ted Kennedy, the hero of liberal Washington, for example, had someone like that advising him on tax policy. But the little Jew could never escape the back room, the way I could.

Charlie may have stated this a little crudely, but what he said comported with what I could see of the state of the world I was entering. Using all his powers, he was able to secure a job for me at *The Washington Post*, the big time for a young journalist. The owner, Katharine Graham, had inherited the paper from her father, a man with a background quite like my own—he was the descendant of Alsatian Jewish peddlers who had a business connection in Don-aldsonville. But she was an Episcopalian (when she died, her quasi-state funeral was held in the National Cathedral), and the heads of the news and editorial departments of the paper were also Epis-copalians, from socially impeccable backgrounds. In those days—and who knows, maybe also now—the ranks of the prominent in Washington were full of secret Jews, because, as Charlie said, the more obviously Jewish you were, the less high you could rise in the world. I had a friend who had come to Washington in the early sixties as a correspondent for a string of Texas newspapers. She secured an interview with C. Douglas Dillon, the secretary of the treasury and head of a white-shoe Wall Street firm. "Mr. Dillon, my readers would like to hear you talk about how your grandfather was a Polish immigrant peddler named Sam Lapowski who opened a store in Abilene," she said. That ended the interview.

The *Post*'s top editors each had a hardworking middle-class Jewish deputy. Howard Simons, the managing editor, had an uncanny ability—or maybe everyone does, so it isn't uncanny—to figure out who in the vast *Post* newsroom was Jewish. He'd establish a special line of communication with each of us, which was wonderful for me. What I could do for Howard was tell him what, behind the veil, life was like for German Jews. For an Eastern European Jew like him, this was catnip, because we were an object of mixed fascination and resentment that was necessarily speculative, because we were so far out of reach. Some years later, Howard produced a book of oral histories called *Jewish Times*, in which I was one of the interview subjects. I suppose I was guilty of dining out on stories that I knew by then would strike mainstream Jews as exotic: the impenetrable rejection of us by the Mardi Gras krewes and the Boston Club, and our own insistent need to distance ourselves from the *Ostjuden*. Father had told me once that back in the 1930s his aunt in Chicago, Nettie's sister, had felt she had to sell her house because Abe Pritzker, the founder of a great fortune but to her simply "Russian," had moved onto her block. That was in my oral history. When Howard's book was published, Father was not happy: not only did it call public attention to our Jewishness, and put us in the company of other Jews from whom we would want to be distinguished, I had also talked about private matters in New Orleans that we were not to acknowledge except in conversations that other people couldn't overhear. He went to all the bookstores in New Orleans—there weren't many— and offered to buy up their stock of the book if they would agree not to reorder it.

MAXIMUM DAYS

By the late 1970s, when I was out of college and working in Washington, Father had pretty well abandoned his project of bringing down the last restrictions against Jews, or at least against us, in the most rarefied restricted precincts of New Orleans social life. Father and Mother were accepted—indeed, loved and admired—by the people from those precincts who accepted them, and they didn't socialize with the people who didn't. They'd give large holiday parties at Quercus, the house fully decorated with a Christmas tree and wreaths, for an overwhelmingly non-Jewish guest list. I think of this period as representing the maximum glory days of Quercus. Mother's most favorite novels were *Buddenbrooks*, *The Magic Mountain*, and *War and Peace*; she used to tell me that she wished she could somehow unread them, erase them from her memory, so she could experience the pleasure of the encounter for the first time again. I was so committed to resisting her career advice in those days that I resisted all her advice. (In those days, I still identified myself most strongly as a Southerner, something Mother never did, so my reading was in search of a submerged Southern liberal tradition I could identify with.) It was years before I read those books and saw what she meant. *The Magic Mountain*'s obvious connection to Mother was through her ongoing and never resolved illnesses, but *Buddenbrooks* and *War and Peace* remind me of the part of New Orleans we inhabited, and I'm sure Mother noticed that too. The ceaseless kaleidoscope-like rearrangings of a coterie of large extended families, who were collectively presiding over a social order in decline—that, not the modern American mainstream, was our world.

Parties are at the center of life in New Orleans—I think of them as almost living things, with their own flow and rhythm. Most of the parties where you might find me now are merely extensions of people's worldly lives, celebrations of some achievement or attempts to raise money for a cause. Parties in New Orleans are purer, I suppose, and if they stand for something larger, it's something social: court-ship rituals or the making and breaking of other alliances. Mother, her middle-class origins a distant memory by now, would spend days preparing for her and Father's holiday parties, hiring extra ser-vants, ordering hors d'oeuvres from caterers, writing out elaborate instructions for the cleaning of floors, windows, furniture. When the evening arrived, the house would be fully alive, filled with the sounds of gregarious, graceful people laughing or whispering con-fidentially. Small clumps of guests, like schools of fish, swirled and eddied through the wide hallways, composing themselves and then dissolving. Works of art—Mother's brightly colored abstract paint-ings, Father's precisely tooled stone and brass sculptures—covered the walls and stood on the floor. Books were everywhere. Uni-formed servants, mostly Creoles whom all the guests had known for years because they worked at everyone's parties, kept people's glasses filled and bantered with them within the careful, inviolable, well-understood unstated boundaries of racial caste. After everyone had left, the house was a landscape of overflowing ashtrays and drinks stashed in odd corners, and Mother would conduct a debrief. We'd cover who'd had too much to drink, who'd flirted with someone they weren't supposed to flirt with, who'd looked lovely, who'd looked dissipated. It felt as if Quercus were the center of its own small civ-ilization, which I suppose is what Father and Mother wanted and what the arrangements they'd made with each other required.

By saying that these were the maximum glory days of Quercus, I suppose I'm raising the question of why those days couldn't have gone on forever. They never do in grand homes, do they? One of the pleasures of *Buddenbrooks* is how slowly and subtly the story of the family's decline plays out. I'm imagining that when Father and Mother built Quercus, Father, at least, may have dreamed that it would stay in the family for generations, like Palo Alto. Even after it became clear that Nancy and I were not going to spend our adult lives in New Orleans, he used to talk about donating Quercus to Tulane. It would be the local version of Villa I Tatti, the estate of the

Jewish art authenticator and all-around aesthete Bernard Berenson outside Florence, now owned by Harvard and one of Father's favorite places. Father was proud to have arranged for Pop's client Sam Zemurray's columned mansion on St. Charles Avenue to be donated to Tulane, and Edgar and Edith Stern's house to become a museum, and several of the old sugarcane plantations outside New Orleans to be opened to the public. For Quercus to become such a site, or a place for scholars to come on fellowships to do research, would have entailed the family fortune's staying in better repair than it did.

Father had a client, a handsome and assured man who owned a barge company, who was convicted of bribery because his company had paid a government official in Chicago to get a garbage-hauling contract. This ensnared Father indirectly in a criminal case, which was about as undesirable at Monroe & Lemann as a divorce case; also, Mother confided to me, Father, overimpressed by his client, had made a substantial personal investment in his company, which was now lost. It was a strict rule of Father's never to discuss money or business at home, because that was vulgar, but I also had the sense that Monroe & Lemann wasn't growing in pace with other prominent New Orleans law firms. Father considered practices like billing lawyers' time by the hour and setting up a marketing department to find new clients also to be vulgar. He became ever more deeply absorbed in his travel, his study of ancient Greek, his prodigious noncontemporary (except for the works of Louis Auchincloss) literary reading, and his ever-changing array of collections and hobbies.

I picture him, in the evenings after dinner, bent over his desk in a corner of the library, enjoying the pleasures of the unusual and self-contained environment he had created. Mother, whose health began to deteriorate seriously when she was in her sixties, would retire to her bed. Father developed an intense interest in Sèvres porcelain—dinnerware produced in prerevolutionary France, expensive, fussy, and too delicate to be put on display. Small, precious, gorgeously colored cups and saucers, decorated with exquisite flowers and gilt curlicues, which Father had located through dealers or at auctions, would arrive at Quercus every few weeks. It couldn't have been Father's conscious intention to torment Mother with these purchases, but they did torment her, as a sign of how completely their tastes and interests had diverged. As much as Mother still had the strength to do things outside the house, they had to do with liberal causes and modern art. New Orleans has a high tolerance for unusual individual choices, so Mother and Father's decisions about how to live didn't raise any eyebrows, as far as I could tell. They'd had to adapt to New Orleans, years earlier, and they had. For years when I was young, I had the idea that I'd find my own, different, but just as local, adaptation, with Jack Burden, Binx Bolling, and Quentin Compson as my guides—and even now, all these decades later, when I write a book, it's usually set in the South and centrally concerned with race, which when I was growing up was the ever-present and unmissable ordering principle of everyday life. But it became clear that I wasn't actually going to live my adult life in New Orleans, and that led me to a different kind of adaptation.

Until I was deep into middle age, I had no idea what the Jewish lives of the people I came from had been like. As Southerners we were proud to be more interested in multigenerational genealogy than Americans typically are, but not on that subject, over which an impenetrably thick curtain had been drawn. When you think about it, it seems obvious that any kind of seriously backward-looking history of our family would have to be about our being Jewish, but that's exactly how we didn't think about it. Instead, we preferred to think about being Jewish as a minor and inconsequential fact about ourselves, like hair color, not to be denied but also not worth being the object of the intense and precise curiosity that Father and Mother applied to other subjects. It wasn't stated, or even consciously felt, but somehow we knew that to probe into the meaning of our Jewishness too deeply would destabilize the comfortable foundation of our lives. But knowing what I know now, it looks as if something that had mattered a great deal to members of my family upstream from Father and Mother was about to be reawakened in me as a young adult. Not knowing it then, it was mysterious as it was happening. Why did being Jewish, and the deeply embedded tension between that and living comfortably in the wider world, keep presenting itself, unbidden and unexpected?

The first time I had lunch with Dominique, my first wife—I was working in Washington, but I had come up to New York, where she lived—she told me a story about herself that she said she hadn't shared with many people. I remember the scene vividly. We'd met in a large, noisy restaurant. Dominique fixed her big, unforgettably pale blue eyes on me and spoke in a low confidential voice that I had to strain to hear. Her father, a surgeon who had grown up in a small town in Kentucky, and her mother, who was from Casablanca, had met and rapidly fallen in love and married during her father's military service. They had settled in a suburban town in Connecticut, where they occasionally went to services at a Presbyterian church. Dominique would regularly visit her father's intensely religious family in a small town in Kentucky, but she had never seen where her mother had grown up—and in any event, they didn't live there anymore, because they had relocated from Morocco to France. During a trip to Paris when she was a college student, Dominique arranged to visit some of her mother's relatives. Over dinner, they told her that they were Jewish—something that would have been obvious from their last name, Chiriqui, and from her mother's maiden name, Benarrosh, to anyone who was familiar with Sephardic Jewish culture. She was shocked; they were amused. How could she not have known?

Back home, Dominique confronted her parents. Was it true? She got back a ruefully told story: her father, a dutiful son, was terrified that his parents would not be able to accept his marriage to a Jew, so he'd be forced to choose between love and family loyalty. But since his bride was from halfway around the world, and there would never be any contact between the two families, why not just tell his parents that she was French? He got her to agree that for the purposes of their life together in America, her Jewishness would be erased, as if it had never existed. Dominique's mother hid that essential part of her identity, not just from her husband's family but from everyone, from her own children. The only time I remember its being mentioned at a family occasion was at the wedding of one of Dominique's sisters, at the church, where her grandmother (who knew I was Jewish) leaned over to me and said in a stage whisper, *"C'est un marriage mixte!"*

What might seem odd about this story is not the anticipated reaction of Dominique's father's family in the rural South, but the need to keep Jewishness secret even in the New York suburbs in the postwar decades. It's easy to forget that even in that time and place, there were many places where Jews were not welcome, and casual antisemitism, even publicly expressed, wasn't seen as unacceptable. Dominique's family lived in Stamford; one town to the west was Greenwich, where, one heard, a Jewish family wouldn't be able to buy a house, and one town to the east was Darien, the Jew-barring town where part of *Gentleman's Agreement* is set. In John Cheever's canonical short story "The Swimmer," set nearby in Westchester County, an obviously Jewish family called the Biswangers, prosperous and socially unacceptable, the kind of people whose dinner party invitations would be politely declined, makes a brief appearance: "They were the sort of people who discussed the price of things at cocktails, exchanged market tips during dinner, and after dinner told dirty stories to mixed company." The doomed but high-society main character, Neddy Merrill, has a brief conversation with Mrs. Biswanger that forces him to leave in disgust, because "she was always talking about money. It was worse than eating your peas off a knife." This appeared in *The New Yorker* in July 1964, the same month that Lyndon Johnson signed the Civil Rights Act.

Dominique at that point had me figured out better than I had myself figured out. She told me later that she'd decided to reveal such an intimate and tightly held secret at such an early point because she sensed that it would matter to me. If I'd been asked about that as an abstract proposition, I don't know that I would have agreed, but of course she was right. By that time, when I was in my twenties, I felt a distinct tug in the direction of Jewishness. I didn't know what to do about it, but it was there, not to be denied. Anything that was demonstrably Jewish—a book, a movie, a restaurant—drew my interest. I was curious, I wanted to know more. It was a doorway into an endlessly extensive hidden realm that was completely mysterious to me, because Father and Mother had determinedly kept it at an inaccessible distance. Anything that was anti-Jewish—a story about exclusion, an obstacle that hadn't come down, a disapproving enumeration of supposedly Jewish traits—was no less fascinating, or possibly more fascinating. Maybe your body knows things your conscious mind doesn't: starting around then, and contrary to the common wisdom about the erotic impulses of Jewish men, I found that knowing a woman was Jewish always made her more alluring. My libido, like Walker Percy's Geiger counter, began rattling. Our small category of humanity was so charged, so demanding of strict limitation—how could it not have that kind of power?

But then what? Once or twice I wandered into a synagogue for services on the Jewish holidays but I felt completely lost, self-conscious. No place, it seemed, had services that had been as aggressively normalized as Temple Sinai's. People would say prayers in Hebrew and Aramaic that I didn't understand, sing tunes I'd never heard, stand up and sit down according to rules that everybody but me seemed to know. All I had really learned, at that point, was how to conform to the broad outlines of being culturally Jewish. What did that amount to? It was at best shallow, merely a stance that didn't entail any real commitment, and at worst a false front. When we were planning our wedding, Dominique located a Reform rabbi who was willing to marry us, knowing that under Jewish law, which holds that anyone with a Jewish mother is Jewish, it was not a forbidden intermarriage. But she was willing to promise not to reveal the secret during the ceremony, so that Dominique's parents' friends wouldn't have to learn that something so important had been concealed from them. The wedding was in a rented mansion in Connecticut, built in 1912 by an oil tycoon. The clerk at the town hall, who issued the marriage license, pulled Dominique aside and asked her if she was really sure she wanted to marry a Jew. Father, when he arrived for the ceremony, spotted the customary basket of *kippot* and hid it away, as he had at his wedding to Mother.

Being married by a rabbi was a first step that meant something to me, more than I would have predicted, but I had no idea what the next step after that was. I had another unbidden but intense Jewish moment when Dominique's father, a kind and generous man, suggested to us that our first child, Alex, not be circumcised. I suppose that it seemed to him to be a barbaric and outdated practice, one that entailed inflicting pain on an innocent newborn. Also, why perform an intimate, marking-for-life ritual whose purpose was to underscore how different Jews are from other people? In the late twentieth century, why couldn't we start to be like other people instead? Hearing the suggestion, I was nearly knocked over by an overwhelming wave of resistance that I hadn't expected. No! Surely I hadn't had such a visceral reaction because I consciously felt committed to God's covenant with Abraham; at that point I don't think I'd ever even read that passage in the Torah. Still, some powerful feeling of peoplehood, of a commandment being violated, swept over me, even though, rationally, circumcision didn't seem to comport with the idea I had been raised on, of Jewishness as a modern mainstream religion that had ridded itself of superstitions, rituals, and ancient bloody practices. Not long afterward, when we moved to a suburban town just outside New York City to raise Alex and his brother Theo, four years younger, I made a point of joining the small and relatively new synagogue there, the Pelham Jewish Center (Pelham was another of those towns that had previously been "restricted"; the older members of the synagogue had stories about the difficulties they had encountered in getting the local officials' permission to buy an old house and convert it).

Consciously, officially, I was doing this for Alex and Theo, so that they would grow up with some sense of Jewish identity. At that point I was aware of four Jewish holidays: Yom Kippur, Rosh Hashanah, Hanukkah, and Passover. For Passover we'd go to a seder at a friend of Dominique, somebody who'd been raised with seders as a familiar family routine, as it wasn't for either of us. For Hanukkah I bought a cheap tinny menorah and found a transliteration of the prayers you say while lighting the candles; I'd try, with only spotty success, to organize a minute or two of candle-lighting on the eight nights. Yom Kippur and Rosh Hashanah presented more of a challenge. The synagogue, a spacious, comfortably shabby old house on a residential street, struck me as an impregnable fortress. It was affiliated with the Conservative movement. That meant everyone there would be wearing *kippot* and *tallitot*—often the men had their own, which they'd bring to the synagogue in a zippered velvet bag that had been given to them on the day of their bar mitzvah— and that the services were interminably long and incomprehensible. I would drag Alex and Theo there as soon as they were old enough to come, but they squirmed and I felt out of place. When the project of keeping them in their seats became insuperably difficult, which was usually within half an hour, we'd slip out. I imagined the other people there staring at us disapprovingly as we left.

As the years passed, I'd go to the synagogue sometimes for a friend's child's bar mitzvah. At a crucial point in every Saturday morning service, the ark would be opened, everyone would stand, the Torah scroll would be brought out, and someone would walk it around the room so that everyone could symbolically kiss it: a quick touch of the prayer book or the fringe of the *tallis*, first to the scroll, then to the lips. After this display of reverence, the scroll—hand-calligraphed parchment made of stitched-together animal skins— would be laid down on a podium and opened, and the rabbi would read that week's portion aloud in a special incantation. At a bar mitzvah, it would be the spindly child, dressed up more fancily than on any previous occasion, who would be called up and handed the staggeringly heavy Torah scroll. Before beginning the procession around the room, the child would intone the essential Jewish prayer, the *Shema*. And at that point, unbidden, I would burst into helpless tears, struggling to keep it quiet enough not to be noticed.

What was happening—why the dramatic effect? Access to this aspect of Jewish life, of the lives of my family going back hundreds of years, through an unimaginable variety of circumstances, had been shut off to me, as firmly as a metal door being welded shut. That must have upset me a great deal, even though I wasn't consciously aware of being upset about it. Now the door was open. I was weeping over the poignancy of my parents' doomed hope that other doors would open if they closed this one. Over how liberating it felt to permit myself the luxury of particularism, of membership in a people, instead of having to insist that whatever I felt and wanted was an expression of universal values, aimed at the benefit of all. Over submitting to the undeniable power of ancient, prerational wisdom.

So maybe this project wasn't actually merely about Alex and Theo. It was about me. The idea that the tradition would continue, no doubt through unforeseen misfortunes, into another generation, and that this was something to proclaim proudly, no matter whether it might seem foreign to non-Jews—that broke through to some very deep place in my soul. What's obvious, if you want to be analytic, is that the way I was brought up, supposedly so liberated, so carefree about what it meant to be Jewish, actually amounted to a heavy burden to bear. The rest of the world seemed to care a great deal about Jewishness, no matter how much we had persuaded ourselves that it wasn't really very consequential. Why couldn't we, or more to the point why couldn't I, make it consequential too? In which case, it might have a positive rather than negative meaning. It's also the case that some things are beyond reason, even for somebody who has been trained to revere reason. The Torah is a sacred object. It contains all the truth in the world. Its continued vitality is a miracle. It is responsible for the unlikely continued vitality of the Jewish people, my people. There, I've said it. I know educated, liberal, open-minded people like me are not supposed to have such thoughts, but I do.

As Alex came into range of his teens, I conceived of the idea of having him bar-mitzvahed. With a group of friends, some of whom were in mixed marriages, I arranged for a Reform rabbi to conduct an abbreviated training program that would culminate in a group bar mitzvah ceremony. This was so as to avoid what seemed to us parents like an insanely rigorous regime of preparations—four hours a week, for years—that was required by the synagogue. When I told Mother and Father about this, during a visit to New Orleans, in the mid-1990s, it did not go well. Father, ever the gentleman, didn't say he was upset, but I could tell he was. He was quiet, his face became grave and drawn. Mother, always less restrained and by now accustomed to acting as Father's proxy in these matters, immediately exclaimed, "That's child abuse!" I have a hard time explaining their reaction to people, or at least to Jews who think of their children's *b'nai mitzvot* as pretty much the greatest days of their lives as parents. It wasn't entirely rational. Father had been confirmed, though not bar-mitzvahed, at Temple Sinai—I have a photograph of some kind of costumed tableau that was part of the ceremony, with him in the front row, a young prince. In Mother's childhood, most Jewish boys, including her brother, were bar-mitzvahed. Still, I don't have any trouble understanding it. We are all prisoners of the limitations of our immediate surroundings—even people as worldly as Father and Mother. A bar mitzvah wasn't just completely out of the context of their adult lives in New Orleans, it was threatening. Some forms of nonconformity are tolerable, others are not. That it was not was an acknowledgment of our high awareness that, at least in our surroundings, everything about Jews was not okay. That was why it was so important that we establish that we were unusual Jews, not like most Jews.

If this had been a movie, I would have stormed out of the house and initiated a breach with Father and Mother. That kind of thing wasn't our style, and anyway, I didn't want to have a breach with them. I sensed that on this issue, because they were still at home and I had left, they were more vulnerable than I was. We negotiated.

Mother and Father agreed to put aside their reservations and come to Alex's bar mitzvah, and in return I agreed that I wouldn't invite anybody from New Orleans outside of our most immediate family or, when I was back home, mention that the ceremony had taken place. At the ceremony, Father was polite and Mother was actually moved by the sight of her adored first grandson, in a suit and tie, being officially a man for the first time. I think she had a picture in her mind of the ceremony's being filled with black-clad guests, the women in wigs, the men wearing side curls, so she was relieved to see a crowd of denizens of the suburbs whose appearance was well within the range of what was familiar to her. The one Lemann relative who came—approved for the invitation list because she didn't live in New Orleans—was a cousin of Father's who lived near us in the New York suburbs. Afterward, she wrote me a note saying that it had been a lovely ceremony but that, because she'd had such a good relationship with her father, she didn't feel the need for God as a substitute for something missing in her life. That struck a familiar chord: the idea that a blowtorch-intense rejection of anything Jewish was properly understood as the healthy, normal, relaxed approach, but a tug in the direction of the way most Jews lived was evidence of an untreated neurosis.

JUDITH

Judith was at the bar mitzvah, as a presence in my life still new enough to limit herself merely to hinting that by her lights the ceremony was less a decisive break with everything I had known than a very small step in the right direction. Dominique and I were divorced by then. I had bought a house a couple of blocks away from the one where we had lived together, and we were raising our sons as joint-custody parents. Judith had just gone to work at a new magazine started by a friend of mine; he had the idea that we might be a good match, so he suggested that I take her out to dinner. Hmm. Judith and I both inhabited a tiny subculture, intellectually inclined journalists, where everyone had at least heard of everyone else. She had a reputation for being intimidating, the kind of person who had mastered most of the difficult books that frightened the rest of us off, probably by reading a version that hadn't been translated into English.

We had actually met once before, a few years earlier. Judith was editing a small magazine that covered the academic world, with a saucy edge, and she'd suggested we have lunch to talk about the possibility of her giving me a writing assignment. She struck me as exotic. I was a rising political journalist by then, married, a father, living in the suburbs. Judith was single, with short curly hair, wearing black clothing and thick-framed glasses, a denizen of a world of people trained in literary theory that was completely unfamiliar to me. We had lunch at a noodle restaurant I'd never heard of. I pictured her life as being a round of smoky, late-running parties in lofts. When my friend made his suggestion, I hadn't seen her except for that one time. I invited her to come out from the city for dinner at my house. That may have been a way of making myself exotic—How often did someone like her take the commuter train to the suburbs?—and it was also a way of making it clear right away that my life had a lot more circumstances than went along with what I imagined to be a typical single man she'd meet.

I remember hearing Judith approaching my house, because, in her context but not mine, it was fashionable for women to wear large, clunky elevated black sandals, along with bright crimson nail polish. I picture her bursting through the door, a big presence, full of gossip, health bulletins, excited reports on newly discovered cultural treats, provocations, warnings of looming danger, digressions. She said things that were more candid and unpredictable than you'd expect to hear at an early encounter. We went through our basic histories. Her grandfather, her father's father, had come to the United States from what is now Belarus, alone, as a young man who spoke no English, in the early 1920s—just under the wire before the passage of the Johnson-Reed Act, the severe 1924 immigration restriction that closed the gates of America and forced subsequent waves of fleeing Jews to Palestine. He made his way to Detroit and soon started a business washing the soiled overalls of workers in automobile repair shops, a task so dirty and onerous that nobody else wanted to take it on. The washing initially took place in the kitchen sink of a small apartment, but it grew into a substantial business. After a series of family disputes, Judith's father had wound up running an offshoot of the original business, an industrial laundry in Puerto Rico. She'd mostly grown up there, as a rebellious, reading-obsessed child living in a small outpost of diasporic Jews: refugees from Hitler, refugees from Fidel Castro, businessmen attracted by the local government's tax breaks.

I countered by giving Judith the outlines of my own family's story. It was instantly clear that I had tapped into a deep reservoir of bad feeling. "Oh! So you're one of the people who met us at Ellis Island and told us we couldn't stay in New York, so we had to go to Detroit," she said. Well, it wasn't me personally; even conjuring up a picture of my grandfather, arms determinedly crossed, personally barring Judith's grandfather from entering New York City, resonant as it was, would be accurate only emotionally. But of course it was true that established German Jews had launched a series of projects to steer Eastern European Jewish immigrants to the American provinces, and also that the two distinct Jewish cultures we'd grown up in mutually disliked and feared each other. Jews like me were raised to think of Jews like Judith as the people who had ruined everything for us by coming here in such overwhelmingly large numbers and by being so obviously foreign in every way. Jews like Judith were raised to think of Jews like me as the people who looked down on them and who, with rare exceptions, hadn't been able to summon enough solidarity to do anything to help European Jews when they were in dire distress. They had a derisive nickname for us: *yekke*, Yiddish for "jacket," meaning someone with money and fine clothes who held himself apart from his countrymen.

For the two of us, though—a Jewish mixed match, I suppose,

each of a type the other had been raised to resent or even to dread—the otherness of the other carried a high-voltage charge. That's how it looks to me now, at least. Judith was presenting herself as a deracinated, stylish denizen of the downtown cultural world. This was, in its way, a not much less marketized way to live than being a trader on Wall Street, except that the commodity being continually repriced wasn't a bond or a futures contract, it was you. It didn't make Judith content in any deep way; she'd started occasionally turning up at synagogues. Her mother, as a housewife in San Juan, feeling the same kind of dissatisfaction that Mother had felt during her early years in New Orleans, had gone through an extraordinary effort to become, in middle age, a member of the first cohort of female ordained Conservative rabbis, which had required her father's agreeing to relocate to New York City. Judith had grown up around this yearning of her mother's. That it went unfulfilled during her childhood made its power only greater. Who doesn't wind up repeating patterns from parents' lives? It didn't require superhuman insight to see that Judith was feeling a strong tug toward a more religious life. Judith was pretty much the only person who knew Judith to whom it wasn't obvious that some version of her mother's evolution was in store for her.

In the days when we were getting to know each other, Alex and Theo were living half of every week at my house and half at Dominique's house. One of my routines was to make a large pot of bolognese sauce during the weekend and then transfer it to small containers and freeze them. Then during the week I would defrost the containers one by one and pour them over pasta, which would take care of the boys' dinner. Once Judith came out to my house while I was doing this—gradually pouring small ladlesful of milk into a slowly simmering pot of ground beef. I saw a powerful, involuntary startled reflex, a horrified recoil, as if she'd seen something outside the ordinary bounds of decent human behavior. "What are you *doing*?" she said. I said I was making bolognese sauce—what was unusual about that? "But it's milk and meat!"—the most basic kosher restriction. This had never occurred to me, but to Judith, who had insisted to me that she didn't keep kosher and didn't intend to, I had violated a fundamental taboo that lived deep inside her, below the level of consciousness.

This moment didn't displease me. I knew by then that I wanted, or even longed for, some access point to what being Jewish meant, not just as a surface cultural style or as a set of political positions but as something profound, something that existed outside and above the standard routines of my life, which were beginning to seem inadequate to my most insistent needs and longings. I didn't know how to get to that—but maybe Judith did. And I had an instinct that I would not be able to find what I was looking for without making some trade-offs, because I had already seen that the option of dropping anything about being Jewish that might inconvenience you in the non-Jewish world leads to a washed-out and unsustainable version of being Jewish. That was why the original version of Reform Judaism had lost its audience: so much had been subtracted that what remained did not have the power to transport you to a different way of being. In the short run, in deference to Judith, I could substitute picadillo (no milk) for bolognese sauce. That's minor. But surely the adjustments wouldn't end there. A meaningful Jewish life can't be entirely frictionless, if you choose to live in the non-Jewish world to any extent. You will always find yourself negotiating the differences between one and the other. That means you always have to be aware of your Jewishness as you proceed through the tiny decisions people make in the course of every day. Maybe that's the point—that kind of always-on awareness is what life in the Diaspora requires if you want not to lose the thread.

If both of us were being drawn toward what Judith called Yiddishkeit (a word that I had never encountered), it's obvious what was in our pairing for me, but what was in it for Judith? She was always hyperaware of Jews who were more Jewish than she was, both in how they lived and in their adeptness at Jewish skills. I think she would have found it difficult to make an adult Jewish life for herself if she had placed herself among these (by her lights) superior Jews who (she imagined) were constantly judging her harshly. If called upon to perform at Sabbath services, would she be able to do so flawlessly, or would she make a mistake in pronunciation or cantillation that those in the know would notice? She certainly didn't have to worry about this with me. Her project could proceed. And there was a kind of bred-in-the-bones Jewish anxiety that sat with her often—with me, generations further down the line, less often. Being with me was calming.

Separately but mutually, I think, we had begun to grow weary of the all-encompassing professional worlds that we had worked assiduously to enter. In the New Orleans of my childhood, people didn't care very much about what you did for a living or even whether you did anything for a living. "What was your mother's maiden name?" was a more typical establishing question than "What do you do?" In the Jewish Puerto Rico of Judith's childhood, most people operated family businesses. In both cases, the lives of people who were bound up in their ascent though major institutions seemed impossibly distant and alluring. We didn't know people like that. But when you make yourself into one of those people, perhaps especially in journalism, with its focus on minutely tracking the doings of important and powerful people—their advances and retreats, the readjustments of their alliances—you begin to understand the psychic shortcomings of living that way. Being Jack Burden, tormented, questing, and rebellious, was not at all the same thing as being a high-achieving journalist in New York; the inside of a Balzac novel isn't such a happy place.

At the synagogue in Pelham where we were members then, people knew we were journalists, but they weren't tuned in to the fine gradations of status within the category, any more than we knew whether the members of the congregation who were accountants were major accountants or minor accountants. All of us who belonged were bound together by something different from professional status. That came as a relief, a vacation from professional anxiety. Being active members, which we were once Judith and I were together, entailed a great deal of mundane activity: making gift baskets for Purim, figuring out who was going to bring the food for the *Kiddush* after services, settling minor disputes within the community. This formed a kind of foundation, a base camp from which one could scale the religious heights and get a glimpse of something holy. It didn't always happen. It didn't even usually happen. But you couldn't skip to it, so there you were, mired, much of the time, and not unpleasantly, in the everyday. I remember once in the early days getting to the end of a Saturday morning service, which hadn't seemed any more or less enthralling to me than services usually were. We sang the final song, *Adon Olam*. Judith turned to me and kissed me full on the mouth. She was happy. I was happy. Maybe we were even something beyond happy.

AFTER MOTHER

One holiday season, before we were married, I brought Judith, Alex, and Theo down to New Orleans. Mother, now in her early seventies, was living as an invalid, her body ravaged by decades of arthritis and of heavy doses of cortisone. She usually moved through the world in a wheelchair, when she went out at all. What was on my mind was that I wanted Mother and Father to get used to the idea of Judith as a member of the family, but something different was on Mother's mind. At the end of the visit, she drew me aside and asked me to come back soon, by myself. Why? Because she was going to die. I thought she was being melodramatic, but one doesn't decline an invitation like that, so I returned a couple of weeks later. What didn't happen that weekend was some kind of emotional reckoning, or a summing up, or the revelation of a secret. We just reminisced and gossiped. I arranged with a movie theater to use a special entrance so that I could take Mother there in her wheelchair. We saw *Shakespeare in Love*. I left still thinking she was being melodramatic. Not long after that, Judith and I were engaged.

A few months later, Father called to say that Mother was in the hospital. I remember his tone as being almost apologetic. We both knew that somewhat mysterious trips to the hospital, usually associated with her heavy intake of pills, well beyond what her doctors had prescribed, happened regularly. This one would surely be like the others, brief and not to be explored deeply. But, for some reason, one of the doctors had asked him to call Nancy and me and ask us to come to New Orleans right away. It was surely unnecessary but he would have been remiss in failing to pass the message on. Both of us instantly booked flights, Nancy from Washington, me from New York.

We arranged to meet at the Atlanta airport and take the second flight together. From there we called Father. He advised us to go home. Everything was going to be fine, there was no need to come all the way to New Orleans. We came anyway, and called Father again as soon as we had landed. He said that while we were in the air between Atlanta and New Orleans, Mother had died. I think he'd gotten so accustomed over their long years together to putting everything that might be troubling out of his mind and focusing instead on the pursuits that made him happy that he couldn't absorb what was happening. At the airport, Nancy and I were standing at the departure gate, stunned, when our across-the-street neighbors, devoutly religious Christians, appeared. They gave us the joyously convivial greeting that is the custom in New Orleans. We told them what had happened. Instantly compassionate and sorrowful, they suggested that we all get on our knees and pray. We said no thanks and came home.

When we arrived at Quercus, we found Father in a kind of daze. But when somebody dies, there's a lot to do, so we got busy. I remember Temple Sinai, which Mother rarely entered, being packed for her funeral. I suppose that at such events there's always the public version of the person being mourned, and dozens of private individual versions quietly playing in people's heads. Surely some people there remembered her as the intermittently tormented young wife and mother rebelling against New Orleans—but, officially, she left the world as a pillar of the community, a beloved local philanthropist.

Should we postpone our wedding, scheduled to take place just three months later, in November 1999? We didn't. I don't think Mother would have wanted us to; she wanted other people's lives to go on, even as she recognized that hers wasn't going to. We got married in the grand headquarters of one of those private men's clubs in New York that surely wouldn't have permitted Jewish members when the building opened a hundred years earlier. Judith's mother officiated. Judith had decided that she wanted a full-on traditional Jewish wedding. She hired a klezmer band to play at the reception. We had an artist make an elaborately hand-lettered and -painted *ketubah*, a religious marriage contract, modeled on the one that my great-great-grandparents had made for their second, religious, wedding ceremony in New York back in 1852, just after Marie had converted and become Miriam. Judith moved out of the house for a few days before the ceremony, and went to a *mikveh*, a ritual bath, to purify herself before entering married life. At the ceremony she circled me seven times. As soon as we were married, we secreted ourselves in a private room for a short while before reemerging. At the reception we were hoisted on chairs by the klezmer-fueled dancing guests. At the meal, at each place setting was a *bencher*, a small white prayer book specially inscribed for the day, and of course there were also specially inscribed *kippot* for the guests to wear at the ceremony.

Against the majestic force of all this, it would have been inconceivable for Father to have tried to engineer a *kippah*-free ceremony at the last minute; instead, surely for the first time in his life, he wore a *kippah* himself. On the morning of the wedding, he and I went together to services at Temple Emanu-El on Fifth Avenue, the great and venerable holy site of the German Jews. There he found reassurance that the old way of being Jewish still had a home, but I sensed that his fierce resistance to any other way of being Jewish, on my part at least, was softening. I didn't know then, and he may not have known either, how fully I was returning to the traditions of our family's earlier generations, but I had a sense that the ceremony officially and publicly announced that I was passing out of one territory, a familiar one, and into another, where there would be mysteries and surprises.

"I have something to tell you," Judith said to me one day very early in our relationship, well in advance of our engagement. We were lying side by side in bed. It sounded ominous: what? "You need to know that if I ever have children, they are going to go to day school. I want them to grow up knowing who they are." I was mystified. I sat up. "What's day school? Instead of night school?" Judith explained that a day school is a school for Jewish children that combines secular and religious education. Her older sister had gone to a day school in Detroit, before the family moved to Puerto Rico, and it was one of the sorrows of Judith's life that there were no day schools in San Juan so she couldn't go to one there. Hence her embarrassingly low (by her standards, not most people's) level of Jewish skills—but we could correct that in the next generation. I had been vaguely aware that there were Orthodox Jewish yeshivas, where the education was entirely religious, but they were far outside the boundaries of my experience. It occurred to me that many people I knew in New Orleans, which is one of the most Catholic cities in the country, had gone to parochial schools: Jesuit, Holy Cross, Sacred Heart, and so on. The local Black elite, heavily Creole, sent its children to all-Black parochial schools, like St. Augustine and Xavier Prep. So, okay, it would be like that. It felt strange to think about this. Judith's children didn't exist yet. How was she so confident about who they were? And here we were talking about this in bed. It was inescapable that I might be their father, and if they were my children, and they went to one of these schools I'd never heard of, they'd wind up quite different from me. But it was obviously nonnegotiable, so I'd better adjust.

Even before we were married, Judith had herself appointed head of the education committee at our synagogue, so that Theo could have a proper bar mitzvah—which meant solo, with a good deal more recitation in Hebrew than Alex had done. Theo was more of a

rebel than Alex; years of quarreling followed, over whether he had
to go to afterschool preparation sessions every Tuesday and Thursday. In the car on the way to the synagogue, he'd ask, it seemed
like every single time, "Why do I have to do this?" Once we got
there, he'd organize the other kids to resist whatever the unfortunate Orthodox teacher who'd been engaged to train them had in
mind. To Judith all this demonstrated the necessity of day school,
because there most of the preparation would be embedded in the
school day, hence no quarrels, and higher-grade preparation. Anyway, didn't I find the thought of having children who were not bilin-
gual in Hebrew and English unimaginable?

At Theo's bar mitzvah, I don't think there were many guests who
noticed any shortcomings. Father by now was married to Sheila
Bosworth, a lapsed-Catholic New Orleans novelist who was able to
nudge him toward being less determinedly resistant to Jewishness.
Somehow this quality of Father's had been woven into the tensions
and tests of wills in his relationship with Mother; she'd been in
close enough range of typical American Jewish life that he had to
keep his guard up. Sheila didn't present this challenge, and she was
grateful to Temple Sinai for being willing to treat the two of them
as an honorable married couple, as her church was not. Father began
attending Yom Kippur services at Temple Sinai, as Pop had done.
He offered no resistance to Theo's bar mitzvah. He wore a *kippah*
there without protest. There's a moment after the service when a
parent gets up and says a few words. I talked about all those fraught
car rides when I had to tell Theo why he had to do this. The car rides
are over now, I said, so I'll explain it one last time, for everyone to
hear. What he'd just done meant that he was in a company that
extended a very long way, both vertically, back in time, and horizontally, around the world. For centuries people he'd come from, people
whose names we didn't even know, had done what he'd done. Now
he was one of them. And he could turn up at a Saturday morning
service anywhere, be warmly welcomed as if he were family, and
assist in the Torah service if asked. The further into this I got, the

harder it was to keep going. It wound up, as usual, with me dissolving into tears. It was as if I had finally granted myself permission to say something I'd always felt, just below the level of consciousness, but had kept tightly under a lid. That's a powerful thing to do. It has a force that can knock you over.

SEPARATION

Alfred Uhry's play *The Last Night of Ballyhoo*, a rare inside look at the culture of German Jews in the Deep South, set during the time when Father was growing up, has what must be one of the great unearned happy endings. Joe, a Brooklyn Jew, has wandered into the life of the superassimilated Freitag family in Atlanta. He has arrived to take a job in the family furniture business, but that doesn't mean he's socially acceptable by the Freitags' lights. Uhry, who grew up in Atlanta, obviously knows the territory intimately, and also knows how aberrant it will appear in the present. He presents Joe as heroic in every way, far past the point of believability, so that his unacceptability in German-Jewish Atlanta in the play is obviously unacceptable to the audience. Joe conceives an occasion to court Sunny, the Freitags' college-age daughter, but it has to be out of town, far away from the family's immediate orbit. Sunny reveals to Joe the true source of her family's peculiar form of Jewishness.

> **SUNNY:** It's only ignorance. I don't know anything. There's a big hole where the Judaism is supposed to be. But I remembered. I do know some Yiddish. I went to my suitemate's house in Chestnut Hill for dinner once and they said it at the table. Shabit Shallim—something like that.

> **JOE:** It's not Yiddish. It's Hebrew. It's the blessing you say Friday night.

> **SUNNY:** Shabbat Shalom.

Once it's clear they are going to wind up together, Uhry cuts away. Then there's a quick closing scene of a Friday night dinner at the Freitag home in Atlanta, which has lost the Christmas tree that has been on stage up to that point. Sunny lights a pair of Sabbath candles and says the traditional one-line prayer that goes along with candle-lighting. Then she and every other member of the family in turn intone the magic words, Shabbat Shalom. Done! Problem solved!

I don't think I had ever been to a Sabbath dinner before Judith came into my life. By that time I had been living away from New Orleans for twenty-five years, and I had been a dues-paying member of a synagogue for ten years. New York might be the best place to be a Jew, the most comfortable, the safest, in the entire history of our people (although, even so, there have to be armed guards stationed at the entrances to synagogues and Jewish schools; the safety of the present is relative to the sweep of Jewish history, not absolute and definitely not permanent). That means being Jewish doesn't require much of you. You self-identify, perhaps you attend the occasional Jewish wedding or bar mitzvah, you're culturally familiar with everyday Jewish life—familiar foods, a rhythm of speech, a set of prevailing attitudes—and that's about it. You don't have to do any-thing as a member of the community. I think that explains how it was possible for me to have become officially Jewish, indeed alarm-ingly Jewish from my family's point of view, without having been to a Sabbath dinner. But now that was going to change.

In *The Last Night of Ballyhoo*, Joe brings perfect Jewish happiness to the Freitag family merely by importing candles and two words of Hebrew. I wonder whether this would have worked so well with his family back in Brooklyn. Would the reborn Freitags, reformed Reform Jews, refrain from turning lights on and off on the Sab-bath, and from cooking? Would they decline all Friday night invi-tations except invitations to other families' Shabbat dinners? Would they locate a kosher butcher in Atlanta? Would they bake a challah? After blessing the candles, would they bless their children, and then the wine, and then ritually wash their hands, and then refrain from speaking until the challah had been blessed and eaten? Would they turn off the radio for twenty-five hours? Would they study Torah? What I found was that Sabbath dinner, like everything else about being Jewish once you've decided to plunge in, was all about compromises and trade-offs. If we were truly strict, it would be hard to go on living the life I'd been living for decades; if we were truly lax, the meaning would melt away. Jews, like everybody else, don't like being excluded, but observing the Sabbath entails self-segregation—leaving the mainstream and dwelling in an all-Jewish world for a day.

Judith's parents of course had a Sabbath dinner every week, but even they couldn't get through the whole day without turning anything electric on or off. What wasn't difficult for them was separating themselves temporarily from the non-Jewish world, because there was no separation during the rest of the week either. Once I asked Judith's mother why, in all the dozens of times I'd been at her apartment for well-attended meals, I'd never encountered anyone who wasn't Jewish, except once when there was a young minister from Sweden or Denmark who was at the Jewish Theological Seminary on an exchange program and had been farmed out to Judith's family. She said, in innocent wonder, "How would you meet someone who wasn't Jewish?" I understood what she meant. Both of Judith's parents had been raised in all-Jewish neighborhoods in Detroit (when they were young, where else were Jews permitted to live?). They had gone to a local commuter college while living at home, they had met in a synagogue, and they had grown up knowing that the big automobile companies and other major employers would not hire Jews, so they'd have to start their own businesses that operated in an all-Jewish economic ecosystem, quite like the one my own earlier-arriving family had operated in during the nineteenth century.

One summer we were in Venice on a vacation—one of Mother and Father's favorite cities, where the concierge at the Gritti Palace, a small monument to tasteful luxury, would greet them as old friends on their regular visits. To look at art there, you wind up going to churches, because that's where most of the greatest paintings are. We were doing this with Judith's father and I noticed he was trembling and sweating. He asked me to come outside with him. He said he just couldn't be in a church—it hit some deep, deep terror nerve. The Talmud specifically forbids Jews to enter churches, but I'm not sure Judith's father knew that. His parents had both been raised in godforsaken shtetls in Eastern Europe, constantly worried about pogroms. His elderly grandmother was transported to a forest, stripped naked, and murdered by the Nazis, a victim of the Einsatzgruppen, the "Holocaust of bullets." He just couldn't make himself comfortable in a monumentally non-Jewish environment.

What I encountered in Judith's parents' apartment, on the Upper West Side of Manhattan, was something just as utterly foreign to me as the church in Venice was to Judith's father: a place where the baseline assumption was that being Jewish was great in every way, a source of boundless gratification and pride. As you entered, there was a mezuzah, a small box containing a scrap of Torah on a parchment, at the front door, as commanded in Deuteronomy 6:8. Then, inside, you'd encounter the art on the walls: just about every picture was explicitly Jewish, with scenes of Israel at least in the plurality. Farther inside, you'd see the books on the shelves, which were overwhelmingly on Jewish topics. On the tables were photo albums of bar and bat mitzvahs and of Jewish weddings. On the shelves that didn't contain books, there were menorahs and Sabbath candelabra. On the sideboard in the dining room there were baskets filled with *kippot*, each one bearing the printed legend of some Jewish special occasion over the years. There were drawers full of *benchers*, bearing similar legends, which would come out for the *birkat hamazon*, the endlessly long grace after meals sung at the conclusion of a Sabbath dinner. None of this would have been remotely possible at Quercus.

An evening at Judith's parents' apartment with no mention of Israel would have been inconceivable, because so many relatives lived there, because visits were constant, and because Zionism and Jewishness were inextricably intertwined for them. I was raised to react to all this the way that Judith's father reacted to being in a church: it felt alarming, unclean, at the most instinctive level. But here it wasn't. I loved it. I felt liberated. Mother and Father, and Judith's parents, lived very differently, but what the ways they had chosen to live had in common was a hyperawareness of antisemitism. Here, unlike at Quercus, Jewishness didn't have to be suppressed at all times—which in no way meant that in New Orleans it wasn't always in our consciousness; our strict avoidance was a tribute to antisemitism. Here you could evaluate things happening in the world according to whether they were good for the Jews. You could interrupt. You could talk about your body. You could talk about what things cost. You could complain about Jews, in ways that, if non-Jews did it, would enrage you. Everything that had been bottled up could be uncorked.

Before the Enlightenment, for pretty much everybody and certainly for Jews, religion was an all-encompassing ordering principle for every aspect of life. Even in the present, I was seeing the residue of this. Practiced, organized religion will get you properly born, married, buried. It will give a temporal structure to your day, your week, your month, your year. It will give you holidays to celebrate, charities to support, a community to belong to. It feeds you. It tells you stories. It has a soundtrack. It offers the most recondite and challenging intellectual pursuits, if you're interested in that sort of thing. All this together, in the Jewish world, doesn't even amount to being truly observant. For that, just to begin, you'd start every day with the morning prayers and you'd use the ritual baths and other forms of purification that play a major part in the Torah and the Talmud, but are much less major in the lives of even the most actively engaged Jews and certainly aren't a part of my life. The more you move in a post-Enlightenment direction, the more you're left to invent everything, or to overvalue whatever is the prevailing wisdom of the present moment, or to try to extract more richness from jobs and casual friendships than they can reliably provide. How can you compare the occasional reunions you try to schedule with people you worked with long ago, or summer block parties with your neighbors, or business meals with colleagues you've come to feel genuinely close to, or a regular tennis game, or a book group, with the absolute inviolability and empyrean grandeur of the Sabbath?

Outside of the Jewish world, I move in two other worlds, journalism and universities. Both of them are overwhelmingly secular, and when people in them find out that I am actively religious—something I don't advertise; it feels potentially disqualifying—they can be incredulous. I get questions like "Do you believe in God?" or even "When you're sick, do you go to a doctor?" Religion means superstition, ignorance, authoritarianism, strife: right-wing fundamentalist voters at home, Islamists abroad. Without it, the world's sorrows would be reduced. The more prosperous countries have become far more secular recently than they have ever been and it doesn't seem to have made life much less tragic. What's more profoundly true is that everybody belongs to a tribe of some kind. Everybody has a set of beliefs, a narrative, that frames the way they experience life. Some people call theirs a religion, others use a political or ethnic identity, or a professed faith in rationality, instead. It's impossible to exist as a completely decontextualized and individualized person all of whose principles are universal.

Once Judith and I went to a lecture on religion by a famous Jewish, but militantly secular scientist. He began by saying that he would define religion as a belief in the supernatural. Okay, then you win, but that doesn't anywhere near describe our own religious life. Is reading Torah belief in the supernatural? Is a seder? Is Zionism? In active Jewishness, as elsewhere, there's an element of reverse snobbery, so in our Jewish world it's common to hear people say they don't believe in God. (In the same spirit, it's better to say that you belong to a small minyan than to a big synagogue.) What that means is that they see concepts like faith and belief as having originated in Christianity and then been backdated into Judaism; real Jewishness is all about trying to understand the eternally daunting and revealing texts, and to abide by as many of the 613 laws as we can. These are bound to be losing battles—it's one thing to forswear idol worship and incest and to observe the major holidays, another not to use a razor and to avoid clothing that contains both wool and linen—but at least we're struggling with them. We're a *kahal*, a community, a remnant of the ancient Jewish self-governing tradition.

If you were inclined to challenge me, you might ask, Well, then why have you chosen this one particular membership and what it entails, when there are many others available? Is it just a personal preference, morally neutral in comparison to the alternatives? There you'd have me. I could say that I have chosen to live the way I live because (as I didn't know when I was growing up, but have learned) it's aligned with the way many generations of the people I came from lived. I could say that I prefer the broader spectrum of experiences and the more profound and forgiving bond of community that being actively Jewish provides to the thinner gruel of living as a member of a socioeconomic formation that is bound to be fleeting. I could say that I concluded that the German-Jewish Reform tradition in which I was raised was so eager to demystify, detribalize, and de-inconvenience itself, continually subtracting from Judaism rather than adding, that it became unsustainable and withered away and I needed to find something to replace it. All true. The harder question to answer is why I have chosen to accord a special reverence to my tradition. Is it just that it's mine? Or that it has lasted so long? Officially, I believe that some collection of human beings produced the Torah: a long-running and not conventionally organized team of writers and redactors. God didn't hand it to Moses (twice) on Mount Sinai. And most of the classic commentators were indisputably human beings, rabbis with bylines. Right? But then why is the sight of the physical scroll so powerful for me? Why do I find rereading it every year so rewarding, so useful? Isn't the idea of commandedness fair to use as a way of capturing this? You've got me there. Not every question has a perfect rational answer.

A JEWISH LIFE

I said that our wedding felt like a passage from one way of living to another, but it's also true that after the band had packed up and the dishes had been cleared away, only a dozen of the guests, at most, picked up the *benchers* that were at their places and stayed in place for the *birkat hamazon*. It wasn't as if everybody we cared about was at an equal level of Jewish observance that we could simply adopt. We had to work it out for ourselves. We wound up moving from the suburbs into the city, partly because we thought a richer Jewish life could be had there. As we'd agreed, we sent our two children, Moses and Josephine, to a Jewish day school through eighth grade. The school put us into an all-encompassing, all-Jewish world. The parents got to know one another, as parents of children who go to school together do. We'd meet at school events, at holiday celebrations, at Saturday morning services, and at Sabbath dinners, which aren't like adult dinner parties because all family members are invited. We joined a large synagogue on the Upper West Side, a lineal descendant of the synagogue where my great-great-grandparents were religiously remarried in the 1850s. Within it we usually went to a small minyan whose members were so well educated Jewishly that it didn't need a rabbi to lead services. All this put us in the major leagues of living a Jewish life, in a way we hadn't been in the suburbs.

I'd insisted that Alex and Theo be circumcised, but I didn't have to be present. Moses had a bris, presided over by a celebrity *mohel* Judith's mother knew, who drove around New York in a chauffeured limousine with personalized license plates that read MOHELPJK (his name was Pesach J. Krohn). Josephine had a baby-naming ceremony. Both of them were called to the Torah, after extensive anxious preparation, at the age of thirteen. Judith learned how to bake challah. We often—Judith more often than me—attended some of the nearly limitless Jewish cultural events (lectures, concerts, study sessions) that are available in New York. After all these years, these innumerable Jewish occasions form a blur. Thinking about them, I'm put in mind of one of Alice McDermott's novels about mid-twentieth-century Irish Americans: there's a texture, a taste, a smell, an accumulated ordinariness of religious occasions, that stays with you as much as the glory of memorializing marriage and birth and adulthood and death. By now I must have been in a thousand basement function rooms with long folding tables covered with paper tablecloths, stacked with plastic plates and utensils, laden with dishes of rugelach, kugel, babka—crumbly, cloying, familiar— and dark, capacious, too-warm apartments in old buildings where the customary baskets of inscribed *kippot* accumulated from innumerable Jewish occasions sit on shelves, waiting for guests.

The two foundations of living a Jewish life are keeping kosher and observing the Sabbath. The first of these I'm not good at. At home, we don't have pork or shellfish and we don't mix milk and meat. When we have friends over who are more observant than we are, we have to turn it up a few notches, sometimes to the point of ordering triple-wrapped food from a kosher caterer and serving it on disposable dishes and utensils. All the traditional religions, as part of being full-service methods of organizing people's lives, have dietary laws. I can see how kosher serves the purpose of enclosing you within the community. Either you don't leave the strict Jewish world, so you never have to think about it, or you operate in the wider world, and you always have to think about it; every time you eat, it's a moment of awareness of being Jewish. Even Judith's mother was willing to eat at non-kosher restaurants, which means she was probably straying even if she only ordered fish and vegetables. For me, it's impossible to feel a bone-deep proscription on non-kosher food because it's what I was raised on. When our children were small, I avoided ordering something obviously non-kosher in a restaurant, like lasagna (milk and meat), because I didn't want to set a bad example, but now that they're older I'm not as strict about that. Contemplating living out my days without ever again tasting gumbo would be like contemplating no more matzoh ball soup might be for someone raised conventionally Jewish. But even in my case, the kosher laws have lodged themselves in my head: food is the immediate daily front end of the never-ending process of negotiating the boundaries between Jewish and American. That seems more authentic than pretending there are no boundaries to negotiate.

The Sabbath feels less arbitrary to me and the rewards are more immediate and palpable. It's an obviously special occasion, not an ongoing limiting proscription like keeping kosher. Still, we are not entirely successful Sabbath observers. We briefly tried not using electricity on the Sabbath. That meant figuring out which lights to leave on and which to turn off in advance of sunset on Friday, forswearing any electronic devices, and cooking all meals in advance. It was too much; I'd always leave the bathroom in pitch-darkness, or want to add one last element to dinner after sunset. But I don't work on Saturdays, and I usually go to services, and we always have Sabbath dinner on Friday, either at home or with friends, scheduled usually weeks in advance. Judith says the blessings—in Hebrew, of course—before we eat because I don't know how. There's work, inconvenience, involved. You have to make plans. An inner countdown begins to run in your head as the week begins. There are things you can't do, invitations you can't accept. We've found that guests who aren't used to it can be intensely uncomfortable being at a table where people say prayers. With small children, there's a measure of squirming and arguing that goes along with the process of bathing and dressing with special care and turning screens off.

One of the books we used to read to the children when they were little—in the category not of great children's literature, but of Jewish exhortation—was about Sabbath dinner. The main character was a little boy named Yossel. It went through the cooking, the baking, the baths, the specially set table, the lighting of the candles, and then, if I'm remembering the book properly, something called Sabbath magic descended on the room. That was the payoff from all the preparation. This was something close to a fairy tale, as it was meant to be—but sometimes, not always, the book had it right. There *was* a kind of magic, a glow. It felt different when you crossed the time barrier separating the Sabbath from the rest of the week. Peace and order descended, cares evanesced, tradition established itself. And this necessarily required separation, from the rest of the week, from work, from money, from rushing, and from the non-Jewish world. So here again was the business of negotiating your place between two different modes of consciousness. It never went away, and if somehow it did go away, so did what mattered about being Jewish.

In 2005, one of my colleagues at Columbia, the university where I work—a colleague I'd never met, an eye doctor who works in the university's medical complex, fifty blocks away from my office—invited me to travel to Tel Aviv to make a speech opposing a movement that was then emerging, and is now at full force, to have universities boycott Israel. If the movement succeeded, the many partnerships between American and Israeli universities would come to an end. Like many of the Jewish things I'd already done, this initially felt like an invitation to violate the German-Jewish version of kosher, because back home in New Orleans we'd had such a strict proscription against any form of public Jewish advocacy, not to mention one that entailed an open gesture toward Israel. Father ended his days never having even considered going to Israel, despite his love of travel and of the ancient world. Scotland, France, Italy, Turkey, Greece—all these were suitable repeated destinations for him, but not the Holy Land.

But I accepted the invitation. The planned trip expanded into a two-week visit, with Judith, the children, and Judith's parents all coming along. I have an oddly precise memory of standing on a grassy hilltop in Jerusalem on the day we arrived. It was hot and bright. Traffic moved chaotically through the streets nearby. Israelis always seem to be rushing somewhere; the people crowding the sidewalks, in sandals and short-sleeved shirts, displayed no sign that they were aware of anything special about where they were. But I thought: how peculiar it feels to be in a place where Jews are not a provisional minority, as I was accustomed to thinking of us as forever and inescapably being. We were in a self-consciously quaint neighborhood called Yemin Moshe, made up of small golden stone houses and cobblestone streets, ornamented with luxuriant flowing vines, which had been founded by Pop's namesake, Moses Montefiore, with additional funds donated by New Orleans's leading Jew, Judah Touro. It should have felt familiar, but instead it felt utterly foreign: a high-voltage jolt of Jewish particularism.

Israel is a very small country, so during our time there we were able to see most of the familiar sights: the old city in Jerusalem, Tel Aviv, the villages along the Mediterranean shore, the Dead Sea. It struck me that being there in 2005 had something in common with what a visit to the United States in 1840 would have been like: at the standard sites, a hortatory national project was overwhelmingly the main point. At Masada you get the legend of a group of heroic Jews on a remote mountaintop who were besieged by Roman soldiers and wound up committing suicide rather than surrendering. At Yad Vashem, the Holocaust museum, after you've made your way through the devastating exhibits, you emerge into the bright desert light and get a sweeping view of the land. The message is unmistakable: nationhood was the obvious and only way to guarantee a better future for the Jews. At the Western Wall, the imposing remnant of the Second Temple, you see an underground archaeological exhibit forcefully establishing the historic and consistent presence of the Jews beginning in ancient times.

Our visit coincided with Shavuot, the holiday that marks the giving of the Torah at Mount Sinai. Moses, having lengthily communed with God at the top of the mountain, emerges, bearing stone tablets inscribed with the law, which he imparts to the Jews waiting below. It's one of the Jewish holidays that I didn't know existed until I was middle-aged. In Jerusalem we were staying at an inn with a view of the old city. We could see a long line of people dressed in white, slowly trudging up an endlessly long stairway to one of the gates in the old walls, so they could stay up all night studying Torah at the Wall. The procession had a solemn dignity, a sense of returning to an unaltered custom from ancient times.

On one of our days in Israel we went to Ramallah, less than fifteen miles away—poor, crowded, barricaded, graffitied—to visit the family of a Palestinian former student of mine. It felt like making the trip in a major American city from the part that officially presents itself to the hard-up, heavily policed margin. On another day we climbed a long flight of stairs up to what Israelis call the Temple Mount, to see the place where the First and Second Temples had stood and where Abraham had bound Isaac to be sacrificed on God's orders. There you stand on a large stone plaza, filled with armed guards and Muslim pilgrims, and look at two of Islam's holiest sites, the gorgeously tiled, gold-topped Dome of the Rock and the dun-colored, columned Al-Aqsa Mosque—from the outside, because Jews aren't allowed to enter. Telling Israelis we knew that we had gone to these places—Arab territory—evoked a startle reflex, like Judith's when she saw me pouring milk into a meat sauce.

My friends who'd had more typical Jewish upbringings than me were raised on the idea that Israel was a light unto the world, whose establishment amounted to a universally admired liberal triumph. That was obviously as much of an illusion as the idea of the early Zionists that Palestine was unpopulated. By the time I got there, Israel had not been under the firm political control of liberal social democrats for many years. It was obviously deeply resented and constantly on guard against attack. Later that year, the government would end its nearly twenty-year occupation of Gaza, which engendered a furious internal opposition that drove the country even further to the right. It touched me deeply to be in this ancient Jewish place, but my first visit hardly convinced me that Zionism was going to prove to be the serene solution, at long last, to the Jewish question.

THE FLOOD

A trip to the Holy Land can't help but put you in mind of fable-level plagues, natural disasters, wars, sufferings. Such things aren't supposed to be part of contemporary life in America—but just a few weeks after we returned from Israel, New Orleans suddenly, unexpectedly, lay in ruin. Hurricane Katrina broke through the city's flimsy flood protection system and left much of it under water. Sweltering, homeless refugees, overwhelmingly Black, crowded into public spaces to survive. The city had always been an affront to nature, low-lying, disease prone, home to mosquitoes and snakes and constantly encroaching junglelike vegetation. What made it worth settling was the potential for resource extraction: cotton, indigo, sugarcane, fur, seafood, sulfur, oil. New Orleans never signed on to the Protestant ethic. People's devotion to all forms of pleasure—food, drink, parties, dancing, sex—provided distraction from the perilousness of the situation. The underlying incentives were always to live in the present, not to plan for the future. The color line enhanced the situation, because the white city fathers, either not wanting the Black majority to prosper or, worse, not believing it was capable of prospering, didn't provide good schools, well-paying jobs, or solid housing. As had been the case since the time of plantation slavery, it was a more Caribbean than American city, charming and seductive but rough and poor behind the curtain.

Back in the second decade of the twentieth century, the time when Pop was establishing his legal practice, a brilliant young engineer named Albert Baldwin Wood devised a system of pumping stations that could drain the swampy parts of the land that lay between the crescent bend of the Mississippi River and Lake Pontchartrain and, supposedly, keep them dry forever. Over the course of the twentieth century, these parts of the city became neighborhoods. (One, Pontchartrain Park, was New Orleans's first planned Black middle-class neighborhood, financed by Edgar and Edith Stern, who had absorbed Booker T. Washington's theory that Black economic progress, rather than integration, should be the primary racial cause.) Hurricane Katrina overwhelmed the pumping system, which made every part of the city built within the previous century flood. Thousands of people sat on their roofs waiting to be rescued by boats traversing what had been streets; many others crowded into the hot, underprovisioned downtown sports arena and convention hall because they had nowhere else to go.

Father, then a few months short of his eightieth birthday, had been through a lifetime of natural disasters, beginning with the great Mississippi River flood of 1927, whose muddy, levee-breaching torrents displaced almost a million people up and down the river. Quercus had a generator to keep the lights on and the air-conditioning running when the city's power system went out, as it regularly did. Father didn't see any reason to obey the order to evacuate, the latest in an endlessly long series, that came down just before the storm hit. But after it had, it was obvious that he and Sheila couldn't stay. Quercus is in a part of the city that had been built up in the late nineteenth century—the part where four generations of our extended family had lived—but the entire city, including the older sections that weren't under water, was uninhabitable. It presented itself to a suddenly attentive world as a site of total devastation. Most of the streets were impassable because of downed branches, garbage, and debris, local government had shut down, the utilities weren't functioning. As always at times of great stress in New Orleans, old racial terrors, rooted in plantation days, that we had supposedly put behind us came straight to the surface: the Black fear of being treated as disposable, barely human, never out of range of being murdered with impunity; the white fear of the murderous Black mob that was just beyond our sight, marching in our direction.

Sitting in New York, I was a wreck. It was late August, just before the beginning of the academic year. I left my office and sat on a bench on the Columbia campus, dazed, taking in air in great gulps, wondering how the students walking past me on the way to class could go about their lives while New Orleans had simply stopped functioning and seemed to be in danger of descending into a state of violence and chaos from which it would never recover. For a time there was no way to reach Father. The internet and the telephone lines didn't work. Then, miraculously, it turned out that

Father's mobile phone could receive, but not make, calls. Somehow a line of communication was established with one of Father's old friends, Brooke Duncan—a former king of Carnival, recently widowed. Brooke, a tall and erect ex-Marine, put on his duck hunter's wading boots, armed himself with a couple of guns, and waded a mile or two to Quercus. Was he rescuing Father or was Father rescuing him? It wasn't clear, but either way they were throwing in their lot together. Father, believing he'd be set upon as soon as he left Quercus, went into his gun collection and armed himself too. He, Sheila, and Brooke got into a car, bearing their small arsenal. Their aim was to escape the city as quickly as possible.

I went online, looking for block-by-block information about which streets were passable. Henry Clay? No, there's a live electric line on the street. Take Webster instead. Left on Pitt? No, a tree is down. Turn on Coliseum. In that fashion I guided the elderly, gun-toting refugees to the edge of downtown where they could take a bridge across the Mississippi River—their exodus's version, I suppose, of the Red Sea—and turn northwest on Highway 90. Finally they arrived in Baton Rouge: hardly the contemporary Canaan, but at least they were safe there. The relief of knowing that left me trembling, overwhelmed. Somehow, everything depended on Father's being able to dwell in the custom-tailored enclosure he'd built for himself at Quercus, which itself was enclosed within a larger, but not all that much larger, environment in New Orleans where he had always lived, and which wasn't quite like anyplace else in its customs and values and rituals, in what it was prepared to take in and what it was not. A provincial, traditional, enveloping place has its own logic. It resists the logic of the outside world. New Orleans *felt* safe. Hadn't it always been the same? Didn't everybody know everybody else? It seemed like a profound violation to have it made manifest that it wasn't *actually* safe, that it was, more than most places, places that to me felt far more unstable, subject to natural disaster and social and political breakdown. The thought of New Orleans, familiar

New Orleans, being taken away—from Father? from me, even though I wasn't there anymore?—was unbearable.

Father and Sheila lived in a hotel in Houston for more than two months and then moved back to Quercus. There was no question of not returning; they were waiting until the moment when the city was at least barely habitable to move back. Soon after that, we visited New Orleans for Thanksgiving. On the way from the airport, Moses, then three years old, exclaimed, "You didn't tell me we were going to Iraq!" I can see why he said that; what he saw was unlike anything he'd encountered outside of a television or movie screen. Unprocessed debris—tree branches, garbage—was everywhere. The waters had receded, leaving a thick residue of brown mud. Much of the city was abandoned, with rusting refrigerators and washing machines on people's front yards and spray-painted symbols, left by emergency workers, on their boarded-up front doors. People debated whether to write off parts of the city as gone forever, but that was a losing argument. Officially, if you truly loved New Orleans you had to want to restore all of it, like the Temple in Jerusalem—so it took many years for the city to appear as it had before the storm. Quercus was far more functional than most of New Orleans, but it was never quite in a full state of perfect repair again. What I can see now is that, like so many of the grand homes in Europe that Father liked to visit on his summer trips, Quercus was premised on the continuance of a social system that didn't last. It took a small army to keep its stone floors polished, its expanses of plate-glass windows cleaned, its lawns mowed and its planting beds weeded. Sheila had to spend a great deal of time and attention assembling a skeleton crew at least to maintain Quercus's appearance, although she probably would have preferred not to be the chatelaine of a large, constantly needy establishment housing only two people. Quercus had become a modern version of a familiar phenomenon, especially in Louisiana: a grand manor in slow, genteel decline.

Something about living in Quercus made Father thrive, though—that has to be part of the reason he lived so long. He had his books, his files, and his treasured objects, not to mention the large, though dwindling, circle of friends of a lifetime. He maintained an office at the law firm where he worked after Monroe & Lemann had dissolved, where he was an adored figure, until the age of ninety. Alex, my oldest son, graduated from college the spring after Hurricane Katrina. He moved to New Orleans for two years, living at Quercus and working for an organization that worked on restoring the city. Moses and Josephine, the children of Judith's and my marriage, were born when Father was in his late seventies, but they still had plenty of time to visit him in situ, to be ushered into his magical corner of the library and given puzzles to solve, games to play, gadgets to admire, mock-prosecutorial questions to answer.

I can't explain why Father loved the things he did, but I had a good idea of what he would love. Anything involving rearranging shapes into a pattern would ring the bell for him; he had dozens of puzzles with this motif. Anything involving disputes over grammar and punctuation, or rules more generally. Anything involving the decline of standards in some institution he'd grown up admiring. Small, perfectly shaped objects, like the miniature granite books of his that I now keep on my desk. Antique keys. These may not sound interesting, but he had a way of taking you into camp, as people used to say when he was young, and getting you to join in his obsessions. On our visits we'd sometimes drive up to Donaldsonville and see Palo Alto and the old Lemann store (now ghostly: it had gone out of business in the 1990s, after Walmart came to town), as I'd done as a child, or go out into the bayou country, where unpainted houses sat on stilts and herons and pelicans perched on tree stumps, or look at plantation houses built before the Civil War, during the Louisiana sugarcane boom that had brought our family to America so long ago.

When I met Judith's father, in 1997, he was sixty-five years old and had just been diagnosed with a rare blood disease and told he had five years to live. Through sheer determination and a limitless appetite for medical interventions, he would up living almost twenty-five years, toward the end getting sicker and sicker, thin and pale, constantly in and out of hospitals. He died in 2020, and Judith's mother's health soon began to fail. She died less than a year later. They had been married for more than sixty years. Judith's father died in a hospital, her mother at home. We gathered and sat with her for the last few days. It wasn't clear how much she was taking in, but Judith, knowing what she would have wanted, sang prayers to her—at the very end, the *Neilah*. "The gates are closing, Ma," Judith whispered, and she was right. After her mother was gone, obeying Jewish law, we took turns sitting with her body, making sure someone was always there until men came to take it away. After that, as the law prescribes, she was placed in a white shroud, with no embalming, and a simple pine coffin, and immediately buried in our synagogue's section of a Jewish cemetery in New Jersey.

For many years I called Father every Sunday—usually getting the greeting "Hello, old-timer!" delivered in a soft Southern accent. On the Sunday after Judith's mother died, I told him we were sitting shiva. "What's shiva?" I explained. "I've never heard of that," he said. "Who made that up?" This was a venerable exchange we'd have, over the years since I began to live a more Jewish life: he'd profess to believe that something I was doing was not authentically Jewish but, instead, was something that Orthodox Jews had recently invented and claimed as traditional. It was hard to tell whether he was kidding. He may not have known himself. In any case, it was a way of saying that what he'd grown up with, in Jewish and many other ways, was what he considered to be normal. About Judith's mother's shiva, he played his trump card: "They must not do this at Temple Emanu-El." But of course they do. I sent him a link to the Temple Emanu-El website to prove it. Things have changed, even there.

Father died in 2023, a few weeks after his ninety-seventh birthday. He lived at Quercus until the very end. Mother, George and Anne Montgomery, and most of the rest of Father's hundreds of friends, the accumulation of a long life lived in one enclosed and deeply emplaced neighborhood, were long gone by then. A few years before the end, a very slow-moving disease that he had contracted as a soldier made it impossible for him to swallow. This set off a serious health crisis. He spent weeks at Touro Infirmary, where he was born and died, where I was born, and where his mother had worked as a surgical nurse—there was a plaque commemorating her service in the hallway outside his room. Finally he was well enough to go home, consigned to be nourished through a feeding tube for the rest of his life.

The Mississippi River overflowed the levees in 1927, causing the most destructive flood in American history. Like a surgeon opening up a patient in an operating room, the flood put on display what was not always so obvious about the social structure of the Deep South. Among the hundreds of thousands of people who were rendered homeless, Black people had it worst—in many cases they were imprisoned, starved, and forced to work at gunpoint. Poorer white people had it second worst, and rich white people were able to protect themselves. For safety not just from the rising waters but also from the disease and disorder that are always a possibility in New Orleans, Father, as an infant, was sent to live with an aunt in Chicago for the better part of a year. I've always thought that left him with an extraordinary ability to make his own self-contained world where he could be happy.

Whether or not that was the origin of it, the ability was evident in his very old age. Tiny, frail, and confined to Quercus for fear of infection, Father first hired someone to help him produce a series of elegant books assembled from the photographs he had made on the long summer trips he took for half a century or more: *Italian Ornaments, Greek Islands, Curiosities and Amenities of Travel, Scottish Glens, Muslim Lands, La France Profonde*. When he was done with that, he turned his attention to buying sculptures online, via a network of dealers he had assembled. (One of them, whom Father especially liked because he was a member of the Sassoon family, British Jewish aristocrats, used to tease Father by telling him that he had two very elderly clients, but he couldn't reveal the other one's name. After they both had died, he told me: it was Queen Elizabeth II, who was Father's exact contemporary.) He spent the last portion of his life surrounded by a careful arrangement of small figures in bronze, granite, marble, dark wood. Bulky wooden crates from abroad, bearing new sculptures, were still arriving after he died. His last word, a text to an art dealer sent from inside an oxygen tent at Touro on the final day of his life, was "Nevelson."

On our last visit, for what turned out to be his final birthday, Father gathered his grandchildren around his wheelchair in Quercus's sculpture-packed living room and, to show that "I still have all my marbles," he proudly pronounced—in ancient Greek, which he'd been studying in weekly sessions with a Catholic priest for decades—he told them what was the longest word ever written, from a play by Aristophanes:

"λοπαδοτεμαχοσελαχογαλεοκρανιολειψανοδριμυποτρ ιμματοσιλφιοκαραβομελιτοκατακεχυμενοκιχλεπικοσσυφ οφαττπεριστεραλεκτρυονοπτοκεφαλλιοκιγκλοπελειολαγω οσιραιοβαφητραγανοπτερύγων."

A few weeks later, Sheila called to say Father had gone into the hospital. It reminded me of Father's call back in 1999, when Mother went into the hospital for the last time. It was nothing major, he'd be back home soon. But then she called again: he was gone. We all headed to New Orleans. Even if the impulse to obey Jewish law had been there, it would have been impossible to follow, because it was the height of Mardi Gras season, the great preemptive event in New Orleans. People had parades and balls to attend, you couldn't expect them to come to a funeral. Even Jews who can't belong to the krewes want to go see the parades they put on, and anyway many of the streets are closed. We who set off the Geiger counter lived by the narrative logic of *The Moviegoer*, just like everybody else. We buried Father—three or four of us, plus the rabbi from Temple

Sinai, shivering against a cold drizzle—in the company of dozens of his relatives in the German-Jewish neighborhood of the non-Jewish Metairie cemetery and returned to New York, where, whether he'd have liked it or not, we sat shiva. More people came than I had expected, not because they had known Father, but simply because it was his due as one of our people.

Then, once Mardi Gras had passed, we flew down to New Orleans for the funeral at Temple Sinai. Even though most of Father's friends had long since died, there was a line of impeccably dressed people that stretched all the way down the cavernous main sanctuary's long aisle, out onto St. Charles Avenue, and almost around the block, making manifest what you get in return for being a dedicated and generous citizen of a highly particular community for almost a century. We went home, and returned a few weeks later so that each of us could pick out a few things of Mother's and Father's to take away. Material that had accumulated in corners and closets over half a century appeared in small mountains on tables and in hallways, for inspection and disposition. Theo shipped a stack of umbrellas to himself—that was another thing Father collected, as long as the umbrellas were made of a single piece of wood. Alex took a few paintings. I boxed up the careful notes Mother had made after every therapy session during the time she was practicing as a child psychologist, plus a stack of albums of old photographs: black-tie dinners in the 1930s, greetings at train stations, group portraits taken in front of the pyramids or the Parthenon. It felt as if we had been transported into the last act of *The Cherry Orchard*, Anton Chekhov's play about a family of Russian aristocrats whom circumstances have forced to sell off the family estate. We set out one last dinner, of takeout food, to eat in the dining room; the days when it would have been cooked, served, and cleared away by servants in crisp white uniforms had long since passed. Then Sheila and my stepsisters, Allison and Charlotte Jane, began preparing Quercus to be put up for sale.

All these routines made instinctive sense to me, but they were difficult to explain back home in New York. Delaying a Jewish funeral in deference to a Christian holiday? Father's enveloping community in New Orleans, with its powerful internal logic, its imperviousness to the direction of the rest of the world, didn't make for a workable match with Jewish law. They were two separate things, impossible to unify.

THE MINYAN

In New York the minyan where Judith and I pray on Saturday mornings meets in a mundane empty room on an upper floor of the synagogue, hardly an architecturally inspiring space. It's comfortable. The old Reform services that Father grew up with were kept short and accessible. People dressed up and sat obediently in their pews for the duration of the service. In our minyan, the service lasts for three hours, and almost none of it would be comprehensible to someone raised as Father was. People dress informally, they gossip, they wander in and out. I still don't read or speak Hebrew, but I've learned at least when to stand and sit and how to recite a few of the prayers from memory. I know when to bow during *Aleinu*. I can struggle through an *Aliyah*, a turn as assistant to the Torah reader, by reading a transliteration of the blessings from a large laminated card on the *bimah*.

What am I doing there? The straightforward answer is that a group of our friends, parents of our children's classmates at their Jewish day school, also go there, so at first it served as a comfortable place socially and a way of maintaining a continuity between school, services, and Sabbath meals. By now it's our Jewish community, whose boundaries extend well beyond the services themselves. Over the years, the members of the minyan have come to understand that I have to be given tasks that don't require Hebrew language literacy, but Judith can take her turn reading a section of the Torah portion, or the accompanying Haftorah (a passage from the prophetic literature that goes with each week's portion), or delivering the D'var

Torah, which requires consulting the Talmud and other rabbinic texts. When she gets one of these assignments, I see that some powerful pull that can't be denied is making itself felt. It impels her to put it at the top of the pile, ahead of whatever she has to do in the non-Jewish part of her life. And there's no question that *leyning*—reading aloud from the Torah scroll—before an audience of fifty or so would take precedence over writing an essay on a secular subject for an audience of hundreds of thousands. Is it fear of making a mistake in front of a crowd that would notice and whose good opinion matters a great deal to her, or the preeminence of obligation to the community over other obligations, or the higher sense of gratification that comes from doing that particular job well, or, more simply, the assumption that sacred duties are the highest duties? Probably all of those. She's a Jew first and everything else second.

People often wind up wandering into a hothouse environment that has its own elaborate internal standards, a detailed prestige system, and an apartness from the mainstream. My original environment in New Orleans was certainly one of these. Our minyan, which otherwise has no area of overlap, is another one. In both cases, in very different ways, I'm something between an insider and an outsider. I don't mind—that's a familiar location for me. I've come to feel at home there. Some Saturdays Judith stays home and I go to services by myself. Even when I don't understand the Hebrew or Aramaic words, even when my attention wanders from the close reading of the Torah portion that I'm supposed to do every week, there's something about the timeless minor-key rhythms that puts me at rest. I try to imagine the settings in which long-ago relatives whose names I'll never know said the same prayers. I think about what's going on in my secular life from a welcome distance. I feel an assumed, though not necessarily researched, confidence that the people I'm with come at life, locate themselves, in the same way I do. That makes me feel less alone in the world.

Many members of our minyan would call themselves Jewish professionals. When I was growing up, that meant you were Jewish and also a doctor or a lawyer or an engineer. In this case, it means that the word *Jewish* appears on your business card, because you are a professor of Jewish studies or you work in a Jewish organization. Most of them sent their children to Jewish schools through twelfth grade, to Jewish summer camps, and to a gap year of study in Israel between high school and college. I imagine that these people don't have to negotiate constantly between their Jewish and non-Jewish identities in the same way that I do. Large sections of my life—New Orleans, my work in journalism, the university—stand completely apart from my life in the minyan. But I suppose that's the point: if you live entirely inside a Jewish environment, you're constantly aware of being Jewish because it determines how you spend your time and with whom, and what you think about all day. If you don't, and you have chosen to try to live a Jewish life, you're still constantly aware of being Jewish because you're always conscious of the adjustments you have to make as you move back and forth.

Moses and Josephine go out into the world every day wearing a six-pointed star on a silver necklace. I wouldn't feel comfortable doing that. We have a mezuzah posted at our front door. It tells anyone who comes to the door that we're Jewish, and it reminds us that we are trying to instill a spirit of holiness in our home. I must have been thirty years old before I saw a mezuzah for the first time, but at this point I wouldn't feel comfortable not having it there. Judith has her mobile phone programmed to display two dates, the secular one and the date on the Jewish calendar. I don't. What it all comes down to is that, if something awful happened to me, if I lost everything, even through my own venality or stupidity, and I reached out to the minyan for help, the minyan would respond—even members who hardly know me would, because I'm one of them. I'm not absolutely sure that most other people in my life would. In our tradition, we understand that everybody makes terrible mistakes. Even the patriarchs and matriarchs whose lives we study in the Torah did. Abraham told Pharaoh that Sarah was his sister, not his wife. Sarah banished Hagar and Ishmael, the concubine and son she'd arranged for Abraham, to the desert. The list goes on and on. Communal solidarity trumps individual worthiness. What would get you kicked out would not be sinning individually, it would be betraying the community.

In New Orleans, the way we defined what it meant to be Jewish was external. We'd figure out what people who weren't Jewish thought Jews were like, and then we'd try to keep the positive parts of that (being smart, being productive) and drop the negative parts (being tribal, being overaggressive). We were trying to fit in completely, to find a version of being Jewish that was fully acceptable, just as pleasing to non-Jews as to Jews. Can that project ever succeed? I'm skeptical that it can; anyway, through all the great length and breadth of Jewish experience, it definitely hasn't happened yet. In the minyan, the meaning of being Jewish is internal and particular: our history, our laws, our customs. They don't have to be justified on anyone else's terms, but that means, inevitably, that we won't fit in perfectly outside of our own community. To me, it seems like a small price to pay for the access you get to a sense of belonging, to a base layer of routines on which the rest of life can stand, and, every once in a while, to a glimpse of the empyrean. Anyway, the lesson of my own life is that the payoff from completely fitting in, in the hope of which you give up so much, never quite fully arrives.

INTO HISTORY

At Columbia, over the years I became someone who was regularly summoned to advise the president and to take on special assignments on his behalf. This role came easily to me. You could say that I represented the third generation of my family to enact some variation on the theme. I'd go to dinners at the presidential residence, a handsome mansion designed by McKim, Mead & White that is one of the largest single-family houses in New York, often in the company of prominent people who'd arrive in limousines, and sit at a long table, where we would eat an elegant meal described on a stiff card left at each place, served by a large, discreet, attentive staff. I understood instinctively how much it was proper to say at these dinners, where the unofficial boundaries of the conversation were set. I carried out my assignments efficiently and discreetly.

Separately, ever since I'd made my first trip to Israel, I had been working with an informal group of Jewish faculty members to oppose the ongoing campaign to sever the university's ties to the Jewish state. The other side would organize a letter and gather signatures, and we'd organize a counter-letter and gather signatures of our own. Just a few weeks after the president I'd served for decades retired, early on a Sabbath morning, soldiers of the terrorist group Hamas breached the fortifications separating Israel from Gaza and carried out the largest mass slaughter of Jews since the defeat of Hitler. Protests and counterprotests immediately dominated the life of the university. I was invited to an audience with Columbia's new president, whom I had never met. She told me she was going to create a task force on antisemitism—would I serve as cochair? Father had died only a few months earlier, and I'm not sure I would have been comfortable accepting the offer if he'd been alive. Here I was, serving with two cochairs who were Orthodox, as a highly public Jewish advocate in the middle of a fierce controversy that seemed to have the rapt attention of the entire world. At the very end of *All the King's Men*, Jack Burden, done with politics, back in Burden's Landing, and turning again to his long-delayed dissertation about a dead relative, tells us that he'd decided to "go out of history into history." I was reversing the direction, going from my period of intense, almost compulsive family research into direct involvement in an all-consuming public battle. But the phrase still felt apt.

My family investigations were research in the literal sense, meant to find out what had happened, but I was also trying to learn something about myself. What did it mean that I was, that we were, Jewish? The word all by itself sits neutrally on the page. It's something you are, one of the many ethnic identities American culture blandly celebrates. It's fine, it's not connected to anything. What my research showed me was that being Jewish was a much more essential part of my family's history in America than I had ever imagined. I hadn't known that my Cajun great-great-grandmother had converted to Judaism. I hadn't known that my German-born great-great grandfather had given money for a synagogue to be built in the village where he grew up. I hadn't known that the two of them had gone to great lengths to make a Jewish life for their children, which included sending their first child, my great-grandfather, from Louisiana to a Jewish boarding school in New York City. I hadn't known that my great-grandfather was a founder of *The Jewish Messenger* and the Purim Association. I hadn't known that Pop, my grandfather, had testified in Congress on behalf of a doomed proposal to bring Jewish children from Europe to America to save them from the Holocaust. I hadn't known that Mother had taught in the synagogue in her hometown in New Jersey. Finding out about all that made it easier, or even imperative, to accept the president's invitation. I was reestablishing an interrupted family tradition of understanding Jewishness as an active state, entailing obligations. Still, this was the most overtly and publicly Jewish thing I'd ever done.

Almost a year before the October 7 attack, our Jewish community in New York went into a state of high alarm when a new right-wing governing coalition took power in Israel. Our synagogue's rabbi announced that he would no longer say the customary prayer for the state of Israel during the Saturday morning service. There were enormous antigovernment protests in Tel Aviv, proportionately the largest and longest-lasting in the world. Judith, along with many of our friends, demonstrated outside the Israeli consulate in New York. It seemed as if the new government was all anybody talked about. Its ascension undercut a core conviction that most of our friends had been raised on and that resided deep in their psyches, that Israel is a nation devoted to liberal principles, not to crude domination over its real and perceived enemies.

That was the context in which the Hamas attack arrived. It touched every ancient fear, revivified every terrifying family story, about the violent mob that is always lurking nearby, waiting for an opportunity to do its worst to Jews, simply because they are Jews—and it also demonstrated that the new government, in addition to everything else, could not keep Israel safe. And that was only the beginning of the evidence that the fundamental shape of our world wasn't what we thought it had been. It had been possible, at least for liberal Jews in New York, to imagine that after three-quarters of a century Israel had become accepted, even admired, that it was well defended, and that the elusive goal of a Palestinian state and a lasting peace was still within reach. All that may always have been an illusion. Now it was gone. Soon Israel launched a ferociously violent counterattack on Gaza, which left tens of thousands more people dead, Hamas members and ordinary citizens, than the October 7 attack had, and flattened large parts of Gaza.

At Columbia, many Jewish students who'd been raised in such a way that they hadn't encountered the idea of Israel as fundamentally bad—the way my own children had been raised—were intensely miserable. (If you prick us, do we not bleed?) We on the task force would go around talking to groups of them and hear stories about *kippot* snatched off heads, mezuzahs torn off dorm-room doors, insults of a kind that aren't supposed to be part of student life on an enlightened campus. A very old phenomenon, the division of Jews into good Jews and bad Jews, was emerging in a new guise: Zionists and anti-Zionists. Zionists couldn't join some clubs, couldn't comfortably study in some academic disciplines, and, outside of the university, had difficulty being published, exhibited, given grants. They were like the scapegoat in the Book of Leviticus, loaded up with the iniquities and transgressions of the Israelites, then banished to the wilderness. Jewish students who weren't unalterably attached to Israel felt pressure to disown it, or at least to avoid it, as the price of belonging.

It all felt oddly familiar. When Father was coming of age, a rarefied group of well-born Protestant Americans had a degree of prestige, even reverence, that's now long forgotten. One of this group's precepts was that Jews in their raw, unadulterated, unacculturated form had to be excluded; Jews who had shed their obviously Jewish characteristics were eligible for a kind of provisional membership. That was one reason that the Reform movement's Pittsburgh Platform had felt moved to renounce Zionism, more than a decade before Herzl published *Der Judenstaat,* his manifesto calling for the establishment of a Jewish state in Palestine. It looks to me now as if, all these years later, under a profoundly different set of prevailing standards, Jewishness still isn't universalizable. The old dream that there might be a completely easy way of being Jewish (at least in the way I have chosen to be Jewish) in the wider world seems once again to have vanished.

One afternoon, on a weekend when Judith and I were visiting Moses at college, I got a call from a colleague—a veteran Columbia administrator, a professional who performed an essential service far removed from the public eye. Why this call, of all the calls I got, has stuck with me, I don't know, but it has. My colleague told me that she considered herself lucky to be alive. Most of her family back in Europe had died in the camps, but somehow her parents had found a way to get to America before it was too late, and she'd been born here after the war. In her household as she was growing up, it was taken as a given that Israel represented the fulfillment of an ancient promise, the seat of a growing civilization, an organized and nearly unprecedented means for Jews to find safety. Like me, she'd been at Columbia for decades. She'd felt comfortable, or even as if she'd arrived in a magical place of learning and tolerance. But now, in meeting after meeting, Israel came up, even when it had nothing to do with the official topic, and it had become clear that Zionists were not welcome. And these attitudes had spread through the culture, to the point that her own children were barely speaking to her. She didn't know what to do.

I couldn't solve her problem, but she was grateful that there was somebody to talk to. After we'd hung up, I sunk into a chair, overwhelmed. I think she had stated forthrightly what I had begun to feel. Moses came over and wrapped his arms around me, reversing the polarity of parent and child. And not long after that, after he'd come home after the end of the school year, on a Saturday night he was walking not far from the Columbia campus when he and another young man jostled each other on the sidewalk. The other guy saw the star of David on Moses's necklace and started shoving him, calling him a dirty Jew. Moses dashed into a bar where people knew him and stayed there until the guy had left. When he came home, he sat in the living room and sobbed. His whole body was shaking. "We can't live here anymore," he said. This time I wrapped my arms around him. I don't know if he meant what he said literally; we're still here now. But what was becoming clear was that I had gone from feeling uncomfortable in the Jewish world to feeling more comfortable in the Jewish world than I did outside it.

WHAT REMAINS

After Judith's mother died, we found a typewritten sheet of paper she'd left behind, a set of wishes to be fulfilled after she was gone. She asked that one of her children say kaddish for her. Judith, the most religious of the three of them, took that on—and she well understood that her mother had in mind saying kaddish every day, for the prescribed eleven months. It's an aspect of the communal nature of Judaism that we are commanded to pray in groups of at least ten Jewish adults, which meant that every day (well, almost every day) Judith found a place to go for services, either in the morning or in the afternoon. If the only available place was Orthodox, she had to sit in a women's section and mouth the words of the prayer silently, because women there aren't permitted to pray out loud. When a conflict between the obligation and feminist principles was unavoidable, the obligation won. Years earlier, I said kaddish for Mother after she died, but every week, not every day, even though it wasn't her wish, and I observe her *yahrzeit* every year. I did the same for Father. The kaddish is a prayer in Aramaic that, oddly, doesn't mention death, mourning, or the person for whom you're saying it; instead, it merely praises God. I take that to mean that one ought to mourn by reminding oneself that our covenant survives, as it has for so many centuries, and that whoever died played a part in that and so belongs to a continuum that extends past the life-span. As much as I've tried, I just can't seem to memorize the kaddish. I have to read the transliteration from the prayer book, and even then I struggle, stumble, and mumble. At Father's funeral, I was pleased to see that Moses and Josephine could say the kaddish perfectly, from memory.

I still haven't gotten used to the idea that Father and Mother are gone, Quercus is gone, and most of the relatives I knew growing up are gone too. I have to figure out what part New Orleans, our family's intermittent home for nearly two hundred years, plays in my life. I still have many relatives and friends there. But the way it looks, the way the moist, sticky air sits on my body, the faint odor of coffee and wet asphalt and gardenias, the whistles of tugboats on the river, the buckled pavements and the paint peeling away from doorframes— all this will always make me feel like I'm home. My family has probably stayed put more than most Americans, and moved around religiously more than most Jews. The time is not so far away when I will take my place in our family's history, rather than our present. That's something I think about. Jacob and Miriam were buried in a Jewish cemetery, not in Louisiana. When I visited, the director told me that there is room for another generation there. The next three generations of Lemanns are buried in the family plot in Metairie cemetery. There's plenty of room there too, but Judith is not crazy about the idea of our being buried in a mostly Christian cemetery.

When we visited Germany and saw the expensive gravestone that Jacob Lemann, as a wealthy middle-aged man, had built for his long-dead father, Judith spotted a pair of outstretched hands engraved at the top of the stone. "You're a Cohen!" she said— the hands, as she knew and I didn't, mean that you belong to the ancient hereditary class of priests, supposedly the descendants of

Moses's brother Aaron, who still have a special prestige in observant communities.

"Does that mean you love me more than you did before?" I asked her, half kidding, but only half.

"Of course it does!"

I consulted my cousin Hanan, the one whose father had converted from Judaism to become a Quaker, and who is now an Orthodox Israeli with dozens of grandchildren. He told me that a Cohen loses his priestly status if he marries a non-Jewish woman, even if she converts, so we are actually former Cohens. We lost our membership when Jacob married Marie—oh well. A couple of years before our trip to Germany, Judith traveled all over Eastern Europe with her sister and one of her cousins to learn what they could about their family's history. There they encountered no signs of intermarriage or assimilation, and no impressive gravestones either—instead, mostly, unmarked places out in the woods where people they came from, after uniformed thugs had removed them from their homes at gunpoint, taken everything they had, and loaded them into wagons, had been lined up and shot, if they hadn't had the foresight to move to America or to Israel. The eternal questions about Jewish life in the Diaspora can't ever be satisfactorily answered. We'll survive, though we will never sit comfortably in the world. But the tradition can't ever, or maybe can't ever be allowed to, disappear.

We'd had three deaths in four years—Judith's parents' and then Father's. After the mourning, we went back to the routines of our lives, now as the older generation of the family. Mundaneness is comforting. For us, some of it was ordinary mundaneness and some of it was Jewish mundaneness. Would we host both Passover seders, or just one? Whom would we invite, and what could we ask the guests to bring? How many days ahead of time should we begin the project of boiling the silverware, eliminating everything non-kosher from the house, and stowing our regular dishes away? After Passover, there was a controversy in the minyan that had to be resolved. There were weddings, bar mitzvahs, other people's shivas, the endless procession of Sabbath dinners. There were starchy, sweet, comfortable *Kiddush* lunches, with babkas, kugel, herring, schnapps. There were lectures, study sessions, museum exhibitions.

One day during this period of mourning and readjustment, I visited Donaldsonville. When Father would take me to visit when I was a boy, we'd go to the family store, B. Lemann & Brother, and be shown, in addition to the merchandise for sale, exotic nineteenth-century items left over from the store's early days. Father's cousin Bubs would take us up to the attic to write our names on a white-washed brick wall with a thick pencil. What could possibly be more permanent? But it wasn't. After 150 years, the store went out of business. The family tried to operate it as a museum of small-town life in the nineteenth century, but not many visitors turned up. Then, for years, the building stood empty, a constant source of worry to my country cousins. Finally there was good news: a developer from New Orleans, who specializes in preserving historic properties, had bought the store. He was going to convert it into an apartment house, with the help of a subsidy from the state. It's now called Lemann Art Lofts, more as a tribute to the terms of the subsidy than to the likelihood of Donaldsonville's reemerging as a mecca for bohemians.

When I visited, DeeDee DiBenedetto, my cousin Peter's partner and the chatelaine of Palo Alto plantation, arranged to take me to meet the developer who had saved the store. It was generous of DeeDee to take the time: she'd been up most of the previous night in connection with her work as a private eye, sitting in her car in the parking lot of a motel, because she was working a matrimonial case. We met at Palo Alto. DeeDee, a powerful presence who has a big mane of jet-black hair and animated, heavily mascara'ed eyes, greeted me with an enfolding hug. We drove across the Mississippi River on the Sunshine Bridge—named after a familiar country song whose popularity a singer named Jimmie Davis rode to the governorship of Louisiana—and then to Houmas House, the site of what

The cornice of the Lemann store in Donaldsonville, photographed during the years after it had gone out of business. CAROL M. HIGHSMITH

was once the largest sugarcane plantation in the United States. It was a short trip, less than twenty miles.

Houmas House presents itself as a full-blown tourist attraction, with a big sign welcoming visitors, three restaurants, a museum, an amphitheater, and an inn. There are splashing fountains, ponds, wandering ducks and geese, colored lights playing across the plantation house at night. At the peak of its life as a working plantation, its owner, John Burnside, controlled six thousand acres of land, made productive for him through the labor of more than nine hundred enslaved Black people. William Howard Russell, the correspondent from *The Times* of London who had been dispatched to the United States to cover the Civil War, visited the plantation in 1861. He reported that the enslaved were not permitted to learn to read or write, or even to go to church. They lived in cabins with no windows.

DeeDee and I had a long lunch with the owner of Houmas House, Kevin Kelly, at the most elegant of Houmas House's restaurants. Kelly is a big, talkative man, florid faced, who is keenly aware of the charges of his critics—he celebrates plantation slavery, he has

Disneyfied Houmas House—and indignantly rejects them. We sat at a dark wooden table laid with graceful china on a crisp white tablecloth, and ordered heavy, rich Southern dishes. Then we got into an elongated golf cart and toured the grounds. Kelly knows his market. He has designed the premises as a restoration of what many white Southerners—even now, and certainly when I was growing up—prefer to think of as a vanished past of wealth and ease. As its website puts it, Houmas House on the eve of the Civil War "contained over twelve thousand acres of the finest quality of cultivable land . . . and was without exception, the finest property possessed by a single proprietor in America."

Kelly lives in the main plantation house himself, as John Burnside and the other previous owners did. Anything that would evoke the South's old racial order in a positive way attracts his interest. He has made a standing offer of one million dollars to the city of New Orleans to sell him the statues of three leading Confederates—Robert E. Lee, P. G. T. Beauregard, and Jefferson Davis—that it took down a few years ago, so he can house them at Houmas House. Just about everything else in New Orleans that has been removed from a public place for being racially offensive, he has acquired and put on display in his museum. One section of his museum is devoted entirely to paintings of Black people eating watermelons. And nearby is an exhibit about country general stores in the Old South, where all the artifacts I used to see on my childhood visits to B. Lemann & Brother, which came into Kelly's possession when he bought the building, are on display. His are the hands into what we once had have passed, so that they can help vivify a wishful version of life in the Old South.

Just as it used to be inconceivable to me that Quercus would one day be somebody else's house, that B. Lemann & Brother would be an apartment building, and that its venerable contents would wind up in a museum celebrating the South's old racial order, I wouldn't have imagined that one day I would feel more Jewish than Southern. But now I do. It's the ancestral seat that has lasted. My adolescent task of finding a usable Southern past has come to feel insuperably difficult, in light of what the explorations and investigations of many people besides me have turned up. Jack Burden took me a crucial distance—I learned that you can't sit easily in the world, that nothing is ever simple, that there's always something—but no further. Through the generations, I came to the view that being Jewish has taken my family further than being Southern did. It feels as if there is more to learn, a more profound moral code, more to build a life around, in the Jewish tradition. It isn't the way I was raised, but over the years it has become comfortable. It's what I'm used to. Sometimes it's more than comfortable—it's an opening into something sublime.

One reason Judith doesn't go to Saturday morning services as regularly as I do is that she wants more from them, though she is rarely able to say exactly what that is—some sort of transcendence she can't locate. I'm less well schooled than she is, so I don't notice what's lacking as keenly. Or maybe it's that I haven't experienced what's possible as often as she has. All the Jewish practices carry with them a hope, a longing, for something that only rarely is realized. A synecdoche for this is sex, which is on the list of commanded activities on the Sabbath. As with all the other rules, nothing happens to you if you ignore the commandment, or if you obey it merely dutifully. But there's always the possibility of something more. We know from the very beginning of the Book of Genesis that men and women are destined to find it difficult to lie together naked and unashamed—but sometimes we can. In the Song of Songs, the rare book in the Hebrew Bible that doesn't mention God, your ointments are fragrant, sweetness drops from your lips, honey and milk are under your tongue.

I remember being with Judith on a Sabbath afternoon once in the early days. She was warm, close, solid. I felt that something long locked away, something glorious, had been opened up for me. Somehow whatever barriers that usually were there for me—for both of us, really—had been breached. We were comfortable, with no need for emotional protection, and I had to wonder whether the Jewish life we had begun to live together, with its enveloping sense of trust and a common purpose, was part of the reason. Had I come home, finally—to my real home, not one of a lifelong series of hoped-for homes? I don't know. You can't ever really know the answer to that kind of question. But I remember thinking: I have never felt this close to another person.

ACKNOWLEDGMENTS

MY FIRST THANKS GO TO MY LATE COUSIN BERNARD Lemann (1905–2000), a professor at Tulane University's architecture school and an early leader of the architectural preservation movement in New Orleans. In the late 1950s or early 1960s, Bernard realized that the copious papers and records kept at B. Lemann & Brother, the family store in Donaldsonville, Louisiana, had real historical value. He began a project of collecting these and other family papers and donating them to Tulane's Louisiana Research Collection. He also wrote a privately published book, *The Lemann Family of Louisiana* (1965). It's this material that served as the foundation for my research for this book.

Brad Snyder, a law professor at Georgetown and a biographer of Felix Frankfurter, persuaded my father, Thomas Lemann, to give him access to the extensive, decades-long private correspondence between Frankfurter and my grandfather, Monte M. Lemann. After reading this material, Snyder urged me to have it transferred to a research library because of its historical importance. My family and I took his advice, for which we are grateful, and now the Louisiana Research Collection has Monte Lemann's papers. Leon Miller, the center's director, made the decision to accept the papers and then supervised the project of organizing them and making them available to the public—including me, for the research for this book. He and the collection's excellent staff, especially Lori Schexnayder, have my thanks for everything they have done to make this book possible.

There is another, smaller collection of Lemann family papers at the American Jewish Archives in Cincinnati. Also at the American Jewish Archives are the extensive papers of my relative by marriage Lazard Kahn (1850–1928); the papers of another relative by marriage, Julian Feibelman (1897–1980), the long-serving rabbi at Temple Sinai in New Orleans; the papers of Max Heller (1860–1929), a previous long-serving rabbi at Temple Sinai; and the papers of the American Council for Judaism. Gary Zola, the archives' director, and, especially, Dana Herman, the director of research and collections there, were superbly and copiously helpful.

Karen Franklin, the director of family research at the Leo Baeck Institute in New York, organized my trip to Germany to learn about my family's life there in the eighteenth and nineteenth centuries. I owe great thanks not only to her, but also to two local historians she arranged for me to work with, Wolfgang Fritzsche in Mainz and Stefan Mossel in Essenheim. Without the three of them, I surely would have been unable to pierce the barrier that separates most American descendants of immigrants from any details about their families' long-ago lives in the old country.

In the office of the Ascension Parish Clerk of Court in Gonzales, Louisiana, Brett Landry, the deputy clerk, provided a great deal of help in guiding me through my family's old records in the clerk's offices there and in Donaldsonville. These records can be daunting: most are handwritten, and many are in French. I could never have found what I needed in them unaided. Also in Donaldsonville, my cousin Peter Lemann and his partner, DeeDee DiBenedetto, shared with me family materials that hadn't been deposited in the Louisiana Research Collection at Tulane. In New Orleans, Milly Heller, great-granddaughter of Rabbi Max Heller, shared some of her family's private papers with me. My cousin Geoffrey Goldberg conducted a long oral history interview with his grandmother, Lillian

Hyman Florsheim, that gives a detailed picture of one branch of my family's life in New Orleans in the early twentieth century. Another cousin, Barbara London Almario, has turned up difficult-to-find details about the history of my mother's family.

At Harvard Business School's Baker Library, Heather Oswald helped me find the reports on Lemann family enterprises, going back to the 1840s, in the library's collection of the credit reports produced by R. G. Dun and Company, the forerunner of Dun & Bradstreet. Leslie Lovett, a high school history teacher in Houston, gave me a copy of her excellent Tulane undergraduate thesis on Jacob Lemann, from 1990.

Several of my fellow members of Minyan M'at, in New York—people far more knowledgeable than me about various aspects of Jewish studies—gave me indispensable advice about this project. They include Barry Holtz, David Roskies, Nancy Sinkoff, Daniel Nevins, and Carol Ingall. In particular, Nancy Sinkoff introduced me to Nina Warnke, a translator who helped me understand old family documents written in German or rendered in the Hebrew alphabet; Daniel Nevins introduced me to Rabbi Roderick Young, of Norfolk, England, who trained me for the sections of the book that entail scriptural interpretation; and Carol Ingall, through her research on the Isaacs family of New York, gave me materials about my great-grandfather, another Bernard Lemann, who was a close friend of the Isaacs family.

In the course of doing research, I got helpful and generous advice from a number of experts on various aspects of the story I tell in this book. I'll thank them individually here: Joy Banner (the Descendants Project), Mark Baumann (Southern Jewish Historical Society), Tobias Brinkmann (Pennsylvania State University), Michael Cohen (Tulane University), James French (James Madison's Montpelier), Richard Kilbourne (independent scholar), James Oakes (City University of New York Graduate Center), Josh Parshall (independent scholar), Lawrence N. Powell (Tulane University), Shari Rabin (Oberlin College), Stuart Rockoff (Mississippi Humanities Council), Caitlin Rosenthal (University of California, Berkeley), Adam Rothman (Georgetown University), Marina Rustow (Princeton University), Jonathan Sarna (Brandeis University), Ismar Schorsch (Jewish Theological Seminary), and Jacob Morrow Spitzer (Yale University).

A number of colleagues and friends agreed to read and suggest improvements to early versions of the manuscript. This is a time-consuming task, and I am profoundly grateful to them for their help, which wound up improving the book greatly. They are Marie Brenner, Faith Childs, Farah Jasmine Griffin, Steven Hahn, Claire Hoffman, Nancy Sinkoff, and Leon Wieseltier.

The work I've been doing for all these years is highly collaborative—it's far closer to putting on a play or playing in a band than self-exiling to a garret. Because it's nonfiction, the underlying material, and the people who help you find and understand it, are essential partners. So are those who help turn thoughts into words and then into a book. I have been working with the same agent, Amanda Urban, for my whole adult life; in general, and in the case of this project, she has been consummately wise, professional, and devoted. This is the first time I have worked with Robert Weil, my editor at Liveright. He is a master at what he does. I don't think there is a paragraph in this book that he didn't urge me to improve—and doing what he suggested did improve it. His close, detailed, patient attention through several drafts helped me to understand how to say what was closest to my heart, in language that was less distanced and journalistic than what I am used to writing. Also at Liveright, Peter Miller, the director of publicity; Steven Pace, the director of sales; Trent Duffy, the copyeditor; and Luke Swann, Robert Weil's assistant, were all supremely encouraging and impressively good at what they do. Kathleen Karcher, who handled permissions, was also very helpful.

I come from a large, close extended family. It can't have been entirely easy for my relatives to have known for these past few years that I've been working on a family history whose result would inevitably be as complicated as honest family histories always are. I appreciate their patience, support, and trust. My particular debt to my wife, Judith Shulevitz, will be obvious to anyone who reads this book. In any number of ways, this project simply would not have been possible without her.

A NOTE ON SOURCES

THIS IS A WORK OF NONFICTION, BUT IT IS NOT A WORK of academic scholarship. Here I will offer a rough guide to my source material, not a specific citation for everything in the book.

It will be obvious to readers that some of the primary material here comes from my own memories. Some of it is in boxes of family materials, mainly from my parents, that I have at home. But a good deal, especially of the older material, is publicly available in library manuscript collections—mainly the Louisiana Research Collection, at Tulane University in New Orleans, and the American Jewish Archives, in Cincinnati. The pertinent collections at Tulane are the Lemann Family Papers (LaRC-168) and the Monte Lemann Papers (LaRC-1124). Some additional material I used is in the Edgar B. Stern Papers (LaRC-235) and the Robert G. Polack Papers (LaRC-231). At the American Jewish Archives, there is a small collection of Lemann Family Papers (MS-383), and more substantial collections of the papers of my relatives by marriage Lazard Kahn (MS-174) and Julian Beck Feibelman (MS-94). I also consulted the papers of the American Council for Judaism (MS-17). At Harvard Business School's Baker Library, I read the R. G. Dun & Company credit reports for my family's businesses in nineteenth-century Louisiana.

I read widely in published sources on a number of topics, particularly Jewish history in Germany and the American South, as well as sugarcane plantations in Louisiana. Below I list a few books and articles that I found particularly useful.

ON SUGARCANE PLANTATIONS

BOOKS

Richard Follett, *The Sugar Masters: Planters and Slaves in Louisiana's Cane World, 1820–1860.*

Richard Kilbourne, *Debt, Investment, Slaves: Credit Relations in East Feliciana Parish, Louisiana, 1825–1885.*

Sidney W. Mintz, *Sweetness and Power: The Place of Sugar in Modern History.*

Solomon Northup, *Twelve Years a Slave.*

Frederick Law Olmsted, *The Cotton Kingdom.*

C. Peter Ripley, *Slaves and Freedmen in Civil War Louisiana.*

Charles Roland, *Louisiana Sugar Plantations During the Civil War.*

Caitlin Rosenthal, *Accounting for Slavery: Masters and Management.*

William Howard Russell, *My Diary North and South.*

J. Carlyle Sitterton, *Sugar Country: The Cane Sugar Industry in the South, 1753–1950.*

ON JEWS IN GERMANY

BOOKS

Leora Batnitzky, *How Judaism Became a Religion: An Introduction to Modern Jewish Thought.*

Amos Elon, *The Pity of It All: A Portrait of the German-Jewish Epoch, 1743–1933.*

Paula Hyman, *The Emancipation of the Jews of Alsace: Acculturation and Tradition in the Nineteenth Century.*

Jacob Katz, *Out of the Ghetto: The Social Background of Jewish Emancipation, 1770–1870.*

Jacob Rader Marcus, *The Rise and Destiny of the German Jew.*

Michael Meyer, *The Origins of the Modern Jew: Jewish Identity and European Culture in Germany 1749–1824.*

David Sorkin, *Jewish Emancipation: A History Across Five Centuries.*

David Sorkin, *The Transformation of German Jewry, 1780–1840.*

Fritz Stern, *Gold and Iron: Bismarck, Bleichröder, and the Building of the German Empire.*

ARTICLES

Salo W. Baron, "Ghetto and Emancipation: Shall We Revise the Traditional View?" *Menorah Journal*, June 1928.

Dana Herman and Jason Kalman, "Jacob Rader Marcus in Berlin, 1936." *The American Jewish Archives Journal*, 2021.

ON GERMAN JEWS IN THE UNITED STATES

BOOKS

Avraham Barkai, *Branching Out: German-Jewish Immigration to the United States, 1820–1914.*

Stephen Birmingham, *"Our Crowd": The Great Jewish Families of New York.*

Eric Goldstein, *The Price of Whiteness: Jews, Race, and American Identity.*

Ande Manners, *Poor Cousins.*

Shari Rabin, *Jews on the Frontier: Religion and Mobility in Nineteenth Century America.*

Brad Snyder, *Democratic Justice: Felix Frankfurter, the Supreme Court, and the Making of the Liberal Establishment.*

ARTICLES

Tobias Brinkmann, "'German Jews?': Reassessing the History of Nineteenth-Century Jewish Immigrants in the United States." In *Transnational Traditions: New Perspectives on American Jewish History*, edited by Ava F. Kahn and Adam D. Mendelsohn.

Tobias Brinkmann, "Jewish Immigrants from Central Europe in Antebellum America." In *By Dawn's Early Light: Jewish Contributions to American Culture from the Nation's Founding to the Civil War*, edited by Adam Mendelsohn, 2016.

Philip Goodman, "The Purim Association of the City of New York." *Publications of the American Jewish Historical Society*, 1950.

Julien Gorbach, "The Non-Jewish Jew: Walter Lippmann and the Pitfalls of Journalistic 'Detachment.'" *American Journalism*, 2020.

Gerald Sorin, "Mutual Contempt, Mutual Benefit: The Strained Encounter Between German and Eastern European Jews in America, 1880–1920." *American Jewish History*, Autumn 1993.

Gary P. Zola, "The Common Places of American Reform Judaism's Conflicting Platforms." *Hebrew Union College Annual*, 2001.

ON JEWS IN LOUISIANA

BOOKS

Elliott Ashkenazi, *The Business of Jews in Louisiana 1840–1875*.
Julian B. Feibelman, *The Making of a Rabbi*.
Emily Ford and Barry Stiefel, *The Jews of New Orleans and the Mississippi Delta*.
Bobbie Malone, *Rabbi Max Heller: Reformer, Zionist, Southerner, 1860–1929*.
Edgar B. Stern, *A Sentimental Journey*.
Peter M. Wolf, *My New Orleans, Gone Away*.

ARTICLES

Anny Bloch, "Mercy on Rude Streams: Jewish Emigrants from Alsace-Lorraine to the Lower Mississippi Region and the Concept of Fidelity." *Southern Jewish History*, 1999.
William F. Holmes, "Whitecapping: Agrarian Violence in Mississippi, 1902–1906." *The Journal of Southern History*, May 1969.
Joe M. Richardson, "Edgar B. Stern: A White New Orleans Philanthropist Helps Build a Black University." *The Journal of Negro History*, Summer 1997.
Stuart Rockoff, "Carpetbaggers, Jacklegs, and Bolting Republicans: Jews in Reconstruction Politics in Ascension Parish, Louisiana." *American Jewish History*, March 2013.
Gary P. Zola, "Reform Judaism's Pioneer Zionist: Maximilian Heller," *American Jewish History*, June 1984.

Nicholas Lemann, a fifth-generation Louisianan, was born and raised in New Orleans. He started his career in journalism there as a seventeen-year-old reporter for an alternative weekly paper, the *Vieux Carre Courier.* He has been writing magazine articles and books since then. His journalistic home for more than twenty-five years has been *The New Yorker,* where he usually covers politics. From 2003 to 2013 he was dean of the Columbia Journalism School. He is a professor there now and also directs a publishing venture called Columbia Global Reports.

Lemann's books use reportage, archival research, and intellectual history to bring to light major and under-chronicled changes in American life: the great Black migration from the rural South to the urban North (*The Promised Land*), the development of a formal meritocratic system (*The Big Test*), the violent overthrow of Reconstruction (*Redemption*), and the ascent of the financial system to dominance of the economy (*Transaction Man*).

The father of three sons and a daughter, he lives in New York City with his wife, the author and critic Judith Shulevitz.